BJ M.....

Sams **Teach Yourself**

Swift™

in **24** **Hours**

SECOND EDITION

 SAMS 800 East 96th Street, Indianapolis, Indiana, 46240 USA

Sams Teach Yourself Swift™ in 24 Hours

ISBN-13: 978-0-672-33765-9

ISBN-10: 0-672-33765-7

Library of Congress Control Number: 2015913414

Printed in the United States

First Printing December 2015

Trademarks

All terms mentioned in this book that are known to be trademarks or service marks have been appropriately capitalized. Sams Publishing cannot attest to the accuracy of this information. Use of a term in this book should not be regarded as affecting the validity of any trademark or service mark.

Warning and Disclaimer

Every effort has been made to make this book as complete and as accurate as possible, but no warranty or fitness is implied. The information provided is on an "as is" basis. The author and the publisher shall have neither liability nor responsibility to any person or entity with respect to any loss or damages arising from the information contained in this book.

Special Sales

For information about buying this title in bulk quantities, or for special sales opportunities (which may include electronic versions; custom cover designs; and content particular to your business, training goals, marketing focus, or branding interests), please contact our corporate sales department at corpsales@pearsoned.com or (800) 382-3419.

For government sales inquiries, please contact governmentsales@pearsoned.com.

For questions about sales outside the U.S., please contact international@pearsoned.com.

Editor-in-Chief
Mark Taub

Senior Acquisitions Editor
Trina MacDonald

Senior Development Editor
Chris Zahn

Managing Editor
Kristy Hart

Senior Project Editor
Betsy Gratner

Copy Editor
Paula Lowell

Indexer
Erika Millen

Proofreader
Sarah Kearns

Technical Editor
Valerie Shipbaugh

Editorial Assistant
Olivia Basegio

Cover Designer
Mark Shirar

Compositor
codeMantra

Contents at a Glance

Table of Contents

About the Author

BJ Miller is an iOS developer for DXY Solutions, a mobile, web, and design consultancy in the Cleveland, Ohio, area. BJ earned his B.S. in Computer Science from Baldwin-Wallace College (now called Baldwin-Wallace University) in Berea, Ohio, the town where he grew up. His latest career path encompassed large-scale enterprise network administration, SQL database administration, and Microsoft SharePoint Server and Microsoft Project Server administration and integration as a contractor for the United States Department of Defense, with all the Microsoft certifications that come along with that. Before that, he spent several years in LAN engineering, designing and implementing network infrastructure, as a Cisco Certified Network Associate.

BJ began iOS development in 2009 after not having programmed for a few years, and he developed a passion for the platform and the Objective-C language. Now, his love has expanded to include Swift, and there is still yet room in his heart for more. In 2013, he released his first app into the iOS App Store, called MyPrayerMap, as a simple tool for managing prayer requests.

When he is not writing in Objective-C or Swift for either work or this book, he enjoys spending time with his wife and two boys, reading, listening to music or podcasts, and playing *The Legend of Zelda* (any game on any system will do). He also co-organizes the Cleveland CocoaHeads Meetup with Daniel Steinberg, http://www.meetup.com/Cleveland-CocoaHeads/, and organizes a submeetup of that group called Paired Programming Fun, which is a casual meetup where the focus is on Test-Driven Development (TDD) in Swift in paired-programming style. BJ often presents iOS-related topics at CocoaHeads and also speaks at other conferences such as MacTech, CocoaConf (Columbus, Ohio), and CodeMash v2.0.1.5. He also blogs from time to time at http://bjmiller.me and is on Twitter as @bjmillerltd.

Dedication

This book is dedicated to my wonderful family and friends who have been incredibly supportive throughout this entire process. Thank you all for your love and encouragement.

Acknowledgments

I would like to thank my wife and two boys for putting up with me while I wrote this book... again. While this book was largely an update versus brand-new content, it was still an exhausting process. I am excited to spend more time with you. I would also like to thank whoever invented coffee; may the Lord bless your soul and keep you. Speaking of the Lord, it is pretty close to not humanly possible that this book would have been completed in time, with all the other obstacles going on in my life, without his loving arms around me and my family; thank you, Jesus.

I would also like to thank my friends, coworkers, and the rest of the Mac/iOS community for all their love and encouragement. If I had not been introduced to someone, who introduced me to someone, who introduced me to Daniel Steinberg, I might not have pursued iOS development further and I might not have written this book. If you ever get the chance to meet that man, your life will be enriched.

Also, I cannot go without thanking the fine people who helped this book come to be: Trina MacDonald (Acquisitions Editor), Chris Zahn (Senior Development Editor), Olivia Basegio (Editorial Assistant), Valerie Shipbaugh (Technical Editor), Paula Lowell (Copy Editor), and Betsy Gratner (Project Editor).

We Want to Hear from You!

As the reader of this book, you are our most important critic and commentator. We value your opinion and want to know what we're doing right, what we could do better, what areas you'd like to see us publish in, and any other words of wisdom you're willing to pass our way.

You can email or write directly to let us know what you did or didn't like about this book—as well as what we can do to make our books stronger.

Please note that we cannot help you with technical problems related to the topic of this book, and that due to the high volume of mail we receive, we might not be able to reply to every message.

When you write, please be sure to include this book's title and author, as well as your name and contact information.

Email: errata@informit.com

Mail: Sams Publishing
           ATTN: Reader Feedback
           330 Hudson Street
           7th Floor
           New York, New York 10013

Reader Services

Register your copy of *Sams Teach Yourself Swift in 24 Hours* at informit.com for convenient access to downloads, updates, and corrections as they become available. To start the registration process go to informit.com/register and log in or create an account.* Enter the product ISBN 9780672337659 and click submit. Once the process is complete, you will find any available bonus content under "Registered Products."

*Be sure to check the box that you would like to hear from us in order to receive exclusive discounts on future editions of this product.

Introduction

At Apple's yearly World Wide Developer Conference (WWDC) in June 2014, Apple announced a new programming language called Swift that the company had been developing since 2010. This was a huge announcement; Objective-C had been the primary language of choice for developing most Mac and iOS apps for many years. The excitement surrounding this language was palpable. Twitter lit up with tweets about Swift, domain names with Swift in the title were being purchased left and right, and within 24 hours of the announcement, more than 300,000 copies of Apple's Swift iBook had been downloaded. People were ready for change.

But a new language brings not only syntactic differences but also idiomatic differences and new conventions. Swift is not just an object-oriented language, but it introduces features gleaned from other languages, such as C#, Haskell, Ruby, and more. Touted to be "Objective-C without the C," Swift has evolved so much over the past year that it is difficult sometimes to see any similarities. Swift builds upon familiar concepts from Objective-C but includes a more modern, safer syntax and multiple paradigms such as object-oriented, functional, imperative, and block structured, as well as reintroducing itself at WWDC 2015 as a protocol-oriented programming language.

Swift is officially at version 2.0 but is still evolving, and even as this book is being written, more changes are entering beta. With that said, this book is current as of Swift 2.0 and Xcode 7. If there are changes that you find in these examples that do not work as described or with screenshots, please check Apple's release documentation and electronic versions of this book as they can get updated a lot faster than the printed book you may have in your hands. Also, all the code examples from this book are available and will be kept up-to-date in the GitHub repository: https://github.com/STYSwiftIn24H/ExamplesV2.

Swift is already proving to be a great language and as of its release is compatible with iOS 7 and up. Swift can also be written for apps running on OS X Yosemite and later. Updates are coming from Apple rather quickly, so if something is not available that you need or if something is not working as expected, consider filing a bug or feature request at http://bugreport. apple.com.

Who Should Read This Book?

This book is designed for a beginner-intermediate level programmer. Even advanced programmers who are not yet familiar with Swift can benefit from this book. You do not have to have a background in software development to make your way through this book, although it may help. If you are not familiar with software development whatsoever, you may benefit from more fundamental books first, although with the examples inside this book, you may be able to follow along just fine.

In this book, I assume you have a passion to learn about Swift and to develop apps for the Mac and/or iOS platforms. I also assume that you are willing to carve out time in your schedule to take this book seriously and learn the concepts herein.

What Should You Expect from This Book?

This book is a guided tour of the Swift programming language, discussing some of the ins-and-outs of Swift, best practices, do's-and-don'ts, and more. It is not just a language reference. By the time you complete this book, you should have a firm grasp on many of the concepts in Swift including the syntax to make them come to fruition.

You should not expect to be able to write award-winning iOS or Mac apps right out of the gate by just reading this book alone, as this book is not meant to be a one-stop-shop for learning everything about app creation. Such a book would be thousands of pages long. Rather, there are more components to writing apps, particularly the Cocoa and Cocoa Touch frameworks, which deserve books in their own right (and many exist). You should write apps via careful planning and development, and depending on how many different technologies your app includes, you may need more resources.

You also do not need to read this book from cover to cover before attempting to write apps of your own using Swift. Feel free to experiment along the way with your own apps, or use this book for reference if you are stuck in an app of your own and need some guidance.

Also remember that this book is current as of Swift 2.0 and Xcode 7, so please understand that changes may be made after this book has gone through final edits and been printed. Code examples will be updated as progressions in the Swift language and Xcode environment change. They are available on GitHub at https://github.com/STYSwiftIn24H/ExamplesV2.

NOTE

Code-Continuation Arrows and Listing Line Numbers

You'll see code-continuation arrows ➥ occasionally in this book to indicate when a line of code is too long to fit on the printed page.

Also, many listings have line numbers and some do not. The listings that have line numbers have them so that I can reference code by line; the listings that do not have line numbers are not called out by line.

HOUR 1

Introducing the Swift Development Environment

What You'll Learn in This Hour:

▶ What Swift is and where it came from

▶ How to install Xcode 7 from the Mac App Store

▶ How to navigate the Xcode Integrated Development Environment (IDE)

▶ How to use playgrounds

▶ How to use Swift's Read-Eval-Print-Loop (REPL)

▶ How to write your first Swift app

Since the introduction of the iPhone in 2007, Apple seems to have lit a fire in the industry for not only consumer-based electronics but also the opportunity for most anyone to be able to write apps for their platform, be it Mac or iOS. This has had a dramatic effect on culture, as you cannot go to a coffee shop or to any business now and not see a slew of MacBook Airs, MacBook Pros, iPhones, iPads, and now Apple Watches. Chances are, if you're reading this book, you are wondering how you can write an app that could appear on the screens of the very people you see at those coffee shops and businesses.

This book is about the Swift programming language, the new programming language announced by Apple at the 2014 World Wide Developer Conference (WWDC). Prior to Swift's introduction, Mac and iOS apps were mainly written in a language called Objective-C, which is a strict superset of the C programming language, meaning that you could write apps in both languages, and sometimes had to. In this book, we explore the Swift programming language and learn its fundamentals, structure, and syntax, which gives you a foundation to write great Mac and iOS apps.

What Is Swift?

Swift is a programming language customized by Apple and introduced as Objective-C without the C. Indeed, this is somewhat true. Not only has Swift taken cues from other languages such as Haskell, Ruby, Python, C#, and several others, it has also matured over the last year with its own style and methodologies. Swift is tuned to work with the existing Cocoa and Cocoa Touch frameworks, which contain all the familiar classes used in modern Mac and iOS apps, to support their interoperability.

Swift is built on three pillars: being safe, powerful, and modern. Swift provides a lot of safety in terms of type checking, constants for immutability, requiring values to be initialized before use, built-in overflow handling, and automatic memory management. With respect to power, Swift was built using the highly optimized LLVM compiler, includes many low-level C-like functions such as primitive types and flow control, and of course was built with Apple's hardware in mind for optimal performance. Swift is also modern in that it adopted many features from other languages to make the language more concise, yet expressive, such as closures, generics, tuples, functional programming patterns, and more that we cover in later hours.

Getting Started

The biggest assumption at this point is that you have a Mac computer already, as without that, you cannot install Xcode, Apple's Mac and iOS Integrated Development Environment (IDE).

NOTE

Download Xcode

Xcode 7 is a free download from the Mac App Store. You must have Mac OS X 10.10.4 or later. Although you can write Swift code in Xcode 6.x, this book will encompass Swift version 2.0, which requires Xcode 7.

Launch the App Store app on your Mac, search for Xcode, and click to install the software. Once the installation is complete, Xcode is listed in your /Applications directory.

Take a Look Around

When you open Xcode, you may be greeted with prompts asking whether you want to install extra tools; go ahead and install them. This should only happen the first time you launch Xcode. Once Xcode is open, you see a standard menu window with options to create a playground, create a new project, or open an existing project, and on the right side is a list of recent projects and playgrounds you've opened (if you've opened any). The window should look like Figure 1.1.

Although in this book we predominantly work in playgrounds, it is good to become familiar with the IDE, so let's do that quickly. Click Create a New Xcode Project to create a new Xcode project. The next screen asks you what type of project you want to create, and for this experiment, just use Single View Application, as seen in Figure 1.2, and click Next.

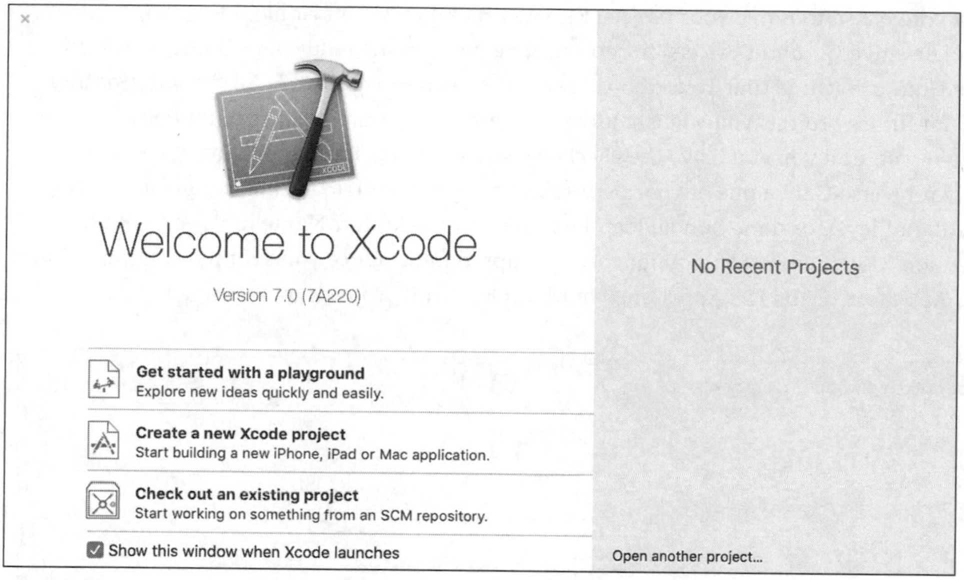

FIGURE 1.1
The Welcome to Xcode screen, where you can choose to create or edit projects and playgrounds.

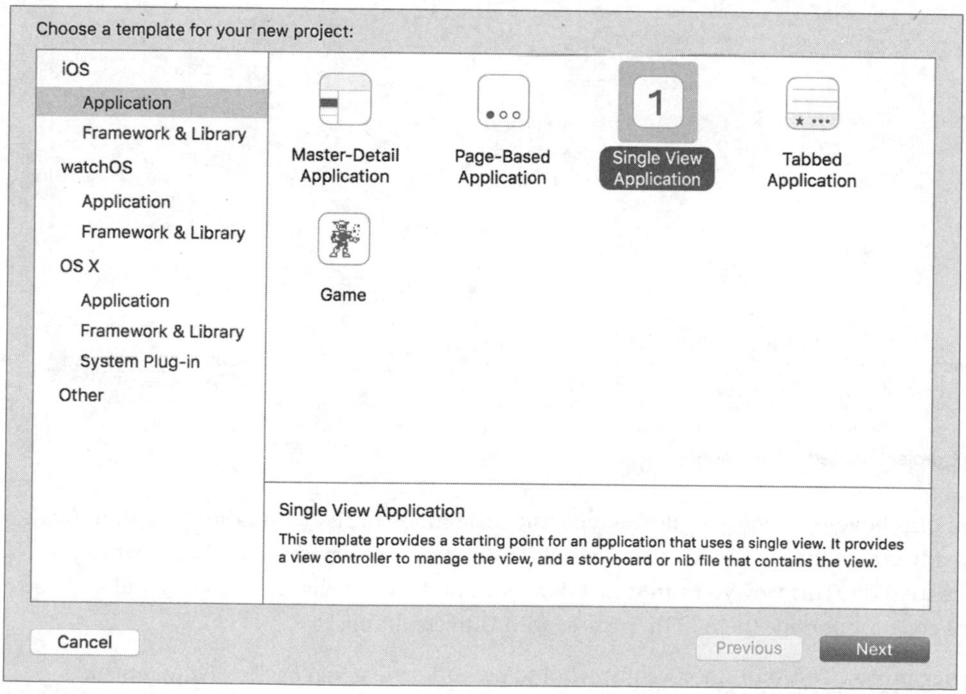

FIGURE 1.2
The project template chooser screen.

Next, you are asked to name your project. Choose an Organization Name, Identifier, Language (Swift or Objective-C), and Device(s) to run on. Here you can also indicate whether you want to use Core Data or include Unit Tests and UI Tests, as shown in Figure 1.3. All this information is useful for future projects you will create, but for our testing purposes, we don't need to worry about them yet, and you can leave the checkboxes as they are. The Organization Identifier is usually a reverse-DNS name of your personal or company URL to ensure uniqueness at an organizational level, and the Bundle Identifier tacks on the Project Name to the end of the Organization Identifier to ensure uniqueness per app bundle. Once you submit an app to either the Mac App Store or the iOS App Store, your bundle identifier needs to be unique.

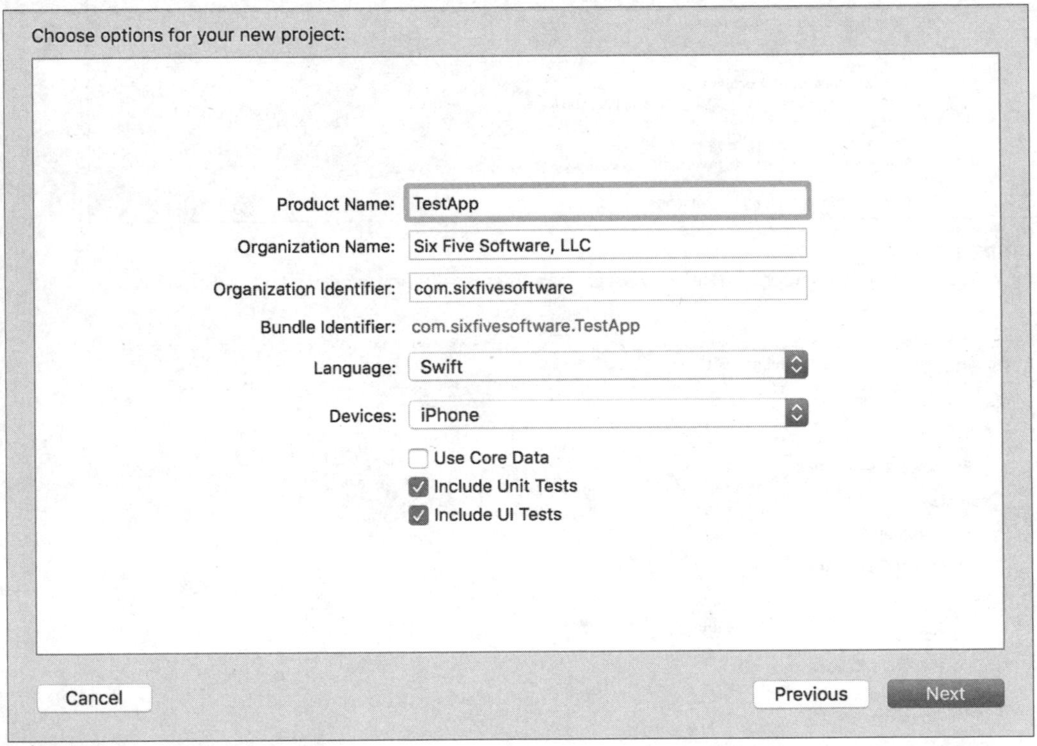

Choose options for your new project:

Product Name:	TestApp
Organization Name:	Six Five Software, LLC
Organization Identifier:	com.sixfivesoftware
Bundle Identifier:	com.sixfivesoftware.TestApp
Language:	Swift
Devices:	iPhone
	☐ Use Core Data
	☑ Include Unit Tests
	☑ Include UI Tests

Cancel   Previous   Next

FIGURE 1.3
Enter your project-related information.

Here you also have the choice for device type, such as iPhone or iPad, and that is so that Xcode can properly create the Storyboard files needed for the device or devices you plan to write your app to be used on. This way you can target different interfaces on different devices, but still use the same code to manage them both, such as with Universal apps.

Name your project TestApp, since we just want to get to Xcode to get acclimated (you can remove this project later). As a general rule, you may experience fewer headaches down the road if you choose project names with no spaces. Choose Swift for the language, and click Next. Xcode opens, and you see the new project you created. It should look something like Figure 1.4.

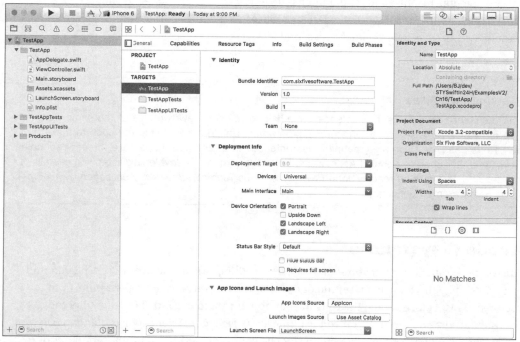

FIGURE 1.4
The initial Xcode IDE layout. The Navigation Pane is on the left, Inspector Pane is on the right, and main content area is in the center. In the top toolbar are buttons to run or stop a build, see error and warning info, and show or hide views.

Xcode is nicely partitioned off into logical sections, as you may be accustomed to from other IDEs; however, it also has some nice features to note. The pane on the left-hand side is called the Navigator Pane. Here, you can choose between different Navigators to view files in your project, warnings and errors, breakpoints, Unit Tests, and more. The pane on the right-hand side is called the Inspector Pane. This dynamic pane changes depending on what element is clicked, such as editing a selected button's text property, or adjusting a control's position in a window.

The main content area in the center is where you'll spend most of your time when working on an actual Mac/iOS project. The content area is where you can change project settings, and most importantly create your app by either writing code or designing the interface in a Storyboard.

The bar along the top left has several useful functions available. Toward the left, you have your standard Mac Red/Yellow/Green buttons for window management. Next, the play and stop buttons are actually *Build and Run* and *Stop* when referring to compiling, building, and running your apps on the Simulator or devices. To the right of that is where Xcode notifies you of current information, such as how many warnings or errors are in your project, and build status.

Finally, the upper right-hand set of buttons can adjust the views you see to show or hide the Navigator Pane, Inspector Pane, Debug Pane, or Assistant Editor, as well as view code comparisons, source code "blame" views, and logs.

NOTE

Viewing Two Files

The Assistant Editor splits the content area in half so you can view two files at the same time. This is helpful, for instance, when you might be writing Unit Tests and also the code to make the Unit Tests pass, or if you are creating a user interface in a Storyboard and have the corresponding View Controller open to connect Actions and Outlets. For more on developing apps with custom interfaces, I recommend reading John Ray's book *Sams Teach Yourself iOS Application Development in 24 Hours*, Sams Publishing.

Xcode Playgrounds

One of the excellent main features of Xcode is something called **playgrounds**. A playground is a scratch pad, if you will, for testing out code to ensure you receive proper results from code segments, before adding the code to your app. It is because of this functionality that playgrounds are so powerful; you can get immediate feedback if your code is going to give you the results you expect without having to compile your code and run it on the Simulator or a device.

You can create a new playground at any time, and you can choose to have it be a part of your project or just as an independent playground file. Since we're already in an open project, click File > New > File, and then in the Source set of files (for either iOS or Mac), choose playground, then click Next. In the Save As dialog, name your playground file (the name MyPlayground is fine for our purposes), and then click Create. Don't worry about the Group or the Targets for now; we aren't building an app yet, so we don't care about that.

NOTE

Mac or iOS Playgrounds

There is a difference in file structure when creating a playground from the Mac section or iOS section. Creating a Mac playground adds the `import Cocoa` statement at the top of the file, and makes Mac frameworks and modules available to you. Creating an iOS playground adds the `import UIKit` statement at the top of the file, and makes iOS frameworks and modules available to you. There is nothing visually different about either playground at first. If you create an iOS playground, but instead want to test Mac app code, or vice-versa, simply create a new playground of the desired type.

Notice that your new playground comes equipped with a few lines of Swift code for your learning convenience. Let's touch on a few of these basics first before moving on. Your playground should look something like this:

```
//: Playground - noun: a place where people can play
import UIKit
var str = "Hello, playground"
```

The first line in the preceding code is a comment and is ignored by the compiler. You can use comments to annotate certain parts of code to be human readable, perhaps explaining for other coworkers (or even yourself) what this particular section of code is for. The // (double forward slash) signifies that the remainder of the line is to be treated as a comment. You can also comment entire sections of code or paragraphs of text, either on the same line or on multiple consecutive lines by enclosing them in /* and */. Swift even allows you to nest comment blocks inside comment blocks, such as /* ... /* ... */ ... */.

The remainder of the preceding code performs a simple task in that it assigns the string "Hello, playground" to a variable str. Even though the code doesn't directly print any output to the console, the playground by default displays "Hello, playground" in the playground's results pane to show the contents of the variable and any subsequent variables or constants you create. This comes in handy when you want to test logic, math, and other operations.

It is also worth noting that the variable str is prefaced with the keyword var. The var keyword lets Swift know that str is a variable, and can change its contents. To create a constant, or an immutable variable, use the keyword let instead of var.

TRY IT YOURSELF ▼

Create Your First Lines of Swift in the Playground

At this point, it makes sense to try out your first lines of code while you're in the playground, so let's do it together here.

1. Type the following onto a new line in the playground:

   ```
   let myNewValue = 40 + 2
   ```

2. Notice the right-hand side of the playground displays "42". Type the following line of code as-is, to insert the value inside a sentence:

   ```
   print("My new value is \(myNewValue).")
   ```

3. To view the printed output in the console, click the View menu, then Debug Area, and then click Show Debug Area. The Debug Area is now visible at the bottom of the screen, and you should see the output of the print() statement:

   ```
   "My new value is 42."
   ```

Congratulations! You have written your very first lines of Swift.

In the preceding Try It Yourself example, you assigned a value of 42 to `myNewValue` in step 1. Then, in step 2, you inserted the value inside a sentence, using something called **string interpolation**, which is a convenient way to interpolate variables or constants inside output. The next hour discusses string interpolation in more detail. The `print()` statement prints output to the console, which is handy for quick debugging or viewing contents of data.

NOTE

Removing Xcode Projects

If you would like to remove this Xcode project (or any Xcode project you may not want any longer), you can simply remove the containing folder on the file system. Say you saved this project in ~/Documents/TestApp. Simply delete the TestApp folder from your Documents directory.

The Swift Read-Eval-Print-Loop (REPL)

Swift also comes packaged with a nice feature called a **Read-Eval-Print-Loop**, or a **REPL** for short. The REPL is an interactive command-line–based version of what we just experienced with playgrounds. Using the REPL is nice for quick tests to make sure code works the way you expect, similar to what you get with a playground, but rather than creating a new file in your project, you can just use this ephemeral REPL to get in, test your code, and get out. Whether to use a playground or the REPL is largely a matter of preference of what you feel comfortable with. If you are already using Terminal.app, or some other command-line utility, it may be easier for you to just open the REPL. On the other hand, if you're already in Xcode, it may be quicker for you to just create a playground and go from there.

To access the REPL, you simply type the following:

```
$> xcrun swift
```

`xcrun` is a command-line tool provided by Xcode for running or locating development tools or properties. So in the preceding line, we're telling `xcrun` to run the Swift REPL. When you press the Return key, you see something like the following (your version numbers might look different):

```
Welcome to Apple Swift version 2.0 (700.0.57 700.0.72). Type :help for assistance.
  1>
```

The `1>` is the Swift REPL prompt where you can start typing Swift code, one instruction per line, and it interprets your code for you, much like the playground did. Let's try another example of writing code, this time in the Swift REPL.

Combine Two Strings Together Using the Swift REPL

Let's do another example of some Swift code here; hopefully this one isn't too difficult yet. If you don't fully understand it, don't worry; we cover this in great detail in the next hour.

1. Open Terminal.app on your Mac.

2. Type `xcrun swift` in the Terminal; then press Return.

3. At the `1>` prompt, enter the following:

```
let firstHalf = "I'm writing Swift code,"
let secondHalf = "and I'm so excited!"
let combined = firstHalf + secondHalf
```

4. Notice how each time you press Return, Swift's REPL displays the name of the constant or variable we used, its data type of `String` (we cover data types in Hour 2, "Learning Swift's Fundamental Data Types"), and its value.

5. Take a look at how using the + operator concatenates the two strings together. Swift is smart enough to know that even though we're dealing with letter characters (as opposed to adding numbers), the + operator adds `String` instances together. More on operators in Hour 3, "Using Operators in Swift."

You're doing great! The Swift REPL keeps constants and variables in memory for the duration of your REPL session. This means that you can reference variables and constants several lines later, which helps you work on tackling problems quickly and easily before you write the code in your actual app. The completed Try It Yourself example should look like Figure 1.5.

To quit the Swift REPL, type a colon (:) to invoke command mode; then type q for quit and press Return. You are returned to your regular Unix shell prompt.

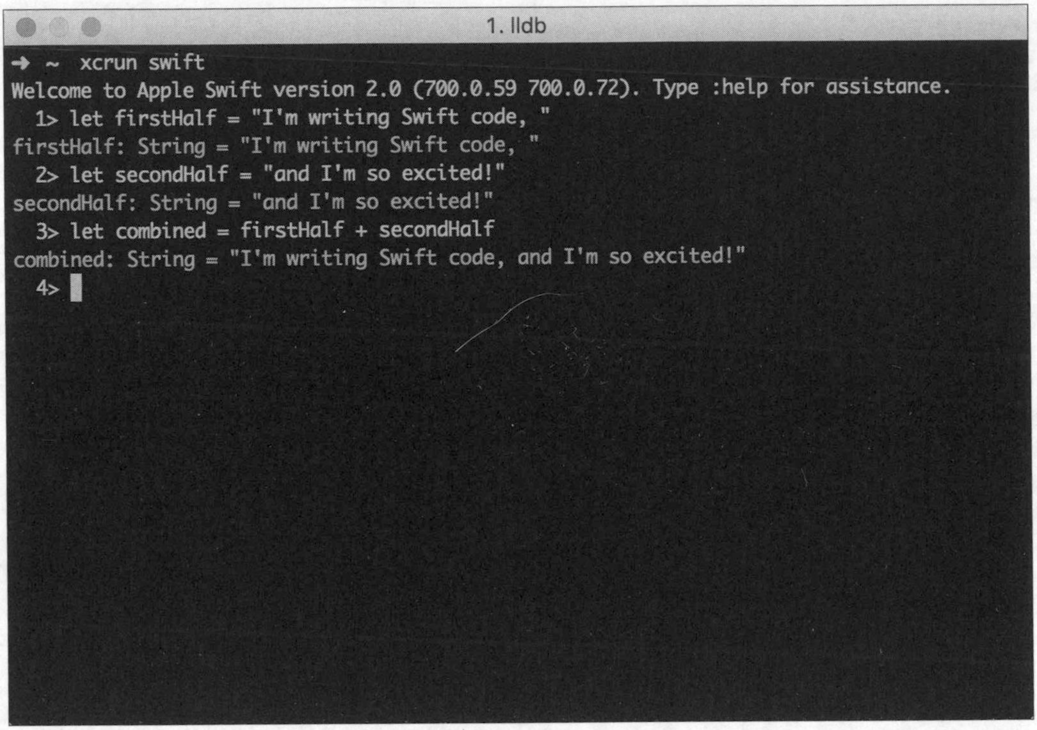

```
● ● ●                            1. lldb
→ ~ xcrun swift
Welcome to Apple Swift version 2.0 (700.0.59 700.0.72). Type :help for assistance.
  1> let firstHalf = "I'm writing Swift code, "
firstHalf: String = "I'm writing Swift code, "
  2> let secondHalf = "and I'm so excited!"
secondHalf: String = "and I'm so excited!"
  3> let combined = firstHalf + secondHalf
combined: String = "I'm writing Swift code, and I'm so excited!"
  4> █
```

FIGURE 1.5
The completed Try It Yourself example using the Swift REPL.

Summary

In this first hour, you learned a brief background on the Swift programming language and what it is built upon. We walked through opening the Xcode environment for the first time and explored some of Xcode's layout, as well as the Swift REPL. You also created your first lines of Swift code and saw how Xcode and the REPL give you instant feedback on what your code is doing.

In the next hour, we cover the difference between variables and constants and explore some of Swift's native data types, such as String, Int, Bool, Character, Double, and Float.

Q&A

Q. Can I have a playground without having to create a full Xcode project?

A. Absolutely. Xcode treats playgrounds as interpretable files, independent of any project.

Q. I am still running OS X Mountain Lion. Can I still use Xcode?

A. OS X Mountain Lion (v. 10.8) can run Xcode, but the latest version of Xcode that can run on Mountain Lion is Xcode 5.x. OS X Mavericks 10.9.3 is the earliest version that can support Xcode 6, and OS X Yosemite 10.10.4 is the minimum required OS for Xcode 7. Xcode 7 is required for Swift 2.0.

Q. I just started learning iOS development, and it seems that Swift is very popular. But, should I still learn Objective-C?

A. Objective-C is still heavily used in many Mac and iOS apps and will still be used for some time to come. This book predominantly teaches the Swift programming language, but if you want to be a developer full-time or in some sort of capacity, you may encounter Objective-C code from an existing code base, so you may benefit from learning some Objective-C. There are plenty of good resources available for learning Objective-C, as it is a seasoned and solid language.

Workshop

The workshop contains quiz questions and exercises to help you solidify your understanding of the material covered. Try to answer all questions before looking at the answers that follow.

Quiz

1. What command opens the Swift REPL?

2. Use a playground to write Swift code that multiplies the numbers 3 and 19 and stores the value in a constant named `result`. What does the code look like?

3. How do you quit the Swift REPL?

4. What is the minimum Mac OS X version that runs Xcode 7?

5. What would be the output of the following Swift code?

```
let age = 33
let outputString = "Someone you know is \(age) years old"
```

Answers

1. `xcrun swift.`

2. `let result = 3 * 19` (the playground result pane displays 57).

3. Type a colon (:), then q, and then press Return.

4. Mac OS X 10.10 is the minimum version to run Xcode 7.

5. The output would be: "Someone you know is 33 years old."

Exercise

Try creating a playground in which you combine two strings together, and then use the `lowercaseString` method on your combined string to convert the string to all lowercase letters. (HINT: In a playground, press the period key (.) immediately after typing the combined variable name to get a list of actions you can take on that string.)

Learning Swift's Fundamental Data Types

What You'll Learn in This Hour:

▶ Understand the differences between constants and variables

▶ How to declare and use constants and variables

▶ How Swift uses type inference for automatic type setting

▶ Swift's common data types

▶ How to specifically declare data types with type annotation

In the first hour, we walked through setting up the Xcode and Swift Read-Eval-Print-Loop (REPL) environment and exposed the Xcode layout to you. We also examined some brief examples of Swift code to show how these environments can be used to help you code and even test your code. We briefly used the Swift keyword `let`, when declaring constants in code and assigned different types of data to them (such as the number 42 or the string "Hello, playground"). During this hour, we take a closer look at how Swift uses the `var` and `let` keywords (called **introducers**) and also how Swift knows how to handle different types of data.

There are two fundamental ways in Swift that we declare data types, and they are **constants** and **variables**. Let's take a look at that now.

Constants in Swift

Constants are a way of telling Swift that a particular value should not and will not change, hence the term constant. This is also called **immutable**, since something that is constant cannot mutate. Swift's compiler optimizes memory used for constants to make code perform better because if Swift knows that the size and/or contents of that memory will not change, it can eliminate a lot of potential mutability aspects it may normally have to check for when working with these values. Constants also provide you, the programmer, with a safety net by providing protection from accidentally overwriting the contents of a constant value.

Think of some times when constants may be necessary. For example, say you're writing an app that calculates distances, and you know that there are 5,280 feet in a mile. You could set a constant called `feetPerMile` and set its value to 5280. That way, whenever you need to reference that value in your code, you can use `feetPerMile` in your calculations.

You can only assign a value to a constant once. Value assignment does not need to happen at the time you define the constant, but after it has been given a value it cannot change. Because of the immutability of constants, if you try to change the value of a constant, Xcode provides a compiler error, stating that you cannot assign to a `let` value. Now, let's take a look at variables.

NOTE

When to Use Constants

Because Swift is a safe language, it is a suggested best practice to use constants with the `let` introducer as often as necessary. This greatly improves safety by preventing accidental data manipulation and even helps Swift's compiler improve performance. Only use constants, however, when you know the value of your constant will never change.

Variables in Swift

As you can see, with as dynamic as apps are and have to be, we wouldn't get far by working with only constants. Swift provides an equally simple way to declare variables as it does constants, and that is with the `var` introducer. Variables, as the name implies, can be variable and are **mutable** by nature. This means that the value of the variable can change whenever you use the = operator, called the **assignment operator** (we discuss operators in Hour 3, "Using Operators in Swift").

Variables are particularly useful for when you know that data could or will change. For instance, if you are building a pedometer app, you know that with every step you or the user of your app takes (assuming the user has a device with the M-series motion coprocessor), the number of steps will increase. That variable will continue to be updated with the number of steps taken up to that very moment.

▼ TRY IT YOURSELF

Assign Constants and Variables

Using a playground or the Swift REPL (whichever you are more comfortable with), try these steps to visualize your knowledge of constants and variables:

1. Assign a constant named `feetPerMile` to a value of `5280`.

```
let feetPerMile = 5280
```

2. Assign a variable named `totalFeet` to a value of `0`, just to initialize it.

```
var totalFeet = 0
```

3. Imagine you walk 3 miles, and you want to know how many feet you traveled. Now, make `totalFeet` equal to 3 times what is stored in `feetPerMile`.

   ```
   totalFeet = 3 * feetPerMile
   ```

4. Suppose the global standard for number of feet per mile changes from 5280 to 6000, due to a standards disagreement. Try to change `feetPerMile` to `6000`.

   ```
   feetPerMile = 6000
   ```

You get an error trying to change `feetPerMile`, don't you?

In the last experiment, you noticed that you can declare a constant, `feetPerMile`, and give it an initial value (of 5280) with no problem. You also declared a variable, `totalFeet`, with an initial value (of zero), equally as easily. Then, you changed the value of the variable, and Swift was okay with that. Now, when you tried to change the value of `feetPerMile`, you received an error that you were trying to change a constant `let` value. This is an example of how Swift's compiler helps keep your code safe from mutation issues.

Keep a few things in mind when naming your constants and variables. You can use any Unicode character in the name of your constants and variables, except that they cannot begin with a number and must begin with a letter. This is an excellent feature if you need to express something in a different language that would not so easily be done with an English keyboard. Names also cannot have punctuation or special characters, as those are often reserved for keywords or operators. You can also now use Emoji for names of constants or variables, such as setting the chicken face character to the string "chicken," and Swift infers the chicken face Unicode character to be of type `String`. As cute as that may seem, a lot of programmers tend to shy away from using Emoji or other special characters for names as it makes referencing those variables and constants difficult while typing, and you have to pause your train of thought to hunt down a particular Unicode character or key combination.

Now that we've discussed constants and variables, let's learn about Swift's data types.

Introducing Data Types

One of Swift's primary safety features is related to handling data types. In this section, we cover four basic data types, their composition, and how Swift infers data types when they aren't explicitly stated.

Type Inference

So far we have not explicitly stated the types of data we want Swift to use for our constants and variables, and we haven't needed to. Swift uses something called **type inference** when a data type is not explicitly declared. Swift does this by analyzing the value that is set to the constant or variable we are declaring and setting the type accordingly. Let's take a quick look at our example from the last hour, where we added 40 and 2:

```
let myNewValue = 40 + 2
```

42 is obviously an integer, so Swift inferred it to be of type Int. The way we explicitly declare the type of a constant or variable in Swift is by appending a colon (:) and then the type (such as Int) to the constant or variable name. This is called **type annotation**. Here is what the code now looks like with type annotation:

```
let myNewValue: Int = 40 + 2
```

Because of type inference, we haven't needed to explicitly state a type, but our examples have been small. In real apps, you may have situations where you need to declare the type for many reasons: so that the compiler can help you for safety reasons, as self-documentation to clearly see what value a constant or variable should hold, or even in stating the return types of values in functions (we explore functions in Hour 8, "Using Functions to Perform Actions").

Data Types

Quite a few data types in Swift can be useful in your apps. The most common ones we talk about here are the following:

▶ Int for integers, which are whole numbers without a fractional component

▶ Double and Float for floating-point numbers (those with a decimal component)

▶ String for working with a collection of characters, words, and so on

▶ Bool for working with true and false values

NOTE

Other Data Types

Many other data types in Swift are available for use to further refine the scope of the data you need to manage. When possible, we outline the data types to know about with relation to the current data type.

CAUTION

Data Types Cannot Be Changed Once Assigned

Once you declare a variable or constant to be of a particular data type, it cannot be changed. Also, you cannot declare a new variable or constant with the same name as an existing variable or constant within the same scope or context.

The `Int` Data Type

Integers are a common data type to use in Swift. Integers are used for things like counting or enumerating through an ordered list or array, counting iterations over a section of code a particular amount of times, and many other practical uses. As you've seen already, the keyword for defining an integer is simply `Int`. On a 32-bit platform, `Int` is a 32-bit integer (or `Int32`), and on 64-bit platforms, `Int` is a 64-bit integer (or `Int64`). This is yet another example of how safe Swift is with its data types.

Another way of using integers is to use an **unsigned integer**, or `UInt`. Unsigned integers are just integers with no negative numerical range, meaning they go from 0 to whatever the upper bound is of the integer you choose. The max upper bound of an `Int` is nine quintillion and change, and its minimum bound is negative nine quintillion and change, so chances are you may never need a number bigger than that. A better illustration is `UInt8`, which is an 8-bit integer. Swift provides 8-, 16-, 32-, and 64-bit versions of `UInt`. Go ahead and see for yourself in this Try It Yourself section.

TRY IT YOURSELF ▼

Find the Minimum and Maximum Ranges of Integers

Open up a playground in Xcode, and try the following examples:

1. Assign a new constant of type `Int` to `Int.max`. What value do you see?

```
let intMax: Int = Int.max
```

2. Assign new constants from `UInt8.max` and `UInt8.min`. Try two more constants, `Int8.max` and `Int8.min`. What values do you see?

```
let uint8Max = UInt8.max
let uint8Min = UInt8.min
let int8Max = Int8.max
let int8Min = Int8.min
```

3. Repeat step 2 for `UInt16` and `UInt32`. What values do you see?

```
let uint16Max = UInt16.max
let uint32Max = UInt32.max
```

4. Now try with `UInt64`. What do you see?

```
let uint64Max: UInt64 = UInt64.max
```

Now you can see the value is 18,446,744,073,709,551,615. That's 18 quintillion.

The completed Try It Yourself section should look like that in Figure 2.1.

```
●  ●  ●                              Ready | Today at 9:59 PM

⊞  |  <   >  | 🖼 Ch02 Int TIY
1  let intMax: Int = Int.max          9223372036854775807
2  let uint8Max = UInt8.max           255
3  let uint8Min = UInt8.min           0
4  let int8Max = Int8.max             127
5  let int8Min = Int8.min             -128
6  let uint16Max = UInt16.max         65535
7  let uint32Max = UInt32.max         4294967295
8  let uint64Max = UInt64.max         18446744073709551615
9
```

FIGURE 2.1
The completed Try It Yourself example finding upper and lower bounds.

TIP

Use `Int` **When Possible**

Although all these types are available for you to use, Apple strongly suggests using `Int` whenever possible, even if you may only need an 8-bit integer, only positive integers (unsigned), and so on. This keeps code consistent, and ensures better interoperability with functions and methods with `Int` return types, preventing you from needing to cast return types to their proper annotation.

The `Double` **Data Type**

`Doubles` are also a common data type to use in Swift. `Doubles` are used when a floating point or decimal value is needed. Akin to `Doubles` are `Floats`, which are similar but with a few differences to note:

▶ `Double` represents a 64-bit floating-point value, and `Float` represents a 32-bit floating-point value.

▶ `Double` has at least 15 decimal digit precision, and `Float` has at least 6 decimal digit precision.

NOTE

When Swift Infers `Double`

Swift always infers `Double` over `Float` when using type inference with floating-point numbers. Because of this, it is suggested to always use `Double` when you need a floating-point number, unless you are working with something designated as a `Float` in another framework. It is also worth noting that if you have a statement in code that involves using an arithmetic operator on integer and floating-point literals, a `Double` return type is inferred. A **literal** is a value that is literally typed into your code as a fixed value, such as 42, -3.14, or "foo".

NOTE

Converting Between Integers and Floating-Point Numbers

There will be times when you need to convert a typed value from one type to another. This is sometimes referred to as **casting**, in that you are casting a variable to behave like another compatible type. For instance, say you have an `Int` with a value of 5, and you need to work with that value as if it were a `Double`. Since a variable cannot change its type once it has been assigned, you must declare a new variable or constant to equal the casted value of the source variable or constant. Consider the following example:

```
let myInt = 5   //this is inferred to be of type Int
let myDouble = Double(myInt)   //myDouble is a Double with the value of 5
```

You can cast a variable or constant by typing the type name and surrounding the variable or constant in parentheses. You can also use casting of variables or constants while adding that value to a value of a different type, so that Swift creates a new variable or constant with the agreed type from the return value, such as the following example:

```
let myNewDouble = Double(myInt) + 1.5
```

Since both `Double(myInt)` and `1.5` are of type `Double`, myNewDouble is inferred to be of type `Double`. You can do the same with numeric literals, but since literals don't have a type until they are assigned, you do not need to cast them. Take this example, with an integer and a floating-point number:

```
let gravity = 9 + 0.8
```

In this case, `gravity` is inferred to be of type `Double`, since Swift operates on the values first (to get 9.8) and then assigns it to `gravity`.

The `Bool` Data Type

Boolean data types are simple because they can only hold the logical values true or false. Boolean types are annotated by the `Bool` keyword. Boolean types are ideal for controlling the flow of app execution, covered in Hour 5, "Controlling Program Flow with Conditionals," and to verify whether a certain condition is `true` or `false`, which then executes a particular block of code. The following is a clear example of how `Bool` values are assigned:

```
let swiftIsCool = true
let objectiveCIsDead = false
```

The preceding example assigns `true` to `swiftIsCool`, and assigns `false` to `objectiveCIsDead`. As there are only `true` or `false` values in Boolean logic, these are the only values that can be assigned.

The `String` Data Type

The next data type to cover is the widely used String data type. A `String` is a logical grouping of characters, and those are, you guessed it, Character data types. Strings are most often what we output to consoles, use as input to text fields, or use as output to screens in labels, text fields, or extended text views.

A `String`, like every type we've talked about thus far, is actually something called a **struct**. A struct is a value type and is a structure that adds functionality to an entity by adding properties and methods. You briefly saw this by getting the maximum value of the `Int` type by calling `Int.max`. An `Int` data type doesn't just hold a number; it also has properties such as min and max and methods such as `distanceTo(other: Int)`.

▼ TRY IT YOURSELF

Find the Properties and Methods on Data Types

Since we know that `Strings`, `Bools`, `Ints`, and `Doubles` (and all variants discussed so far) are structures, you can easily find out what properties and methods are available to use for each data type.

1. Open Xcode and create a playground. Either a Mac or iOS playground is fine.

2. Type the following code:

```
let myInt: Int = 5
let myBool: Bool = true
let myString: String = "Hi"
let myDouble: Double = 1.5
```

3. Hold down the Command key on your keyboard and click the `Int` keyword. Xcode takes you to the definition of `Int`, where you can see, in Swift language, how `Int` was created and what properties and methods are available on the `Int` struct and instances of `Int`s.

4. Click the Back button (a left-pointing arrow) in the bar immediately above the playground's text area, and that takes you back to your code. Hold down the Command key on your keyboard, and this time click the `Bool` keyword. Xcode takes you to the definition of `Bool`, where you can see properties and methods for the `Bool` type.

5. Click the Back button in the bar immediately above the playground's text area, and repeat the previous steps for the `String` and `Double` types. Do you see the differences in how these data types are structured and what is available to you?

`String`s are a mechanism for storing a sequence of values of the `Character` data type. `Character`s are just that, one single character stored in its memory space. This allows us to do many things easily in Swift with regard to strings; we can easily count the number of characters in a `String` instance by using an instance method `someStringValue.characters.count`, and it returns however many Unicode characters represent that `String` called someStringValue. We can also quickly iterate over strings to get each character value at a time with fast enumeration in a for-in loop (we cover loops in Hour 7, "Iterating Code with Loops"). The following example shows a string and how its data is stored:

```
let myStr = "Hi!"
//myStr contains the following: "H", "i", "!"
```

Strings also can easily be concatenated, or joined together, much like adding numbers with the + operator. You already saw an example of this in Hour 1, "Introducing the Swift Development Environment," but it deserves mention here with the `String` discussion. This is a powerful feature and allows for concise but readable code. To concatenate two strings, simply add them when you are assigning them to a new value or using them together for output to the user:

```
let firstString = "Four score"
let secondString = "and seven years ago"
let newString = firstString + secondString
```

The `newString` constant now contains "Four score and seven years ago".

Because strings are so fundamental to Swift, it is now incredibly easy to insert string values, as well as other non-string values, into strings when creating some text to display to the user or to the output console, with something called **string interpolation**. String interpolation allows you to insert the values directly inline in a string literal, by typing the \ (backslash) key, and then surrounding the value with parentheses. Here is an example:

```
let year = 2015
let currentYearText = "The current year is \(year)"
```

The output of the preceding code is a string that contains "The current year is 2015", and sets it to the constant `currentYearText`. Compared to Objective-C, Apple's language of choice for Mac and iOS apps that has been around for almost 30 years, Swift's `String` implementation is a dream. Take a quick look at how the year example looked in Objective-C:

```
NSInteger year = 2015;
NSString *currentYearText = [NSString stringWithFormat:@"The current year is %d",
    ➥year];
```

NOTE

Differences Between Swift and Objective-C

Notice that each statement in Objective-C ends with a semicolon (;). This was to indicate to the compiler that it had reached the end of the statement. Swift infers the end of each statement when you press Return, so you do not need to explicitly type a semicolon, although you can.

Also, Objective-C relied on you, the programmer, to utilize the asterisk (*) character when using **pointers**. All Objective-C objects were pointers to memory in the heap. Swift does not require you to use the pointer indicator, and in fact, you don't use it. We discuss instances in Swift further in Hour 10, "Learning About Structs and Classes."

Before you go off on your own to explore more of these types and how you can work with them, there are a few other smaller things to mention. Swift allows string mutability, simply by declaring a `String` with the `var` introducer instead of the `let` introducer. That way, you can change the contents of a `String` variable simply by setting it to another `String` literal, concatenating one or more strings to it, or setting it to another string variable's value. Mutability with the `var` introducer is not just limited to `String`; I merely wanted to use it as an example.

Swift's `String` struct also provides a property that returns a `Bool` value called `isEmpty`. This is convenient if you need to check whether a `String` instance has any characters in it, such as in an `if-else` block.

Initializing Values

Swift requires that constants and variables be declared before they are used. That means that you use the `let` or `var` introducer to declare a constant or variable with a name and a type (optionally, unless it can't be inferred or you specifically use type annotation). You also can immediately initialize your constants and variables, which is common. You can do this in two ways. First, you can directly assign a literal value to the new constant or variable. Second, you can use that structure's or class's **initializer**. We cover initializers in more depth in Hour 13,

"Customizing Initializers of Classes, Structs, and Enums." Here's a brief example of some sample initializers:

```
let wheelsOnABicycle = 2 // assigns the numeric literal 2
let wheelsOnATricycle = Int(3)  // uses Int's initializer, with the parameter of 3
let emptyString = String() // the empty parentheses indicate an empty String
let piVal = Double(3.14)  // uses Double's initializer, with the parameter of 3.14
```

These seem a little redundant, since you could just as easily type `let piVal = 3.14` instead of using `Double`'s initializer, but you need to get used to this syntax for future lessons, so it is worth explaining now.

One last item to mention for the `String` data type is that since we discovered how to use string interpolation to use non-string values inside strings, you can convert strings with only integers in them to actual `Int` types by using the `toInt()` method on an instance of a `String`. For example:

```
let degreesOutsideString = "80"
  //inferred to be a String because of the double-quotes
let degreesOutsideInt = Int(degreesOutsideString)!
  //returns 80 to degreesOutsideInt as an Int
```

NOTE

Unwrapping Optional Values

Swift has a concept called **optionals**, where a variable may have a value, or it may not. In that case, to remain safe from runtime errors, Swift introduced optionals as a way to wrap values, or lack of values, in a wrapper to be safely passed around and used. The exclamation point (!) in the preceding example tells Swift to explicitly unwrap what is returned from converting the string to an integer because theoretically `degreesOutsideString` could have a value with any character, such as the degree symbol, or "eighty," which is not convertible to an integer. We discuss optionals more in Hour 6, "Understanding Optional Values."

Summary

In this hour, we covered a lot of material regarding the basic data types in Swift, including `Int`, `Double`, `Bool`, and `String`. We learned what types of data each one stores, how to initialize them with proper data, and even how to investigate the full list of data type properties and methods by command-clicking the data type's keyword in Xcode. We even covered some more in-depth topics such as type conversion and string interpolation.

We also really learned how Swift can derive types by using type inference based on the value or values given to a constant or variable, and what it means to have a constant or variable in your code.

In the next hour, we discuss operators, such as +, -, =, ==, and more, and how to work with operators with the data types discussed in this hour. It will be beneficial to jump to operators first before diving into more advanced data types like arrays, dictionaries, and sets, which are discussed in Hour 4, "Working with Collection Types."

Q&A

Q. Will I harm anything by trying out data types with different values?

A. Absolutely not. Playgrounds offer a great way to test your code while providing immediate feedback. Have fun!

Q. Should I always explicitly declare a data type?

A. Not necessarily. There may be situations where it is best to declare a data type, but in simple applications, it is not always necessary to do so. Generally you decide this on a case-by-case basis.

Q. Do all variables have to contain values?

A. No. Swift allows us to use optionals, where a variable can either have a value or not. Optional variables are declared with a question mark: `var myOptInt : Int?`. We learn more about optionals in Hour 6.

Workshop

The workshop contains quiz questions and exercises to help you solidify your understanding of the material covered. Try to answer all questions before looking at the answers that follow.

Quiz

1. What is the difference between `let` and `var`?

2. In the following code, what will Swift infer the data type as?

   ```
   var hasComment = false
   ```

3. What is an unsigned integer?

4. In the following code, what will Swift infer the data type as?

   ```
   var customerAge = "25"
   ```

5. What character is used to concatenate strings in Swift?

Answers

1. The introducer `let` indicates a constant. The introducer `var` indicates a variable.

2. Swift will infer the data type as `Bool`.

3. Unsigned integers can hold a large positive number but cannot contain negative values.

4. Swift will infer the data type as `String`. The actual value is an `Int`, but since the value is wrapped in quotes, Swift will assign the `String` data type.

5. The plus sign (+) is used to join (or concatenate) strings in Swift.

Exercise

Create a new playground. Create two constants to hold your first and last name. Create another constant to hold your favorite quote. Join and display the variables by using concatenation and string interpolation. Next, try to get the count of how many characters are in your joined string.

HOUR 3
Using Operators in Swift

What You'll Learn in This Hour:

▶ How to identify unary, binary, and ternary operators

▶ How to use arithmetic operators

▶ How to use logical operators

▶ How to use assignment and equality operators

▶ How to use operators with strings

▶ How to use range operators

Operators are a key ingredient to every app. In fact, it's difficult to write an app—other than the standard "Hello, world!" example—that doesn't contain at least one operator. Operators are symbols or a set of symbols that change or assign values, combine values, or check or verify values in your code. In this hour, we learn about most of the basic operators in Swift and understand why and how to use them.

All operators in Swift can be categorized as **unary**, **binary**, or **ternary**. Unary operators perform an action upon a single operand, binary operators perform an action upon two operands, and ternary operators perform an action involving three operands.

Unary Operators

A unary operator operates on a single value. A unary operator can be **prefix** or **postfix**, meaning that it can come before a variable or constant (prefix, such as ++count), or immediately follow a variable or constant (postfix, such as count++). Some unary operators can be either (prefix or postfix), while some can be only one or the other. A unary operator cannot have any whitespace between itself and the variable or constant. Unary operators act upon numeric and Boolean types in Swift. Let's take a look at Swift's unary operators.

Increment and Decrement Operators

Two similar operators are the **increment operator** and the **decrement operator**. The increment operator, denoted by ++, increases a numeric value by 1, and the decrement operator, denoted by --, decreases a numeric value by 1. The increment operator is short-hand for a longer expression; a++ is the same as a = a + 1, and a-- is the same as a = a - 1. Both the increment and decrement operators can be prefix or postfix.

There is a key difference in behavior, however, between the increment and decrement operators concerning prefix and postfix. That is the order in which the value is incremented or decremented and when assignment occurs. A prefixed decrement operator decrements the numeric value by 1 and returns the newly assigned value. Likewise, a prefixed increment operator increments the numeric value by 1 and returns the newly assigned value. The postfixed decrement operator first returns the numeric value before decrementing; likewise, the postfixed increment operator returns the numeric value before incrementing. Take a look at the following code example to see this behavior in action:

```
var x = 1
print(++x)
//++x - x increments first, new value is displayed
x = 1
//just resetting value for demonstration
print(x++)
//now x is incremented, but after the print function has already occurred
print(x)
//notice the different value now when this line is printed?
```

Logical NOT Operator

The logical **NOT** operator inverts the value of a Boolean variable. In other words, if a variable's value is true, the variable will now be false, and vice versa. The logical NOT operator is always a prefix operator. We discuss the logical NOT operator and other logical operators a little more in depth later in this hour. Here is what the logical NOT operator looks like in code:

```
let a = true // a is a Bool equaling true
let b = !a // b is a Bool equaling false
```

CAUTION

The Logical NOT Operator Must Be a Prefix Operator

Using (!) after a special type of variable, called an **optional value**, has another meaning, which is covered in Hour 6, "Understanding Optional Values."

Unary Minus Operator

The unary **minus** operator is short-hand for multiplying a variable's value by -1, and returning the result. The unary minus operator is always a prefix operator and can prefix variables, constants, or numeric literals. Here is what the unary minus operator looks like in code:

```
let c = 5
let d = -c // d is equal to -5
let e = -42 // e is equal to -42
```

Swift also has a unary **plus** operator, by prefixing a + before any variable or constant, but it doesn't actually change the value of a numeric variable, because any negative multiplied by a positive is still a negative. The unary plus operator is more for distinction in your code to show that a certain value should be positive. It is very rarely used, but it is available.

Binary Operators

Binary operators are operators that affect **operands**, which are the values on either side of the operator. For example, take a + b. In this expression, a and b are operands, and + is the operator. All Binary operators are **infix**, meaning they are in between two operands.

Standard Arithmetic Operators

Swift provides the four standard arithmetic operators that are binary operators for all numeric types, which are addition (+), subtraction (-), division (/), and multiplication (*). To use these operators in code, you use them exactly the way you would write them in a math equation:

```
let a = 5 + 5 // a equals 10
let b = 3 - 2 // b equals 1
let c = 8.0 / 5.0 // c equals 1.6
let d = 4 * 4 // d equals 16
```

Remainder Operator

Swift includes a **remainder operator**, annotated by the % sign. In other languages, this operator is called the **modulo operator**, which has slightly different behavior. Swift calculates the remainder operator by figuring out how many times b evenly divides a, and returns the remainder. In other words, a = (b * multiplier) + remainder, with `multiplier` being the largest number b could multiply against to not produce a value higher than a.

In languages like C and Objective-C, the modulo operator behaved similarly, but unlike Swift, it could not perform against floating-point numbers; you would get a compiler error as the modulo operator cannot take floating-point numbers as its operands. This is another reason that Swift's remainder operator is truly a remainder operator, because Swift gives the remainder of what is left over from `a - (b * multiplier)`. Listing 3.1 displays the modulo operator in C.

LISTING 3.1   Modulo Operator in C and Objective-C

```
int a = 8;
int b = 6;
int c = a % b; // returns 2, as expected
int d = -8;
int e = d % b; // returns -2, as expected
```

In C and Objective-C, the modulo operator is pretty straightforward, as long as you're providing integers. Listing 3.2 displays the remainder operator in Swift, which not only works with integers like C, but can also operate on `Double` types.

LISTING 3.2   Remainder Operator in Swift

```
let a = 8
let b = 6
let c = a % b // returns 2, just as in C
let d = 8.0
let e = 2.5
let f = d % e // returns 0.5, Swift allows remainders for Double types
```

The Assignment Operator

There is just one **assignment operator** in Swift, as in other languages, and that is the equal sign (=). The assignment operator takes the calculated or literal value on the right side of the equal sign and assigns it to the variable or constant on the left side of the equal sign. We have seen the assignment operator many times throughout this book already, and every single line in Listing 3.1 and Listing 3.2 utilizes the assignment operator.

Compound Assignment Operators

Compound assignment operators in Swift utilize the previously mentioned assignment operator (=), coupled with another operator, to perform a combined effect. Table 3.1 details each operator, what code it is short for, and a description.

TABLE 3.1　Compound Assignment Operators

Operator	Example	Longer Expression	Description
+=	a += b	a = a + b	Add, then assign
-=	a -= b	a = a - b	Subtract, then assign
*=	a *= b	a = a * b	Multiply, then assign
/=	a /= b	a = a / b	Divide, then assign
%=	a %= b	a = a % b	Compute remainder, then assign

Table 3.1 shows some of the basic compound operators. However, there are many more compound operators, all of which are more advanced than the scope of this book, such as bitwise and logical compound operations. For more information on these operators, see the chapter on expressions in *The Swift Programming Language*, Apple, 2015.

Comparison Operators

Comparison operators in Swift are similar to those of other programming languages. Each one returns a Boolean value describing whether the expression was true or false. Table 3.2 lists the basic comparison operators.

TABLE 3.2　Comparison Operators

Operator	Example	Description
>	a > b	Returns true if a is greater than b, else false.
<	a < b	Returns true if a is less than b, else false.
>=	a >= b	Returns true if a is greater than or equal to b, else false.
<=	a <= b	Returns true if a is less than or equal to b, else false.
==	a == b	Returns true if a is equal to b, else false.
!=	a != b	Returns true if a is not equal to b, else false.

As with comparison operators, there are other advanced operators. We cannot discuss them all in this book, but we cover two more of them in Hour 10, "Learning About Structs and Classes."

NOTE

Using Comparison Operators

Most often, comparison operators are used in conditional statements, such as an `if` block, or in loop statements, such as a `while` block. Examples would be `if a > b { print("a is greater than b" }`, or `while a < 100 { ++a }`. We cover conditionals and control flow in Hour 5, "Controlling Program Flow with Conditionals," and loops in Hour 7, "Iterating Code with Loops."

Range Operators

Range operators in Swift are denoted by two dots and a left angle bracket (`..<`) or three dots (`...`) depending on what type of range you need. There are two types of range operators: **half-closed range operators** and **closed range operators**.

A half-closed range operator uses two dots and a left angle bracket to indicate a range of integers from its left-hand operand up to but not including the right-hand operand. The expression `1..<5` defines a range of four integers, 1 through 4, but not including 5. You can also use variables or constants with range operators, such as `1..<a`. The half-closed operator is called as such because its range contains its initial value but not the final value.

A closed range operator uses three dots to indicate a range of integers from its left-hand operand up to and including the right-hand operand. The expression `-2...2` defines a range of five integers, from -2 to +2. The closed range operator can also use variables or constants as operands, such as `a...b`. The closed range operator is called closed range because the range is closed on each end by including both operands.

Both half-closed range operators and closed range operators are useful in iterative expressions. Closed range operators are good for ranges where you want both the first and last values of the range to be included. Half-closed range operators are especially good for zero-based lists such as arrays, where the index of the first element is 0, followed by 1, then 2, and so on. Arrays are discussed in more detail in Hour 4, "Working with Collection Types." Consider the code in Listing 3.3—it illustrates the differences in the two range operators.

LISTING 3.3   Different Range Operators

```
for a in 1...5 {
    print(a)
}
//This closed range prints the following:
//1
//2
//3
//4
//5
```

```
let arrayLength = 3
for b in 0..<arrayLength {
    print(b)
}
//This half-closed range prints the following:
//0
//1
//2
```

CAUTION

Ranges Must Progress in a Positive Direction

Ranges in Swift must progress in a positive direction. The starting index (left-hand operand) must be less than or equal to the ending index (right-hand operand). Attempting to progress in a negative direction will result in a compiler error if detected when coding or a run-time error and crash if detected while the app is running. You might want to validate that the left-hand operand is less than the right-hand operand if your operands are not known at compile time.

Logical Operators

Swift provides three **logical operators**, AND (&&), OR(||), and NOT (!). These operators are called logical operators because they evaluate upon and return Boolean value types based on logic. The three logical operators compare the bits inside their given operands, perform the operation against them, and then return the result. These three operators are similar to those you would find in other languages, but we discuss them here if you're not familiar.

Logical AND Operator

The **logical AND operator**, sometimes referred to as just AND, performs a logical AND operation against both operands and returns the result. Let's illustrate how AND operates and comes up with a return value. Look at the truth table in Table 3.3.

TABLE 3.3 Logical AND Operator Truth Table

Operand 1	Operand 2	AND Result
True	True	True
True	False	False
False	True	False
False	False	False

Let's say you're comparing two Boolean values, a and b, in the following code sample:

```
let a = true
let b = false
let c = a && b
```

What value does c have? You're right; c is false. The AND operator is useful when every value in a certain set of conditions needs to be met first before executing an expression or set of expressions. For example, the following code snippet illustrates what use of the AND operator looks like if you were to try to get access to a device's motion data:

```
if CMPedometer.isStepCountingAvailable() && userAcceptedUseOfMotionProcessor {
    /* it's now ok to get step data */
} else {
    print("cannot get step data")
}
```

If step counting is not available (known by the Boolean return value of CMPedometer. isStepCountingAvailable()) or if the user has explicitly stated it's not okay for us to have access to the device's motion coprocessor, then we cannot count the user's steps.

Logical OR Operator

The logical OR operator is similar in syntax to the AND operator but behaves slightly differently. The OR operator evaluates two operands and decides whether either one is true or not, no matter which one, and then returns its result. The truth table in Table 3.4 details the OR operator's behavior.

TABLE 3.4 Logical OR Operator Truth Table

Operand 1	Operand 2	OR Result
True	True	True
True	False	True
False	True	True
False	False	False

The OR operator returns true if either operand in the expression is true. Let's take another look at a simple code snippet to illustrate OR:

```
let a = true
let b = false
let c = a || b
```

What is the value of c? Again, you're right; the value is `true`. A more realistic example might look something like this:

```
if userHasCellularConnectivity || userHasWifiConnectivity {
    // assume user has an internet connection, start talking to web service
} else {
    // warn user to enable connectivity hardware
}
```

In the previous example, if either of the two operands (`userHasCellularConnectivity` or `userHasWifiConnectivity`) is true, then the first block of code executes. If neither operand is true, the second block of code executes. We cover conditionals with `if` statements in Hour 5.

Logical NOT Operator

The last logical operator, NOT, as mentioned earlier, simply inverts the value of a Boolean variable or constant. Although not a binary operator, NOT is listed here in the logical operators section for completeness. For example, see Table 3.5 for the truth table illustrating the values resulting from the NOT operator.

TABLE 3.5 Logical NOT Operator Truth Table

Operand	NOT Result
True	False
False	True

Combining Logical Operators

Logical operators can be combined into larger expressions where multiple lines of logic may be required. The expression `a && b || !c` combines all three logical operators and can be read as "a and b must be true, or not c". While not required, you can insert parentheses to explicitly state the order of operations you want in your code, such as `(a && b) || (!(c && d))`.

Ternary Conditional Operators

Swift has only one ternary conditional operator, and it is written as short-hand for a longer expression that checks a particular case or condition and provides a value for the true branch and another value for the false branch. We cover the ternary conditional operator in greater detail in Hour 5, since it is a more succinct substitution for a longer conditional expression.

Summary

In this hour, we covered a lot of material regarding operators. Most operators are straightforward, but if you don't understand any, don't worry; operators are used frequently throughout the book, and you will pick it up by repetition. Logical operators manipulate and/ or combine Boolean values `true` and `false`. Unary operators act upon a single target, binary operators act upon two targets, and ternary operators compare a Boolean value to execute one of two expressions. Operators can be prefix, postfix, or infix, meaning they can be written immediately in front of an operand, immediately after an operand, or in between two operands, respectively. Most of these types of operators are familiar from other languages.

A set of operators in Swift that are new to some C and Objective-C programmers are range operators. These prove to be powerful for iterating over ranges of values, items in a list, and others. Range operators come in two types: half-closed range operators, which include the first but not the last values given, and closed range operators, which include the first and the last values given. We use these operators multiple times throughout this book.

In the next hour, we discuss collection types including `Arrays` and `Dictionaries`. `Arrays` and `Dictionaries` are crucial to many apps, in that they keep lists of multiple objects in memory to be used for things such as data sources, data retrieved from networks, or even to store preferences between app launches.

Q&A

Q. Is it better to use postfix or prefix?

A. This depends on the needs of your calculations. There is no performance gain using one or the other; it purely depends on how you need to use them. For instance, ++a and a++ both increment a, but the former increments before returning its value, and the latter returns its value and then increments. Be careful of this distinction in your code.

Q. Why are there two range operators? Wouldn't it be simpler to just use one?

A. Having two range operators allows you to express intent a lot more clearly in code. In the case of a zero-based list, you may have 10 items but the last item's index is 9, so a half-closed range operator (0..<count, for instance) would be a better fit. If you know you have a finite number of times something should loop, a closed-range operator (1...10, for instance) clearly indicates a range of 1 to 10.

Q. What is a practical example of using remainder?

A. Imagine an app that shows a progress bar when loading. In this case, the progress is only checked occasionally (every nth time) throughout the loading loop, or when the count of the loop % n is equal to 0. This becomes clearer in later hours when we cover conditionals and control flow in Hour 5 and loops in Hour 7.

Workshop

The workshop contains quiz questions and exercises to help you solidify your understanding of the material covered. Try to answer all questions before looking at the answers that follow.

Quiz

1. What is the difference between postfix and prefix unary operators?

2. In the following code, what is the value of the constant c?

```
let a = 11
let b = 5
let c = a % b
```

3. In the following code, what is the value of the variable a?

```
var a = 5
let b = 6
a *= b
```

4. In the following code, what is the value of the constant b?

```
let a = 5
let b = -a
```

5. What is the difference between two dots with a left angle bracket (..<) and three dots (...) in a range operation?

Answers

1. The postfix increment does not increase the value of its operand until after it has been evaluated. The prefix decrement increases the value of its operand before it has been evaluated.

2. The value of c after the remainder operator is 1.

3. The value of a after the compound assignment is 30.

4. The value of b after the unary minus operation is -5.

5. The two dot with left angle bracket range (..<) is a half-closed range because the upper limit is noninclusive. The three dot range (...) is a closed range because the upper limit is inclusive.

Exercise

Create a new playground. Create two variables to hold two separate numbers, 1 and 10. Use different comparison operators to compare the two values. Next, display the numbers using both the half-closed and closed ranges.

Working with Collection Types

What You'll Learn in This Hour:

▶ The structure of arrays

▶ The structure of dictionaries

▶ The structure of sets

▶ How to create instances of collections

▶ How to use subscripts and keys to access data

▶ How to use tuples to access key-value pairs

In this hour, we explore the three types of **collections** in Swift: **arrays**, **sets**, and **dictionaries**. We also cover a data structure called a **tuple**, which isn't a declarable data type like an array, set, or dictionary but can be used to get data of varying types from dictionaries and other structures. Collections are common structures used in everyday apps because they are great for things like storing data source information, storing retrieved data from a network resource, storing ordered or even unordered lists of information, and more. We can do a lot of things with collections, so let's get started.

Arrays

Let's start by learning about arrays. Arrays are ordered sets of data, and every member inside an array must be of the same type. This means that if you have an array of integers, all the members must be of the integer type, and you cannot insert a `Double`, `Character`, `String`, or any other data type into the array. Swift's array structures behave this way to help with type safety to prevent the incorrect data type from entering an array and having potentially harmful side effects.

Declaring an array in Swift is simple. As you have done already with types such as `Int`, `Double`, `String`, and so on, you do something similar with the array type, with one small twist. You have to specify the type of data that will be stored in the array, and that type is placed inside open and closed chevrons. Here is what an array declaration looks like in Swift:

```
let myArray: Array<Int> = [1, 2, 3]
```

As you are familiar with by now, the `let` introducer signifies that the array is a constant. `myArray` is the name of the constant, and `Array<Int>` tells Swift that `myArray` is an array of `Int`s. Placing comma-separated values inside square brackets, as you see with `[1, 2, 3]`, is an array literal and is a way to provide elements to an array quickly.

CAUTION
Array Member Types Cannot Change

Keep in mind that once you declare an array, even with the `var` introducer to make it a mutable array, its member's types cannot change. This helps keep type safety consistent, and Swift warns you even before compiling if it notices you are trying to insert a value of a different type. If you need an array to store different types than an array you currently have, declare a new array with that desired member type.

As with many things in Swift, there is another way (and yes, an even shorter way) to declare an array of a particular type. From the previous example, let's declare `myArray` as an array of `Int`s again but now using Swift's short-hand syntax for declaring an array:

```
let myArray: [Int] = [1, 2, 3]
```

`[Int]` is Swift short-hand for declaring `myArray` of type `Array<Int>`. The same could be done for `[Double]`, `[String]`, `[Bool]`, or even if you had a custom class, struct, or other type, you could create an array of that type too, such as `[MyCustomClass]`. However, because of Swift's tremendous power to infer types, we can shorten this declaration even further:

```
let myArray = [1, 2, 3]
```

Excellent! Because of the square brackets, Swift infers `myArray` to be an array. Then, Swift analyzes the data inside the square brackets and senses that they are all integers, so it declares `myArray` to be `[Int]` for us.

NOTE
Best Practice for Declaring Instances of `Array`

Unless necessary, it is suggested for consistency and readability to use `Array` short-hand syntax with the enclosing square braces, such as `[Int]` rather than `Array<Int>`. This is because it visually models more closely the structure of an `Array`.

In the event you just want to declare an empty array, you can use either of two methods: use open and close parentheses after the open and close brackets with the member type inside, or assign an empty array literal after declaring the type annotation. Both are shown here:

```
var todoItems = [String]()
var moreTodoItems: [String] = []
```

[String] indicates to Swift that you want a variable array to hold instances of type String, and in the first line, the () short-hand syntax indicates to Swift to initialize the array with no items, as an empty array. Likewise, in the second line, you are simply telling Swift what type moreTodoItems is and then assigning an empty array literal. Either method is acceptable; use whichever you prefer.

NOTE

All Values Must Be Initialized to Be Used

Remember that all instances in Swift must be initialized before they are used; thus, the short-hand initializer syntax is common. You may find yourself using it frequently when you don't know the values needing to be stored in an array yet.

Indexes and Subscripts for Accessing Values

Each member in a Swift array has an associated **index**. This behavior is the same as C and Objective-C, as well as many other languages, in case you have experience there. You can use this index to reference a member inside the array. All arrays in Swift are **zero-based**, which means that the first index in an array is always zero (0), the second index is 1, the third is 2, and so on. Why is that important to mention? If you have an array that has five elements—let's say "A," "B," "C," "D," and "E"—to get the value "E," you ask the array for the value at index 4, because index 4 is actually the fifth element's index in the array. To access the data in an array, you use a **subscript**. Subscripts are indexes enclosed inside square brackets immediately following the name of the array in code. Let's take a minute to try this out.

TRY IT YOURSELF ▼

Create and Access Data in an Array

We just learned a lot about creating arrays, how arrays handle member types, and setting initial data. Walk through these exercises to get comfortable with arrays and their syntax.

1. Open Xcode and create a new playground. Either an iOS or Mac playground will work for this example.

2. In the playground, declare a variable array named myArray to hold String values and initialize the array to have the values "Foo", "Bar", and "Baz".

   ```
   var myArray = ["Foo", "Bar", "Baz"]
   ```

3. On the next line, type just the name of your array and watch the results pane to see how Xcode displays the contents of arrays.

   ```
   myArray
   ```

▼

4. Use subscript syntax to access the second element in the array. Did Xcode return "Bar"?

```
myArray[1]
```

5. This time use subscript syntax to change the value for the first element to "Dog", by using the assignment operator we learned about in Hour 3, "Using Operators in Swift." Then type the name of the array again to see the resulting array.

```
myArray[0] = "Dog"
myArray
```

Figure 4.1 shows the resulting playground from the Try It Yourself example.

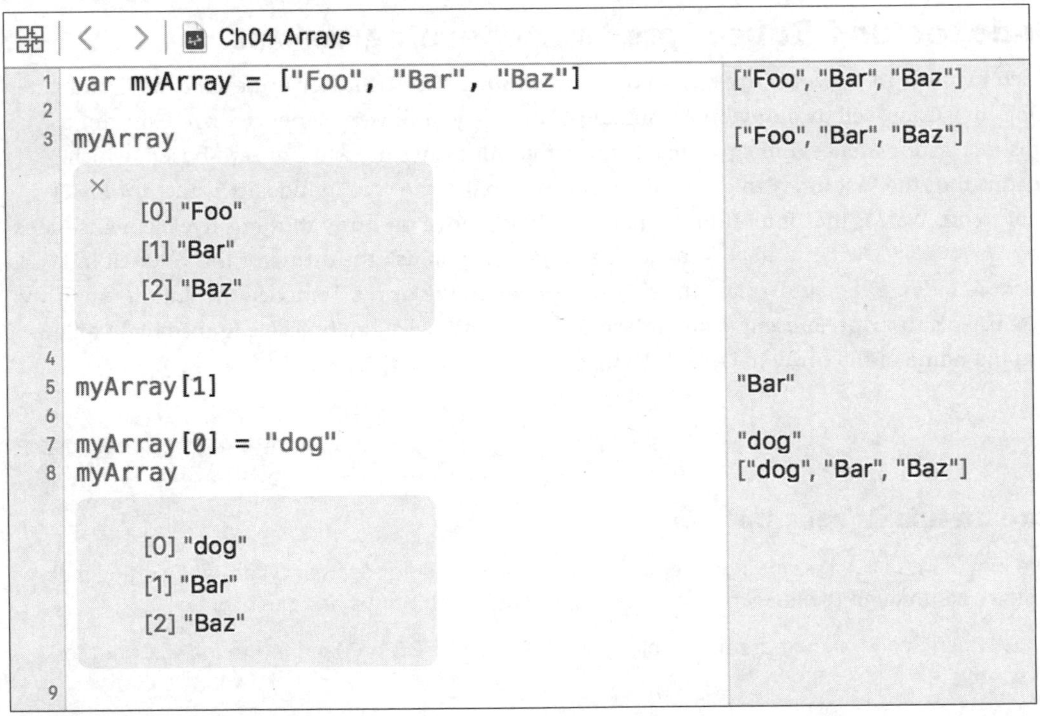

```
 ⊞⊟  <  >  📄 Ch04 Arrays

 1  var myArray = ["Foo", "Bar", "Baz"]            ["Foo", "Bar", "Baz"]
 2
 3  myArray                                        ["Foo", "Bar", "Baz"]

       ×
            [0] "Foo"
            [1] "Bar"
            [2] "Baz"

 4
 5  myArray[1]                                     "Bar"
 6
 7  myArray[0] = "dog"                             "dog"
 8  myArray                                        ["dog", "Bar", "Baz"]

            [0] "dog"
            [1] "Bar"
            [2] "Baz"

 9
```

FIGURE 4.1
The resulting playground.

Manipulating Arrays

In the preceding Try It Yourself section, step 5 walks you through changing the value of one of an array's members. You can use subscripts to change a value inside an array. Just be sure that you are inserting data of the proper type.

Adding Elements to Arrays

Another action you may want to take on arrays is appending elements to an array. For instance, say you're building a To Do manager, where the user inserts tasks to remind himself to do things. It wouldn't be an effective app if the user wasn't allowed to add tasks. Thankfully, Swift gives us an easy method to use on an array instance to append a value, and it is called **append**. Take a look at Listing 4.1 to see how appending to an array works.

LISTING 4.1   Appending an Element to an Array

```
var tasks = [String]()  // initializes empty array to tasks
tasks = ["Clean house", "Walk dog"]  // tasks now has 2 elements
tasks.append("Wash the car")  // tasks now has 3 elements
print(tasks)  // displays: [Clean house, Walk dog, Wash the car]
```

You can append items to arrays by not only using the append(someValue) method on your array instance, but you can also use the addition-assignment compound operator, discussed in Hour 3. To add items this way, you must enclose them inside square brackets as an array literal, even if you are appending one item. Using the code in Listing 4.1, see Listing 4.2 for a continuation.

LISTING 4.2   Appending an Array with the Addition-Assignment Operator

```
tasks += ["Milk the cow"]  // tasks now has 4 elements
tasks += ["Rake leaves", "Mow lawn"]  // tasks now has 6 elements
tasks.count  // displays 6
```

In the previous example, we used the addition-assignment operator to add array literals to our existing array. This illustrates some of Swift's power, with concise syntax.

CAUTION

Be Careful with Subscript Syntax

You cannot append items to an array by using subscript syntax. Doing so, such as assigning "Fill gas tank" to index subscript 10, would result in an **out of bounds** error because the compiler checks first to see whether an element at that index exists, which it doesn't. You can always determine how many elements are in an array by using the count property on an array. It returns the number of elements in that array. Just remember, if there are five elements in an array, the last index is 4, because arrays are zero-based.

Inserting Elements into Arrays

Remember that arrays are ordered lists, and when you append an item to an array, it tacks the new item on to the end of the array. Table 4.1 illustrates an abstract representation of how an array can be visualized.

TABLE 4.1   Array Visualization

Index	Value
0	"Clean house"
1	"Walk dog"
2	"Wash the car"
3	"Milk the cow"
4	"Rake leaves"
5	"Mow lawn"

Suppose in our To Do app, our user wants to take a shower after milking the cow. We could change the value at index 4, but then he or she wouldn't be reminded to rake the leaves. Swift provides a way to insert elements into an array at a particular index, with the `insert(someValue)` method. Building upon Listing 4.1 and Listing 4.2, Listing 4.3 illustrates how to insert an item into our existing list of tasks.

LISTING 4.3   Inserting an Element into an Array

```
tasks.insert("Take a shower", atIndex: 4)   // tasks now has 7 elements
```

Now our array of tasks should look like Table 4.2.

TABLE 4.2   Array Visualization After Insertion

Index	Value
0	"Clean house"
1	"Walk dog"
2	"Wash the car"
3	"Milk the cow"
4	"Take a shower"
5	"Rake leaves"
6	"Mow lawn"

Replacing and Updating Items in an Array

Replacing values at a particular index is as easy as using subscript syntax denoting the index you want to update, and using the assignment operator (=) to set the new value. For example, to update "Walk dog" to "Walk Boudreau", simply type the following code:

```
tasks[1] = "Walk Boudreau"
```

Swift even has syntax for replacing ranges of values inside arrays. The range lengths don't have to be the same either, as Swift resizes the array to fit the new length. Perhaps you know that "Wash the car," "Milk the cow," and "Take a shower" are all part of your daily routine, and you don't need them spelled out for you. You could replace them with a new array literal or values from another array. The inserted value must be an array of the same type as the receiving array, even if you're only inserting one value. The following example illustrates the concept of replacing ranges:

```
tasks[2...4] = ["Daily routine"]
```

Removing Items in an Array

Swift's array structure provides many ways to remove elements from an array instance. Removing an item in an array deletes the item itself, and if necessary, shifts all the affected indexes so that they are once again sequential from 0 to count-1. Depending on the method used to delete items from an array, you might also be returned the item being deleted, which can be useful for comparisons and such. Before we move on to dictionaries, let's try removing some items from our tasks list.

TRY IT YOURSELF ▼

Remove Items from the Tasks List

Use several different methods to remove items from the tasks list.

1. Open Xcode and create a new playground. Either a Mac or iOS playground is fine.

2. Create and populate the array tasks by writing all the code from Listings 4.1, 4.2, and 4.3.

3. Our user cleaned the house, so remove the first item in the tasks list:

```
tasks.removeAtIndex(0)
```

4. Our user decided not to mow the lawn, and since it's the last item in our array, we can simply remove the last item:

```
tasks.removeLast()
```

5. Our user just got lazy, and decided not to do anything. Clear the tasks array all at once:

```
tasks.removeAll(keepCapacity: false)  // or...
tasks = []  // either line would remove all items and set size to 0
```

The complete set of tasks is shown in Figure 4.2.

```
31
32   // Hour 4 TIY #2
33   tasks.removeAtIndex(0)                     "Clean house"
34   tasks.removeLast()                         "Mow lawn"
35   tasks.removeAll(keepCapacity: false)       []
36   tasks                                      []
37   tasks = []                                 []
38   tasks                                      []
39
```

FIGURE 4.2
The completed Try It Yourself section, illustrating how to remove items from an array.

Common Array Methods and Properties

Swift's array structure provides many methods for getting information from an array instance. Probably the most common is `count`. `count` is an instance property of type `Int` that tells you how many items are in the array. You can simply use `myArray.count` to return to you the number of items.

Another helpful instance property of arrays is the property `isEmpty`. `isEmpty` returns a `Bool` as to whether the array is empty or not. This is commonly used in conditional statements (more on conditional statements in Hour 5, "Controlling Program Flow with Conditionals"), such as an `if` statement, because `if` statements evaluate Boolean expressions. Consider the following code example to illustrate the `isEmpty` and `count` properties:

```
if myArray.isEmpty {
    print ("There are no items in myArray!")
} else {
    print("There are \(myArray.count) items in myArray.")
}
```

Arrays have many other methods and computed properties as well, where you can tell the array instance to perform a particular task or ask it for data. Two such properties are `first` and `last`. These two properties are pretty self-explanatory; they return a single item from the array instance, whether the first item or last, respectively.

To get a look at what all you can do with arrays, as well as with any types, hold down the Command key and click the type (in this case, type `Array<Int>` and Command-click the word "Array" in Xcode), and Xcode takes you directly to the type's definition. Anything you see with a `var` introducer is a property, and anything that starts with `func` is a function or method. Most often, too, Apple provides documentation in its code in the form of comments above methods or properties that need explanation. This is a great way to learn what's available if you are the type of person who likes digging through code!

Dictionaries

Dictionaries in Swift are similar to arrays in that they hold lists of data, except dictionaries are unordered lists, and instead of accessing them via indexes, dictionary values are accessed via **keys**. A key is a unique identifier for every value in a dictionary. Keys can be `Ints`, `Doubles`, `Strings`, `Bools`, and even enum members, because a key must be **hashable**. Hashable means that the value can be made uniquely identifiable via a hash algorithm. Swift uses hashes for keys behind the scenes because this makes finding values for keys perform better. Don't worry about hashes, though; you won't have to interact with them directly.

NOTE

Enum Members as Dictionary Keys

A value type we've not yet discussed are enumerations, sometimes referred to as simply enums. Enums hold a unique group of related values, and because of this, can make great unique keys for dictionaries—and you get the benefit of code completion for safety, rather than potentially misspelling key names. We discuss enums in Hour 12, "Harnessing the Power of Enums."

Key-Value Pairs

Data is stored in dictionaries in **key-value pairs**. A key-value pair is similar in concept to arrays where a value has an associated index, although dictionaries are unordered, and data members are referenced by their keys. Each key and value in a dictionary must have a data type, and it must remain consistent throughout the life of the dictionary. For instance, to declare a dictionary with keys of type `String` and values of type `Double`, it would look like the following code example:

```
var myDictionary: Dictionary<String, Double> = ["pi" : 3.14]
```

The preceding dictionary declaration is similar to arrays in that you specify the types to be used inside the dictionary in between the open- and closed-chevrons. The differences here are that there are two types inside the chevrons rather than just one, represented as `<key-type, value-type>`, and the dictionary literal we assigned as our initial value uses `"pi"` as the key string, and the literal `3.14` as the value. This satisfies Swift's type safety requirements.

Dictionaries in Swift are slightly different than Objective-C's `NSDictionary` and `NSMutableDictionary` classes, which can store any type of object as their keys and values, and no information was provided about the type of data stored in these dictionaries. Often you, the developer, had to perform introspection on a retrieved object, meaning you asked it what type of class it was first before you could do anything with the returned value. Swift allows you to do something similar by telling a dictionary to use the `Any` type for the value type, but it is not the default behavior, and you should make sure you explicitly state the data type if it is known.

NOTE

Using Swift's `Any` **and** `AnyObject` **Types**

Swift provides two generic data types, `Any` and `AnyObject`. `Any` refers to an instance of any type at all, not including function types. `AnyObject` refers to an instance of any class type. We discuss `Any` and `AnyObject` more in Hour 15, "Adding Advanced Type Functionality."

Initializing Dictionaries

As mentioned already, instances of all types in Swift must be initialized first before use with at least a zero value or empty array or dictionary. There are two ways to declare an empty `Dictionary` in Swift for easy initialization. The following four lines are functionally the same, just written differently to illustrate the differences in how you can initialize a `Dictionary` instance:

```
var newDictionary = Dictionary<String, String>()
var newDictionary: Dictionary<String, String> = [:]
var newDictionary = [String : String]()
var newDictionary: [String : String] = [:]
```

The first line uses the open- and closed-parentheses to tell Swift to use `Dictionary`'s default `init()` method, which returns an empty instance of a `Dictionary<String, String>` structure. The second line initializes a `Dictionary<String, String>` instance by giving it an empty dictionary literal (`[:]`). The third line uses short-hand syntax for declaring a `Dictionary` of type `[String : String]`, similar to `Array` short-hand, and uses open- and closed-parentheses to initialize. The fourth line uses short-hand syntax again and then assigns an empty dictionary literal. Any of these methods of initialization is correct and acceptable. Here we make the dictionary a `var` because if we declare a constant dictionary with `let`, it won't allow us to modify it in the future.

NOTE

Best Practice for Declaring Instances of `Dictionary`

The suggested best practice for declaring instances of `Dictionary` is to use the short-hand syntax from the third and fourth lines of the previous example. This is for consistency and readability, as it visually models the structure of a `Dictionary` better than `Dictionary<KeyType, ValueType>`.

Type Inference with Dictionaries

Swift can also infer the types of the keys and values of dictionaries by the types of the values given during initialization. Listing 4.4 shows how to explicitly declare a dictionary with typed keys and values, and then also by using Swift's type inference.

LISTING 4.4   Using Type Inference to Reduce Code

```
// First, declare a Dictionary with explicit types
var myDictionary: [String : Double] = ["pi" : 3.14]
// Next, we'll declare the same Dictionary using type inference
var myDictionary = ["pi" : 3.14]
```

As you can see, not only did Swift infer that myDictionary is a Dictionary based on the provided dictionary literal, but it also inferred the types of the keys and values inside the dictionary. That is powerful! In addition to Swift's type inference saving us some time typing, type inference also greatly reduces the risk of errors occurring down the road, because Swift is checking for type safety any time your variable or constant is used.

Adding Data to Dictionaries

As seen previously, you can initialize dictionaries with dictionary literals, such as ["pi" : 3.14]. You can provide more than one key-value pair in a literal by separating each pair with a comma. For instance, Listing 4.5 initializes a dictionary with two key-value pairs.

LISTING 4.5   Initializing a Dictionary with Multiple Key-Value Pairs

```
var specialNumbers = ["pi" : 3.14, "gravity" : 9.8]
```

The Dictionary instance from Listing 4.5 now holds two key-value pairs and can be visualized abstractly in Table 4.3, much like we did previously with arrays.

TABLE 4.3   Dictionary Visualization

Key	Value
"pi"	3.14
"gravity"	9.8

Rarely will you ever have all the data you need upon initialization, so we need a way to later add data to the dictionary variable after it's been initialized. Swift provides two ways for us to add data to a dictionary: use the updateValue(value:, forKey:) method or use subscript syntax. The updateValue(value:, forKey:) method syntax looks a little intimidating if you haven't seen Objective-C's method names before, and we cover functions and methods in more detail in Hour 8, "Using Functions to Perform Actions." Dictionaries in Swift, unlike arrays, can create a key-value pair simply by using subscript syntax to add a value for a given key, even if the key doesn't exist yet. Swift adds the key-value pair when you reference a key that doesn't exist, when using the assignment operator (=). Listing 4.6 builds upon Listing 4.5 by adding a new key-value pair to the existing dictionary.

LISTING 4.6   Adding a New Key-Value Pair

```
01:  specialNumbers["this year"] = 2015  // adds 2014.0 for key "this year".
02:  specialNumbers.updateValue(2014, forKey: "last year")  // adds 2014.0 for
➥key "last year"
```

Did you see how Swift automatically adds the .0 to the end of both 2014 and 2015? That's because the specialNumbers dictionary holds Doubles for its values. Even though we entered integer values, Swift converted them to Double values to satisfy its type safety requirement.

In Listing 4.6, line 1 used subscript syntax, and line 2 used the updateValue(value:, forKey:) method to illustrate another way to add data to a dictionary. Both lines are functionally the same. However, the updateValue(value:, forKey:) method returns the previous value for the specified key, if any. This can be helpful if you want to verify that an update actually took place. If there were no existing key-value pair, updateValue(value:, forKey:) returns nil, which we discuss more in Hour 6, "Understanding Optional Values."

Despite the intimidating syntax, updateValue(value:, forKey:) should be read aloud as plain English and maybe it will make sense: "Update value 2014 for key 'last year'." The difference here over what you may have seen in C, C#, or another language is that instead of placing parameters inside parentheses one after another, Swift shares some commonality with Objective-C by placing parameter names as part of the method signature to make the code more readable and to make how parameters are used more understandable.

Removing Pairs from Dictionaries

Since dictionaries are unordered lists, no index-shifting needs to happen when removing items from a Dictionary instance. There are two ways to remove items from a dictionary: subscript syntax or the removeValueForKey(key:) method. Listing 4.7 illustrates both ways of removing items from our dictionary, building upon Listing 4.6.

LISTING 4.7   Removing Pairs from Dictionaries

```
specialNumbers["this year"] = nil // setting a key's value to nil removes the pair
specialNumbers.removeValueForKey("last year") // removes the pair
➥where key = "last year"
```

Common Dictionary Methods and Properties

As with arrays, a variety of properties and methods is available for dictionaries as well. The count property exists on Dictionary also, which returns the number of key-value pairs inside. You can also retrieve an Array instance of just the Dictionary's keys or values, by using the myDictionary.keys property or myDictionary.values property, which can be helpful when using iteration loops. As mentioned earlier with arrays, you can Command-click the Dictionary type wherever you have it in Xcode to be taken directly to the Dictionary struct's definition for more information.

Sets

The third collection type to discuss, which is new as of Swift 1.2, is a **Set**. A set is an unordered collection of unique items. Sets are a great way to store values just like an array or dictionary, but when ordering does not matter and you need to ensure uniqueness.

Much like the keys in a dictionary, set values must be hashable. This means that you cannot have a set of just any type, the type of its members must be the same, and its members must be uniquely identifiable. Swift's basic types, `String`, `Int`, `Double`, and `Bool`, are all hashable.

Creating a Set

Just like when defining arrays and dictionaries, you have a few options. You can declare a set with the `Set<Type>` type annotation, or you can use the `Set` struct's initializer and it will infer the inner type. Listing 4.8 illustrates these methods of creating a set.

LISTING 4.8   Creating a Set

```
let firstSet: Set<Int> = [1, 1, 2, 2, 3, 3]   // set consists of {1, 2, 3}
let hyrulianWarning. Array<String> = ["It's", "dangerous", "to", "go",
   ➥"alone!", "Take"]
var hyrulianSet = Set(hyrulianWarning)
```

In Listing 4.8, we create two sets. The first set is declared with the `Set<Int>` type annotation, and then provided values from an array literal. Notice how there are duplicates in the array literal, but the set only contains one of each integer. It is also a constant, defined with the `let` introducer.

The second set, `hyrulianSet`, is created by passing an array (which I purposefully defined as `Array<String>` to illustrate that it was an array and not a set) into the `Set` initializer. I created it as a `var` because we will mutate it shortly. Do you see how the set's members are stored in potentially a different order than the array? You might see different results, but my first time entering the code from Listing 4.8 displayed the following:

```
{"dangerous", "It's", "Take", "to", "go", "alone!"}
```

The preceding doesn't really make sense because it's not a complete sentence either in the array or the set, so let's take a look at adding elements to a set.

Adding Elements to Sets

Because sets don't have indexes, keys, or any sort of indexed or sorted storage, to add an element after the set has been initialized, you simply insert it using the `insert()` method. Listing 4.9 continues the set created in Listing 4.8 by inserting the last word needed to complete the famous phrase told by the old man from *The Legend of Zelda*, and add another phrase.

LISTING 4.9   Using the `insert` Method

```
hyrulianSet.insert("this.")
// Now my set looks like: {"dangerous", "It's", "this.", "to", "go", "alone!",
  ➥"Take"}
hyrulianSet.insert("It's")
hyrulianSet.insert("a")
hyrulianSet.insert("secret")
hyrulianSet.insert("to")
hyrulianSet.insert("everybody.")
// If you're coding with me, did you notice the set only has one "It's"?
```

Retrieving Elements from Sets

Now that we have a set populated with some items, we need a way to get elements out of the set. Remember that sets are unordered, unindexed collections, so we cannot just simply ask the set for a particular item of our choosing; we can only ask for a single item, or all items.

Asking a set for all of its items is simple; there is not even a method for it. If you are storing data in a set to keep uniqueness, but your data source for what is displayed on screen is an array, you can simply feed the set into a new array's initializer, such as the following:

```
dataSource = Array(hyrulianSet)
```

NOTE

Sets Are Unordered

Keep in mind that your `dataSource` instance might not be sorted the way you want it to be, so you will need to do that separately. We briefly discuss sorting methods in Hour 9, "Understanding Higher Order Functions and Closures."

Retrieving a single element from a set is quite simple as well—you just ask a set for its first element. This is a little confusing, because as sets are unordered, having a "first" element doesn't really make sense, like it does for an array. The expression used to be called any, indicating that you just wanted any item available. `first` is named the way it is to indicate that Swift will return to you the first item it comes across in the set.

```
let first = hyrulianSet.first  // returns "dangerous"
```

Removing Elements from Sets

After learning how arrays and dictionaries handle removing items, sets are not that different at all. Listing 4.10 illustrates the various methods for removing items from a set.

LISTING 4.10   Using Different Removal Methods

```
hyrulianSet.remove("dangerous")
hyrulianSet  // see "dangerous" has been removed from the set
let takeIndex = hyrulianSet.indexOf("Take")
hyrulianSet.removeAtIndex(takeIndex!)
hyrulianSet.removeFirst()
hyrulianSet.removeAll()
```

As you can see from Listing 4.10, you can remove items that match an existing item in a set ("dangerous"), you can get the SetIndex object of an item and remove an item of a particular set index, and finally you can remove the first or all items in a set. Option-click these methods on hyrulianSet to see Apple's documentation on them. There, you will see their intended purpose, and if they return the element being removed or not.

Powerful Things You Can Do with Sets

Depending on the needs of your app, you may or may not ever need to use a set. You might only need to get one item from a set, such as when reacting to touch events on a view, in which you can override one of a few UIView instance methods; for instance, touchesBegan(touches: Set<UITouch>, withEvent: UIEvent?). Because iOS cannot tell which finger is which on the screen, but it knows how many are on the screen, and can guarantee that each touch represents a unique finger, the Set<UITouch> type is the perfect choice. You can ask the set for how many fingers touched down, if you need to start an action with perhaps two or more fingers, by using touches.count.

There are many more things you can do with sets, and I'll list a few here along with some descriptions. Then, you will test your knowledge of them in the following Try It Yourself section.

▶ **union**—When providing another set or sequence, a new set is returned with elements from both.

▶ **intersect**—When providing another set or sequence, a new set is returned that includes only those elements that belong to both.

▶ **isSubsetOf**—Returns true if all elements in the initial set are members in the provided set, and false if otherwise.

▶ **isSupersetOf**—Returns true if all the initial set at least contains all elements in the provided set, and false if otherwise.

▶ **isDisjointWith**—Returns true if no members in the initial set are in a provided set or sequence, and false if otherwise.

▶ **exclusiveOr**—When providing another set or sequence, a new set is returned with elements that occur in either the initial set or the provided sequence, but not both.

Now let's try these actions in a Try It Yourself section.

▼ TRY IT YOURSELF

Perform Actions on Sets

Use several different methods to analyze differences and similarities in sets.

1. Open Xcode and create a new playground. Either a Mac or iOS playground will be fine.

2. Create and populate four sets: one with odd integers 1 through 7, one with even integers 2 through 8, one with all integers 1 through 10, and finally one with odd integers 1 through 19.

```
let odd = Set([1, 3, 5, 7])
let even = Set([2, 4, 6, 8])
let firstTen = Set(1...10)
let oddToTwenty = Set([1, 3, 5, 7, 9, 11, 13, 15, 17, 19])
```

3. Find the resulting union and intersecting sets between the `odd` and `even` sets. Then, using `firstTen` and `oddToTwenty`, use `intersection` to create a set with odd numbers below ten. What results do you see in the results pane?

```
let union = odd.union(even)
let intersection = odd.intersect(even)
let oddToTen = firstTen.intersect(oddToTwenty)
```

4. Use the `isSubsetOf` method to inspect whether the `odd` set is a subset of `firstTen`, whether `odd` is a subset of `even`, and whether `oddToTwenty` is a superset of `oddToTen`.

```
odd.isSubsetOf(firstTen)
odd.isSubsetOf(even)
oddToTwenty.isSupersetOf(oddToTen)
```

5. Use `isDisjointWith` to determine whether `even` is disjoint with `odd`, and whether `even` is disjoint with `firstTen`. Then find the resulting set by using `exclusiveOr` between `oddToTwenty` and `firstTen`.

```
even.isDisjointWith(odd)
even.isDisjointWith(firstTen)
oddToTwenty.exclusiveOr(firstTen)
```

Your completed Try It Yourself section should look like the playground in Figure 4.3.

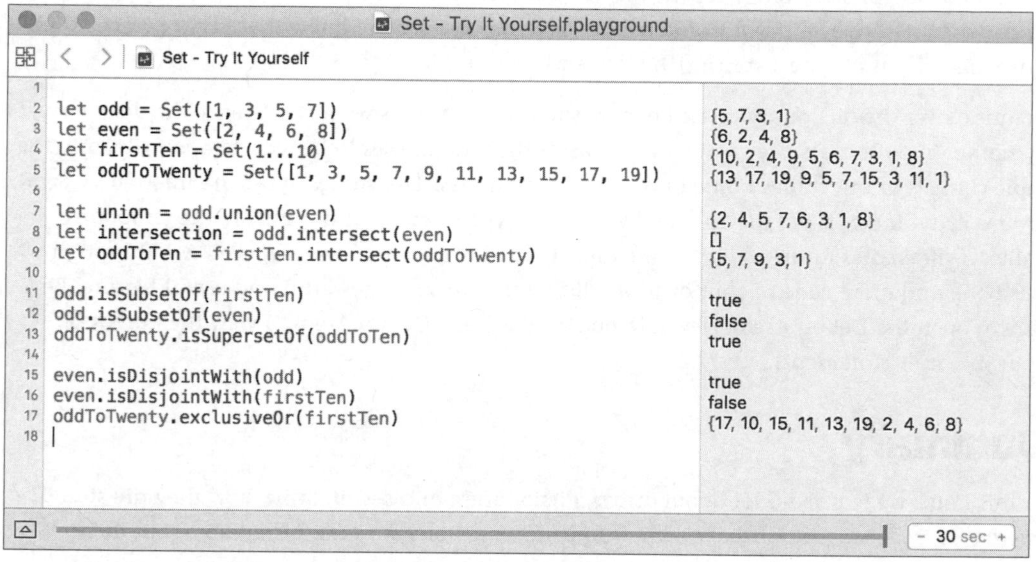

FIGURE 4.3
The completed Try It Yourself playground utilizing multiple different methods on sets of data.

Tuples

Tuples are a feature of Swift that is new to most C and Objective-C programmers. Tuples are an interesting case in Swift in that they represent a grouping of values as a compound value, but Tuple itself is not a type you can declare like you can an Array or Dictionary. Tuples can be used to extract the index and value from an Array item, or the key and value from a Dictionary item, as a pair that can extract those values to individual temporary values. Tuples are often used in for-in loops, and Listing 4.11 illustrates using tuples for arrays and dictionaries.

LISTING 4.11   Using Tuples with Arrays and Dictionaries

```
let anArray = ["Mary", "had", "a", "little", "lamb"]
let aDictionary = ["fleece color" : "white as snow",
    "Mary's location" : "lamb was sure to go"]
// first use tuples in anArray
for (index, value) in anArray.enumerate() {
    print("Index: \(index), value: \(value)")
}
// next, use tuples in aDictionary
for (key, value) in aDictionary {
    print("Key: \(key), value: \(value)")
}
```

In Listing 4.11, we use tuples for iterating over both an array and a dictionary. Notice that we write `anArray.enumerate()` for the array, versus just the name `anArray`. If we had just written `anArray` to iterate over, Swift would require us to not use a tuple but rather just a `String` type since `anArray` is of type `[String]` by inference.

Iterating over the dictionary is a little more straightforward, as we just reference the dictionary by name. In both cases, we create a tuple inside the parentheses to be used temporarily, and the tuple consists of the values named inside the parentheses. The values' types are inferred by Swift; for `anArray`, index is of type `Int`, and value is of type `String`, and these are the temporary values Swift creates for us as part of the tuple to extract from the array. As you work through this book and more code of your own, you'll find that this is a powerful and useful feature. Be sure to open the Debug Area (View > Debug Area > Show Debug Area) to view the output of your `print()` statements.

Summary

In this hour, we learned a lot about arrays, dictionaries, and sets in Swift, how they are stored, referenced, indexed, initialized, and how to perform actions or get information about them. We also learned about tuples and the role they play with arrays and dictionaries.

In the next hour, we explore conditional statements and how to use them to control program flow.

Q&A

Q. Arrays and dictionaries seem similar. What is the difference?

A. Arrays involve a set of sequentially stored data objects with random access to those objects. Dictionaries store key-value pairs of the objects. This makes arrays ideal for a collection that has a logical order, and dictionaries ideal when objects need to be referenced by something more meaningful than an integer, such as "name" or "city," and when order is not necessary.

Q. Can an array contain values with differing data types?

A. No. Array elements must be of the same type.

Q. What is a good use case for using a set?

A. In addition to the `touchesBegan(...)` illustration earlier, Apple uses sets in Core Data (Apple's data persistence framework) to represent relationships between objects. For instance, a person might own many dogs. The order of dogs is not necessary and each dog is unique. A `Set` is an appropriate type to represent that relationship.

Workshop

The workshop contains quiz questions and exercises to help you solidify your understanding of the material covered. Try to answer all questions before looking at the answers that follow.

Quiz

1. How can you find the total number of items in an array in Swift?

2. In the following code, what is the value of `petArray[0]`?

```
var petArray = ["Dog", "Cat", "Bird", "Fish"]
```

3. What is wrong with the following code?

```
let petArray = ["Dog", "Cat", "Bird", "Fish"]
petArray.append("Fish")
```

4. Given the following code, how could you update Player One's score to 125.0?

```
var highScore = ["Player One" : 99.0, "Player Two" : 99.7]
```

5. What would be the result of the following code?

```
let seussArray = ["One", "Fish", "Two", "Fish", "Red", "Fish", "Blue", "Fish"]
let seussSet = Set(seussArray)
```

Answers

1. `count` returns the number of elements in an array.

2. The value of `petArray[0]` is `Dog`.

3. You cannot add or remove elements to array constants.

4. You could update it like this:

```
highScore.updateValue(125.0, forKey: "Player One")
```

5. The set would look something like:

```
{"Fish", "One", "Red", "Blue", "Two"}
```

Exercise

Create a new playground. Create an array that contains your first and last name as values. Create a variable that points to the same array to make a copy. Add, remove, and alter values in each array and observe the results.

Now use the same values in a dictionary. Attempt to add and remove items from the array and dictionary.

Finally, create a few sets of data with members of similar types (such as two instances of `Set<String>`). Explore the methods available to you with the sets and discover some other methods that we did not have a chance to discuss here to find out what they do to your sets.

Controlling Program Flow with Conditionals

What You'll Learn in This Hour:

▶ How to use `if` statements to control logic

▶ How to use `switch` statements to control logic

▶ How to use pattern matching for controlling flow

▶ How to transfer control of code execution

In programming, you often need to make decisions in code based on the state of a value, what type of device is being used, what screen is presented, or any of a multitude of other decision points. These decision points are called **conditions**, and based on the value of a condition (whether true or false), a particular path of logic is then executed in code.

In this hour, we discuss how Swift uses conditional operations to enable you to modify the path of code executed and customize application flow. The two conditional operations provided in Swift are the `if` statement and the `switch` statement. Both make possible conditional branching of code, or put differently, they make possible execution of different expressions, behaviors, or code paths based on a given set of criteria.

The `if` Statement

The first method of using conditional programming in Swift is by using the `if` statement. The `if` statement is perhaps the most common and simple conditional logic checking paradigm in computer programming. We have already seen the `if` statement utilized a few times throughout this book so far in simple use cases, and you probably have an idea of how to use a basic `if` statement just by context. Let's discuss the syntax a little more here and get a better feel for what you can do with `if` statements, and when they are appropriate to use.

If you are coming from the C or Objective-C world, you are accustomed perhaps to the syntax looking something like the code in Listing 5.1.

LISTING 5.1   The `if` Statement in C/Objective-C

```
BOOL valueToCheck = YES;
if (valueToCheck == YES) {
    // code to execute if valueToCheck is true
}
```

The `== YES` is redundant, as is `== true` in Swift, and can be removed. Next, Listing 5.2 shows how the same section of code looks in Swift.

LISTING 5.2   The `if` Statement in Swift

```
let valueToCheck = true
if valueToCheck {
    // code to execute if valueToCheck is true
}
```

The thing to notice here is that C and Objective-C require parentheses around the condition being checked, and Swift does not require it, although you can insert parentheses if it assists with readability.

Although there is that slight difference in syntax between Swift and C/Objective-C, they behave exactly the same way as with pretty much most any other programming language. The `if` statement has been around for a long time in many programming languages.

The basic `if` statement that we covered only executes code inside its curly braces if the condition is true. But what if we want an alternate expression to execute if the statement is false? Swift, as with most every other language, provides an `else` clause, which executes code inside a different set of curly braces when the condition is false. Since the syntax is exactly the same as C and Objective-C, minus the parentheses around the conditions, I won't have separate listings describing the differences; Listing 5.3 shows the same logic check as Listing 5.2, but this time adds the `else` clause.

LISTING 5.3   Using an `if-else` Statement in Swift

```
let valueToCheck = true
if valueToCheck {
    print("valueToCheck is true")
} else {
    print("valueToCheck is false")
}
```

Adding an `else` clause to execute code based on a false condition is done simply just by adding `else { ... }` immediately after the closing brace of the true block. If read aloud, this code could be dictated as "If valueToCheck is true, then execute the first block of code. Else, execute the second block of code." The else clause acts as a way to catch any non-true condition and execute a certain block of code, when all else fails.

To add more potential paths of execution to an `if` statement, you use the `else if` syntax. The `else if` syntax simply gives you more chances to verify a true value and execute a particular block of code before resuming execution of code or having an `else` clause catch any non-true condition. Listing 5.4 illustrates the `else if` syntax.

LISTING 5.4   Using `else-if` Syntax

```
let myColor = "blue"
if myColor == "red" {
   print("Stop signs are red")
} else if myColor == "blue" {
   print("The sky is blue in Ohio...sometimes")
} else {
   print("I don't know what color myColor is")
}
```

The `if`, `else-if`, and `else` syntax in Swift is straightforward. The condition being tested must evaluate to either true or false, and depending on which operator and operands you use in your `if` or `else if` statements, the appropriate block of code is executed. You could test whether a number is greater than or equal to another number, check strings for equality, verify whether a certain character is in a string, or many other conditions, as long as they return a `Bool` value. Before we move on, let's work an example together. We use a Foundation function called `arc4random()` to generate a random integer for us and use the remainder operator (`%`) to keep the random number within a small range to check its values easily with an `if` statement.

TRY IT YOURSELF ▼

Use `if`, `else-if`, `else` Conditional Statements in Practice

Write a random number generator and check the values using `if`, `else-if`, and `else`.

1. Open Xcode and create a playground. Either a Mac or iOS playground will be fine.

2. Remove all the existing code in the playground, and import the Foundation framework, so we can access the `arc4random()` function.

```
import Foundation
```

3. Use the `arc4random()` function to create a random number and limit its scope to 0–9. Also, create an implicitly unwrapped string variable to hold our result.

```
let randomNumber = arc4random() % 10
var result = ""
```

4. First, check whether our `randomNumber` value is 0.

```
if randomNumber == 0 {
    result = "Zero is the first index in an array"
}
```

5. Next, check whether our `randomNumber` value is 1. (I'll include the closing brace from the initial if block, since the `else if` command belongs on the same line.)

```
} else if randomNumber == 1 {
    result = "One is the loneliest number... "
}
```

6. Add an `else` block to act as a default block of code to run, if none of our conditions are met. (Again, I'm including the final brace from the `else-if` block for continuity.)

```
} else {
    result = "Our random number is \(randomNumber) "
}
```

7. Finally, we can simply put the name of our result variable on a single line, and the playground displays its value in the results pane to the right.

```
result
```

You might have seen that the value of our random variable was shown in the Xcode playground's results pane, so this test may seem frivolous. However, the point of this example was to get you familiar with the structure of using if, else if, and else statements to execute code based on meeting certain conditions.

Try your code against different random values generated by re-executing the playground (click the Editor menu, and then click Execute Playground). You see the random number change, and the result variable should adjust accordingly. Figure 5.1 shows what the playground should look like upon completion.

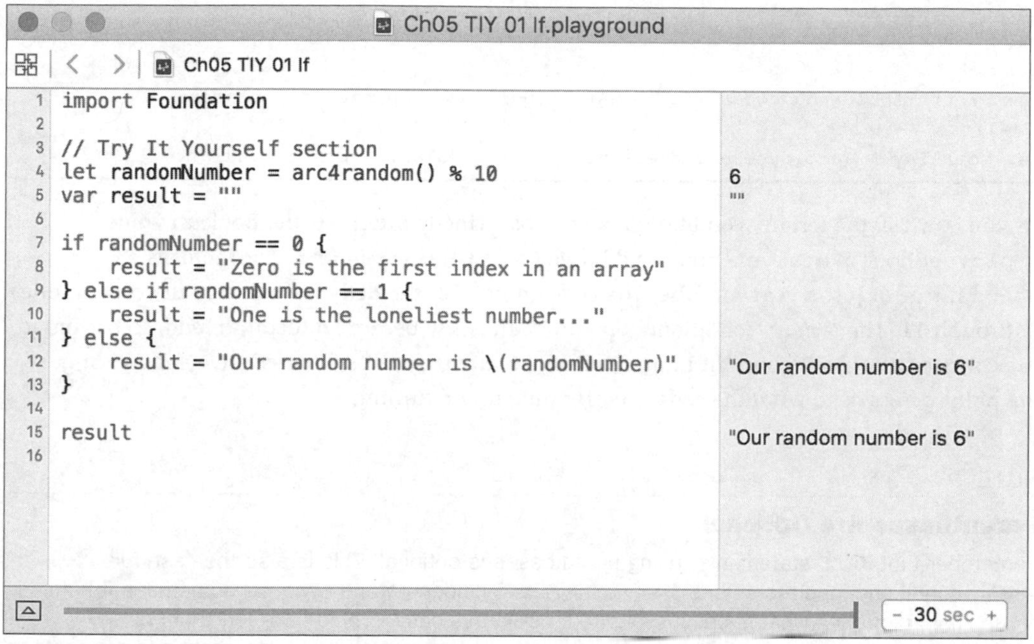

FIGURE 5.1
The completed Try It Yourself example for `if` statements in a playground.

Ternary Conditional Operators

Hour 3, "Using Operators in Swift," discussed unary and binary operators, but there is a third type of operator in Swift that returns values based on a conditional check, called a **ternary conditional operator**. Swift has only one ternary conditional operator, and it is written as short-hand for a longer if-else expression that checks a particular case or condition and provides a value for the true branch and another value for the false branch. Let's take a look at a common `if` block to show how a regular `if-else` conditional block would look as a ternary operation in Listing 5.5.

LISTING 5.5 Using Ternary Conditional Operators

```
01: let salary = 50000
02: let bonus = 10000
03: var totalPay = 0
04: let employeeShouldReceiveABonus = true
05:
06: // the following code is a traditional if block
07: if employeeShouldReceiveABonus {
08:     totalPay = salary + bonus
09: } else {
```

```
10:     totalPay = salary
11: }
12:
13: // the following code is a ternary conditional operation replacing
    ➥lines 7-11 above
14: totalPay = (employeeShouldReceiveABonus) ? salary + bonus : salary
```

As you can see, the ternary conditional operator succinctly interprets the Boolean value
employeeShouldReceiveABonus and based on its value (true or false) returns salary +
bonus if true or just salary if false. The code on line 14 is exactly the same as the code in lines
7 through 11. The ternary conditional operator can easily become difficult to read, so be sure to
use concise variable or constant names, but make sure they are still descriptive enough to get
the point across as to what the code is performing and returning.

NOTE

Parentheses Are Optional

Remember that in if statements, using parentheses is optional. This is also the case for
ternary conditional operators. Line 14 in Listing 5.5 included parentheses, as sometimes it helps
readability or knowing what is being evaluated, but in this case I could have left them out.

The switch Statement

Swift also provides another condition checking mechanism, and that is the switch statement.
The switch statement compares a value against a set of possible matching patterns. Not only is
the syntax structured a little differently than an if statement, the way you can match values is
also different.

The switch statement compares different **cases**, in which each case is a value or pattern to
compare against the value being considered in the switch statement itself. If a match is found,
the block of code corresponding to the matched case is executed. Switch cases are checked in
sequential order, meaning that the first is checked, then second, and so on. If two cases provide
a positive match, be sure to structure your switch cases in the order you prefer, because only
one of them will get executed.

Every switch statement must be **exhaustive**, meaning that you must either provide a case
clause and a subsequent block of code to execute for every value or pattern to match, or provide
a **default case**. The default case is much like the else block in an if statement, in which if
no condition or pattern match is met, the default block of code is executed. Let's rewrite the
random number example from earlier in this hour with a switch statement in Listing 5.6.
Note: If you're following along with your own playground, either an iOS or Mac playground will
work with this example.

LISTING 5.6   Using the `switch` Statement

```
01: import Foundation
02:
03: let randomNumber = arc4random() % 10
04: var result: String!
05:
06: switch randomNumber {
07: case 0:
08:     result = "Zero is the first index in an array"
09: case 1:
10:     result = "One is the loneliest number..."
11: default:
12:     result = "Our random number is \(randomNumber)"
13: }
14:
15: result
```

The syntax is a little different, but the concept is the same for this example. In fact, the length of the program increased by one line. So why would we use `switch` statements when we could use `if` statements? You may not always need to, but `switch` statements can do a lot more advanced pattern matching than `if` statements can. Let's start by discussing what can be matched in `switch` statements.

Match More Than Just `Int` Values

Switch statements in other languages, such as C and Objective-C, require the value to be compared to be an integer. C and Objective-C also require a `break` keyword at the end of every case block, because program execution would go to the next case (which may also be true but not desired) and inadvertently execute code you don't want executed. In Swift, `switch` cases can match many more types than just integers, such as strings, characters, doubles, floats, Boolean values, ranges, and tuples. You can even match multiple values with one case statement, rather than needing a case statement for each value to match. Also, `switch` statements do not **fall through**, which means that once the code in a specified case executes, code execution does not fall to the next case in the absence of a break command; rather, execution leaves the entire `switch` block.

NOTE

Explicit Break or Fall Through in `switch` Cases

Although Swift does not require an explicit `break` command at the end of every case block, you can add the `break` statement for clarity or to show specific intent. If, on the other hand, you want to opt in to fall-through behavior, you can add the `fallthrough` statement to the end of a case block, and program flow continues executing the next case if it matches or default case, if one exists.

Listing 5.7 illustrates how to use Swift's `switch` statement to match against multiple values with a single case statement. This can be useful for when you want the same block of code to be executed if more than one value could satisfy the match.

LISTING 5.7   Matching Multiple Values in a Single Case

```
let farmAnimal = "chicken"
switch farmAnimal {
case "cow", "pig", "goat":
   print("cow, pig, or goat was matched")
case "chicken", "rooster":
   print("chicken or rooster was matched")
default:
   print("unrecognized farm animal")
}
```

Switch Range Matching

`switch` statements in Swift can also match cases using range operators, discussed in Hour 3. This enables you to compare a value to check whether it is between a specified range of values, and if so, execute the first case block that satisfies the match. Say, for example, that you are writing an app that compares a student's exam score to the A-B-C-D-F grading scale, where an A is 90 to 100, a B is 80 to 89, a C is 70 to 79, a D is 60 to 69, and an F is below 60. Since you are already familiar with using the half-closed range and closed range operators, let's walk through this together in the following Try It Yourself section.

▼ TRY IT YOURSELF

Determine a Student's Grade Letter

Use a `switch` statement and range matching cases to determine a student's grade letter.

1. Open Xcode and create a new playground. Either iOS or Mac playground will work.

2. Remove all the existing code in the playground and import the Foundation framework, so we can access the `arc4random()` function.

   ```
   import Foundation
   ```

3. Use the `arc4random()` function to create a random number and limit its scope to 0–100. Also, create an empty string variable to hold our grade.

   ```
   let examScore = arc4random() % 101 // generates random number between
      ➡0-100, inclusive
   var grade = ""
   ```

4. Begin the `switch` statement by comparing `examScore`'s value. Xcode automatically adds a closing curly brace after pressing Return.

```
switch examScore {
```

5. Place the cursor on the line in between the curly braces and add a case statement for the closed range of 90 to 100, followed by a colon (`:`). On the next line, set the grade to "A".

```
case 90...100:
    grade = "A"
```

6. On the next line, add a case statement for the half-closed range of 80 to 90, followed by a colon. Then set the grade to "B".

```
case 80..<90: // this could have also been 80...89
    grade = "B"
```

7. Repeat step 6 for "C" (half-closed range of 70 to 80), and "D" (half-closed range of 60 to 70).

```
case 70..<80:
    grade = "C"
case 60..<70:
    grade = "D"
```

8. To finish the `switch` statement, add a default clause, where the grade will be "F". Here, the closing curly brace of the `switch` statement is shown.

```
default:
    grade = "F"
}
```

9. Display a string in the playground using string interpolation to display a message and what grade the student earned. This is sometimes quicker in playgrounds than using `print(...)`.

```
"Student received: \(grade)"
```

If you followed the Try It Yourself example, your code should look like Figure 5.2.

```
1  // Try It Yourself setion 2
2
3  import Foundation
4
5  let examScore = arc4random() % 101        90
6  var grade = ""                            ""
7
8  switch examScore {
9  case 90...100:
10     grade = "A"                           "A"
11 case 80..<90:
12     grade = "B"
13 case 70..<80:
14     grade = "C"
15 case 60..<70:
16     grade = "D"
17 default:
18     grade = "F"
19 }
20
21 "Student received \(grade)"               "Student received A"
22
```

FIGURE 5.2
The completed Try It Yourself example for switch statements using range matching.

Switch Tuple Matching

As you saw in Hour 4, "Working with Collection Types," tuples are powerful and lightweight constructs. Tuples can be used in switch statement cases to match multiple values or even ranges of values. Some other tools available to you are **wildcards** and **value binding**. A wildcard, denoted by the underscore (_), means that any value in the considered value is a match for that place in the tuple. With value binding inside a tuple, you can declare a temporary constant or variable to the matched value in any place in the tuple. You can also reference values in the switch's considered value's tuple with dot syntax by appending a number corresponding to the place of the desired value in the tuple (tuples are zero-based like arrays). The example in Listing 5.8 illustrates some of the different ways you can match patterns, use wildcards or ranges, and even use value binding inside a tuple and switch case, and how to use the values inside a case's execution block.

LISTING 5.8   Using Tuples for Pattern Matching Inside Switch Cases

```
01: let carInventory = ("Ford", 55) // carInventory is a tuple of type (String,
    ➥Int)
02:
03: switch carInventory {
04: case (_, 50...100):
05:     "We have too many \(carInventory.0) cars. Sell! Sell! Sell!"
06: case (let make, 0...20):
07:     "We are low on \(make). Buy more inventory."
08: case ("Ford", let num):
09:     "We have \(num) Fords in stock."
10: default:
11:     "Unrecognized make"
12: }
```

In Listing 5.8, we declare a tuple of type (String, Int) in line 1 and assign it to carInventory. Line 2 is left blank for readability. In line 3, we begin our switch statement, considering the carInventory value. The first case, on line 4, compares a tuple with any kind of string as its first value (because of the underscore wildcard), and the closed range of 50 to 100. If that passes, then we use carInventory.0 using dot syntax to display the first value in the carInventory tuple in line 5. In line 6, our case uses value binding to assign the constant make to whatever value is in the first field in the tuple, and then matches the number in inventory to the closed range of 0 to 20. If this case is true, then we can use make inside our code block because we temporarily bind the value to make. Here, value binding is just an explicit way to clearly outline in code our intention of using the value in code, rather than just using carInventory.0. Line 8 compares the string "Ford" directly and uses value binding for how many Fords it matches, and then uses the bound num in its resulting code branch. Finally, in line 10, we have our default case if no matches are made until this point, because switch statements must be exhaustive, and then close with the curly brace. Xcode warns you if you do not have an exhaustive switch statement, because Swift needs exhaustive checks to ensure safety.

Refining Switch Cases with the where Keyword

Swift's where keyword can be used in line with a case statement to refine the condition to be validated. Use the where keyword along with value binding into temporary constants, and you then can have dynamic value checking inside the case statement's conditional check. Listing 5.9 illustrates this, as it is much easier to see the where keyword in action, where we determine by the amount entered whether a word should be pluralized with an extremely generic use case. An actual pluralization implementation would have a more robust solution.

LISTING 5.9   Using the `where` Keyword in a Switch Case

```
01: let wordTuple = ("car", 2)
02:
03: switch wordTuple {
04: case let (word, amount) where amount == 1:
05:      "You have \(amount) \(word)."// if amount == 1, would print
   ➥"You have 1 car."
06: case let (word, amount) where amount == 0:
07:      "You have no \(word)s."// if amount == 0, would print
   ➥"You have no cars."
08: case let (word, amount):
09:      "You have \(amount) \(word)s."// would print "You have 2 cars."
10: }
```

A lot happens in these 10 lines of code, so let's break it down. In line 1, we create a simple tuple of type (`String`, `Int`) and assign it to `wordTuple`. Then in line 3, we consider `wordTuple` in the `switch` statement. Line 4 has the first case, where we use value binding to assign the (`word`, `amount`) tuple temporarily and extract individual values from it to compare the value of amount. It is obvious here that (`word`, `amount`) is equal to (`"car"`, `2`) because we declared that in line 1. However, there may be times when you're iterating over a list of items and you may not know the contents of the tuple, and this type of checking comes in handy. Line 5 uses the constants from the tuple with string interpolation to print the singular representation of word. Likewise, line 6 checks for `amount == 0`, which pluralizes word with a custom sentence. Finally, line 8 uses value binding to catch any value, so no default case is necessary, and makes the `switch` statement exhaustive. Line 9 assumes that any value other than 1 will be plural and appends an "s" to the end of the word constant.

NOTE

Tuples Can Hold More Than Two Values

Remember that tuples can be more than just a pair of values. Tuples can contain any number of items inside and can be used to quickly group together like objects or values. Tuples can even be used as return values for functions as a way to return more than one value or object from a function—something that wasn't available in C and Objective-C. We cover tuples as return types in Hour 8, "Using Functions to Perform Actions."

Transferring Control of Execution

In an effort to make code execution more efficient and flexible, Swift has four ways to control program execution. Three of the methods are familiar if you are coming from a C or Objective-C background: `break`, `continue`, and `return` statements. The remaining method of control transfer is the `fallthrough` statement. Swift's execution flow with `switch` statements is similar to that of Pascal-based languages, where control of the program is transferred to the statement immediately following the closing curly brace of the entire switch statement. In contrast, C and Objective-C fall through to subsequent case statements and require a specific break statement at the end of each case, unless your program requires fall-through.

This hour discusses only the break and fallthrough statements, as they pertain to switch statements. The continue statement is discussed in Hour 7, "Iterating Code with Loops," and the return statement is discussed in Hour 8.

The break Statement

Although not specifically necessary in switch cases, the break statement can be useful in terms of efficiency. The break statement breaks execution of the current switch statement or enclosing loop and transfers control to the first line of code after the ending curly brace of the switch or loop statements. To use, simply insert a break statement after the last line of code you want executed before you want to break out.

In Swift, break is implied after each case statement's code has executed. The following snippet shows what a break statement looks like in code:

```
let someValue = 0
switch someValue {
case 0:
    "someValue is 0."
    break
default:
    break
}
"I am executed immediately following the break statement"
```

TIP

Use Break for Empty Cases

Because switch statements must be exhaustive and every case accounted for, break statements by themselves in a case block can be used to denote that no special code should execute for that case.

The fallthrough Statement

The fallthrough statement, as mentioned before, enables you to opt in to fall-through behavior in a switch statement. By nature, switch statements break their execution once they reach the end of a matching case's block, and control resumes after the switch's ending curly brace. However, you can add the fallthrough statement at the end of a matching case's block to explicitly have your code's execution fall through to the next case, or the default case, whichever may match first. The following code snippet illustrates this behavior:

```
let anotherValue = 15
switch anotherValue {
case 0..<20:
    "\(anotherValue) is between 0 and 19"
    fallthrough
case 10..<20:
    "\(anotherValue) is between 10 and 19"
default:
    "default branch."
}
```

Here, we can see that the given value 15, stored in anotherValue, is within the half-closed range of 0 to 20 and is also within the half-closed range of 10 to 20. In a conventional Swift switch statement, switch cases are evaluated in sequence; the first case would execute and then immediately exit the switch statement entirely. However, we add the fallthrough statement, which means that since anotherValue is also within the half-closed range of 10 to 20, that case's code also executes. Swift behaves this way for safety purposes so that you don't accidentally have other potentially passing cases execute inadvertently, and you must opt in to fall-through behavior if you want to have it.

Slightly More Advanced Pattern Matching

Introduced in Swift 2.0 is a new feature to the language allowing more powerful and flexible pattern matching. You can now use the case statement from a switch expression inside if conditional statements, as well as in for loops, which we will discuss in Hour 7. What this allows you to do is rather than have an exhaustive case statement, or even a default case when you don't really need it, you can simply have a one-line if statement matching a pattern much like a switch statement can do.

The syntax for this form of pattern matching is a bit backwards at first appearance, but if you think about it as the same general structure as a switch case statement, it can grow on you. Listing 5.10 illustrates a very small example of how you can use it. We will use this method of pattern matching much more throughout the remainder of this book, because it can be applied to many more concepts, so do not fret if you don't understand the purpose or power of this type of pattern matching yet.

LISTING 5.10   Using Advanced Pattern Matching

```
let age = 34
if case 0..<50 = age {
    "you're younger than 50"
}
```

```
if case 30..<40 = age where age % 2 == 0 {
    "You're in your thirties and your age is even"
}
```

In Listing 5.10, we can see that we needed to quickly check in a conditional the value of age. If age is within the range of 0 to 50 (half-closed), then we print the result that the age is younger than 50. We can also use the where clause, much like a switch statement, to further refine our conditional. It is a little odd to see the range check first and only have a single equal sign to make the comparison, but it's really making a temporary assignment inside the if statement, which can either succeed or fail. In a real application, you may have a more meaningful check and even action to be performed, rather than just printing output, but hopefully you can see the power in these few lines. You were neither required to have a default case, nor have two different comparisons combined with the logical AND operator (if age >= 0 && age < 50). Later in this book, when using pattern matching with looping, optional value comparison, and more, you will see just how powerful and nice it is to have at your fingertips.

Summary

This hour discussed both methods Swift uses to conditionally branch and execute different paths of code depending on evaluated criteria: the if statement and the switch statement. These statements are commonly used, so go back and reread any parts you may not feel completely comfortable with yet.

This hour also discussed the simplicity and power of pattern matching with switch statements, from matching ranges of values, tuples, and value binding. We also covered using the where statement to further refine switch cases by providing conditions that must be met to match that case. You also learned how to provide multiple matches for a single case statement, such as in the farm animal example, providing a way to reduce the amount of code needed to fulfill a specific purpose.

You also learned about controlling the transfer of execution by opting in to fall-through behavior with the fallthrough statement, as well as explicit breaking behavior with the break statement.

Finally, you learned a bit of advanced pattern matching, which will serve you well in hours to come. This form of pattern matching is very powerful and you will find yourself using it quite frequently.

All these topics help equip you to better understand the upcoming hours, so let's move on to discussing optional values, which is how Swift handles the absence of a value.

Q&A

Q. Is it better to use `if-else` or `switch`? They seem similar.

A. The `switch` and `if-else` statements are similar, but as you saw in this hour, the syntax is different. This is another case where you should pick the one that works best for the context of the application that you are developing.

Q. Can you use nested `if`, `else if`, and `switch` statements in Swift?

A. You can use nested `if`, `else if`, and `switch` statements in Swift, and often may need to. In the next hour, we cover ways to accomplish this without a nasty nested structure. Always be careful to ensure the readability of your code when using nested statements.

Q. Since switch statements must be exhaustive, what should I do if I do not want anything to happen in one of the cases?

A. This would be a perfect place to use `break`. The `break` statement enables you to declare that nothing should happen if the given case is true.

Workshop

The workshop contains quiz questions and exercises to help you solidify your understanding of the material covered. Try to answer all questions before looking at the answers that follow.

Quiz

1. Find the error and correct the code snippet:

```
let savingsAmount = 500
if (savingsAmount = 500) {
    print("Goal has been reached!")
}
```

2. What is the purpose of the default case in a `switch` statement?

3. What is `fallthrough` used for?

4. Create a constant named `x` with a value of 3. Create a `switch` statement to check whether the value of the constant `x` is between 1 and 4 or between 5 and 7. Nothing should happen if `x` is not in this range.

5. Create a constant to hold a student name and number. If the student number is equal to 1, display the text, "The first student name is `student name`". Do not display anything if the student number is not equal to 1.

Answers

1. The conditional must have two equal signs (==). Remember that one equal sign (=) denotes assignment, while two equal signs (==) denotes equality comparison.

```
let savingsAmount = 500
if (savingsAmount == 500) {
    print("Goal has been reached!")
}
```

2. The default case handles what actions should occur if no other case in the `switch` is true. Swift case statements must be exhaustive, so the default case is helpful.

3. By default, Swift exits a `switch` statement after it has found a match and executed the respective code segment. The use of `fallthrough` allows execution to continue from one case to the next to potentially match another case.

4. Solution:

```
let x = 3
switch x{
    case 1...4:
        println("The value is \(x). \(x) is between 1 and 4")
    case 5...7:
        println("The value is \(x). \(x) is between 5 and 7")
    default:
        break
}
```

5. Solution:

```
let studentInformation = ("jDoe", 1)
switch studentInformation {
    case let (studentName, studentNumber) where studentNumber == 1:
        "The student name is \(studentName)"
    default:
        break
}
```

Exercise

Create a new playground. Create a tuple containing two integers. Use a `switch` statement to match a pattern in your tuple. Let the first case extract both values where the second value is equal to twice the first value. Let the second case extract both values where the second value is three times the first value. The default case should do nothing. Print appropriate output to the playground depending on what case was executed.

Understanding Optional Values

What You'll Learn in This Hour:

▶ What are optional values

▶ Why optionals were introduced in Swift

▶ How optionals assist with type safety

▶ How to declare a variable as optional

▶ What `nil` values are, and how to handle `nil`

This hour we discuss a new concept that is not yet in most programming languages called optional values. We have learned so far about Swift's type safety and how Swift requires variables and constants to have a data type, whether explicitly annotated or inferred, and also be initialized with a value. Optionals in Swift are a way to handle the absence of a value, which can and does happen in many cases. This hour's content can be a little bit of a mind-stretch, but it is important to cover this foundational concept now before continuing any further. If you need to re-read this chapter another time or two, please do so before moving on and getting lost or frustrated later. Let's dive in to discuss what being an optional value means.

What Are Optional Values?

Explicitly unwrapped optionals, or just **optionals**, in Swift are instances that may or may not have a value. Swift's idea of an optional value is to help prevent you from writing code that could access the absence of any value, which is denoted by a keyword called **nil**, when you meant to access an actual value. nil is a familiar concept if you come from the Objective-C world, where nil is a pointer to an empty object. In Objective-C, you could use nil to your advantage; if an object were nil and you sent it a message (such as asking for its array contents in reverse order), nil would just stifle the message sent. Then, you could check for nil in your code and assume that if nothing happened or you received no array, the object was nil. Then you go on your merry way by creating an instance of that object yourself.

In Swift, however, interacting with `nil` is handled a little differently. `nil` is the absence of a value, and because Swift variables and constants must have an initialized value (in other words, a non-`nil` value), variables and constants as we've seen in examples thus far cannot themselves be `nil`. As opposed to Objective-C, Swift's `nil` applies only to a single enumeration value type, not any reference type, like the way Objective-C used nil. Think of it this way: Let's say you have two variables, a and b, where a equals 5 and b is `nil`. You try to create c = a + b, but because b happens to be equal to `nil`, the app would crash because `nil` is the *absence* of a value, not just 0.

To create a safeguard around the issue of `nil` values, Swift uses optionals. Anytime you have a variable that you know could have a `nil` value, you designate the variable to be an optional variable, and what Swift does is create a **wrapper** around the variable's value, just in case it may be `nil`. If the value is `nil`, you are protected from runtime errors that would crash your app by otherwise directly accessing `nil`.

NOTE

Value Types and Reference Types

It was mentioned that Swift's `nil` value only applies to a single enumeration value type, whereas in Objective-C any instance of a reference type (i.e., a class) could have a `nil` value. We cover the differences in greater detail in future hours on classes and structs, but for now just know that a reference type creates one instance and can have many variables point to it, and an instance of a value type can only have at most one variable pointing to it. All types we have seen thus far including `Strings`, `Arrays`, `Bools`, `Ints`, and so on are all value types in Swift.

How to Designate a Variable as Optional

An optional is a type that can contain a value of any type, much like `Array`. Declaring an `Array` to contain the type `Double` looks like `Array<Double>`, and each element in the array instance is of type `Double`. Optionals are no different, except that they can only hold one value, whereas an array can hold many. To declare an instance of an optional `String`, you would declare it as follows:

```
var myOptionalString: Optional<String>
```

The Swift-ier syntax for designating a variable as optional is simply appending the question mark character (?) to the end of the variable's type in its declaration. The following code declares the same variable as an optional `String`:

```
var myOptionalString: String?
```

Because we are not initializing `myOptionalString` with any value, and we haven't made an initial assignment, it has no value yet. But, since `String` values cannot be `nil` (nor can any other value of any type, for that matter), we tell Swift that it is optional with the question mark character after the type. Swift's compiler recognizes this and knows that `myOptionalString` must use special operations to **unwrap** it before use.

NOTE

Optionals as Variables and Constants

As a general best practice, it is suggested that you use the `let` introducer to create constants as often as possible where necessary in your code as an optimization feature, and, of course, for safety. Optionals can either be variable or constant, and usage depends on the needs of your situation. If you know a variable could be assigned `nil` or any other value at any point after initial assignment, make it a variable with the `var` introducer. If you only need to store the result of something, from a function, for example, for temporary inspection but it will never need to change, then you can create it as a constant with the `let` introducer. Xcode will suggest usage of the `let` keyword when it senses that a variable never mutates, but always double-check because sometimes the compiler incorrectly deduces things.

Wrapping and Unwrapping Optional Variables

These terms are not uncommon to most programmers, as often a particular app or framework requires you to wrap a value or object inside another object to be passed around to another function or method, or for storage. Apple's Foundation framework includes data types such as the `NSArray` and `NSDictionary` classes, which are similar to Swift's `Array` and `Dictionary` structures. A big difference, though, is that `NSArray` and `NSDictionary` store their values as type `id`, which is a pointer to any type of *object*. This means that to store a value, let's say the integer 6, into an `NSArray` or `NSDictionary`, you have to wrap it into an `NSNumber` object. Then, to get the value out to use it, `NSArray` and `NSDictionary` would return the object of type `id`, so you would have to explicitly unwrap, or *cast down* to the desired type—in this case, `int`. (Note the lowercase `int`. In C, scalar types are lowercase. In Swift, the equivalent is `Int`.)

Wrapping and unwrapping in Swift work similarly, except that with optionals, you aren't converting the type to another, per se. A better way to think about optionals is to think about your variable in front of you and then imagine a big box around it, keeping it safe from the elements. There may be something inside the box, or there may be nothing inside the box. But Swift allows the box to represent your value as it exists in your app and gets used and passed around. When you need to access the value, you explicitly unwrap (or, in this analogy, unbox) the value and access it directly.

Optional values are wrapped by default, so you don't need to explicitly wrap them. To unwrap, however, you can do that several different ways. Let's discuss what those methods of unwrapping are and what would be the best cases in which to use them.

Forced Unwrapping with the Unwrap Operator

First and foremost, Swift provides an **unwrap operator**. We didn't discuss this in Hour 3, "Using Operators in Swift," because it wouldn't have made any sense to you yet, having not learned about optionals at that point. The unwrap operator is simply the exclamation point (!) character immediately following the optional variable's name in code. This is called **forced unwrapping**. Listing 6.1 shows the declaration of an optional `String` variable and then using it in code.

LISTING 6.1   Declaring and Unwrapping Optional Values

```
var optStr: String?  // declares optStr as an optional String, with no value yet
optStr = "I'm an optional string"
let unwrappedString = optStr!  // unwraps and assigns the actual string value
print(unwrappedString)  // prints "I'm an optional string" to the console
```

As you can see from Listing 6.1, declaring, assigning, and unwrapping optional values do not look too daunting. It's a nice safety measure that Swift implements to reduce the potential for apps to crash by accessing `nil`.

CAUTION

Ensure You Don't Forcibly Unwrap a `nil` Value

The unwrap operator forcibly unwraps an optional variable and should only be used when you know that the variable contains a value. If you unwrap an optional variable that contains `nil`, your app will crash at runtime, logging the message "Fatal error: Unexpectedly found nil value while unwrapping an Optional value."

Forced unwrapping is handy and easy to do when you know that the variable contains a non-`nil` value. But what if you aren't sure that the value isn't `nil`? We can use **conditional binding**, also called **optional binding**, to check the variable's value first before using it.

Optional Binding to Unwrap Variables

Because we may not know the inner value of a wrapped optional value at the time we receive it, we cannot always use the force unwrap operator to get at the value inside, because it may be `nil`. Swift has a mechanism called optional binding, used in an `if let` statement, to help us both unwrap a value and test it for validity before using it. Optional binding is useful because it assigns the unwrapped value to a temporary constant for use within the scope of the `if let` statement.

Listing 6.2 shows an example of how to use optional binding in an `if let` block to illustrate how, depending on whether the value inside the optional wrapper is `nil`, different statements or expressions will be executed.

LISTING 6.2 Using Optional Binding to Unwrap and Use Optional Values

```
var optionalString: String? = "I am a string."
if let unwrappedString = optionalString {
    print("unwrappedString is not nil, and equals \(unwrappedString)")
} else {
    print("optionalString contains nil")
}
```

Using optional binding, we were able to assign the unwrapped value inside `optionalString` to `unwrappedString`, if it is not `nil`. If `optionalString`'s value is `nil`, then the `else` block executes and prints "optionalString contains nil". If you were following along and typing the code here, did you find the same results, giving `optionalString` a string value or `nil`?

NOTE

Optionally Bound Values Live Only in Their Declared Scope

Keep in mind that when using optional binding, the constant declared in the `if let` (or `if var` for a bound variable) statement is used for only the life of the `if` block. Once execution passes outside the last curly brace, be it for the first `if` block, an `else if` block, or an `else` block, the variable or constant is deallocated and you cannot use it any longer. Attempting to use the constant or variable outside of its declared scope will result in a compiler error about use of undeclared variables.

Implicitly Unwrapped Optionals

Swift has a concept called **implicitly unwrapped optionals**, wherein you declare a variable as an optional, but with the intention that it won't have a `nil` value any time after it gets initialized with a value. To declare a variable as an implicitly unwrapped optional, you use the exclamation point character (!) immediately following the type name, rather than the question mark character (?). Here is what an implicitly unwrapped optional variable's declaration looks like:

```
var implicitInt: Int!
```

No initial value is given, but when it is initialized with a value (such as in an `init()` method, which we discuss in more depth in Hour 13, "Customizing Initializers of Classes, Structs, and Enums"), it will be known to have a value always, until it is deallocated from memory. An implicitly unwrapped optional is still an optional at heart, and can certainly be assigned `nil` at any time after initialization. The difference between an implicitly unwrapped optional and an explicitly unwrapped optional is that you do not need to do anything special to the optional value, and you can treat it in syntax as if it were not optional (in other words, you do not need to unwrap it to use it); an implicitly unwrapped optional is still allowed to be `nil` at runtime, so take care when using them.

There are several benefits to using implicitly unwrapped optionals. First, sending known good input to a class that returns an optional value would normally mean a lot of checking for a value inside the optional variable, when you know that the returned value is a valid value inside the optional. Second, implicitly unwrapped optionals remove the need to use the force unwrap operator on optional variables before accessing the value or calling methods on the variable. This leads to cleaner and more easily readable code and less confusion about accidentally calling methods directly to an optional versus the underlying value.

CAUTION

Implicitly Unwrapped Optionals Are Still Optionals

Even though Swift handles the unwrapping of implicitly unwrapped optionals without your need-ing to, it is worth it to mention this again. If the optional value is `nil`, you will still have a run-time error and the app will crash. Make sure the value has been initialized to a non-`nil` value before use.

Listing 6.3 illustrates implicitly unwrapped optionals, including declaration, receiving optional return values, and usage in the app. The listing uses a method on `Dictionary` that we discussed earlier, `updateValue(value:, forKey:)`, which returns the old value after successfully updating, or `nil` if the key-value pair did not exist prior. Since it could return `nil`, `updateValue(value:, forKey:)` returns an optional value of the same type as the value we updated.

LISTING 6.3   Using Implicitly Unwrapped Optionals

```
var optionalInt: Int!  // optionalInt is an implicitly unwrapped optional
var myDictionary = ["life" : 32]  // myDictionary is a mutable Dictionary
optionalInt = myDictionary.updateValue(42, forKey:"life")  // updates value for
  ➥key and returns 32 to optionalInt
let sixtyFour = optionalInt * 2  // we can use optionalInt normally,
  ➥without forced unwrapping
print(sixtyFour)
```

If you are following along in your own playground, and you entered in the code from Listing 6.3, go ahead and change `optionalInt` from `Int!` to `Int?`. What error do you see?

Nil Coalescing Operator

Another new operator to discuss is the **nil coalescing operator**. The nil coalescing operator is an infix operator and is denoted with two question marks (??) in between two operands. The left-hand operand is an optional value, and the right-hand operand is any non-`nil` value. The operator returns the unwrapped value of the optional if one exists or the operand on the right if the left-hand optional is `nil`. Here is an example of the nil coalescing operator:

```
let result = optionalString ?? "No value"
```

In the preceding example, if `optionalString` is `nil`, then `"No value"` is assigned to `result`. Otherwise, the unwrapped `optionalString` value is assigned to `result`. Regardless of which expression was evaluated, `result` is inferred to be a non-optional instance of `String`. The nil coalescing operator is perhaps one of my favorite operators in Swift because of its succinctness and power, and it allows you to evaluate an expression in one line of code that might otherwise take you several more.

Unwrapping Multiple Optionals

There may be instances where you have multiple optional values that you need to unwrap and use, such as after parsing some JSON data from a web service, and you need to take all the optional values and create a model object from them. Your model object might require that every property is a non-optional property, and to create an instance of the model object, you need every optional value unwrapped. This is not an uncommon case at all.

You could use nil coalescing to provide a default value for each optional value, but a default value might not make sense for some properties. In fact, your requirements might define that if any value is missing, to not even create the model instance at all.

You could also use conditional binding to unwrap each optional value, but this would result in a nasty nested mess of `if let` statements, affectionately called *the pyramid of doom*. Because this was a big (and common) problem, and many people needed a much more elegant solution, Apple introduced the ability to unwrap multiple optional values in the same line, separated by commas. Listing 6.4 illustrates *the pyramid of doom*, and Listing 6.5 illustrates how to use multiple bindings to make for a more elegant and readable solution.

LISTING 6.4   The Pyramid of Doom

```
let jsonDictionary: [String : Any] = ["artist": "Incubus", "song":
    ➥"Absolution Calling", "yearReleased": 2015]

if let artist = jsonDictionary["artist"] {
    if let song = jsonDictionary["song"] {
        if let yearReleased = jsonDictionary["yearReleased"] {
            print("\(song) by \(artist) was released in \(yearReleased)")
```

```
        }
    }
} else {
    print("some information was missing.")
}
```

LISTING 6.5 Using Multiple Bindings

```
let jsonDictionary: [String : Any] = ["artist": "Incubus", "song":
    ➥"Absolution Calling", "yearReleased": 2015]

if let artist = jsonDictionary["artist"],
    song = jsonDictionary["song"],
    yearReleased = jsonDictionary["yearReleased"] {
        print("\(song) by \(artist) was released in \(yearReleased)")
} else {
    print("some information was missing.")
}
```

With multiple bindings, you separate each assignment by a comma, and you can even separate them onto different lines for readability. This makes for a nice, linear flow of your code, versus the indented mess that Listing 6.4 could get into for a JSON dictionary with many more key-value pairs than shown. You also reduce the amount of curly braces needed from $n * 2$ to just 2, where n is the number of pairs.

NOTE

Don't Overthink Optional Values

Remember in the first paragraph of this hour when I said that your mind could be stretched a little? This is one of those parts that made me think to mention that. In fact, understanding optional values is so important in Swift, I wrote an article with videos solely dedicated to understanding them at http://www.informit.com/articles/article.aspx?p=2359760. The content of the article relies heavily on understanding enumerations, so I suggest reading that article after studying Hour 12, "Harnessing the Power of Enums." Don't try to overthink optional values and all that you can do with them. They really are a simple concept, just very foreign at first to some.

You can also refine your multiple binding statements with leading conditional checks, as well as conditional `where` clauses after a binding. The leading conditional enables you to exit early from potentially calculating several unwrap operations, as well as allocating a bunch of memory that would never get used. Likewise, the conditional `where` clause allows you to only unwrap and assign a value to a new constant if the unwrapped value matches a particular pattern or criteria. Having that validation in-line can be tremendously powerful.

Use Case for Optionals

A real-world situation where you would use optional variables would be something like writing an iOS app that allows a user to log in to a web service with a username and password. You might have to send the username and password variables to another controller to be validated, and perhaps perform more UI-based interaction with your user, such as asking for more information like an email address, and so on.

The object doing the validation might already exist by the time you send the username and password to it for validation, and having the two properties set to default values might not make sense; making them optional values with no initial assignment makes more sense.

Let's imagine that the requirements for a username and password are simple: The username must be at least 10 characters and begin with the letter e, and the password must simply be at least 8 characters. Let's work through these requirements in the following Try It Yourself section.

TRY IT YOURSELF ▼

Validate User Input with Multiple Bindings and Conditional Checking

Walk through an example using an Xcode playground to understand handling user data, using multiple bindings with conditional checking, and unwrap optionals appropriately.

1. Open Xcode and create a new playground. Either a Mac or iOS playground is fine. Clear the contents of the playground file.

2. Create two properties to store the username and password, each of type `String?`. Also create a Boolean variable to track whether the user is allowed to log in or not.

```
var username: String?
var password: String?
var ableToLogin = true
```

3. Assign values to the username and password variables, simulating receiving them from another object passing them in to ours.

```
username = "e14052729082"
password = "1qaz2wsx"
```

4. Now we can use conditional checking with multiple bindings. First, check to see whether the user is able to log in; then unwrap the username where the username is greater than or equal to 10 characters and also begins with the letter e. In the same binding, unwrap the password if its character count is greater than or equal to 8. Print the username and password if these checks and bindings succeed; otherwise, print an error message.

```
if ableToLogin,
    let unwrappedUsername = username where unwrappedUsername.characters.count
    ➥>= 10 && unwrappedUsername.hasPrefix("e"),
```

```
        let unwrappedPassword = password where unwrappedPassword.characters.count
        ➡>= 8 {
            print("\(unwrappedUsername) and \(unwrappedPassword) are valid.")
    } else {
        print("Please enter valid input.")
    }
```

Congratulations are in order if you stuck with it and finished the Try It Yourself example and got the expected results! This was a difficult example, and it utilized not only optional binding to unwrap optional values but was a good exercise in defining logic and appending that logic to each binding. This example required the let keyword to be used for each binding because we used in-line where clauses for each binding. If you do not use a where clause after each binding, or only use a where clause after the last binding, you may omit the let keyword from every binding except the first, as shown in Listing 6.5. Figure 6.1 shows the completed Try It Yourself example for you to compare results.

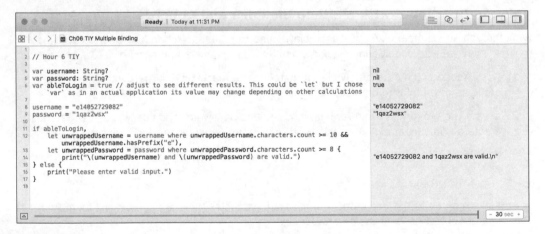

FIGURE 6.1
The completed Try It Yourself example with optional binding to unwrap optionals.

There is a lot more to optionals in Swift, but we need to cover a few more concepts first. We return to optionals in Hour 12, "Harnessing the Power of Enums," and also in Hour 19, "Working with Optional Chaining," as well as many more. Optional chaining is a powerful feature in Swift that enables you to traverse object hierarchies of optional values in one line of code without having separate checking mechanisms for each optional value. For now, let's move on to Hour 7, "Iterating Code with Loops."

Summary

This hour introduced optional variables, a relatively new concept not yet implemented in many programming languages, as a way to better safeguard variables from being accessed while containing `nil`. This is a major player in Swift's language, and you will find yourself regularly using optional values.

You learned how to declare a variable as an optional with the optional declaration operator (?), and what being an optional variable means. You also learned several different methods for unwrapping: forced unwrapping by using the force unwrap operator (!); implicit unwrapping by declaring an optional variable with the implicit optional operator (!) immediately following the variable's type; and `if let` statements, which both unwrap and compare the unwrapped value against `nil` to determine whether a value exists and execute the appropriate section of code. You also learned how to add conditional checking before an optional binding expression, unwrap multiple optionals in one expression, and also qualify each unwrapping by verifying its unwrapped value with `where` clauses.

In the next hour, we discuss more about controlling program flow with loops and how you can use loops to execute statements repeatedly as many times as needed.

Q&A

Q. What are some differences between using `nil` in Objective-C and optionals in Swift?

A. Objective-C uses `nil` with pointers. Optionals in Swift work for all types, while `nil` in Objective-C works only with classes. As we learned, optionals are safer in Swift when coupled with the built-in unwrap operations.

Q. Do I have to use a where clause with each optional binding in a multiple binding expression?

A. No, you do not need to use a `where` clause all the time. You may use them if you need to perform some conditional checking or pattern matching on the unwrapped value(s). If you do not use in-line `where` clauses, you may omit the `let` keyword for every binding after the first.

Q. Will a `nil` optional that is force unwrapped give a compile-time error?

A. No. The compiler assumes that the optional does indeed have a value since forced unwrapping was used. The error occurs when the app is run.

Workshop

The workshop contains quiz questions and exercises to help you solidify your understanding of the material covered. Try to answer all questions before looking at the answers that follow.

Quiz

1. A variable that holds a phone number in an app may contain a value or it may not. The following code snippet was used, but it is incorrect. How would you correct it?

```
var phoneNumber: String = nil
```

2. How do you use forced unwrapping of optionals in Swift?

3. What is optional binding in Swift?

4. Create an implicitly unwrapped optional that contains a user's score in a game.

5. Is it safer to use nil coalescing to unwrap an optional than to use forced unwrapping?

Answers

1. An optional should be used instead: `var phoneNumber: String?`

2. Forced unwrapping can be completed by adding an exclamation point (`!`) character immediately following the optional variable's name:

```
var phoneNumber: String?
phoneNumber = "555-555-5555"
let unwrappedPhoneNumber = phoneNumber!
```

3. When used in an `if let` statement, optional unbinding unwraps a value and tests it for validity before using it.

4. Implicitly unwrapped optionals can be created by adding an exclamation point (`!`) instead of the question mark (`?`) immediately following the type name:

```
var userScore: Int!
userScore = 100
```

5. Yes, it is safer because there will always be a known safe value returned. Be careful, however, that the default value is what you want and that a default value is appropriate to have.

Exercise

Create a new iOS playground. Create a string optional that can hold a value for user feedback in a game app. Practice assigning a value to the optional and using forced unwrapping. Next, use optional binding to unwrap and use the optional value. Try unwrapping the value with nil coalescing, too, and provide default values where appropriate. Finally, rewrite the optional as an implicitly unwrapped optional.

Iterating Code with Loops

In Hour 5, "Controlling Program Flow with Conditionals," we discussed controlling program flow with conditionals in which you can directly manipulate the path of execution of an app based on certain criteria. This hour also touches on controlling program flow, but in a different manner; we discuss how to loop certain blocks of code, expressions, and even iterate through items in arrays and dictionaries. Looping enables you to perform specific actions repeatedly or on each item in a collection. We also touch on transferring control of execution from within loops, much like we did with the `break` and `fallthrough` statements from last hour, but we discuss another control transfer statement and how each control statement behaves within loops.

Two Categories of Loops

Swift has two major categories of loops, often referred to as **while loops** and **for loops**. Many languages support both types of loops, and the concepts have been around for a long time. First, let's take a look at while loops.

While Loops

While loops will loop a set of statements until a certain condition is met. This is much like what we did in the Hour 5, where we used `if` and `switch` statements to check whether a condition was met to execute a certain set of statements. While loops are similar. However, they execute the given set of statements inside their block repeatedly until a condition is met.

Swift, like many other languages, has two types of while loops: **while loops** and **repeat-while loops**, formerly called a **do-while** loop. The major difference is that while loops evaluate the condition at the beginning of the loop before the statements inside the block execute, and a repeat-while loop executes the first iteration automatically and then checks the condition at the end.

NOTE

How a While Loop Evaluates Conditions

While loops evaluate their conditions to ensure that they should execute the code within their block of statements or not. This means that while loops evaluate logical values just like `if` and `switch` statements do; if a condition is true, the set of statements gets executed. If a condition is false, the statements do not get executed. Loops determine whether a condition is true, and if so, execute the loop *one time*. Then, they re-evaluate the condition to see whether they should execute the loop again, and so on until the condition is met. Conditions are not limited to Boolean variables or constants. You can have a complex expression as your condition, as long as it evaluates to either true or false.

The While Loop

I hope I haven't confused you by saying that a while loop is a type of while loop. The while loop is like a song on an album of the same name. Programmers generally categorize both repeat-while and while loops as "while loops." With that distinction made, let's discuss the while loop, its syntax, and behavior.

As mentioned already, a while loop first checks its condition to see whether it should even execute the code inside its block. If the condition is true, the code inside the block executes once, and then the condition is checked again. If false, the statements inside the block do not execute, and program execution resumes on the next line after the while loop's ending curly brace. Listing 7.1 illustrates a simple while loop displaying 10 numbers in the console.

LISTING 7.1   While Loop Syntax

```
01:  var count = 0
02:  while count < 10 {
03:      print("count is \(count)")
04:      ++count
05:  }
```

In line 1, we create a simple variable, `count`, of type `Int`, and set it to 0, as it will be used in the while loop's condition. Line 2 uses the `while` statement to begin the while loop and checks the condition first before any loop execution. In this case, 0 is less than 10, which returns true, so the program execution enters the loop. Line 3 simply prints a string showing the contents of `count`, and then line 4 increments `count` using the prefixed increment operator. When execution reaches the curly brace on line 5, the while loop *always* returns back to the line where it checks the condition (in this case, line 2). The reason that it always goes back to check the condition, even on the last iteration, is that the computer doesn't know it has reached the last iteration until its condition returns false. Once `count` is equal to 10, and the expression `while 10 < 10` is evaluated, the expression is false, and code would resume execution on line 6 (which is not shown here).

While loops are appropriate when the execution of statements inside the loop are strictly dependent upon a passing condition. In other words, the code inside a loop may never execute if the condition fails during its first validation. Be sure, however, that your while loops are structured in such a way that it will eventually evaluate to false and move on.

CAUTION

Be Aware of Infinite Loops

If you are not careful, you may experience what's called an infinite loop. An infinite loop can happen when the condition that gets evaluated each iteration is never false, so it just keeps going and going until the app either runs out of memory or is killed by some other means. Such an example would be if we never incremented `count` in the preceding example and it never was made equal to 10. Always be sure that your loop conditions will be met eventually.

The Repeat-While Loop

The repeat-while loop is similar to that of the while loop, with one small difference; the repeat-while loop performs the statements inside the loop exactly once before evaluating the loop's condition. If the condition is true, the statements inside the repeat-while loop are executed again. If the condition is false, control is transferred to the statement immediately following the while condition.

The repeat-while loop syntax has the condition at the end of the loop after the closing curly braces. Having the condition at the end of a repeat-while loop is nice, because not only does it make readability easier, but it also provides the visual validation that the statements inside the loop will run at least once until the condition is evaluated. Listing 7.2 rewrites Listing 7.1's code with a repeat-while loop instead of a while loop.

LISTING 7.2   Repeat-While Loop Syntax

```
01:   var count = 0
02:   repeat {
03:       print("count is \(count)")
04:       ++count
05:   } while count < 10
```

As you can see, the general concepts of the repeat-while loop are the same as a while loop. But the biggest difference is that the repeat-while loop executes the statements inside the loop block *first*, denoted by the `repeat` statement on line 2, before evaluating the condition, whereas the while loops evaluates the condition first. You'll need to consider this knowledge when writing your own apps, as one loop is not better than another; rather, it depends on how you want the flow of your app to be.

▼ TRY IT YOURSELF

Use a Repeat-While Loop to Compare Values

Let's walk through an example and use random numbers to simulate rolling a pair of dice, to see how many times it takes for us to roll the same number on both dice.

1. Open Xcode and create a new playground. Either a Mac or an iOS playground is fine. Clear the contents of the playground.

2. Start by importing the Foundation framework, as we need that for the random number generator.

```
import Foundation
```

3. We need a few variables: two for the dice and one to count how many rolls it takes to get matching numbers.

```
var timesRolled = 0
var rollOne: Int
var rollTwo: Int
```

4. We can begin the repeat-while loop now, so write `repeat` and an open curly brace. (Note that when you type an open curly brace and press Return, Xcode automatically places a closing curly brace on the following line to help prevent you from accidentally forgetting to add it.)

```
repeat {

}
```

5. Inside the curly braces, generate two random numbers and assign them to our two roll variables. We use a different random number generator, which has a more uniform distribution. The `arc4random_uniform(6)` function generates a random number between 0 and 5. Then add 1 to make the final number between 1 and 6, such as the sides on a die.

```
rollOne = Int(arc4random_uniform(6)) + 1
rollTwo = Int(arc4random_uniform(6)) + 1
```

6. Here it is helpful to print each result so you can see the actual dice rolls, and then increment the `timesRolled` variable to denote that we rolled the dice.

```
print("one: \(rollOne), two: \(rollTwo)")
++timesRolled
```

7. That's all we need inside the repeat-while loop, so after the closing curly brace, add the `while` statement with the condition we need to evaluate.

```
} while rollOne != rollTwo
```

8. Print the final value of how many times we rolled the dice to get both dice equal.

```
print("You rolled the dice \(timesRolled) times to get
    ➥ matching dice values.")
```

9. Hold the Command and Shift keys together and press Y to show the Debug Area, where the results from the `print(...)` statements will display, showing your results.

NOTE

Differences in Random Number Generators

Notice in step 5 in the preceding Try It Yourself section that we use a new random number generator than the `arc4random() % x` expression we used previously. The `arc4random_uniform(x)` function returns a random number using uniform distribution between 0 and *x*, and avoids modulo bias. Modulo bias can favor some remainders over others, depending on the "ceiling" number provided. Read more on modulo bias on Wikipedia at http://en.wikipedia.org/wiki/Fisher-Yates_shuffle#Modulo_bias.

This Try It Yourself example is perfect for the repeat-while loop because to find out whether our first roll has matching dice results, we need to roll at least once. The repeat-while loop lets us roll first before evaluating our condition. Remember, you can keep re-executing the playground to regenerate new random numbers to test your code by opening the Editor menu and then clicking Execute Playground. If you did everything correctly, your playground should look like Figure 7.1.

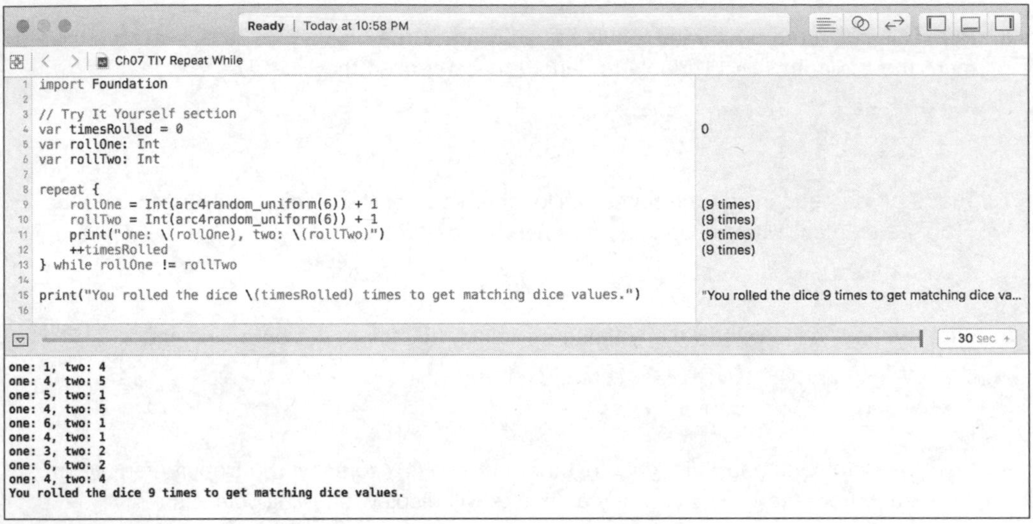

FIGURE 7.1
The completed repeat-while loop example, with code and results.

For Loops

The other type of loop in Swift is called a **for loop**. For loops iterate over statements of code a finite number of times, given in the syntax of the for statement. Like while loops, there are two types of for loops: the **for-condition-increment** loop (often just dubbed a *for loop*) and a **for-in** loop. Let's take a look at both for loops now.

The For-Condition-Increment Loop

The for-condition-increment loop, from here on out just called the *for loop*, is similar to the same loop in C, just with a small syntactic difference; Swift does not require any parentheses in the for loop, while C does.

The first thing a for loop does is initialize the variable that will serve as a counter; typically this is set to 0 or 1, or whatever counter number makes sense for your app. Then, a semicolon (;) is required to complete the second part of the for loop: the condition. The condition is much like what we have seen so far, where you must evaluate a condition to return true or false, so that the loop knows whether it should begin execution inside its loop or resume program flow after its final curly brace. After the condition is another semicolon, and then the incrementor. The incrementor could also be a decrementor, depending on the direction in which you are traversing numbers. You don't have to increment/decrement by 1; you could do so by 5, 17, or whatever number you need. All you're doing is telling the for loop how to change the counter variable once it has gone through an iteration of its loop.

Listing 7.3 illustrates both a for loop in C and a for loop in Swift, writing the same loop in both languages.

LISTING 7.3 For Loops in C and Swift

```
01:  // in C
02:  int result = 0;
03:  for (int count = 1; count <= 10; ++count) {
04:      result += count;
05:  }
06:  printf("%d", result);  // prints "55"
07:
08:  // in Swift
09:  var result = 0
10:  for var count = 0; count <= 10; ++count {
11:      result += count
12:  }
13:  print("\(result)")
```

In C, you can see in line 3 that the parentheses are required around the entire for statement, minus the keyword for itself, and ending before the starting curly brace. The only other differences are just the way that Swift and C declare variables differently, and also C uses printf(...) and Swift uses print(...) to print to the console.

Did you notice anything else? The for loop syntax reminds us a lot of the while loop from earlier in this hour. In fact, its behavior is identical to the while loop, in that there is an initialization, condition, statements to execute, and an increment. For these types of iterations, a for loop is many times preferred over a while loop, as its intent is clearer; the nature of a for loop is a known number of iterations, whereas while loops are designed to handle a variable number of iterations until a condition is met. In other words, while loops are not always dependent upon a counter that gets incremented. A while loop could have a condition to loop while itemFound == false, say for iterating over an array to find an element inside, which would then set the Boolean flag itemFound to true and exit the loop.

For loops are often used to iterate over a collection or list of items, such as arrays, because the count of arrays can always be retrieved by their count property. This way, you can easily access values at particular indexes, because your for loop counter will always be a valid index of the array. The following code snippet illustrates using a for loop over a collection of items:

```
let daysOfWeek = ["Mon", "Tue", "Wed", "Thu", "Fri", "Sat", "Sun"]
for var i = 0; i < daysOfWeek.count; ++i {
    // do something with the day
}
```

CAUTION

Stay in Bounds

Be careful while using for loops that you stay within the bounds of an array if you are iterating over one. Arrays are zero-based, which means their first index is zero, so your for loop should start at zero also and increment its way up (if working from the beginning to the end of the array). The for loop should always stop at `array.count - 1`, though, because `count - 1` is the last index of the array. Trying to access an element at index `count` in an array will throw an out of bounds exception, and your app will likely abort.

The For-In Loop

Another type of for loop is called the for-in loop. If you're coming from Objective-C, you may be familiar with the for-in loop already. The for-in loop is designed to iterate over every item in a collection, range, string, or progression made up of multiple items. The syntax of a for-in loop is more easily understood than that of a traditional for loop, in that it reads more closely like a sentence in the English language than a for loop. The make-up of a for-in loop looks like the following:

```
for item in items {
    // do something with item
}
```

The for-in loop also begins with the `for` keyword just like the for loop, but here you assign inline a constant to work with (`item`), followed by the `in` keyword and then the collection, range, or progression to traverse (`items`). The `in` keyword denotes that we're going to inspect every item in the `items` collection. The for-in loop gives us a nicer way to iterate through an entire collection of items without having to know the count of how many objects are in the collection, keep a variable to count our current index, or worry about incrementing anything. This simplified behavior in a for-in loop is called **fast enumeration**. It enables us to quickly iterate over every item in a collection, range, or progression without having to write code to manage other parts of the loop.

NOTE

Scope and Declaration of For-In Loop Items

By including the name `item` in our previous example, Swift automatically declares `item` a constant of whatever type is held in the collection, range, or progression. Say you are using a for-in loop's fast enumeration to iterate over an array of `String` objects. Each instance of `item` is newly declared by Swift as a constant of type `String` and is only available within the braces of the for-in loop and disposed of at the end of each iteration. The `item` constant is not available outside the for-in loop.

Iterating Through Different Data Types with For-In Loops

Here is where some of Swift's power really shines. When iterating through different ranges, collections, progressions, and so on, Swift can automatically declare a constant of the necessary type by using type inference, including tuples of multiple types, for each item. Swift lets you use fast enumeration for any type or range that is a collection of something. The reason that Swift declares a constant is that the item evaluated should not be altered while using fast enumeration, because that would alter the sequence being enumerated.

Let's first discuss ranges. In Swift, you can use the for-in loop to iterate over a given range, using either the half-closed range or closed range operators. The item to be evaluated is a constant of type Int. Where we had incremented the count variable in the past, we cannot increment a constant value, so Swift discards the current item and creates a new one with a value one greater than the last value. The code in Listing 7.4 illustrates a for-in loop iterating over a closed range of numbers.

LISTING 7.4   For-In Loop with Ranges

```
01:  for count in -2...2 {
02:      print("count is \(count)")
03:  }
```

The code in Listing 7.4 should be pretty easy to understand by now. In line 1, we use a for-in loop, with the constant count to iterate through the given range. The range is a closed range, which consists of integer values -2, -1, 0, 1, 2. Since each iteration assigns the next value to count, we can print the current value of count in a print(...) statement. If you're typing this as we go in a playground, remember to press Command-Shift-Y to show the Debug Area, which shows the console output of your print(...) statements. A half-closed range would have worked here as well, but the loop would not have included the final 2 value.

Iterating over ranges is useful and less code to type than the traditional for loop, which can accomplish the same functionality. Sometimes you may just need to iterate over a collection a certain number of times, but you don't care for or need the counted value inside your loop. You can replace the constant count with the underscore (_), which lets Swift bypass storing the current count in a value usable by you and simply performs the iteration the given amount of times. This is useful if you need to perform an action using each item in a collection but don't care about the current count. The first line would look like for _ in -2...2 { in this case. In an actual program, you may want to start at a sensible value such as 0 or 1 for your iteration, rather than -2; this was just for illustration.

Next, let's look at for-in loops for Strings. As we covered in Hour 2, "Learning Swift's Fundamental Data Types," String instances are actually made up of individual Character instances. This means that we can quickly and easily loop over every character in a string to do something with it. Listing 7.5 illustrates how to do this.

LISTING 7.5   Using For-In Loops with Strings

```
01:  let myWord = "Supercalifragilisticexpialidocious"
02:  var numberOfEsFound = 0
03:
04:  for eachChar in myWord.characters {
05:      if eachChar == "e" {
06:          ++numberOfEsFound
07:      }
08:  }
09:  print("I found \(numberOfEsFound) e's in \(myWord)")
```

Iterating through `String` instances is pretty easy now that you know the basic syntax of for-in loops. In line 1, we declare a constant `String`, and in line 2, we declare a variable `Int` to keep track of how many instances of the letter e we would find in the given word. In line 4, we iterate over `myWord` by getting each character and storing it into `eachChar` at every iteration of the for-in loop. Lines 5–7 should be familiar to you from the previous hour, and then finally on line 9, we print the output.

Next, let's take a look at some more advanced types to iterate through with for-in loops, starting with the `Array` type. As we know, an array is a collection of items of the same type. So just like iterating over a `String`, which is a collection of objects of type `Character`, an `Array` of type `String` can be easily iterated through in a for-in loop in exactly the same way. Let's examine this type of iteration in a Try It Yourself example.

▼ TRY IT YOURSELF

Iterate Through Arrays with For-In Loops

Create an array and then iterate through each item using a for-in loop. Then use a `switch` statement to check each case for conditionally creating output.

1. Open Xcode and create a new playground. Either a Mac or iOS playground will work.

2. Remove all the default contents inside the playground to start with a clean file.

3. Declare an array of type `[String]`, and initialize it with an array literal.

   ```
   let bears = ["Papa bear", "Mama bear", "Baby bear"]
   // bears is of type [String]
   ```

4. Use the for-in loop to iterate over each bear string in the bears array.

   ```
   for bear in bears {
   ```

5. Use a `switch` statement to evaluate the `bear` constant and conditionally branch the code depending on which bear is the current bear. Depending on which bear is the current bear,

the appropriate temperature of porridge should be printed to the console. Have a default case in the event that you don't know what bear is in the array. Don't forget the ending curly brace for the for-in loop.

```
switch bear {
    case "Papa bear":
        print("My porridge is too hot!")
    case "Mama bear":
        print("My porridge is too cold!")
    case "Baby bear":
        print("My porridge is just right!")
    default:
        print("Unrecognized bear. Intruder alert!")
    }
}
```

6. Hold the Command and Shift keys and press Y to display the Debug Area, if it's not already shown. There, you'll see each line printed in the console, because we only supplied known bears to our array.

7. Add a different bear to the array, re-execute the playground (select the Editor menu, then click Execute Playground), and see what results you receive in the console in the Debug Area.

The completed Try It Yourself example should look like Figure 7.2.

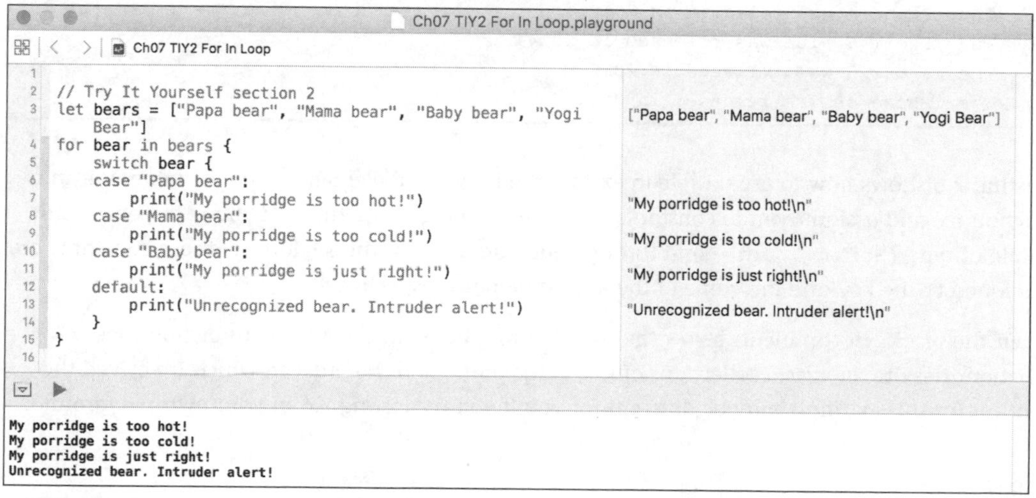

FIGURE 7.2
The completed Try It Yourself example for using for-in loops with an array.

Another facet of fast enumeration with for-in loops is iterating through dictionaries. The idea of iterating through dictionaries is similar to what we have discussed thus far, with one small difference; since dictionaries are built upon key-value pairs, we cannot just use a for-in statement such as for item in myDictionary. How would Swift know whether you mean the key or the value to assign to item?

Here is where we can use a tuple to iterate through a dictionary, by assigning temporary constants inside a tuple to both the key and the value at each iteration of the pairs in the dictionary. The syntax and an example are shown in Listing 7.6.

LISTING 7.6   Using For-In Loops with Dictionaries

```
01:  let retinaiPhonesAndYears = ["iPhone 4" : 2010,
                                  "iPhone 4S" : 2011,
                                   "iPhone 5" : 2012,
                                  "iPhone 5C" : 2013,
                                  "iPhone 5S" : 2013,
                                   "iPhone 6" : 2014,
                              "iPhone 6 Plus" : 2014]
02:  for (iPhone, year) in retinaiPhonesAndYears {
03:      print("The \(iPhone) was released in \(year).")
04:  }
// displays:
//   The iPhone 6 was released in 2014.
//   The iPhone 5C was released in 2013.
//   The iPhone 5S was released in 2013.
//   The iPhone 4 was released in 2010.
//   The iPhone 6 Plus was released in 2014.
//   The iPhone 5 was released in 2012.
//   The iPhone 4S was released in 2011.
```

Listing 7.6 shows how to use a tuple to extract the individual elements of a key-value pair in a dictionary and assign them to constants, as shown in line 2. The tuple (iPhone, year) is a tuple of type (String, Int), and through each iteration in the dictionary, those constants are assigned to the key and the value of the key-value pair, respectively.

I left the results in comments below the code to bring back up a point about dictionaries. Dictionaries are *unordered* collections of key-value pairs, and the order in which I received the output for this example may be different for you if you try Listing 7.6 in your own playground.

NOTE

Sorting Dictionary Key-Value Pairs

While dictionaries are inherently unordered, you can sort dictionaries before using them to get a sorted dictionary to work with. We briefly cover sorting using the sort(...) instance function provided in Swift's standard library in Hour 9, "Understanding Higher Order Functions and Closures."

Using tuples with for-in statements to iterate through dictionaries is useful. But there may be times when you don't need both items in a tuple, and maybe only need to iterate through just the keys or just the values. You can use the wildcard underscore (_) in place of a constant's name inside the tuple, and Swift ignores the value in place of the underscore. For instance, with the iPhone release years in Listing 7.6, if you just need the year values to know how many releases there were per year, you could have a for-in loop that looks like this instead:

```
for (_, year) in retinaiPhonesAndYears {
    // do some calculation for the years, such as add how many released in 2013
}
```

Pattern Matching and Filtering Inside For-In Loops

As we saw in the last hour, some pretty advanced pattern-matching abilities have been added to conditional statements as of Swift 2.0. Well, it should not come as a surprise that these pattern-matching abilities have been brought to for-in loops as well. Using a `where` clause, you can iterate over a collection where a certain condition is true, resulting in fewer iterations and potentially saving battery and CPU cycles. Let's take a look at how this works, with one more example of using tuples in for-in loops with arrays. It is possible to get the index and the item's value at the same time with fast enumeration, and that is by calling the `enumerate()` function on the collection in line in the for-in loop's statement. Listing 7.7 illustrates how this is done.

LISTING 7.7   Using For-In Loops with Enumerated Arrays and Filtering

```
let beatles = ["Paul", "John", "Ringo", "George"]
var ringoIndex = 0
for (index, name) in beatles.enumerate() where name == "Ringo" {
    ringoIndex = index
}
print("Ringo is at index \(ringoIndex) in the beatles array.")
// Displays:
//   "Ringo is at index 2 in the beatles array."
```

Staying with the Beatles for a moment, we can also use pattern matching with for-in loops quite easily. The syntax looks a bit odd, much like it did for conditional statement pattern matching from Hour 5, but it is indeed consistent. To use pattern matching with for-in loops, you use the `case` statement, much like you would in a `switch` expression. Listing 7.8 illustrates how to do this, by storing an array of tuples containing a handful of Beatles albums and their year, and then our for-in loop only needs to execute its body when a certain criterion is met.

LISTING 7.8   Using For-In Loops with Pattern Matching

```
let albums = [("Twist and Shout", 1964),
    ("A Hard Day's Night", 1964),
    ("Yellow Submarine", 1969),
```

```
    ("Let It Be", 1970)]

for case let (album, 1964) in albums {
    print("\(album) came out in 1964")
}
```

You can see in Listing 7.8 that our for-in loop matches any pattern of tuple that contains any album (which will be assigned to the constant `album` during each iteration that matches) but only the year 1964. If you are following along in your own playground, how many results do you get printed in your Debug Area console? You should have two: Twist and Shout, and A Hard Day's Night.

Despite the funky syntax, you can easily parse this down to understandable chunks. The `for` keyword indicates the beginning of a loop, simple enough. Next, the `case` keyword indicates that there will be a pattern to match. The `let (album, 1964)` is the temporary constant applied to each iteration for matching, and finally the `in albums` means that `albums` is the collection we are iterating over and matching against. We will see more of this syntax later, so it will be good for you to get comfortable with it now.

Transferring Control in Loops

In the previous hour, we discussed methods of transferring control of your app's execution with the `break` and `fallthrough` statements, with regard to the conditional `switch` statement. Swift makes it possible to transfer control of execution from loops as well, and we discuss the two statements that enable you to do that: the **continue** and **break** statements. The `continue` and `break` statements can be used in both while loops and for loops.

Transferring Control with the `continue` Statement

Inserting the `continue` statement into a loop halts execution of the current loop's iteration, bypasses any remaining code in the loop, and resumes execution at the next iteration of the loop. The `continue` statement can be useful if you are checking a condition inside the loop, you know that no more execution needs to occur within this iteration, and you can safely move on to the next iteration. Any counter constant or temporary constant assigned as the current item in the iteration is discarded, and the counter is recreated with an incremented value, or the item points to the next item in the collection. Listing 7.9 shows a brief example of how a `continue` statement might be used.

LISTING 7.9 Using `continue` to Transfer Control

```
01:  var results = [Int]()  // creates an empty array of Ints
02:
03:  for count in 1...100 {
```

```
04:        let remainder = count % 7
05:        switch remainder {
06:        case 1...6:
07:            continue   // bypasses any further execution in this iteration
08:        default:
09:            results.append(count)
10:        }
11:        print("\(count) is divisible by 7")
12:    }
```

The code in Listing 7.9 should all be familiar to you, outside the `continue` statement in line 7. By placing the `continue` statement in the case matching any integer among 1 to 6, we tell the compiler to bypass any further code in the for-in block and resume at the next iteration. That means that line 11 will not execute unless `count` is divisible by 7.

Transferring Control with the `break` Statement

The `break` statement, when inserted inside a loop, terminates the current loop iteration and also ends the loop entirely, and resumes execution on the line after the loop's closing curly brace. This can be useful when you need to iterate over every item to check for a certain condition, or whether an item exists, and then exit the loop when the condition is found. Listing 7.10 illustrates an example of how you might use a `break` statement in a for-in loop.

LISTING 7.10   Using break to Transfer Control

```
let word = "Supercalifragilisticexpialidocious"
for eachChar in word.characters {
    print(eachChar)
    if eachChar == "x" {
        print("\(word) contains an 'x'")
        break
    }
}
```

Our for-in loop in Listing 7.10 checks to see whether the letter "x" appears. If so, a message is displayed, and control is transferred out of the loop entirely. The reason is that once we've found the "x," we don't care about any further characters. You may run across many scenarios in your development career where you need to iterate through collections of some sort, and once you've found what you're looking for, there is no need for execution to continue. It is good to keep this in mind, because every line of execution means a little bit of your user's battery gets depleted, whether an iOS device, Apple Watch, or Macbook Pro/Air laptop. So be a good programming citizen, and don't needlessly execute code you don't have to.

Summary

In this hour, we covered many facets of Swift's two methods of iterating code: for loops and while loops. We also learned that for loops consist of for-condition-increment loops and for-in loops, and while loops consist of while loops and repeat-while loops, with examples of each type of loop.

We discussed different data types that could be iterated through, as well as how to handle iterating through collections with tuples to temporarily extract their values into constants to work with inside the loops. We also discussed how to use filtering and pattern matching with for-in loops to more efficiently loop over collections where a condition should be met first.

Then we discussed transferring control of program execution with the `break` and `continue` statements. These statements assist in more efficient code execution, by bypassing unnecessary statements when the situation allows.

Q&A

Q. Is it better to use for loops or while loops?

A. While they seem similar, there is a big difference between for and while loops. A for loop is often used to iterate over arrays or where the end of the condition is known. A while loop is a little more flexible because you can add other data types to the condition. Carefully examining your need for a loop helps you determine the best type of loop to use in your program.

Q. Is it possible to use a for loop without creating a new counter variable?

A. Yes. It is not necessary to create a new variable when using a for loop, as you can reuse an existing variable if one has not yet been created. However, you will most likely want to reset the variable to a more sensible starting value.

Q. Will I break anything if I accidentally create an infinite loop?

A. An infinite loop can crash a program or an app or even lock up the user interface, depending on where you have created the infinite loop. You can quickly see an infinite loop in the playground, stop it, and correct the issue.

Workshop

The workshop contains quiz questions and exercises to help you solidify your understanding of the material covered. Try to answer all questions before looking at the answers that follow.

Quiz

1. Find the error and correct the code snippet so that output is displayed:

```
let count = 0
while count < 10 {
    print("count is \(count)")
    ++count
}
```

2. What is the purpose of the `break` statement inside a loop? The `continue` statement?

3. What is the best way to iterate over a collection of items, such as ranges and numbers?

4. Rewrite the following while loop as a for loop:

```
var count = 20
while count < 100 {
    println("first count is \(count)")
    count += 20
}
```

5. How would you write a for-in loop using a range from 1 to 100 and printing the current index number to the console, but only if the current index number is even?

Answers

1. The constant `count` should be a variable so that it can be incremented inside the loop.

```
var count = 0
while count < 10 {
    println("count is \(count)")
    ++count
}
```

2. When the `break` statement is used inside a loop, it terminates the current loop iteration and also ends the loop entirely. Execution then continues on the line after the loop's closing curly brace. The `continue` statement causes the current loop iteration to end, but resumes looping if the ending condition has not been met.

3. The for-in loop is the best way to iterate over collections of items.

4. The while loop can be rewritten as a for loop, as shown in the following code:

```
for var count = 20; count < 100; count += 20{
    println("count is \(count)")
}
```

5. Use a `where` clause to filter the for-in loop's iteration:

```
for a in 1...100 where a % 2 == 0 {
    print("\(a)")
}
```

Exercise

Create a new playground. Think of a few household items that you would want to add to a household inventory tracker, and their respective values. Create an array of tuples, with each tuple containing the household item and its value. Iterate over the array, and use pattern matching to print information on only the items greater than a particular value of your choosing.

Using Functions to Perform Actions

So far in this book, you have learned some of the basic syntax of Swift, constants and variables of general data types in which we store values, and a fairly procedural approach to developing software. By procedural, I mean that our code starts running at line 1 and executes one line after another until the last line (with the exception of loops, which just reiterate the same lines of code until completion). In this hour, we take a look at **functions**, which are self-contained blocks of code designed to perform a specific task, which may or may not execute in the same linear order as we have done so far.

Functions are a bit of a stretch from what we've covered so far, but follow along closely and you should be okay. As you can see from the preceding "What You'll Learn in This Hour" list, we have a lot to cover. Some concepts of functions might be confusing, but it is appropriate to discuss functions now before we move any further in this book, as most every other hour relies heavily on functions.

Because functions are a key element of Swift programming and because they are used extensively throughout the remainder of this book, I suggest following along in your own playground or REPL in any listing or code snippet, in addition to the Try It Yourself sections, to get practice at typing functions. Truly, the more you do it, the more you will learn.

With that, let's start with a basic introduction to functions, their composition, and how to think about functions as more than they appear to be.

The Nature of Functions in Swift

As mentioned previously, functions are self-contained blocks of code designed to perform a specific task. The code inside a function can be similar to the examples we have done thus far in this book, such as iterating through collections to find a particular piece of data, use conditional switches and if statements to branch execution based on conditions, and so on. Functions can be as long or as short as they need to be to accomplish the task they are given.

NOTE

No Required Length of a Function

As noted, functions can be as long or as short as you need to perform the desired tasks. Many believe that functions should be less than 10 lines of code, no more than 4 lines of code, or what have you. The goal of a function is to accomplish a certain task, and if that task requires too many lines of code, you may want to investigate *refactoring* your code to isolate and extract parts that can be easily repeated, shortened, or even eliminated, all of which can help make your code cleaner, easier to read, and perhaps even more efficient.

The code inside a function, unlike code we have written so far, is not executed until it is **called**. To call a function, you simply call it by name and provide any parameters inside a pair of parentheses. You have already seen one function that fits this description—the `print()` function. It's a little easier to understand when you can see, so let's cover the syntax and structure of functions.

General Function Syntax and Structure

Functions in Swift follow a simple layout. All functions begin with the `func` keyword and then are given a name. After the name, a set of open and closed parentheses is required, inside which can be any number of parameters or values passed into the function to be used by the function. This is followed by the return type, the type of value the function returns. The function name, list of parameters, and return type all make up what is known as the function's **definition**. Finally, a pair of open and closed curly braces is required, inside which is the code your function performs when called. Figure 8.1 illustrates the syntax breakdown of a function.

```
func funcName ( param1 : Type ,  param2 : AnotherType ,..) -> ReturnType {
    return someValue
}
```

FIGURE 8.1
The syntactic structure of a function in Swift.

The syntax can be broken down as follows:

▶ `funcName`: This is the name of the function. Swift functions generally begin with a lowercase letter and then capitalize every word thereafter and contain no spaces, such as `addTheseTwoNumbers` or `findMeanMedianAndMode`. Function names should be descriptive as to what the function does.

▶ `param1:Type, param2:AnotherType,..`: This syntax should be familiar to you; the only nuance is that each parameter is separated by a comma. Parameters are values sent into a function by the caller. Not all functions have, or even need, parameters. Each parameter looks like a typical Swift variable declaration, just without the `let` or `var` introducer, in that you name the parameter, enter a colon (`:`), and then provide that parameter's type. Finally, the trailing `..` signifies that there may be more parameters and is just for illustration. You do not need to put any trailing dots in your function definitions.

▶ `-> ReturnType`: This is the type of value that the function returns. The `->` symbol (a dash followed by the right angle bracket) indicates "this function returns data of type ReturnType." `ReturnType` could be `Int`, `String`, `Bool`, `Char`, and so on, or even a custom type that you create.

▶ `{ and }`: These curly braces indicate the beginning and the end of a function. This is exactly the same as the curly braces you are familiar with from such statements as `switch` and `if`, and `for` and `while` loops. Once execution reaches the ending curly brace, the function is done, and execution resumes on the next line, or the next line after the caller.

▶ `return someValue`: In a function that indicates a return type (with `-> ReturnType`), you must have a `return` statement, followed by a value of type `ReturnType` to return. This value gets passed back to the line of code that called the function. If the function does not have a return type indicated, you do not need to write an explicit return statement. You learn more about returning values later in the hour.

The structure of a function in Swift is a little different than you might be used to if you are coming from a C or Objective-C background. Having the return type at the end certainly takes some getting used to. However, Swift's function syntax does make it more clear what the intent is, that it is indeed a function, what its parameters are, and what it will ultimately return. To me, it reads more like a sentence: "This function is named `addTwoNumbers`, it takes two numbers of type `Int` as parameters, and it returns a value of type `Int`."

Now that we understand the syntactic structure of a function, let's examine functions at an easy level and move our way up. As mentioned earlier, you see a lot of code in this hour, so get your playground or REPL ready, and let's get going.

Functions with No Parameters and No Return Type

The most basic function accepts no parameters and returns nothing. The function definition is short and only contains the function name and an empty set of parentheses. Listing 8.1 illustrates a function with no parameters and no return type, which simply prints a line inside its curly braces.

LISTING 8.1   A Function with No Parameters and No Return Type

```
01:  func printHelloWorld() {
02:      print("Hello, world!")
03:  }
```

The function in Listing 8.1 should be easy to understand. In line 1, we see the `func` keyword, followed by the name of the function, `printHelloWorld`. Then, we see the empty set of parentheses indicating there are no parameters, followed by the open curly brace, signifying the beginning of the code inside the function. Line 2 simply prints "Hello, world!" as any good sample app should. Line 3 closes the curly brace for the function, indicating the end of the function.

If you typed this into your playground, or the Swift REPL, you notice that nothing printed to the console output window. Why not? We never *called* the function. Here's how we call our `printHelloWorld` function:

```
printHelloWorld()
```

That's it. Now, you should see "Hello, world!" in the console output in Xcode's Debug Area or in the console output of the Swift REPL.

The Type of a Function

Before we go any further, an important piece to discuss about functions is that they have a type, consisting of the parameter types and the return type. For instance, let's say we have the `printHelloWorld` function from Listing 8.1. The type of this function is `() -> ()`. This literally means "a function that takes no parameters and returns an empty tuple." When defining a function that returns an empty tuple (also known as a type called `Void`, which is the same as saying the function returns nothing), we don't write the `-> ()` because it's redundant and unnecessary, but under the hood, that's part of the type. It is important to know the type of a function, and throughout this hour, I make a note of the type of a function whenever it is necessary. In the next hour, we discuss some advanced function topics, such as passing functions as function parameters, in which you need to know the function type.

Because a function has a type, just like String or Int are types, it is helpful to think about functions as first-class objects, too. The syntax can get a little difficult to understand, but as long as you understand this point about function types, you should have no problem later.

Functions with Parameters

As we've seen in the function structure example in Figure 8.1, you can place parameters inside the parentheses of a function. This enables you to send values to a function and have that function work with or manipulate those values as part of its greater task. A function can have as many or as few parameters as necessary, if any, to accomplish its task. However, having too many parameters may indicate that your function could be trying to do too much, and you may need to refactor into smaller, more manageable functions.

Let's take a look at a function that takes a single parameter, of type Int, and prints a line of output as many times as the parameter tells. For instance, if the parameter is equal to the number 3, it prints out 3 lines of output. Listing 8.2 shows us how to do that.

LISTING 8.2   A Function with One Parameter

```
01:    func printHelloTimes(times: Int) {
02:        for _ in 1...times {
03:            print("Hello to you!")
04:        }
05:    }
06:
07:    printHelloTimes(3)
// Displays the following output:
//  Hello to you!
//  Hello to you!
//  Hello to you!
```

The declaration of the function in line 1 should be well-understood by this point. We declare the function with the func keyword, give it a name (in this case, printHelloTimes), and then inside the parentheses, we provide a parameter with an associated type, times: Int. times is known to the function as an **internal parameter**, or **local parameter**, in that times can only be used inside the **scope** of the function.

NOTE

Scope of Variables and Constants

A scope is a defining context inside which a variable or constant lives. In Listing 8.2, the scope of the parameter times is considered only to be inside the function because it is defined in the function's parameter list. The scope of a variable or constant defines what elements can and can't access it. In other words, because the times parameter is scoped to the printHelloTimes function, it cannot be used or accessed outside of that function.

`times` is also a constant. If you try to modify `times` inside the function, you receive a compiler error. To change the value of a parameter inside the function, use the `var` introducer before the parameter name inside the parentheses, as shown in the following function definition snippet:

```
func functionWithVariableParameter(var name: String) { ... }
```

Finally, line 7 calls our `printHelloTimes` function and provides the number 3 as an **argument**. An argument to a function is the value you give to a parameter. If a function has required parameters, you must supply valid arguments to it.

If you remember from Figure 8.1, to have multiple parameters in a function, you separate the parameters and types by a comma. Listing 8.3 is a modified version of the function in Listing 8.2, adding a second parameter and using both parameters inside the function.

LISTING 8.3 Using Multiple Parameters Inside a Function

```
func printWord(word: String, numberOfTimes: Int) {
    for _ in 1...numberOfTimes {
        print("Hello \(word)")
    }
}
printWord("wonderful person reading this book", numberOfTimes: 4)
```

The function in Listing 8.3 takes two parameters, one `String` and one `Int`, separated by a comma. Notice how the names of the parameters, along with the name of the function, help describe what the function is and does. If you come from Objective-C, you're probably familiar with that naming convention, as parameters to methods extended the name of the method and combined made it easy to read and understand what the method was intended to do, return, or both.

Also notice that the name `numberOfTimes` for the second parameter is required in calling the function, but the first, `word`, is not. In Swift 2.0, the structure of calling a function changed to show the parameter names after the first one, enabling better readability of functions, and a better understanding for what each parameter is intended. Naming your functions to be readable and naming them such that there is no question as to the purpose of each parameter is a great goal to strive for. Your coworkers and your future self will thank you.

NOTE

Argument Validation

In the interest of keeping these examples brief and explanatory, I left out value validation. If, for instance, I had entered -4 instead of 4 as the argument to `printWord(word: numberOfTimes:)`, I would not have gotten the intended results at all. We won't cover validation in this book, but to validate values, you can simply check to make sure values fit a certain criteria before using them, with if statements, switch statements, and the like.

Functions with Variadic Parameters

Now that we've discussed using parameters inside function definitions, Swift offers us another way to add parameters but of an unknown length. **Variadic parameters** are parameters that can have an unknown number of elements, and when the function is called, the variadic parameters are stored in an array with a length equal to the number of arguments sent from the caller. The syntax for variadic parameters is simple: Just append three dots (. . .) to the end of the type of the parameter, such as (numbers: Int...). Of course, for consistency and readability, it may behoove you to name the parameter with a plural name to indicate that it can take many values as arguments.

Prior to Swift 2, variadic parameters had to be the last parameter in a list of parameters, if there are multiple parameters in a function definition. Now they are not required to be the last parameter and can be anywhere in the parameter list. This is to facilitate flexibility in function naming so that readability makes sense. You can still, however, only have one variadic parameter in your list of parameters.

Variadic parameters can also take zero elements, at which time the function creates an array with zero elements, or in other words, an empty array. This can be used to our advantage, without having to use any special code to check for nil or whether any arguments were passed at all, although you could check whether an array is empty with the .isEmpty property if your app logic required. Listing 8.4 details the use of variadic parameters by adding all the numbers passed in as arguments to the function.

LISTING 8.4   **Using Variadic Parameters in Functions**

```
01:  func addVariadicNumbers(numbers: Int...) {
02:      var result = 0
03:      for eachNum in numbers {
04:          result += eachNum
05:      }
06:      print("Sum total of numbers: \(result)")
07:  }
08:
09:  addVariadicNumbers(1, 2, 3, 4, 5)
10:  addVariadicNumbers(4)
11:  addVariadicNumbers()
// Displays:
//   Sum total of numbers: 15
//   Sum total of numbers: 4
//   Sum total of numbers: 0
```

Right in line 1, we see the use of the variadic parameter inside the parentheses. Since Swift translates all the arguments provided into an array at runtime, we can use numbers as an array, so we use fast enumeration with a for-in loop (lines 3 through 5) to quickly add all the values into a results variable and then print the result. Lines 9 through 11 show different ways to call the function with variadic parameters, the first with many arguments, then one argument, and no argument.

NOTE

Arguments Can Be Constants or Variables

In these examples, we used `Int` literals as arguments passed to functions. Don't forget that you can pass constants or variables too, as long as they are the same type as the receiving parameter.

After seeing a function like the one in Listing 8.4 performing an arithmetic task, it would be nice if we could return the value to the caller so that further processing could take place, or even display a value to the user on the screen. Good news: Swift provides a `return` statement that we can use to return a value, object, tuple, or even another function back to the caller. Let's discuss returning variables next in a basic context and work our way up to more complex scenarios.

Functions with Return Types

So far, our examples of functions have only printed out lines of text to the console. While it's helpful to see them while learning the structure and usage of functions, it really doesn't help you with anything much applicable to solving real problems with code. Some of the power of functions comes in their capability to return data to their caller to be used after the function has finished execution, and that is by using the `return` statement.

If you recall from Figure 8.1, the return type of a function is introduced with the `->` symbol, followed by the return type itself. You do not provide a return name, just a type. If we take the example in Listing 8.4 and change the function to return a value instead of just printing it, the example looks like the following in Listing 8.5.

LISTING 8.5   Returning Values from Functions

```
01:  func addVariadicNumbers(numbers: Int...) -> Int {
02:      var result = 0
03:      for eachNum in numbers {
04:          result += eachNum
05:      }
06:      return result
07:  }
08:
09:  let sum = addVariadicNumbers(7, 4, 9)
// sum is a constant Int, and is equal to 20
```

The major changes in Listing 8.5 from Listing 8.4 are that line 1 adds an `Int` return type, and line 6 uses the `return` statement, rather than just printing with `print`, to return the results variable. This satisfies the function's return type of `Int`. Then, in line 9, we assign the returned value to a constant `Int` named `sum`.

NOTE

Use Return to Transfer Control

If you remember from Hour 5, "Controlling Program Flow with Conditionals," and Hour 7, "Iterating Code with Loops," regarding control flow with conditionals and loops, we discussed four statements that Swift uses to transfer control of execution: `break`, `continue`, `fallthrough`, and `return`. `return` is the last one, and we had not yet talked about it until now, because it didn't then make sense outside the context of functions. The `return` statement ends execution in a function, and returns a value specified (or no value if `return` is used by itself in a function without a return type). You are not limited to one `return` statement inside a function; rather, you can have as many as makes sense for your purposes, such as inside cases in a `switch` statement. Keep in mind, though, that once the `return` statement is executed, no more code inside the function will be executed.

A feature native to Swift, but new to C and Objective-C developers, is the concept of returning multiple values from functions. This is accomplished using tuples, and the syntax looks identical to how you define parameters for a function. To define a tuple of values as the return type, you put the values and return types inside parentheses, as usual. The values are in the format `(value1: Type, value2: AnotherType, ...)`. When you have a tuple as the return type, the return statement must also return a valid tuple, matching the types in the function's definition. To illustrate this, examine the following code snippet to inspect the syntax for defining a tuple return type and returning a tuple:

```
func thisFuncReturnsATuple() -> (a : Int, b : Int, c : Int) {
    return (1, 2, 3)
}
```

The code snippet uses named parameters inside the tuple. You can also create an **anonymous tuple**, which would look like `(Int, Int, Int)`, but having names in the tuple makes extracting values a bit more obvious if you need to do so.

Let's walk through an example of a function returning a tuple in this next Try It Yourself section.

▼ TRY IT YOURSELF

Create a Function to Return Mean, Median, Mode

We take everything you've learned up to now about functions and combine them in this example. Write a function that accepts a variadic parameter of integers and returns the mean, median, and mode.

1. Open Xcode and create a new playground. Either an iOS or Mac playground will work.

2. Clear the playground's existing code and declare a function named `meanMedianMode` that takes a variadic parameter of integers and returns a tuple of a `Double` and two `Int`s named mean, median, and mode. Don't forget the opening curly brace for the function.

   ```
   func meanMedianMode(numbers: Int...) -> (mean: Double, median:
   ➥ Int, mode: Int) {
   ```

3. Find the mean by finding the sum of all numbers in the variadic parameter, and then dividing by the total number of arguments. We have to cast `sum` and `numbers.count` to type `Double`, because our average could contain a decimal value.

   ```
   // find mean
   var sum = 0
   for number in numbers {
       sum += number
   }
   let mean = Double(sum) / Double(numbers.count)
   ```

4. Find the median by sorting the array of numbers and then finding the item in the middle of the array. (Note: This step uses something called a closure, which we discuss in detail in Hour 9, "Understanding Higher Order Functions and Closures." The syntax may look scary, so for now, just type the code and know that it sorts the array.) For simplicity, this function rounds up the `midIndex` for arrays with an even number of elements, although actual median calculations might average the middle two elements or round the index down.

   ```
   // find median
   let sortedNumbers = numbers.sort { num1, num2 in
       return num1 < num2 }
   let midIndex = numbers.count / 2
   let median = sortedNumbers[midIndex]
   ```

5. Finding the mode is a bit more complicated, so we split the process into multiple steps. First, declare an empty dictionary of type `[Int : Int]`. This stores each number in numbers as a key and the number of times that number is in the numbers array as the value.

   ```
   // find mode
   var occurrences: [Int : Int] = [:]
   ```

6. Iterate through each number in the numbers array and increment its associated value in the occurrences dictionary or set a new value of 1 for that key.

```
for number in numbers {
    if var value = occurrences[number] {
        occurrences[number] = ++value
    } else {
        occurrences[number] = 1
    }
}
```

7. Now we have a dictionary that holds each number as a key and how many times that number appears in numbers as that key's value. Declare a variable tuple to store the highest pair, iterate through the occurrences dictionary to find the highest value, and assign that pair to the highest pair tuple. Assign a constant for mode equal to the highest pair's key.

```
var highestPair: (key: Int, value: Int) = (0, 0)
for (key, value) in occurrences {
    highestPair = (value > highestPair.value) ? (key, value) :
➡ highestPair
    }
let mode = highestPair.key
```

8. Now that we have all three values, we can return them in a tuple. Close the curly brace of the function.

```
// return tuple of results
    return (mean, median, mode)
}
```

9. Assign a constant to the returned value of meanMedianMode(1, 1, 2, 3, 5, 8, 13).

```
let mmm = meanMedianMode(1, 1, 2, 3, 5, 8, 13)
```

10. View the values of each member in the tuple by using dot-notation.

```
mmm.mean      // displays 4.7142857142857...
mmm.median    // displays 3
mmm.mode      // 1
```

This Try It Yourself section contains a lot of code, but you should be familiar with all the code used in it, outside the closure in step 4. The completed playground should look like the image in Figure 8.2. Check your results against the results in the image to make sure you got it all right. If you are an experienced developer, you may be looking at that code and thinking that it is horribly inefficient. Yes, it can be refactored and reduced, and by the end of this hour and next, we reduce most of these chunks of code down to one line each. We are just scratching the surface so far concerning how powerful Swift can be with regard to functions.

```
 1  // Find mean, median, and mode of a set of numbers, from Try It Yourself section
 2  func meanMedianMode(numbers: Int...) -> (mean: Double, median: Int, mode: Int) {
 3      // find mean
 4      var sum = 0                                                          0
 5      for number in numbers {
 6          sum += number                                                   (7 times)
 7      }
 8      let mean = Double(sum) / Double(numbers.count)                      4.714285714285714
 9
10      // find median
11      let sortedNumbers = numbers.sort { num1, num2 in                    [1, 1, 2, 3, 5, 8, 13]
12          return num1 < num2 }                                           (6 times)
13      let midIndex = numbers.count / 2                                    3
14      let median = sortedNumbers[midIndex]                               3
15
16      // find mode
17      var occurrences: [Int : Int] = [:]                                 [:]
18      for number in numbers {
19          if var value = occurrences[number] {
20              occurrences[number] = ++value                              2
21          } else {
22              occurrences[number] = 1                                    (6 times)
23          }
24      }
25      var highestPair: (key: Int, value: Int) = (0, 0)                   (.0 0, .1 0)
26      for (key, value) in occurrences {
27          highestPair = (value > highestPair.value) ? (key, value) : highestPair   (6 times)
28      }
29      let mode = highestPair.key                                         1
30
31      // return tuple of results
32      return (mean, median, mode)                                        (.0 4.714285714285714, .1 3, .2 1)
33  }
34
35  let mmm = meanMedianMode(1, 1, 2, 3, 5, 8, 13)                         (.0 4.714285714285714, .1 3, .2 1)
36  mmm.mean                                                              4.714285714285714
37  mmm.median                                                            3
38  mmm.mode                                                              1
39
```

FIGURE 8.2
The completed playground for the Mean, Median, Mode function.

NOTE

Return Values Can Be Ignored

The returned values from functions can also be ignored if you don't need their data. Sometimes you just need to call a function to perform a particular task, but you don't care about its return value. In that case, you would just not assign a variable or constant to the returned value and just call the function directly.

External Parameter Names

So far, we have only discussed internal parameter names in functions. This means that the function can use the parameters by name inside the function, but the caller has no reference to the name of the first parameter when calling the function. This used to be a source of confusion when calling functions because the order is important, and functions with only internal parameter names did not give indications as to what parameter aligned with what purpose. This changed in Swift 2.0.

Swift provides a way to specify external parameter names when declaring function definitions, which helps make coding easier for three reasons: First, the caller has a better frame of reference for which argument is necessary and in which order each parameter is expected. Second, it can help shorten the internal parameter to be used within the function, saving time by not having to type perhaps verbose parameter names every time you need to reference that parameter. Finally, it helps the definition of the function read more like a sentence, giving a better understanding of what the function's purpose is.

The way to make an external parameter is to provide an external name, a space, then the internal name, a colon (:), and then the type, such as (externalName name: String). For example, see Listing 8.6 to see how using external parameters can be used to benefit the function and the caller.

LISTING 8.6   Using External Parameter Names

```
func multiply(thisNumber num1: Int, byAnotherNumber num2: Int) -> Int {
    return num1 * num2
}
let result = multiply(thisNumber: 6, byAnotherNumber: 7)
// result is equal to 42
```

Reading the function definition aloud sounds like "multiply this number by another number and return a value of type Int." It is also clearer to the caller just what the intention of the function is and what each argument is for. Internal to the function, we simply just use num1 and num2, saving ourselves some keystrokes.

Functions do not always need external parameters. In fact, if you choose the naming of your function well, you can use an internal name for the first parameter and external names for a better description with the remaining parameters. A rewritten function definition from Listing 8.6 could look like the following snippet:

```
func multiplyThisNumber(num1: Int, byAnotherNumber num2: Int) -> Int {
```

Calling this method now reads more like a sentence:

```
multiplyThisNumber(3, byAnotherNumber: 7)
```

If your internal parameter name is sufficient for use inside and outside a function, and you want or need to specify an explicit external parameter name, you can repeat the internal parameter name. This tells Swift that the caller must use the parameter name, and calling the function can use the same parameter name. Listing 8.7 illustrates this parameter shorthand syntax.

LISTING 8.7   Providing Explicit External Parameter Names

```
func append(lastName lastName: String, toFirstName firstName: String) -> String {
    return firstName + " " + lastName
}
let fullName = append(lastName: "Miller" toFirstName: "BJ")
// fullName is equal to "BJ Miller"
```

Default Parameter Values

A nice feature of Swift is that you can provide default values for parameters in functions, and thus remove that argument from the function call if you decide to use the default value. Assigning a default value in a function definition is as easy as assigning the value directly in line with the declaration, just as you normally would with any variable or constant. You may use a default parameter in any place in the function signature, not necessarily as the last parameter. If you have multiple default parameters, they can be listed anywhere in the function signature. Listing 8.8 illustrates how to use default parameter values.

LISTING 8.8   Using Default Parameter Values

```
func addExercise(exercise: String, withDuration duration: Int = 20) {
    print("You did \(exercise) for \(duration) minutes.")
}
addExercise("walking")
addExercise("cycling", 30)
// Displays:
//   You did walking for 20 minutes.
//   You did cycling for 30 minutes.
```

Change Argument Values with In-Out Parameters

Earlier in this hour, we discussed briefly how to make a parameter into a variable instead of a constant, to be used inside a function. Making a parameter a variable works only within the scope of the function and does not impact the arguments supplied to the function from the caller. You may need to swap the values of two variables or sometimes even get valuable error data if something goes wrong, and often it is easier to use **in-out** parameters instead of a return value. In-out parameters actually change the value of the variable such that it is retrievable from outside the function.

To declare a parameter as an in-out parameter, simply add the `inout` keyword before the parameter name inside the function's description parentheses. Then, to call a function with in-out parameters, you must place the ampersand operator (&) immediately prefixing the name of the variable. The ampersand tells the compiler that the function can directly change the value of the variable. Let's take a look at Listing 8.9 to see how in-out parameters work and can be beneficial.

LISTING 8.9   Using In-Out Parameters

```
func reverseWords(inout firstWord: String, inout secondWord: String) {
    var tempWord = firstWord
    firstWord = secondWord
    secondWord = tempWord
}
var first = "I am first"
var second = "I am second"
reverseWords(&first, &second)
print(first)    // displays "I am second"
print(second)   // displays "I am first"
```

Objective-C did not have the ability to return multiple values inside a return type like Swift can with tuples. To get around that, Objective-C utilized in-out parameters (with slightly different syntax) to accomplish this goal. In-out parameters are useful but are not as obvious as a function having a return type and a return statement. In-out parameters should be used when you want changes to a variable to persist after a function has manipulated it, rather than returning a value and storing the result in a new variable or constant.

Exiting Early

New syntax was added to Swift 2 to enable nicer means for exiting a function early and not leaving you writing most of your function's logic inside the else branch of a conditional statement, indented farther to the right than it need be.

The concept of exiting a function early is not new. Many programmers have done this in many languages for many years. But with the addition of the **guard** statement in Swift 2, early exits are much easier to identify.

The syntax for a guard statement is almost identical to an if statement; however, the guard statement must have an else keyword after its conditional check, and the code that executes the early exit (most often just a return keyword) goes inside the curly braces. Normal execution resumes after the guard statement. If you use conditional binding in your guard statement, using guard let just like if let, then that bound constant lives throughout the remainder of the enclosing function. Listing 8.10 illustrates using several guard statements in different ways to show how it can be used and even used multiple times in a function.

LISTING 8.10   Using guard Statements for Early Exits

```
func printAnEvenNumber(number: Int?) {
    guard let unwrappedNumber = number else { return }
    guard unwrappedNumber < 100 else { return }

    if unwrappedNumber % 2 == 0 {
        print("\(unwrappedNumber)")
    }
}

printAnEvenNumber(nil)   // trips first guard statement
printAnEvenNumber(101)   // trips second guard statement
printAnEvenNumber(5)     // fails test for being even
printAnEvenNumber(4)     // prints "4"
```

The guard statements in Listing 8.10 might seem trivial, but as you work in Swift more and more, you will realize just how useful these simple statements are and might end up using guard statements for these exact purposes. The goal is to exit a function as early as possible to save CPU cycles and battery consumption before any processing happens, to save resources and time. Seeing the guard keyword in code is a great visual indication that this is a test for exiting a function early, whereas an if statement could be a traditional conditional statement and might or might not indicate early exit. The guard statement could easily be one of my favorite additions to the Swift language!

Deferring Execution

Another new feature to the Swift language that was introduced with the guard statement is the defer statement. The defer statement enables you to defer execution of a group of statements until the end of a function. The power of the defer statement really shines when there could be multiple exit points in a function, but you need to have a particular piece of code execute upon exiting the function, no matter what.

To use the defer statement, you simply use the defer keyword, following by a pair of curly braces. Inside the curly braces, you place any code you want to execute at the end of the function. This becomes useful if you start using resources like opening a file on the file system or opening a network socket; these resources will need to be closed at some point. Best practices suggest implementing a defer block immediately after creating or opening a resource that needs your attention later for closing or deallocation. Listing 8.11 shows a brief example of using a defer statement that will get executed upon exiting its containing function each time.

LISTING 8.11   Deferring Execution

```
func functionThatUsesDefer(value: Int?, anotherValue: String?) {
    defer {
        print("finally leaving the function")
    }

    if let value = value {
        print("value is \(value)")
        return
    }

    if let anotherValue = anotherValue {
        print("anotherValue is \(anotherValue)")
        return
    }

    for _ in 0..<10 {
        print("not going anywhere yet...")
    }
}

functionThatUsesDefer(5, anotherValue: nil)
functionThatUsesDefer(nil, anotherValue: "Hello")
functionThatUsesDefer(nil, anotherValue: nil)
```

If you are following along in your own playground, you'll see that the defer statement executes each time there is a return statement that is executed and also when the end of the function has been reached. The defer statement is great for cleaning up resources, calling delegate methods, and many other reasons that you might think of that need to get executed once a function has finished or returned early.

Summary

This hour provided a lot of information, and some concepts about functions are difficult to understand if you've not worked with them in the past. Go back over this hour again if you feel you need to rehash any of the information. Over the next hours, we use functions a lot more, so it is important to understand their structure, syntax, and use.

We discussed the basic structure and syntax of a function in Swift, how to use parameters with functions, and how to return values from functions. We also discussed how to identify the type of function, which is important to know when working with functions, parameters, and return types. As for parameters, we discussed how to use variadic parameters to pass in an unknown amount of arguments at once and convert it to an array, as well as using internal and external names for function parameters. After that, we discussed changing variable values externally with in-out parameters and prepopulating parameters with default parameters.

Finally, you learned how to easily and safely exit functions early using the `guard` statement, as well as deferring execution until a function finally ends using the `defer` keyword.

We aren't done with functions yet. In the next hour, we discuss higher order functions, as well as closures, which are a special type of function and are a powerful feature of Swift.

Q&A

Q. Why would you need to use default parameters?

A. Default parameters are handy for developers. If you have existing functions and find that you need to add another parameter to the function, a default parameter could prevent your function from breaking your current code base. If you set a default parameter value, all existing function calls will still function normally.

Q. What are the naming rules for creating function names in Swift?

A. You want to avoid using any function names that are built into Swift. Functions must start with a letter and cannot contain spaces. It is also a generally accepted practice to use lower camel case for function names.

Q. Can a function have more than one variadic parameter?

A. No, a function can have at most one variadic parameter. If other parameters are used in the function, the variadic parameter must appear last in the parameter list to avoid confusion and errors.

Workshop

The workshop contains quiz questions and exercises to help you solidify your understanding of the material covered. Try to answer all questions before looking at the answers that follow.

Quiz

1. What is wrong with this code?

```
func showUserID() -> Int {
    print("Hello there!")
    return 5
    return 6
}
```

2. When you want to use explicit external parameter names, the external and internal names are the same. How can you tell Swift that the caller must use the parameter name, and the function can use the same parameter name?

3. By default, are all parameters constants or variables?

4. If you want to modify a variable inside the body but you want the changes to persist outside the body, what can you use?

5. What is wrong with the following code?

```
func welcomeUser(userName: String, withEmail: String = " ", userID: Int) {
    print(userName)
}
```

Answers

1. Once the return statement is called, no other values can be returned.

```
func showUserID() -> Int {
    print("Hello there!")
    return 5
}
```

2. You can repeat the internal parameter name to tell Swift that the caller must use the parameter name, and the function can use the same parameter name.

3. By default, all the function parameters are constants in Swift.

4. If you want to modify a variable inside the body but you want the changes to persist outside the body, you can define the parameter as an in-out parameter. This is also known as a pass-by-reference.

5. The parameter with a default value should occur last in the parameter list.

Exercise

Create a new OS X playground. Create a function that displays the current stock name and price for multiple stocks. Practice using default parameter values, variadic parameters, and different return values.

HOUR 9

Understanding Higher Order Functions and Closures

What You'll Learn in This Hour:

▶ What higher order functions are
▶ How to accept functions as parameters and return functions
▶ How to nest functions
▶ What a closure is
▶ How to use reduce code with closures

The last hour introduced and discussed functions in Swift in great detail, from the general structure of a function to the different ways to add parameters and return values of different types. This hour we dive even deeper into functions with higher order functions and add a new term to our vocabulary: **closures**. Grasping the concepts and really understanding the syntax of functions from the last hour is important to moving forward this hour, so if you feel you still need to strengthen your skills with functions, take the time to reread or practice the code samples again.

Let's begin this hour by continuing our discussion of functions with higher order functions.

Higher Order Functions

While Swift is not a full-fledged functional programming language, it does have some functional aspects to it that are helpful. Swift utilizes **higher order functions**, which is just another way of saying that functions in Swift can take functions as parameters, or even return functions.

NOTE

Functional Programming

Wikipedia describes functional programming as "a programming paradigm, a style of building the structure and elements of computer programs that treats computation as the evaluation of mathematical functions and avoids state and mutable data." Further, "the output value of a function depends only on the arguments that are input to the function." Functional programming deserves an entire book devoted to it (and several have been written already), so we won't dig too deeply into the topic, and it doesn't require you to do anything specific in your code; I merely point this out as information about the kind of code we are writing here. We cover thinking in a functional fashion in Hour 24, "Functional Thinking in Swift."

Returning Function Types

Since functions have a type, just as a variable could be a `String`, `Bool`, `Int`, or what have you, a variable can be of a function type. That means that we can store references to functions in local variables or constants, make a function be parameters of a function, or have a function's type be the return type of a function. Using functions as return types is easy in Swift; simply put the type of the function you'll be returning after the `->` symbol in the function definition. Function syntax can get a little tricky to read once you start returning functions, but this is yet another reason why it makes sense to have return types at the end of a function definition, instead of at the beginning as in C and Objective-C; the structure still has a readable flow. To return a function that takes an `Int` and returns a `String` looks something like the following code snippet:

```
func someFunc() -> (Int) -> String
```

This function reads aloud as "A function named `someFunc` that takes no parameters, and returns a function that takes a single `Int` parameter and returns a `String`." Also, the parentheses around the `Int` type are optional and are purely a matter of your choice of style. Some programmers prefer them for readability; others prefer not to have them.

In Listing 9.1, I'll rewrite the `meanMedianMode` function from Hour 8, "Using Functions to Perform Actions," to separate out each average into its own function with its own return type. Although not mathematically necessary, for the purpose of having uniform function definitions, each math function takes `[Int]` and returns `Double`—you'll see why shortly. Then I'll have a central function that receives a string as a parameter and returns one of the average functions. Note that the median function rounds `midIndex` up for an array with an even count, which is fine for the purposes of this example. If you are following along on your own, feel free to alter the median function to calculate a true median by finding the middle two values, adding them together, and then dividing by two. Also note that I have changed the variadic parameters to arrays.

LISTING 9.1   **Returning Function Types from Functions**

```
01: func mean(numbers: [Int]) -> Double {
02:     var sum = 0
03:     for number in numbers {
04:         sum += number
05:     }
06:     let mean = Double(sum) / Double(numbers.count)
```

```
07:        return mean
08:    }
09:
10:    func median(numbers: [Int]) -> Double {
11:        let sortedNumbers = numbers.sort({ (num1: Int, num2: Int) -> Bool in
12:            return num1 < num2
13:        })
14:        let midIndex = numbers.count / 2
15:        let median = Double(sortedNumbers[midIndex])
16:        return median
17:    }
18:
19:    func mode(numbers: [Int]) -> Double {
20:        var occurrences: [Int : Int] = [:]
21:        for number in numbers {
22:            if var value = occurrences[number] {
23:                occurrences[number] = ++value
24:            } else {
25:                occurrences[number] = 1
26:            }
27:        }
28:        var highestPair: (key: Int, value: Int) = (0, 0)
29:        for (key, value) in occurrences {
30:            highestPair = (value > highestPair.value) ? (key, value) :
   ➥highestPair
31:        }
32:        return Double(highestPair.key)
33:    }
34:
35:    func performMathAverage(mathFunc: String) -> ([Int]) -> Double {
36:        switch mathFunc {
37:            case "mean":
38:                return mean
39:            case "median":
40:                return median
41:            default:
42:                return mode
43:        }
44:    }
45:
46:    var mathFunc = performMathAverage("mean")
47:    mathFunc([1, 1, 2, 3, 5, 8, 13])                    // 4.714285714285...
48:    mathFunc = performMathAverage("median")
49:    mathFunc([4, 5, 6])                                 // 5.0
50:    mathFunc = performMathAverage("mode or not mode")
51:    mathFunc([1, 1, 2, 3, 5, 8, 13])                    // 1.0
```

The first thing to notice is that all three averaging functions share the same types for parameters and return types in lines 1, 10, and 19. This becomes useful later when we return and call those functions. The code for the mean, median, and mode calculations is the same; they're just now inside their own respective functions, of type `([Int]) -> Double`. In line 35, we create a new function called `performMathAverage`, which takes one parameter, of type `String`, and returns a function of type `([Int]) -> Double`. Since our averaging functions all are of type `([Int]) -> Double`, our `performMathAverage` function can return any of our averaging functions as its return value. Line 46 then stores a returned function from `performMathAverage` based on what string we provide as an argument, which is `"mean"`. Now `mathFunc` is a variable of type `([Int]) -> Double`. See how that works? If `mathFunc` is a variable of type `([Int]) -> Double`, we can call it with an array of `Int`s and it should provide us with a `Double`. And line 47 verifies our assumption, by returning 4.714285714285. Then in line 48, we reassign `mathFunc` to the median function and send it a new array of `Int`s on line 49, resulting in 5.0 being returned. I agree that if this is new to you, the syntax is a little difficult to understand, but the more you practice it, the more fluent you'll become with Swift functions.

NOTE
_____

Syntax for Returning Functions

Notice in `performMathAverage`, inside the switch cases, we return either mean, median, or mode, and not `mean()`, `median()`, or `mode()`. This is because we are not *calling* the methods; rather, we are returning a *reference* to it, much like function pointers in C. When the function is actually called to get a value, you add the parentheses suffixed to the function name.
_____

Any of the average functions could be called independently without the use of the `perform-MathAverage` function. This is because mean, median, and mode are called **global functions**. If we want to hide functions from the global scope so that only our `performMathAverage` function (or whatever containing function you might be using at the time) can access particular functions, we can use **nested functions**.

Nesting Functions within Functions

It shouldn't surprise you, with as powerful and flexible as Swift is, that we can nest functions within functions. Nested functions are simply written inside a containing function, and therefore are only accessible within the containing function, not globally like standard functions. This can be useful for providing a layer of abstraction or privacy when necessary, to avoid certain functions from being called directly, or to be returned from a containing function when a particular criterion has been met. The mean, median, and mode functions in Listing 9.1 could be nested inside `performMathAverage`, and the example would behave the same.

Nested functions also have access to constants and variables from the containing function's scope. This means that if we declare a function, and directly inside that function we declare a sum variable equal to `0.0`, we could then create a function inside the first function, where we would be able to access sum without any issue. If we alter the sum value inside the nested function, Swift creates a *reference* to that value so that we can modify sum's value directly. If we do not alter sum inside the nested function, but rather just use it for its value, Swift creates a *copy* of the value to be used in our nested function.

CAUTION

References Versus Values in Nested Functions

As mentioned earlier, if a nested function accesses a property (a variable or constant) of the containing function's scope, Swift either makes a reference to or a copy of the value. Accessing by reference means that you are directly accessing or modifying the contents of the variable at that location in memory. Accessing by value means that Swift creates a copy of the value for you to use without modifying the original. Swift does this because you may have two nested functions that both need access to a property in the containing function's scope. One function needs to modify the value, but the other function needs to have a copy of the property's original value. If both nested functions used a reference to the property's value, the function that needed the unchanged value would now have the changed value, and your app could experience unwanted behavior.

Let's rewrite the mean, median, and mode average functions to be nested functions inside the `performMathAverage` function. This makes it possible for us to publicly declare a variable of type `([Int]) -> Double`, which enables us to have that variable change to any average function we want. Listing 9.2 illustrates our `performMathAverage` function with nested functions. For brevity, I have commented out the code inside the median and mode functions as it is the same as Listing 9.1.

LISTING 9.2   Nested Functions

```
01:   func performMathAverage(mathFunc: String) -> ([Int]) -> Double {
02:       var sum = 0
03:       func mean(numbers: [Int]) -> Double {
04:           for number in numbers {
05:               sum += number
06:           }
07:           return Double(sum) / Double(numbers.count)
08:       }
09:
10:       func median(numbers: [Int]) -> Double {
11:           // insert median code here
12:       }
13:
14:       func mode(numbers: [Int]) -> Double {
15:           // insert mode code here
16:       }
17:
```

```
18:        switch mathFunc {
19:            case "mean":
20:                return mean
21:            case "median":
22:                return median
23:            default:
24:                return mode
25:        }
26:    }
27:    var mathFunc = performMathAverage("mean")
28:    mathFunc([10, 11, 10, 12, 10, 13])  // displays 11.0
29:    mathFunc = performMathAverage("median")
30:    mathFunc([10, 11, 10, 12, 10, 13])  // displays 11.0
31:    mathFunc = performMathAverage("mode")
32:    mathFunc([10, 11, 10, 12, 10, 13])  // displays 10.0
```

This example shows you how functions can be nested but still be accessible outside the scope of their containing function by returning a reference to them. Notice also in line 2 that sum is a variable scoped to the performMathAverage function, but it is still accessible inside the mean function. If you tried to assign mathFunc = mean, you would get a compiler error, "Use of unresolved identifier 'mean'." In line 27, we assign performMathAverage("mean") to mathFunc, which is of type ([Int]) -> Double, and refers to the mean function. Since mathFunc is a variable of type ([Int]) -> Double, we can also use performMathAverage to assign different returned functions to it of that same type, which is what we do in lines 29 and 31. Lines 28, 30, and 32 all send integer array literals as arguments to the function that mathFunc refers to at that time and receive the respective output.

Using Functions as Function Parameters

Just as you would specify the function type as a return value, using functions as parameters to functions is similar. The only difference, however, is that you name the parameter to be of a function type, rather than just specifying the type when returning. Figure 9.1 illustrates the syntax of using functions as parameters in a function definition.

```
func someFunc(externalParamName internalParamName: ( FuncParamType ) -> FuncReturnType ) -> ReturnType {
    // write some code...
    return someValue
}
```

FIGURE 9.1
The structure of a function definition with a function as a parameter.

So why would you want to send functions as arguments to functions? Perhaps you want to perform a particular function upon a particular piece of data, and you can send both as arguments to a function that will perform that task.

Now, let's do a Try It Yourself, using a function as parameters to a function.

Perform a Function on Each Member of an Array

Create a function that takes an integer array and a function, and returns a new array with the elements modified by the function argument.

1. Open Xcode and create a new playground. Either a Mac or an iOS playground will work. Clear the contents of the playground.

2. Create a function that simply squares a number given to it. We use this as the function to pass as an argument later. Make it simple; just require the function to take an `Int` parameter and return an `Int`.

```
func square(num: Int) -> Int {
    return num * num
}
```

3. Create a function to iterate over each element in an array of integers and then call the supplied function with the array element as its argument. Then, return the new array.

```
func mapEachElement(inArray arr: [Int], withFunc aFunc: (Int) -> Int) ->
    [Int] {
    var returnArray = [Int]()
    for num in arr {
        returnArray.append(aFunc(num))
    }
    return returnArray
}
```

4. With the functions built, create an array to pass in to `mapEachElement` as an argument.

```
let firstArray = [1, 2, 3, 4, 5]
```

5. Assign a new array to the result of calling `mapEachElement` with `firstArray` and the `square` function.

```
let squareArray = mapEachElement(inArray: firstArray, withFunc: square)
```

Hopefully that wasn't too bad, and you're getting the hang of functions. If you followed along and did the example correctly, your playground should look like Figure 9.2. Incidentally, with this example, you've just written a modified version of a Swift standard library function called **map**. The map function is powerful, and we further explore it later in this book.

```
 1  //
 2  // Ch09 Map Each Element Try-It-Yourself example
 3  //
 4
 5  func square(num: Int) -> Int {                                          (5 times)
 6      return num * num
 7  }
 8
 9  func mapEachElement(inArray arr: [Int], withFunc aFunc: (Int) -> Int) -> [Int] {
10      var returnArray = [Int]()                                          []
11      for num in arr {
12          returnArray.append(aFunc(num))                                 (5 times)
13      }
14      return returnArray                                                 [1, 4, 9, 16, 25]
15  }
16
17  let firstArray = [1, 2, 3, 4, 5]                                       [1, 2, 3, 4, 5]
18  let secondArray = mapEachElement(inArray: firstArray, withFunc: square) [1, 4, 9, 16, 25]
19
```

FIGURE 9.2
The completed playground for the `mapEachElement` exercise.

Closures

Closures are self-contained chunks of code. They resemble functions in that the code inside their curly braces is only executed when acted upon or called, but the biggest difference is they can be anonymous. Some closures don't have a name, so you can't just arbitrarily call a closure to be executed. You see how they are executed shortly, but first let's cover some definitions.

There are three types of closures in Swift, and we've already discussed two of them: global functions and nested functions. Global functions are really closures that are named but do not capture any values from a containing context. Nested functions are named closures and can capture values from their containing function. The last type of closure, **closure expressions**, do not have a name but can capture values from their containing context. The act of capturing outside values and references to be used inside a closure is called **closing**, hence the name closure. Closure expressions are often just called *closures*.

Since we already covered global functions and nested functions, let's take a few minutes to examine closures, their syntax and structure, and walk through some of their powerful capabilities to express code quickly and succinctly without losing clarity or readability.

Structure of Closures

Closures in Swift follow the general syntactical structure illustrated in Figure 9.3.

```
{ ( param : ParamType , paramTwo : AnotherType ,..) -> ReturnType in
    // code inside closure goes here
    return someValue
}
```

FIGURE 9.3
The structure and syntax of a closure expression in Swift.

Inside the curly braces (because, remember, closures do not have names), you define the parameters and their types inside parentheses like you would a global or nested function, and then provide the return symbol (->) and a return type. Immediately following the return type is the keyword in, which denotes the separation of the closure's definition from the code to execute. After the in keyword, you write the code to execute inside the closure expression, and then end the closure with the ending curly brace, just like any other function.

This seems straightforward, considering it is reasonably similar to the structure of global or nested functions. The difference is that the closure signature goes inside the curly braces versus outside. However, wouldn't it be nice if we could shorten the syntax to be a little less verbose and a little more powerful? It turns out we can, and over the next several examples, we reduce the size of a function by utilizing Swift's powers of type inference, implicit returns, shorthand syntax, and **trailing closures**. These make it clearer in one to two lines of code what we are accomplishing, rather than five lines of standard for loops to manipulate the return value.

Let's take a look at how we start accomplishing this goal in Listing 9.3, by using the mean function from Listing 9.1. We use an **instance method** on Array called **reduce**, since our input parameter is an array of integers. The reduce function iterates through each item in the array and recursively builds a return value based on the function operation in the closure expression.

NOTE

Instance Methods

Instance methods are functions that can be called on an instance of a class, struct, or enum, rather than on the type itself. We discuss instance methods and type methods more in Hour 10, "Learning About Structs and Classes," Hour 11, "Implementing Class Inheritance," and Hour 12, "Harnessing the Power of Enums."

Before starting Listing 9.3, let's quickly look at the syntax of the reduce instance method. The syntax is a little strange, so examine Figure 9.4.

```
func mean2(numbers: [Int]) -> Double {
    sum = numbers.reduce( initial: T , combine:  (T, Self.Generator.Element) throws -> T )
}
       M  T  reduce(initial: T, combine: (T, Self.Generator.Element) throws -> T) rethrows

       Return the result of repeatedly calling combine with an accumulated value initialized to initial and each
       element of self, in turn, i.e. return combine(combine(...combine(combine(initial, self[0]),
       self[1]),...self[count-2]), self[count-1]).
```

FIGURE 9.4
Xcode's auto-complete feature displaying the syntax for the reduce instance method.

What's with the letter T, the `Self.Generator.Element` type, and the `throws` and `rethrows` keywords? In Swift, the letters T, U, or any other single capital letter or word with a beginning capital letter are commonly used to denote a **generic placeholder type**, which means that you can use any type you want, as long as wherever else you see a T or U (or whatever other letter is assigned), you use that same type. So for instance, if we set a variable of type `Double` to the `initial` parameter, we would also have to use a `Double` as the first parameter and the return type inside the function for the `combine` parameter. We discuss generics more in Hour 20, "Introducing Generics." We discuss the `Self.Generator.Element` type in Hour 24, "Functional Thinking in Swift," and the `throws` and `rethrows` keywords in Hour 22, "Handling Errors."

LISTING 9.3 Using the `reduce` Function on an Array

```
01:  func mean2(numbers: [Int]) -> Double {
02:      var sum = 0
03:      func meanCombine(num1: Int, num2: Int) -> Int {
04:          return num1 + num2
05:      }
06:      sum = numbers.reduce(0, combine: meanCombine)
07:      return Double(sum) / Double(numbers.count)
08:  }
09:  mean2([5, 6, 7])  // displays 6
```

In the `reduce` function, the first parameter is a starting value with which we build an aggregate value, and the second parameter is a function that takes a parameter of any type (`T`) and another of type `Int`, and returns a value of type `T`. So, on line 3, we created a nested function that takes two `Int` parameters and returns an `Int`. The nested function returns the two parameters added together. Line 6 is the call to the `reduce` function itself, but notice that we don't have the parentheses after `meanCombine` for the combine parameter in the `reduce` function. Do you know why? We are passing in a *reference* to the `meanCombine` function, not *calling* it directly; the `reduce` function calls `meanCombine` for us during its execution, so for now `reduce` just needs to know what chunk of code to execute. The `reduce` function automatically passes in the necessary arguments to the `meanCombine` function for us when it calls `meanCombine` from its execution. Finally, line 9 shows that when we call mean2 with an array of Ints, it returns the appropriate result.

Great, you're learning about the reduce function and how to use a closure as one of the arguments to pass in to it. But this looks like a lot of work compared to the simple, straightforward approach to the mean function in Listing 9.1. Let's take a look at how to simplify this by removing the line that initializes sum to 0, because we can just assign it to the returned value of the reduce function. In addition to that, let's remove the nested meanCombine function and use a closure expression instead. Listing 9.4 illustrates how we accomplish these objectives.

LISTING 9.4   Using Closure Expressions as Parameters

```
01:   func mean3(numbers: [Int]) -> Double {
02:       let sum = numbers.reduce(0, combine: { (num1: Int, num2: Int) -> Int in
03:           return num1 + num2
04:       })
05:       return Double(sum) / Double(numbers.count)
06:   }
07:   mean3([2, 3, 4, 5, 6, 7])  // displays 4.5
```

This is looking better, and we reduced our function by 2 lines to 4. Take a look at line 2, where we declare the closure expression's parameters and return type. We know that Swift is powerful when it comes to type inference, so can't we use type inference here? Yes! Listing 9.5 reduces the size of the closure by removing the types, because they are implied by the combine parameter, simplifying the closure expression's structure.

LISTING 9.5   Using Type Inference in Closure Expression Definitions

```
01:   func mean4(numbers: [Int]) -> Double {
02:       let sum = numbers.reduce(0, combine: { num1, num2 in
03:           return num1 + num2
04:       })
05:       return Double(sum) / Double(numbers.count)
06:   }
07:   mean4([1, 1, 2, 3])  // displays 1.75
```

Our function is looking easier to read without the extra type information in the closure expression's definition, letting us clearly see the parameter names and closure structure without distraction. We even dropped the parentheses around num1 and num2.

Our function didn't reduce any lines of code, though. Let's further refine our example by utilizing a feature in Swift called **implicit returns**. Since our closure expression really only calculates the addition of two numbers, it is referred to as a **single-expression closure**, and therefore the return can be implied. Listing 9.6 shows how this is done.

LISTING 9.6 Using Implicit Return Statements in a Closure Expression

```
01:  func mean5(numbers: [Int]) -> Double {
02:      let sum = numbers.reduce(0, combine: { num1, num2 in num1 + num2 })
03:      return Double(sum) / Double(numbers.count)
04:  }
05:  mean5([7, 7, 11])  // displays 8.3333
```

We have no more return statement inside the closure expression since it is implied, and the closure expression is still readable and understandable. We also reduced the length of the function down to two lines. But why stop now?

Swift provides **shorthand argument names** when used inline inside closures, which is denoted by the dollar sign ($) and the number of the argument, starting with zero (0). For instance, the first parameter could be referenced as $0, the next as $1, and so on. Using shorthand argument names enables you to remove the closure expression's argument list, as well as the in keyword since all that is left is the body of the closure, further reducing the code needed to cleanly express our intent with the operation and return value of the closure. Listing 9.7 illustrates using shorthand argument names in our function.

LISTING 9.7 Using Shorthand Argument Names

```
01:  func mean6(numbers: [Int]) -> Double {
02:      let sum = numbers.reduce(0, combine: {$0 + $1})
03:      return Double(sum) / Double(numbers.count)
04:  }
05:  mean6([10, 11, 12])  // displays 11
```

This is really getting fun! Because of our need to return a value of type Double, we still have to cast sum to be of type Double, but isn't this much clearer? Let's take this another step closer to being as concise and clear as possible.

As a good rule of practice, functions in Swift should typically have any function parameters as the last parameter in the list of parameters. When a function has a function parameter as its last parameter, you may use a **trailing closure** for the final argument. This places the closure *outside* the ending parenthesis and is useful if the closure expression is long. But if we use a trailing closure, what happens to the combine parameter name? You got it—it's gone, too. Listing 9.8 illustrates our mean function with a trailing closure and then simplifies it one more step with another iteration of the function, which makes the function one simple line.

LISTING 9.8 Using Trailing Closures

```
01:   func mean7(numbers: [Int]) -> Double {
02:       let sum = numbers.reduce(0) {$0 + $1}
03:       return Double(sum) / Double(numbers.count)
04:   }
05:
06:   func mean8(numbers: [Int]) -> Double {
07:       return Double(numbers.reduce(0) {$0 + $1}) / Double(numbers.count)
08:   }
```

In line 2, you can see the use of the trailing closure, which is really the final argument to the reduce function. Isn't this so much clearer? Line 3 has come along with us as the final line since Listing 9.3, so in the second function (mean8), we bring up the division statement to the end of the line and return the final value on line 7.

Thanks to the power of Swift's capabilities for type inference, implicit returns, shorthand syntax, and trailing closures, we simplified our mean function from 6 lines to 1, and kept the clarity and readability.

Some closure expressions in Swift require a Boolean return value, such as with sorting. Using **operator functions**, you can reduce a final parameter to just an operator, such as < or > for sorting, as shown in the following snippet:

```
let a = [5, 4, 1, 3, 2]
let b = a.sort(<)   // b is equal to [1, 2, 3, 4, 5]
```

Also, if a function only requires one parameter, and it is of a function type, you can supply the trailing closure to the function as its only argument, and you may remove the parentheses completely. The parentheses would not be necessary since the argument to the function is the trailing closure.

I hope you're really grasping the power of closures in Swift and getting comfortable writing them in concise syntax that still makes sense to you. Take a few minutes to let these concepts sink in and repeat any material you may not have understood. When you're ready, let's walk through an example in this next Try It Yourself section.

▼ TRY IT YOURSELF

Rewrite the `median` Function

Rewrite the `median` function to be as concise as possible, while still being clear in intent and readable. Change the function to return an `Int`, as it only receives `Int` values, and our median function returns the value at the middle of the array. This would break the ability to return `median` from `performMathAverage`, as its definition would change, but that's okay for this example since this will be a new playground. Again, this is not the mathematically precise median average for arrays with an even number of elements; feel free to adjust this example to calculate the true median by averaging the two middle values of an array with an even number of elements. The goal of this exercise is to understand using functions to simplify code. And to reduce naming collisions while showing each function, I gave each function a successive number, such as `median`, `median2`, `median3`, and so on.

1. Open Xcode and create a new playground. Either a Mac or iOS playground will work. Clear the contents of the playground.

2. Write the entire `median` function, as it was in Listing 9.1, but change the return type to `Int` from `Double`.

```
func median(numbers: [Int]) -> Int {
    let sortedNumbers = numbers.sort({ (num1: Int, num2: Int) -> Bool in
        return num1 < num2
    })
    let midIndex = numbers.count / 2
    return sortedNumbers[midIndex]
}
```

3. Use type inference to remove the parameter types and return type from the closure expression.

```
func median2(numbers: [Int]) -> Int {
    let sortedNumbers = numbers.sort({ num1, num2 in
        return num1 < num2
    })
    let midIndex = numbers.count / 2
    return sortedNumbers[midIndex]
}
```

4. Use implicit return syntax to remove the return statement.

```
func median3(numbers: [Int]) -> Int {
    let sortedNumbers = numbers.sort({ num1, num2 in num1 < num2 })
    let midIndex = numbers.count / 2
    return sortedNumbers[midIndex]
}
```

5. Use shorthand argument names to shorten the single-expression closure.

```
func median4(numbers: [Int]) -> Int {
    let sortedNumbers = numbers.sort({ $0 < $1 })
    let midIndex = numbers.count / 2
    return sortedNumbers[midIndex]
}
```

6. Use trailing closure syntax to clarify that the closure is the only argument to the sorted instance method. The parentheses are not necessary when calling the sorted function because the only argument is the trailing closure.

```
func median5(numbers: [Int]) -> Int {
    let sortedNumbers = numbers.sort { $0 < $1 }
    let midIndex = numbers.count / 2
    return sortedNumbers[midIndex]
}
```

7. Use an operator function to remove the shorthand argument names and reduce the closure expression even further.

```
func median6(numbers: [Int]) -> Int {
    let sortedNumbers = numbers.sort(<)
    let midIndex = numbers.count / 2
    return sortedNumbers[midIndex]
}
```

8. Reduce the entire `median` function to a single line.

```
func median7(numbers: [Int]) -> Int {
    return numbers.sort(<)[numbers.count / 2]
}
```

Upon completion, your playground should look like the playground in Figure 9.5. The playground in Figure 9.5 has different function names for each step in the Try It Yourself section, to prevent name conflicts.

```
1  //
2  // Ch09 Try It Yourself - median function re-write
3  //    Each function here has a new name to allow us to visualize each step in the TIY section without
       name conflict here in the Playground.
4  //
5  func median(numbers: [Int]) -> Int {
6      let sortedNumbers = numbers.sort({ (num1: Int, num2: Int) -> Bool in     [1, 2, 3, 4, 5]
7          return num1 < num2                                                    (4 times)
8      })
9      let midIndex = numbers.count / 2                                          2
10     return sortedNumbers[midIndex]                                            3
11 }
12
13 func median2(numbers: [Int]) -> Int {
14     let sortedNumbers = numbers.sort({ num1, num2 in                          [1, 2, 3, 4, 5]
15         return num1 < num2                                                    (4 times)
16     })
17     let midIndex = numbers.count / 2                                          2
18     return sortedNumbers[midIndex]                                            3
19 }
20
21 func median3(numbers: [Int]) -> Int {
22     let sortedNumbers = numbers.sort({ num1, num2 in num1 < num2 })           (5 times)
23     let midIndex = numbers.count / 2                                          2
24     return sortedNumbers[midIndex]                                            3
25 }
26
27 func median4(numbers: [Int]) -> Int {
28     let sortedNumbers = numbers.sort({ $0 < $1 })                             (5 times)
29     let midIndex = numbers.count / 2                                          2
30     return sortedNumbers[midIndex]                                            3
31 }
32
33 func median5(numbers: [Int]) -> Int {
34     let sortedNumbers = numbers.sort { $0 < $1 }                              (5 times)
35     let midIndex = numbers.count / 2                                          2
36     return sortedNumbers[midIndex]                                            3
37 }
38
39 func median6(numbers: [Int]) -> Int {
40     let sortedNumbers = numbers.sort(<)                                       [1, 2, 3, 4, 5]
41     let midIndex = numbers.count / 2                                          2
42     return sortedNumbers[midIndex]                                            3
43 }
44
45 func median7(numbers: [Int]) -> Int {
46     return numbers.sort(<)[numbers.count / 2]                                 3
47 }
48
49 median([1, 2, 3, 4, 5])                                                       3
50 median2([1, 2, 3, 4, 5])                                                      3
51 median3([1, 2, 3, 4, 5])                                                      3
52 median4([1, 2, 3, 4, 5])                                                      3
53 median5([1, 2, 3, 4, 5])                                                      3
54 median6([1, 2, 3, 4, 5])                                                      3
55 median7([1, 2, 3, 4, 5])                                                      3
56
```

FIGURE 9.5
The completed playground for the median rewrite Try It Yourself section.

Using Trailing Closures

You will find in your career as a Swift developer that you use trailing closure extremely often. It becomes second nature to see a closure after a function call, and you just know that it is most likely a completion handler of some sort to be executed either over each iteration of a loop or to be executed after some long-running process has completed.

One such example of a function with a trailing closure is a simple one, using iteration. There is another way to loop execution, but I omitted it from Hour 7, "Iterating Code with Loops," intentionally because the syntax would not have made sense to you without covering the information in this hour first. The function is called `forEach`, and it is an extension on sequence types, such as `Array`, and even ranges.

The `forEach` function takes a function as its only parameter, and that function gets applied to each element in the sequence or range. The signature of the function parameter is `Self.Generator.Element -> ()`, which means the function can take a parameter of any type (denoted by `Self.Generator.Element`, meaning the type of each element in the sequence or range, which we cover in Hour 24), and returns nothing. Listing 9.9 illustrates two ways to use the `forEach` function.

LISTING 9.9 Iterating Sequences and Ranges with `forEach`

```
01: let names = ["John", "Jacob", "Jingleheimer Schmidt"]
02: names.forEach { print("\($0)") }
03:
04: (0..<5).forEach { item in
05:     print("\(item)")
06: }
```

Listing 9.9 shows two different uses for the `forEach` function. The first, in lines 1 and 2, shows creating an array of `String` instances then using the `forEach` function on that array to print the name. We use the shorthand argument name, `$0`, representing the element in the current iteration. Because the `forEach` function takes one argument, we can use `$0` to reference that argument.

Lines 4 through 6 iterate over a half-closed range from 0 to 5, and this time we declare the argument to have a name `item`. You might be saying that this looks an awful lot like using a for-in loop, and you'd be right. But there is one major difference in the behavior of `forEach` versus a for-in loop: `forEach` loops cannot exit early. In a for-in loop, you can exit the loop with the `break` statement, whereas a `forEach` loop will iterate over each item without stopping early. Keep that difference in mind if you are choosing which loop fits your needs.

Summary

Hopefully by now you are becoming familiar with functions and closures, and the structure and syntax are becoming easier to understand. We use them frequently throughout the remainder of this book, so if you don't understand anything regarding functions or closures, I suggest reviewing the previous hour and this current hour to really get a good grasp on the concepts and syntax.

In this hour, we continued Hour 8's discussion on functions by introducing higher order functions. Higher order functions can accept functions as parameters or return functions. Then we discussed nested functions as a way to create functions for use within a containing function but which are not available globally. To use a nested function globally, we introduced a way to return a reference to the nested function from the global function and store the reference in a variable. Sending arguments to the variable executed the nested function with those arguments.

Then we discussed in great detail closures in Swift. Closures are a powerful feature, enabling you to send a closure as an argument to a function and drastically reduce the amount of code needed to not only complete the task but also clearly describe what the code should be doing in the closure expression. Swift closures can be reduced in length but retain their clarity with the use of five key features: type inference, implicit returns, shorthand argument names, trailing closures, and operator functions.

In the next hour, we discuss two Swift building blocks, structs and classes, and how you can build your own custom data types.

Q&A

Q. **What are higher order functions?**

A. Higher order functions are functions that can take functions as parameters or return functions.

Q. **How are nested functions and global functions different?**

A. Nested functions are defined inside other functions and are only accessible from within the containing function. They also have access to constants and variables found in the containing function's scope. Global functions are accessible from anywhere in our program.

Q. **Is it better to use named parameters or shorthand argument names inside inline closures?**

A. The answer to the question depends on your code. You should choose whichever style makes your code clearer and easier to understand.

Workshop

The workshop contains quiz questions and exercises to help you solidify your understanding of the material covered. Try to answer all questions before looking at the answers that follow.

Quiz

1. At the end of the following code snippet, what are the values of `firstHello` and `secondHello`?

```
func sayHello() -> String {
  return "Hello!"
}
let firstHello = sayHello()
let secondHello = sayHello
```

2. What are the three types of closures discussed in this hour?

3. What does the following function do?

```
func someFunction(x: Int, y: Int, f: (Int, Int) -> Int) -> Int {
    return f(x,y)
}
```

4. If you use the function `someFunc` from the previous question in the following expression, what value will be assigned to `result`?

```
let result = someFunction(2, 3, { (a, b) -> Int in return a * b})
```

Answers

1. `firstHello` contains the string "Hello!", but `secondHello` is a reference to the function `sayHello()`.

2. Global functions, nested functions, and closure expressions.

3. The function `someFunc()` takes three arguments and returns an integer. The first two arguments are integers `x` and `y`. The final argument is a reference to a function that accepts two integers as arguments and returns an integer.

   When provided with two integers `x` and `y` and a function `f`, `someFunc(x,y,f)` will call `f` with arguments `x` and `y` and return the result.

4. The arguments to `someFunc()` are the integers 2 and 3 and a function that multiplies two integers together. The result of the function is therefore 6.

Exercise

Create a new OS X playground. We're going to practice passing functions as arguments to other functions.

Write a function `min` that finds the minimum value in an array of integers and returns it and a function `max` that finds the maximum value in an array of integers and returns it. Test your functions to make sure they work as expected.

Next, create a function that returns an integer and takes an array of integers and a reference to a function as arguments. This new function should apply the supplied function to the array and return the result. Now, pass an array of integers and a reference to `min` and make sure that you get the correct value back. Repeat the process with `max`.

Learning About Structs and Classes

What You'll Learn in This Hour:

▶ How to define and create structs and classes
▶ How to declare properties in structs and classes
▶ How to create methods in structs and classes
▶ How Swift handles value and reference types
▶ How to inherit properties and methods from superclasses
▶ How to use memberwise initializers in structs
▶ How to specify security through access controls

In this hour, we discuss two building blocks in Swift that you have seen previously in this book but haven't really examined until now: structures (called **structs**) and **classes**. Structs and classes are flexible constructs that allow you to easily and quickly create custom types for storing, manipulating, and returning data. By using instances of these constructs, and making them interoperate with instances of other types, we form entire apps. We discuss structs and classes together in this hour because, in Swift, the lines delineating the two constructs are somewhat blurred as compared to what you may find in other languages in terms of what you can do with them. Once you learn about structs and classes, object-oriented programming becomes much easier, and the concepts discussed in this book thus far become far more applicable.

Overview of Structs and Classes in Swift

Structs and classes are blueprints to data types that you can create and that are already provided in Swift. Some structs that you have already seen are the data types `String`, `Int`, `Bool`, `Array`, and `Dictionary`, to name a few. In fact, almost all of the Swift standard library data types are structs.

Before we get into how structs and classes are structured and the syntax of creating and using them, let's take a look at some delineating definitions of both structures.

Swift structs are value types with which you can create properties (either variables or constants) to save data about a struct instance and create functions (called **methods**) to add functionality to that instance.

Swift classes are reference types with which you can create properties (either variables or constants) to save data about a class instance and create functions (called methods) to add functionality to that instance.

Those two definitions look awfully similar. In fact, they are identical except for one big difference: Structs are **value types** and classes are **reference types**. Obviously, these are oversimplified definitions, and we discuss more differences throughout this and future hours, but the type difference is important. Being a value type, a struct is *passed by value*, meaning that any time you need to send a struct to a function or even create another variable or constant of an existing struct, a complete copy is made of the struct and the new copy is used in the new variable or constant. This means that the original struct property is kept intact, even if the copy changes.

Classes, however, behave differently. Because classes are reference types, this means that instead of a copy being created and manipulated, a reference to the actual sole instance is passed around and/or used and can be modified directly by a second variable assigned to that reference. To visualize the differences between structs as value types and classes as reference types, see Figure 10.1.

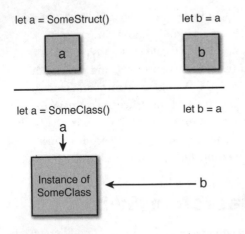

FIGURE 10.1
Diagram illustrating the differences between value types and reference types in memory.

In Figure 10.1, the top half of the diagram illustrates declaring a to equal an instance of SomeStruct and assigning b to be equal to a. When you use assignment with value types, a copy is made, and this is denoted by b having its own unique instance; it just happens that all of b's properties and methods start out the same as a's, and they are of the same type from the assignment.

NOTE

Efficient Copying

With regard to copying value types, Swift is optimized to only actually copy values when necessary. This means that when you set a new struct instance to equal another, Swift waits to physically copy the data into a brand-new instance until the time where any values change and having two separate instances in memory becomes necessary. This "copy on write" behavior is an optimization to decrease the amount of memory your app consumes.

In the lower half of the illustration, a is assigned a reference to an instance of `SomeClass`, hence the letter a being above the instance's shape and pointing to the instance, rather than inside the shape like the a struct value. Then b is assigned a reference to the same instance that a references, so b doesn't actually get its own instance like the struct example; b receives a reference to the existing instance of `SomeClass` that a also references.

That's enough for now in terms of differences between classes and structs. Let's now take a look at their similarities and begin creating classes and structs in code.

What Swift Structs and Classes Have in Common

Classes and structs in Swift share a few common features. The basic syntax structure is also identical outside the initial keyword `class` or `struct` for defining a class or a struct, respectively. Both can define variables and constants (called **properties**) that can be used to store values, and both can define functions (called methods) that can be used to add functionality to their structures. We cover these concepts in detail this hour. There are other similarities that both classes and structs share, such as custom subscripts, custom initializers, extensions, and conformance to protocols, but we discuss those in later hours.

Before we dive into defining methods and properties in our classes and structs, let's first examine the syntax of both constructs. See Figure 10.2 for an example of what each definition looks like in code.

```
struct MyCustomStruct {

}
class MyCustomClass {

}
```

FIGURE 10.2
The syntax for creating structs and classes is nearly identical, with the exception of their keywords.

As you can see in Figure 10.2, to create a struct, you use the `struct` keyword, and to create a class, you use the `class` keyword. Then you name the structure and provide the open and closed curly braces, where the body of the structure will go.

NOTE

Naming Conventions

There are no laws, per se, for how you should name classes and structs and their corresponding properties and methods. There are, however, widely accepted naming conventions, and it is highly suggested that you follow these conventions for consistency. Swift types should use **upper camel case**, such as `MyDataType`. Swift properties and methods, as well as instances of types, should use **lower camel case**, such as `myStringInstance`.

Defining Properties

One of the basic ideas behind structs and classes is that you can create **properties** to store data in an instance of a struct or class. Properties can be either constants or variables, declared with the `let` or `var` introducers, respectively, just as we've seen earlier in this book.

Let's take a look at how to declare variable and constant properties inside a struct. We start by creating a point on a coordinate system, which is a common use for structs in many languages. The `Point` struct should have an x and y coordinate, so let's make those of type `Double`. Listing 10.1 illustrates creating our `Point` struct.

LISTING 10.1   Creating a Point Struct

```
struct Point {
    var x: Double
    var y: Double
}
```

Because the x and y properties store data directly without any sort of calculation, they are referred to as **stored properties**. We cover computed properties in Hour 14, "Digging Deeper with Properties."

Creating a struct in Swift is simple. Structs are great data types when you need a small structure to hold values and perhaps a little extra functionality by adding methods. We add methods shortly, but first, let's declare an instance of our `Point` struct. Listing 10.2 shows how to declare a couple instances of `Point`.

LISTING 10.2   Creating an Instance of the Point Struct

```
let pointA = Point(x: 1.0, y: 2.0)
let pointB = Point(x: 4.0, y: 6.0)
pointB.x                        // displays 4
```

Notice when we declare our instances, Xcode forces us to include the x and y parameter names and arguments inside the parentheses. In Swift, this is called a **memberwise initializer**. Because there is no specific initializer method inside the struct, and all Swift variables and constants need to be initialized with a value before use, Swift requires us to set values upon instantiation. This is not only for safety, but this is also a pretty nice convenience. It suggests to you, the developer, that there are properties that need values, their type, and how many properties there are. Memberwise initializers are specific to structs; classes do not have memberwise initializers.

TIP

Initializing Properties in Structs

To avoid requiring the memberwise initializer for your struct, you can initialize your properties to have a value when you define them. This is done exactly the way you have done in the past by typing something such as var x: Double = 0.0, or more simply var x = 0.0. Then to declare an instance of Point, you can simply type var pointC = Point(). This only applies if all properties in the struct are given initial values when defined.

We declared these instances as constants, because for now we do not need them to change. But what if our struct instances are constants but our struct's instance properties are variables? If our struct instance is a constant, we cannot change any of its properties; even if they are variable properties, our struct instance is constant.

In the third line, we typed pointB.x. This gets the x property's value from the pointB instance. Using the instance name, a dot, and then the property name is known as using **dot syntax**. Dot syntax is a simple and powerful way to access properties and methods on an instance, and even properties on instances inside instances, and so on. You will see a lot more of dot syntax throughout this book, as you will use it daily in your Swift programming life.

Instance Methods

Let's continue this example by adding a function, called an **instance method**, to our Point struct. Say we want to find the distance to any arbitrary coordinate. This functionality is a perfect task for an instance method.

To accomplish this calculation, we need the Pythagorean Theorem. If I just gave you bad memories of high school, my sincere apologies. The Pythagorean Theorem states that given a right triangle with a known base and height, we can calculate the length of the side opposite the right angle, in a formula well-known as $a^2 + b^2 = c^2$. Let's do this in the next Try It Yourself section. You need to import the Foundation framework to be able to access some built-in math capabilities (such as absolute value and square root) and add an instance method called `distanceTo(point:)`. This is just like creating a function as we did in Hour 8, "Using Functions to Perform Actions," and Hour 9, "Understanding Higher Order Functions and Closures," so you should be able to follow along just fine.

▼ TRY IT YOURSELF

Add an Instance Method to a Struct

Create the Point struct here and add an instance method to the struct that calculates the distance to another point using the Pythagorean Theorem.

1. Open Xcode and create a new playground. Either a Mac or iOS playground will work. Clear the contents of the playground.

2. Begin by importing the Foundation framework.

   ```
   import Foundation
   ```

3. Define the `Point` struct.

   ```
   struct Point {
   }
   ```

4. Add two properties of type `Double` for the x and y coordinates inside the curly braces.

   ```
   var x: Double
   var y: Double
   ```

5. Define the `distanceTo(point:)` method, which takes a parameter of type `Point` and returns a `Double`. Use an explicit external parameter name to make the internal parameter name the same as the external parameter name, as it makes calling the method more readable.

   ```
   func distanceTo(point point: Point) -> Double {
   }
   ```

6. Inside the `distanceTo(point:)` method, calculate sides a and b of the right triangle by finding the absolute value difference between the x values and y values.

   ```
   let a = abs(self.x - point.x)
   let b = abs(self.y - point.y)
   ```

7. After assigning values to a and b, we can now calculate and return c. (Note: We could just return the calculated value without assigning to c, but creating c fulfilled the Pythagorean Theorem of $a^2 + b^2 = c^2$.)

```
let c = sqrt(a * a + b * b)
return c
```

8. That's all for the method, and that's all for the struct. Create two instances of the struct now, outside the struct's curly braces.

```
let pointA = Point(x: 1.0, y: 2.0)
let pointB = Point(x: 4.0, y: 6.0)
```

9. Now that we have two points, calculate the distance between them by using our new instance method.

```
let distance = pointA.distanceTo(point: pointB)    // displays 5
```

NOTE

The self Keyword

Notice in step 6 that we use self.x and self.y. While not completely necessary to use in the preceding example (Swift infers that you mean to use x and y instance properties), it sometimes helps readability to be explicit about which properties you are using in an expression. The self keyword refers to the instance currently being operated on. There are some times when the self keyword is necessary, such as inside closures or to remove ambiguity between input parameter names and instance property names. We discuss using self inside closures in Hour 16, "Understanding Memory Allocation and References," and using self to remove ambiguity inside initializers in Hour 13, "Customizing Initializers of Classes, Structs, and Enums."

In step 5, you add the distanceTo(point:) instance method to our Point struct, which should be familiar to you by now. Step 6 uses the Foundation function abs(x: T) to find the absolute value (which returns a non-negative number) of a number or equation, and then step 7 calculates the distance by taking the square root (using the sqrt(x: Double) Foundation function) of $a^2 + b^2$.

Upon completion of the Try It Yourself section, your code should look similar to that in Figure 10.3.

The only difference between functions as we've known them and instance methods is that we don't call the instance methods directly in the Try It Yourself example; we call them with dot syntax as part of our instance. We can, however, call instance methods from within other instance methods in a class or struct, and calling a function is as simple as calling it as we did in Hours 8 and 9: directly and providing any arguments if necessary.

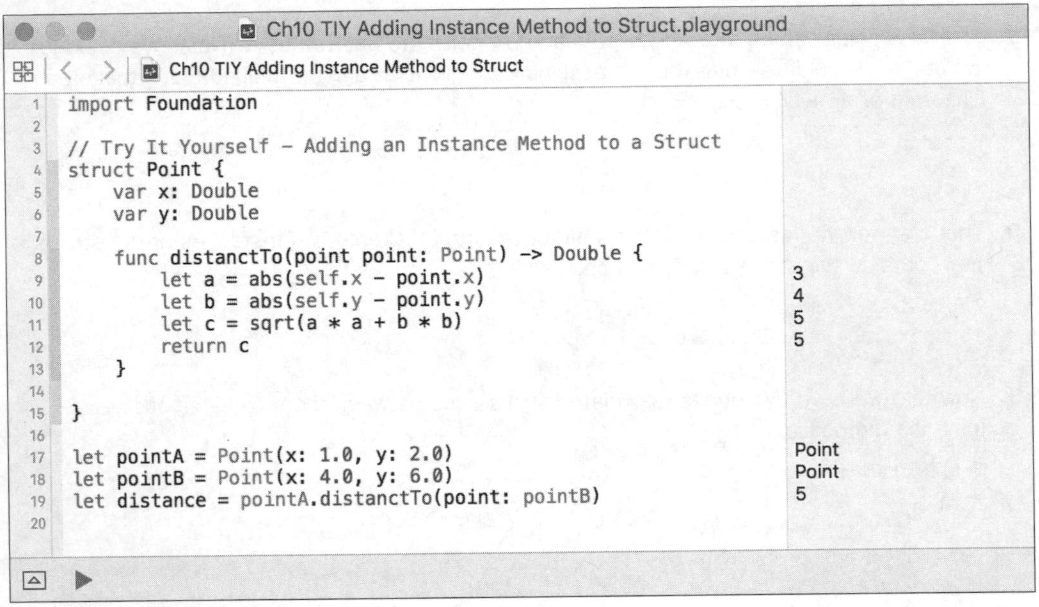

FIGURE 10.3
The completed Try It Yourself example, adding an instance method to the `Point` struct.

Let's say we want to have a method to return half the calculated distance. We can call the
`distanceTo(point:)` instance method from within another instance method to assist in calculating the value. Listing 10.3 illustrates how to call an instance method from another instance
method.

LISTING 10.3 Calling Instance Methods from Instance Methods

```
01:  struct Point {
02:      // properties go here
03:      func distanceTo(point point: Point) -> Double {
04:          // Pythagorean calculation here
05:      }
06:      func halfDistanceTo(point point: Point) -> Double {
07:          return distanceTo(point: point) / 2.0
08:      }
09:  }
10:  let halfDistance = pointA.halfDistanceTo(pointB)
```

The big difference is that on line 6, we add the instance method `halfDistanceTo(point:)`,
which simply gets the distance from the `distanceTo(point:)` method by passing a copy of the
point value, and then divide by 2.0. I divided by 2.0 for consistency; Swift can infer that I want
to return a `Double`, but sometimes it helps code readability to be explicit with literals.

Armed with your knowledge of functions from the previous two hours, you should be familiar with the syntax of creating a function with a parameter and calling it with an argument. The exact same thing is happening here; the difference is that our function belongs to our instance of the `Point` struct, so we must call the instance method as part of the `point` instance.

Struct and Class Similarities

So far this hour, almost everything discussed with structs and shown in examples can be done with classes too, the only exception being that structs can use memberwise initialization as default behavior without you needing to provide an initializer. The syntax is identical (except you'd use `class` instead of `struct` to define a class); you can use properties to store data and methods to perform tasks and return values. In fact, to illustrate these points about classes, let's walk through an example in the following Try It Yourself section.

NOTE

Memberwise Initialization Is Only for Structs

Although we were discussing the similarities of structs and classes, the only difference in code we saw, other than the `struct` or `class` keyword, is that structs use memberwise initialization. This method of initialization is Swift's way of ensuring that all non-optional properties have a value. You can create your own initializers for structs, but we cover that in Hour 13.

TRY IT YOURSELF ▼

Define a Class with Properties and Methods

Now that we've defined a struct with properties and methods, let's make a class that has properties and instance methods.

1. Open Xcode and create a new playground. Either a Mac or iOS playground will work. Clear the contents of the playground.

2. Import the Foundation framework to gain access to standard math functions and create a class called `Circle`.

   ```
   import Foundation
   class Circle {
   }
   ```

3. Inside the curly braces of the class, create a variable of type `Double`, named `radius`, and initialize it to 0.0.

   ```
   var radius = 0.0
   ```

4. Create a function that returns the diameter of the circle.

```
func diameter() -> Double {
    return 2 * radius
}
```

5. Create a function that returns the area of the circle.

```
func area() -> Double {
    return M_PI * radius * radius
}
```

6. With your property and two methods inside the class's curly braces, our class is finished. After the closing curly brace, create an instance of the `Circle` class, as a constant.

```
var circle = Circle()
```

7. Assign your circle instance a radius of 5.0.

```
circle.radius = 5.0
```

8. Call your circle instance's methods to find the diameter and area of your circle.

```
"Circle diameter: \(circle.diameter()), area: \(circle.area())"
```

This Try It Yourself section walked you through creating a class named `Circle`, creating a `radius` property inside it, and two instance methods that returned calculations for the area and diameter of a circle. When finished, your code should look like the code in Figure 10.4.

```
import Foundation

// Try It Yourself — Define a Class with Properties and Methods
class Circle {
    var radius: Double = 0.0

    func diameter() -> Double {
        return 2 * radius                                    10
    }

    func area() -> Double {
        return M_PI * radius * radius                        78.53981633974483
    }
}

var circle = Circle()                                        Circle
circle.radius = 5.0                                          Circle
"Circle diameter: \(circle.diameter()), area: \(circle.area())"    "Circle diameter: 10.0, area: 78.5398163397448"
```

FIGURE 10.4
The completed Try It Yourself section for creating a `Circle` class with properties and instance methods.

Differences Between Structs and Classes

Structs and classes also have their fair share of differences. For instance, as mentioned earlier, classes are reference types and structs are value types. To get a quick glimpse at what this actually means, open the playground you just worked in where you created a `Circle` class and modify the declaration of your circle variable to the following:

```
let circle = Circle()
```

Did you notice that you don't get any compiler errors about modifying a constant? That's because classes are reference types. Swift retains a constant pointer to the `Circle` instance, and that's what is constant, not the values of the properties inside (unless the properties themselves were declared as constants). If you declare a constant struct, the struct is immutable and so are its values even if they were defined as variable properties, because structs are value types. You've been doing this all along, as `Int`, `String`, `Bool`, `Array`, `Dictionary`, and several others we've used are structs.

Listing 10.4 illustrates what happens when you make copies of struct and class instances and how modifying the copy impacts the original, if at all. We reuse the `Point` struct and `Circle` class from previous examples for brevity.

LISTING 10.4 Copying Struct and Class Instances

```
01:   var newPoint = Point(x: 4.0, y: 3.0)
02:   var newPointCopy = newPoint
03:   newPointCopy.y = 17.4
04:   print(newPoint)                       // displays Point(x: 4.0, y: 3.0)
05:   print(newPointCopy)                    // displays Point(x: 4.0, y: 17.4)
06:
07:   var newCircle = Circle()
08:   circle.radius = 3.0
09:   var newCircleCopy = newCircle
10:   newCircleCopy.radius = 7.5
11:   print(newCircle)                       // displays  7.5
12:   print(newCircleCopy)                   // radius 7.5
```

As you can see in Listing 10.4, line 1 creates an instance of `Point`, and then line 2 creates a copy of the `newPoint` instance. What Swift effectively does is create a new variable in memory to hold `newPointCopy` with its own properties and instance methods, with starting values given from `newPoint` (so `newPointCopy`'s initial x and y values are 4.0 and 3.0, respectively). Changing any property in `newPointCopy` has no impact on `newPoint`'s properties, since they are separate values.

The `Circle` instance, however, behaves differently. Being a reference type, when we created a new `Circle` instance in line 7 and set its `radius` property in line 8, Swift created a space in memory for the `newCircle` instance, just like it does for a struct. The difference comes when we create a new variable, `newCircleCopy`, and assign it to `newCircle` in line 9. Swift actually gives `newCircleCopy` a reference to the same instance `newCircle` refers to, so now two variables point to the same instance of `Circle`. This means that `newCircle` is a reference to a `Circle` instance just as `newCircleCopy` is a reference to the same `Circle` instance. In C and Objective-C, variables of a reference type are called **pointers**, and your pointer actually pointed to the physical memory address where the instance was stored. Swift instead, in the name of safety, does not let you alter that memory location directly, but still gives you the capability to use reference types to have multiple variables or constants pointing to the same instance.

Let's take a look at some more differences, starting with structs.

Mutating Struct Properties

Swift structs can have instance methods, but those instance methods cannot mutate the properties inside a struct by default. This is because structs are intended to be inherently immutable data types. To allow them to do so, add the **mutating** keyword before the `func` keyword of the instance method that you want to have change one or more property values. Listing 10.5 illustrates how this can be done. Also, I omitted the `distanceTo(point:)` function for brevity.

LISTING 10.5   Mutating Struct Properties from Instance Methods

```
01:   struct Point {
02:       var x: Double
03:       var y: Double
04:
05:       mutating func moveToZero() {
06:           self.x = 0.0
07:           self.y = 0.0
08:       }
09:   }
10:   var point = Point(x: 3.5, y: 6.0)
11:   print(point)          // displays "Point(x: 3.5, y: 6.0)"
12:   point.moveToZero()
13:   print(point)          // displays "Point(x: 0.0, y: 0.0)"
```

Swift classes do not require you to prefix the `mutating` keyword before a method definition because class instance methods can alter properties as part of their normal behavior.

Comparing Class Reference Equality

There will be times when you need to compare two class instances. To compare class equality, we use the *identical to* operator (===), which is used to compare class instance references to determine whether they point to the same instance. Likewise, we can use the *not identical to* operator (!==) for class instances. Listing 10.6 illustrates using the equal to and identical to operators for classes in simple if statements.

LISTING 10.6   Using Identical To Operator

```
01:  let circleOne = Circle()
02:  circleOne.radius = 5.0
03:  let circleTwo = Circle()
04:  circleTwo.radius = 5.0
05:  let circleThree = circleOne
06:
07:  if circleOne === circleTwo {
08:      "circleOne is identical to circleTwo"
09:  } else {
10:      "circleOne is not identical to circleTwo"
11:  }
12:
13:  if circleOne !== circleThree {
14:      "circleOne is not identical to circleThree"
15:  } else {
16:      "circleOne is identical to circleThree"
17:  }

// displays:
"circleOne is not identical to circleTwo", and
"circleOne is identical to circleThree"
```

Despite circleOne and circleTwo both having radius values of 5.0, they are not identical instances. circleOne and circleThree, however, are identical instances, because we assigned circleOne's reference to circleThree in line 5. See Figure 10.5 for a visual representation of the instance assignments in Listing 10.6.

In Swift, when we declare a struct or class and use the TypeName() syntax, we initialize a new instance of that type. This is why circleOne and circleTwo are *not* identical, even though they both have a radius value of 5.0. They are two separate instances in memory.

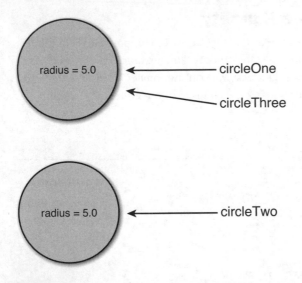
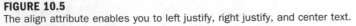

FIGURE 10.5
The align attribute enables you to left justify, right justify, and center text.

Comparing Instance Equality

Comparing class and struct equality is not as easy. To check equality, we would have to provide our own mechanism for validating two struct instances or two class instances are equal, because Swift cannot infer what makes a custom struct or class equal, and we may have our own definition for equality. We discuss how to create custom equality functions in Hour 24, "Functional Thinking in Swift."

When to Use a Class or a Struct

Classes and structs are similar, so when do you use a class and when do you use a struct? Here are some general guidelines, but each case will be different, and depending on your code, you may need to choose one or the other for different reasons.

A struct is good for when you need to encapsulate small, simple data values, when you want values copied rather than passed by reference, and/or when you know that there is no need to inherit from another type. Some examples of structs are the common data types you're familiar with such as `Int`, `Double`, `Bool`, `Array`, and `Dictionary` to name a few. You may also want a struct for 2D or 3D coordinate instances, geometric shape instances, or other simple structures that are value based. Value types like structs are also inherently **thread-safe**, meaning they do not share state across threads of execution, causing potentially unstable state or unintended state changes.

A class is a good choice for when you need to pass a construct by reference, inherit functionality from a parent class, or have a larger structure to manage than just holding simple data structures. Classes are also often used when representing visual elements on a screen, because having an individual representation of an element makes sense. Classes do come with a cost, however, and there are memory implications as well as inheritance overhead involved. We discuss memory allocation with regard to reference types in Hour 16.

Currently Apple suggests using structs until the need for class behavior arises, and over the past year since Swift's release, this has been heavily emphasized. Classes and references types certainly do have their place, but think clearly about the intent of each type you create, and whether it can be a struct or if it needs to be a class. I don't want to scare you away from using classes because as a Swift developer, you will surely use your fair share of them; it is just very important to know the differences and implications of each.

Summary

This hour introduced constructs known as structs and classes and examined the similarities of and differences between each. In Swift, the functionality of the two is much closer than what some programmers may have experienced in other languages.

We explored what it means when we say structs are value types and classes are reference types. You also learned the basic structure of both classes and structs, by adding properties and instance methods to add stored data and functionality to the constructs. These concepts were discussed and even visualized with diagrams illustrating what is actually happening in memory when we allocate new classes or structs and also when we copy them.

Throughout the remainder of this book, we explore more functionality available to structs and classes, as well as a new value type, called an enum, discussed in Hour 12, "Harnessing the Power of Enums." There are more differences and more similarities to cover, and each deserves its own hour.

Q&A

Q. What is a reference type?

A. The most important thing to remember is that when you copy a reference type, by passing it as an argument, initializing it, or assigning to it, you are actually creating a new reference to the existing instance. This means that if you make changes to the copy, you'll be changing your original instance, too.

Q. What is a value type?

A. Unlike reference types, when you copy a value type, you are creating a unique instance of the variable. This means that changes in the copy won't be reflected in the original.

Q. **How do I know if I should use a class or a struct?**

A. The answer isn't always clear, but in general, you should use structs if you have small, simple data values and you want to be able to make copies with independent state. You should use classes when dealing with larger, more complex structures. In the next hour, you'll learn about class inheritance, which gives you a better understanding of when to prefer classes to structs.

Q. **What does the identical to operator (===) do?**

A. The `===` operator compares two references (variable or constant) and evaluates to true if they reference the same instance, and evaluates to false if they do not reference the same instance. This means that two structs will never be identical to (`===`) one another, even if one is a direct copy of the other.

Workshop

The workshop contains quiz questions and exercises to help you solidify your understanding of the material covered. Try to answer all questions before looking at the answers that follow.

Quiz

1. Are classes value types or reference types? How about structs?

2. What model is `newCar` after we run the following code? What model is `usedCar`?

```
struct Car {
    var make: String
    var model: String
}
var newCar = Car(make: "Ford", model: "Explorer")
var usedCar = newCar
usedCar.model = "Focus"
```

3. What's wrong with the following code?

```
class Car {
    var make: String
    var model: String
}
var newCar = Car(make: "Ford", model: "Explorer")
```

4. What does the `mutating` keyword do?

Answers

1. Classes are reference types; structs are value types.

2. Structs are value types, so when we set `usedCar` equal to `newCar`, we create a whole new copy of the object. So when we change the model of `usedCar`, we don't change anything about `newCar` meaning that at `usedCar.model` is "Focus" but `newCar.model` is still "Explorer."

3. Classes do not provide memberwise initializers by default. If this were a struct instead of a class, the code would work.

4. The `mutating` keyword enables a member function in a struct to change the values of that struct's properties.

Exercise

Create a new OS X playground. Create a struct called `Person` with properties `firstName`, `lastName`, and `age` of appropriate data types. Add a method that allows you to change a person's last name. Create an instance of `Person` with your information and test your method to make sure it works.

Now, change `Person` to a class and repeat the process. Notice the differences in the initializer and in the name-changing method.

Implementing Class Inheritance

What You'll Learn in This Hour:

▶ What is class inheritance

▶ How to create subclasses from base classes

▶ How to build a class hierarchy

▶ How to access properties and methods in a superclass

▶ How to override methods in a subclass

▶ How to prevent overriding

▶ What class identity is

▶ When to use class inheritance

In the last hour, we discussed both classes and structs as blueprints for creating instances of data. This hour focuses solely on classes, and some of the extra functionality available in Swift, called **inheritance**. Class inheritance is a concept that has been around for a long time in many object-oriented languages, so if you are familiar with inheritance, you should follow along easily. If you aren't familiar with inheritance, fear not. We discuss the many aspect of inheritance as it relates to Swift and emphasize your learning with examples you can follow. Let's start by defining what inheritance is and why you may want to use it in your apps.

What Is Inheritance?

As mentioned, inheritance is a concept that has been a part of many object-oriented languages for a long time. Inheritance is the practice of inheriting characteristics from another class, in terms of properties, methods, and subscripts. This enables you to create a hierarchy of classes that more appropriately define what an instance of a class should look like, clearly outline responsibilities of a class at a particular level, as well as keep classes small and manageable.

You may want to inherit functionality of a class so that you can customize its behavior or further refine the type of object you are dealing with. For instance, let's say you are working with instances of musical instruments. There are many categories of musical instruments, but ones of note (pun intended) are percussion, winds, and strings. Winds can be broken down into woodwinds and brass. I'm sure there are many other further classifications we could identify, but I think you get the idea. There are common functionalities of all musical instruments and some that are particular to percussion, some to strings, and some to winds. This type of analysis on objects is how we identify relationships and realize how to use class inheritance to our advantage when writing software. But how do we find a good starting point?

Identifying a Base Class

A **base class** acts as the root object of a hierarchy. Base classes do not inherit from any other class; they serve as the class from which other classes inherit functionality. In Swift, unlike Objective-C, you do not need to inherit from a base class, either directly or indirectly, for every class you create. Objective-C classes have to inherit from a base class, most commonly NSObject, to provide mechanisms for allocating memory and initializing the instance and for providing many standard properties and methods, such as a printable description of the object and a hash value. Swift does not require a base class, which is nice because your class instances now do not come with a lot of extra baggage that you may not need, keeping your instances leaner.

Not every app needs a robust hierarchy to describe the required model instances, but the musical instrument example is a good illustration of how to start with a somewhat generic base class, and through each subclass in the hierarchy, start to implement functionality particular to that class. The hierarchy idea is similar to the biological classification system of life, domain, kingdom, phylum, class, order, family, genus, and species. Each level of the classification gets more specific and shares commonalities between ancestors. Figure 11.1 illustrates what our MusicalInstrument class hierarchy might look like, with MusicalInstrument being our base class.

As a best practice, you may want to keep your base classes small, but be sure to put as much functionality inside that is common to all classes that inherit from the base class. Our MusicalInstrument base class may only have one method, called makeSound, but that may be all we need in the base class, the act of making a sound. Every subclass can modify that method, or **override** that method, to customize its own particular sound.

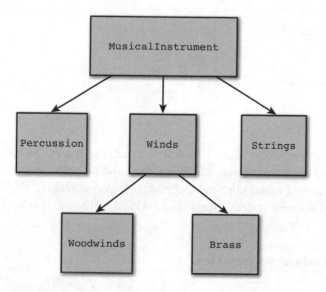

FIGURE 11.1
The `MusicalInstrument` base class with more specific subclasses inheriting from superclasses in a class hierarchy.

Creating a Subclass

What makes a class a base class is the fact that you designate other classes to inherit from it. This begins a hierarchical relationship between the two classes in which the class being inherited from is called the **superclass**, and the class inheriting from a superclass is called a **subclass**. A subclass is simply a class composed of everything it directly implements plus everything it inherits. A subclass inherits properties, methods, and subscripts from not only its direct superclass, but everything up the hierarchy chain up to and including the base class.

NOTE

Other Terminology for Superclass and Subclass

Sometimes superclasses and subclasses are called **parent** and **child** classes because of their relationship to each other, but throughout this book, we call them superclasses and subclasses.

There is no special syntax to defining a base class; you simply create a class as you normally would. Creating a subclass has one small syntactical difference from a normal class declaration: After the class name, append a colon (:) and then the class name from which you want to inherit. Figure 11.2 shows sample syntax of a class inheriting from another class.

```
class  SomeClass  :  SomeOtherClass  {

}
```

FIGURE 11.2
The syntactical structure of defining a subclass to inherit from a superclass.

In Figure 11.2, we see the class `SomeClass` inheriting from `SomeOtherClass`. This is great for an example, but let's take a look at how we might implement our own classes and take advantage of inheritance. Listing 11.1 illustrates how we would implement a base `MusicalInstrument` class and then create the three types of instrument classes from the base class. For now, the subclasses do not have anything in them.

LISTING 11.1   Creating a Base Class and Subclasses

```
class MusicalInstrument {
    func makeSound() -> String {
        return "I make no sound yet."
    }
}

class Percussion : MusicalInstrument {
}
class StringedInstrument: MusicalInstrument {
}
class WindInstrument: MusicalInstrument {
}
```

I chose `StringedInstrument` instead of `String`, because `String` is already the name of a Swift struct, and followed suit with `WindInstrument`. Right now our subclasses don't do anything. However, since our subclasses are composed of everything they directly declare, plus what they inherit, what would happen if we tried to call `makeSound()` on an instance of `WindInstrument`? Let's find out in Listing 11.2.

LISTING 11.2   Declaring an Instance of a Subclass and Calling Inherited Methods

```
let clarinet = WindInstrument()
clarinet.makeSound()   // displays "I make no sound yet."
```

Well, this clarinet is no good! It doesn't make any sound yet. How can we change inherited behavior in our subclasses? We use **overriding**.

Overriding Inherited Methods

Overriding is a concept that enables you to replace the functionality of an inherited property, method, or subscript, to be tailored to the responsibility of the class. It is common when overriding, though not required, to call the superclass's implementation of the characteristic being overridden, to add your own functionality to the existing functionality. If you want to replace the existing functionality, you would not call the super class's implementation. We see an example of that later in this hour.

To override a method inherited from a superclass, you redeclare the method with the same definition but add the `override` keyword at the beginning of the line, before the `func` keyword. Listing 11.3 illustrates just the `WindInstrument` class, to keep the example brief; if you are following along with your own REPL or playground, feel free to override the `makeSound()` function in the other subclasses.

NOTE

Xcode Provides Help with Overriding

Overriding characteristics of a superclass in your custom subclass must be done properly. In other words, you cannot override a method that is not defined in your superclass, and you cannot redefine a method in a subclass that is defined in the superclass without using the `override` keyword. Xcode's compiler will catch these issues and will actually offer to use the `override` keyword in its auto-complete feature or warn you that you cannot override a nonexistent method.

LISTING 11.3   Overriding an Inherited Method

```
01:   class WindInstrument : MusicalInstrument {
02:       override func makeSound() -> String {
03:           return "I use a mouthpiece and make a beautiful sound."
04:       }
05:   }
```

On line 2, you can see that we use the `override` keyword to declare that we are modifying the inherited method. Then, in line 3, we return a different string to refine our `makeSound()` method's return value. Now, calling `clarinet.makeSound()` displays our new return value.

Let's take a look at another implementation of inheritance in this Try It Yourself section. You create a base class of a generic `Shape` with a few properties and a function to calculate the area. Then, you subclass the `Shape` class to a more specific shape and override its `area()` method to make it return the calculated value of the area of that shape since area formulas are different for different shapes.

▼ TRY IT YOURSELF

Override an Instance Method

Utilize what you've learned so far to create a base class and a subclass and override an instance method.

1. Open Xcode and create a new playground. Either a Mac or an iOS playground will work. Clear the contents of the playground.

2. Create your base class, called `Shape`.

```
class Shape {

}
```

3. Declare a variable named `title` and give it an initial value of `"shape"`. Place this inside the `Shape` class's curly braces.

```
var title = "shape"
```

4. Define the `area()` function, but since we don't know what type of shape this generic shape is, simply return 0.0 for now.

```
func area() -> Double {
    return 0.0
}
```

5. Next, define a method called `description()`, and it will serve as a verbose description of our `Shape` instance.

```
func description() -> String {
    return "I am a \(title). My area is \(area())."
}
```

6. That's all for our `Shape` base class. Next, define a subclass of `Shape` called `Square`.

```
class Square : Shape {

}
```

7. Our `Square` class needs to have measurements for its `sideLength`, so make that variable initialized to 0.0, so Swift infers it to be of type `Double`.

```
var sideLength = 0.0
```

8. Now that we know we are a `Square`, with a proper `sideLength` length, we can override the `area()` method to provide a valid calculation for the area of a square.

```
override func area() -> Double {
    return sideLength * sideLength
}
```

9. Now that we have both classes created, declare constant instances of `Shape` and `Square`, and call their `area()` and `description()` methods.

```
let shape = Shape()
let square = Square()
shape.area()
shape.description()
square.area()
square.description()
```

10. Notice that you can call the `area()` and `description()` methods on `square`, although they aren't directly defined in our `Square` class, because they are inherited. Set the `sideLength` and `title` properties of the `square` instance.

```
square.sideLength = 4
square.title = "SQUARE"
```

11. After modifying the square instance, compare it with the shape instance by calling the `area()` and `description()` methods again. Notice that although `Square` is a subclass of `Shape`, the instances are separate instances, and modifying one does not impact the other.

```
shape.area()
shape.description()
square.area()
square.description()
```

When you've finished this Try It Yourself section, your code should look like the code in Figure 11.3.

`Square` is a class just like any other class, and even though it inherits from the `Shape` class, it does not have to override any methods if it is not necessary but can happily use them. Also, you could implement any new methods on `Square` that are not a part of `Shape`, as well as properties or subscripts.

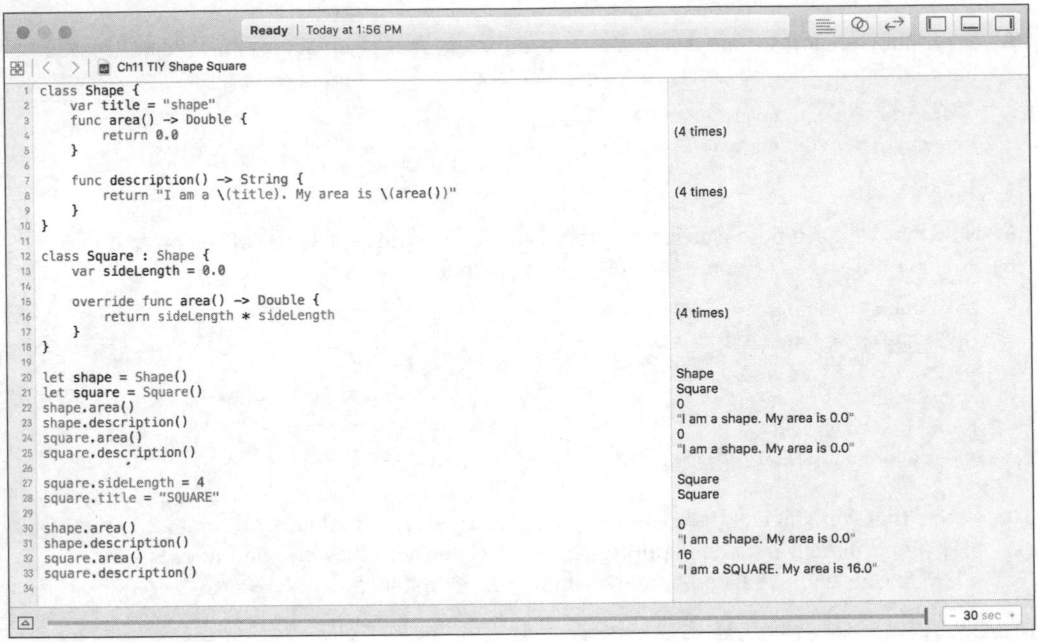

FIGURE 11.3
The completed Try It Yourself section for creating the `Shape` base class and `Square` subclass.

Accessing `super`

You may have methods in your superclass that are not overridden in your subclass, or you have methods in your subclass that might be appending behavior to the superclass's implementation, and you need to access the superclass's methods, properties, or subscripts. To do this, you use the `super` keyword to access the current subclass instance's superclass functionality. Swift is a **single inheritance** language, meaning that any given class can have no greater than one immediate superclass. In future hours, we discuss how to obtain functionality from different sources other than a superclass, but for now, we focus on inheriting from one single superclass.

The `super` keyword in your subclass is used just as if it were an instance itself. You can call any attribute of the superclass with dot syntax, just as you would a normal instance of any class. To illustrate this more visually in code, take a look at Listing 11.4.

LISTING 11.4 Accessing `super` from a Subclass

```
import Foundation
class Shape {
    var title = "shape"
    func area() -> Double {
```

```
            return 0.0
        }
        func description() -> String {
            return "I am a \(title). My area is \(area())"
        }
    }


    class Circle : Shape {
        var radius = 0.0
        override func area() -> Double {
            return M_PI * radius * radius
        }
    }


    class Sphere: Circle {
        override func description() -> String {
            return super.description() + ". My volume is \(volume())"
        }
        func volume() -> Double {
            return (4.0 * super.area() * radius) / 3.0
        }
    }

    let sphere = Sphere()
    sphere.title = "SPHERE"
    sphere.radius = 2.0
    sphere.area()  // which doesn't really make sense for a sphere, but shows that
        ➥Sphere still inherits this method
    sphere.volume()         // displays 33.51...
    sphere.description()  // displays "I am a SPHERE. My area is 12.56... My volume
        ➥is 33.51..."
```

In Listing 11.4, we see a similar structure as the Try It Yourself section, including creation of a Circle subclass. However, this time we go one subclass further and create a Sphere class, inheriting from Circle. So now the chain of inheritance goes Shape => Circle => Sphere. This means that Sphere inherits everything not only from Circle, but also Shape. The Sphere class overrides the description() method but appends a string to super.description(). Looking at the playground result output, it's easy to understand what impact calling super. description() has. Then in the volume() function, Sphere calls super.area() to get the value of the area of a circle, because the area (pi * r²) can be used as part of the volume equation (4/3 * pi * r³).

You will find that calling super.method() or super.property will be a fairly common occurrence for you, especially in the Cocoa and Cocoa Touch frameworks. As you become more familiar with creating apps, you'll discover something called view controller lifecycles, for example.

In an iOS app, each time a view comes onscreen, it is controlled by a **view controller**, and each view controller has methods you can implement to customize the behavior of the class at certain points in time of the view controller's lifecycle. For instance, when a view controller is instantiated and a view comes onscreen, a method called `viewDidLoad()` is called right before the view is shown onscreen. It is a common practice to call `super.viewDidLoad()` to ensure that the view controller's superclass has a chance to execute its implementation of `viewDidLoad()` and so on up the inheritance chain, and then perform actions in this method.

Preventing Overrides

There may be times when you want or need specific attributes of a class to not be overridden. To prevent overriding of any property, method, subscript, or even prevent a class from being subclassed, prefix the declaration with the `final` keyword. This tells the Swift compiler that any subclass that inherits from the current class can still access the current superclass implementation but should not be able to provide its own custom implementation. Let's go through preventing overriding a method in this next Try It Yourself section.

▼ TRY IT YOURSELF

Prevent Overriding a Superclass Method

Spheres don't have an area like a circle does, but they can have a surface area, which is a completely different attribute, as well as calculation. Prevent overriding the `area()` method in `Circle` to avoid an ambiguous definition of area and provide a surface area function for clarity.

1. Open Xcode and create a new playground. Either a Mac or an iOS playground will work. Clear the contents of the playground.

2. Add the `Shape`, `Circle`, and `Sphere` classes, as in Listing 11.4.

```
import Foundation
class Shape {
    var title = "shape"
    func area() -> Double {
        return 0.0
    }
    func description() -> String {
        return "I am a \(title). My area is \(area())"
    }
}
class Circle : Shape {
    var radius = 0.0
    override func area() -> Double {
```

```
            return M_PI * radius * radius
        }
    }
    class Sphere : Circle {
        override func description() -> String {
            return super.description() + ". My volume is \(volume())"
        }
        func volume() -> Double {
            return (4.0 * super.area() * radius) / 3.0
        }
    }
```

3. Modify the `Circle` class implementation to prevent the `area()` method from being overridden.

```
    class Circle : Shape {
        var radius = 0.0
        final override func area() -> Double {
            return M_PI * radius * radius
        }
    }
```

4. Modify the `Sphere` class implementation to add the `surfaceArea()` method.

```
    class Sphere : Circle {
        override func description() -> {
            return super.description() + ". My volume is \(volume())"
        }
        func volume() -> Double {
            return (4.0 * super.area() * radius) / 3.0
        }
        func surfaceArea() -> Double {
            return 4.0 * M_PI * radius * radius
        }
    }
```

5. Now that `Circle`'s implementation of `area()` Is final, try to override the `area()` method in the `Sphere` class. What compiler error do you receive?

```
    override func area() -> Double {    // Error!
```

As you can see in step 4 of the Try It Yourself section, we can still access and retrieve a return value from the `area()` method from step 3. This is because even though the `area()` method is marked as `final`, we can still access it and retrieve its return value. We just cannot override the method to provide our own implementation of it, as you can see in step 5. The completed code, as well as the error, should look identical to Figure 11.4.

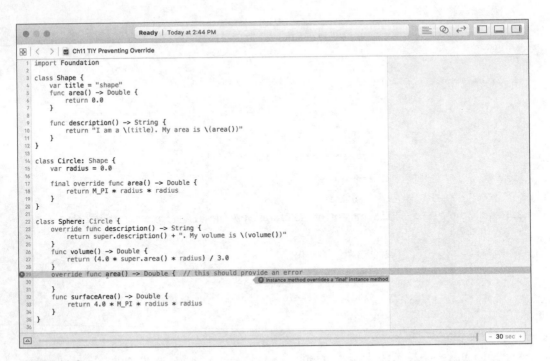

FIGURE 11.4
The completed Try It Yourself section, preventing overriding the `area()` method.

Class Identity

At first sight, subclassing may seem understandable and a fairly easy concept to learn. But it may leave you wondering, "Why would I need to do this?" In Objective-C, each class had an **isa pointer** inside it for identity. It basically said "this class *is a* <insert class name here>". This means, using the same *is a* terminology, that an instance of our Sphere class *is a* Shape, too, because it inherits from Shape. Often, to keep functions or other sections of code generic enough to handle multiple kinds of types for a single argument, you could set the parameter type to the most generic superclass; that way, your function could accept any instance of that class or a subclass thereof.

Let's take a look at this in Listing 11.5. We create a generic function that takes a parameter of type Shape. Look what happens when we send the function different instances of different subclasses of Shape. The class definitions have been omitted for brevity, as nothing in them changes for this example.

LISTING 11.5   Class Identity

```
func printDescriptionForShape(shape: Shape) {
    print(shape.description())
}

let sphere = Sphere()
sphere.title = "SPHERE"
sphere.radius = 4.0

let square = Square()
square.title = "SQUARE"
square.sideLength = 5.0

printDescriptionForShape(sphere)   // displays "I am a SPHERE. My area is
    ➥50.265... My volume is 268.082..."
printDescriptionForShape(square)   // displays "I am a SQUARE. My area is
    ➥25.0"
```

Notice how calling the `description()` method for each instance called that respective instance's `description()` implementation and not the `Shape` class's `description()` method. Structuring your code this way can be beneficial, as you can see from Listing 11.5. We do not need to create two different functions, `printDescriptionForShape` and `printDescription-ForSquare`, as well as for our other shapes, because any class instance that is a `Shape` can be passed in as our argument and satisfies Swift's type safety requirement.

When to Use Class Inheritance

As you have seen in the examples and text of this hour, class inheritance is simple and powerful. It is used in many different areas of Mac and iOS development, but does require you to keep some things in mind.

First, classes do carry some overhead. There is a different process for creating a class object in the heap than there is with creating a value type on the stack, and classes are not as cheap as structs due to extra overhead such as reference counting. Second, with inheritance, you inherit *everything* from a superclass. This is tremendously beneficial when it is an appropriate use case, but can introduce bugs or other unintended behavior if unnecessary for your application.

The musical instrument example earlier is a great visualization of using class inheritance. Each instrument is represented by a class instance with an appropriate level of inherited properties and actions, and can be passed around without being duplicated, or else the law of conservation of mass would be revoked. A hierarchical representation and grouping of objects such as instruments is a great use case for class inheritance.

Another great usage is with UI development. You will often need to use classes to represent elements on screen, and subclass them to create desired behavior or visualization effects. This is so extremely common in iOS and Mac development that this type of inheritance may be your most commonly used application of it. For instance, you may have a view in your application that is commonly used, and its background must always be green. It would make sense to subclass `UIView` into your own custom subclass, perhaps named `GreenView`, and in its initialization set the `backgroundColor` property to green (such as `UIColor.greenColor()`). Then anywhere in your application where you need that view, you would set its class to `GreenView` rather than `UIView`, and the green color will automatically be set. Such a convenience saves time and costly programming errors if you were to forget to set the `backgroundColor` property for every view that needed it.

A use case that might not be so good for class inheritance is that of the hierarchy of species. Although you might think it would work, many complications make species hierarchy not appropriate for class inheritance. The platypus, for example, is one case. A platypus is a mammal, but it does not give live birth; it lays eggs. So the birthing characteristic of mammals would be inappropriate for a platypus to inherit. I've also heard of another example called the "Frogosaur." Feel free to search online for more information on that topic.

The bottom line is to be judicious about whether you need inheritance and understand the implications of using it. We discuss an alternative to class inheritance using value types and protocols in Hour 17, "Using Protocols to Define Behavior," and also Hour 21, "Understanding Protocol-Oriented Programming," involving composing instances with the relevant pieces they need rather than obtaining everything from an inherited super class.

Summary

In this hour, we discussed the concept of inheritance. Inheritance is simply the act of creating a subclass from another class in which the subclass is a composition of everything it implements directly as well as everything from the superclass. Subclassing is important in object-oriented programming, and it is something you will find yourself doing frequently in your career as a software developer.

Once you understood base classes, superclasses, and subclasses, we examined a process called overriding. Overriding enables you to customize the implementation of whatever attribute you are overriding. You can also call the superclass's implementation inside your overriding method by using the `super` keyword.

You then learned how to prevent a subclass from overriding particular attributes by prefixing the `final` keyword to a method, property, or subclass declaration. This leaves the attribute still accessible by a subclass, but the compiler marks the attribute as unable to be overridden.

Finally, you learned about class identity, meaning that any subclass of a given class is a class of the superclass's type too. This can help reduce the amount of code needed to accomplish tasks and makes code more reusable.

In the next hour, we dive into enumerations. Enumerations are value types just like structs, but they have a wildly different implementation than in other languages, so we're in for some fun next hour.

Q&A

Q. Does every Swift class have a superclass?

A. No. Classes in Swift do not have to inherit from a superclass.

Q. Why would I ever need to create a subclass?

A. Subclassing enables you to inherit the behaviors of a superclass and then refine them to better suit your needs. By creating a subclass instead of starting from scratch with a new class, you can save yourself a lot of work, and finding bugs will be easier because you'll have less code to look through.

Q. Can a Swift class inherit from more than one superclass?

A. Not directly. Swift is a single inheritance language, which means that a class can inherit from at most one superclass, but a class's superclass may have a superclass itself, from which our initial class inherits functionality as well. Swift does support similar functionality with a feature called protocols, which is covered in Hour 17.

Q. Can a Swift class have more than one subclass?

A. Yes, a class can have as many subclasses as you want. Single inheritance in Swift means that a class can't have more than one superclass but does not restrict the number of subclasses you can create.

Workshop

The workshop contains quiz questions and exercises to help you solidify your understanding of the material covered. Try to answer all questions before looking at the answers that follow.

Quiz

1. When writing a new subclass, how do you change the behavior of a method that already exists in your superclass?

2. Can you create a class that can never have subclasses?

3. What's wrong with the following code?

```
class Vehicle {
  var speed: Double = 0
}

class Car : Vehicle {
  var wheels: Int = 4
}

func showVehicleInfo(vehicle: Vehicle) {
  print("My current speed is \(vehicle.speed).")
}

func showCarInfo(car: Car) {
  print("I have \(car.wheels) wheels");
}

var myCar = Car()
var myVehicle = Vehicle()

showCarInfo(myVehicle)
showVehicleInfo(myCar)
```

4. True or false? If my class overrides a method defined by its superclass, my class can never access the superclass's implementation of the method.

Answers

1. Write the method as you normally would, but prefix the method definition with the `override` keyword. Make sure your new method has the same signature as the one you're replacing, or you'll end up overloading the method instead of redefining it.

2. Yes! The `final` keyword can be used on classes, properties, subscripts, and methods. If you prefix your class definition with `final`, then no other class can ever inherit from it.

3. The function `showCarInfo()` takes an object of type `Car` as an argument, but we're trying to pass it an object of type `Vehicle`, which is an error. Notice that `showVehicleInfo(myCar)` is just fine because `Car` is a subclass of `Vehicle`, so `myCar` is a vehicle as far as our program is concerned.

4. False. A subclass can access a superclass's implementation of an overridden method by using the `super` keyword. For example, `super.description()` would call the description method in the parent class, not the version defined in the current class.

Exercise

Create a new OS X playground. Create a `Building` class that has properties that hold the number of floors in the building and the building's address. Create a subclass of `Building` called `House` that has properties for the number of bedrooms and the number of bathrooms in the house. Create a second subclass of `Building` called `Store` that contains the name of the store and the name of the store manager.

Add description methods to all three of your classes. These methods should display all the information about the class. Remember that stores and houses are both buildings, so they should show address and number of floors as part of their descriptions.

Finally, write a function that takes any kind of building and prints out that building's address.

Harnessing the Power of Enums

What You'll Learn in This Hour:

▶ What an enumeration is

▶ How to use enums to group related items

▶ How to access enum raw values

▶ How to use associated values

▶ How to use `switch` statements with enums

▶ How to add methods to enums

Enumerators are simply a structure of data that groups together related values. By that definition, it may not seem much different from any other topic we've talked about thus far, namely, structs, classes, dictionaries, arrays, and tuples. Swift enumerators, called enums, are a special kind of grouping structure in that they can keep a logical list of items, either with an ordered or unordered backing value, and are incredibly useful when working with items that can have only one option selected. Swift enums are a lot different than enums from other languages, as can be seen in the preceding list of topics. So let's get started and dive into what makes enums so special and powerful in Swift.

Understanding Swift Enums

If you come from a C background, you may be familiar with enums. C enums are integer-based. They are used to give a more meaningful representation to a numeric list of values, such as the colors of the rainbow. Consider the following scenario: We want to easily store the colors of the rainbow with a corresponding integer, so that we can have the user enter a number 1 through 7 and get a color in return. In C, we would either have to define seven `#define` statements, assigning each color an integer, or seven `const int` values each with a color being assigned an integer value. Using these in code would cause a lot of extra effort to ensure that each matched the same type, and each value was sequential (versus accidently giving two colors the number 6, for example).

Enums solve that problem nicely. In C, an enum might look like the following code snippet:

```
// enums in C
enum ColorsOfRainbow {
    red,
    orange,
    yellow,
    green,
    blue,
    indigo,
    violet
};

// how to use the enum in code
enum ColorsOfRainbow myColor = green;   // myColor is equal to 3
```

Here, we create an enum called `ColorsOfRainbow` and provide it with the seven colors in a rainbow. Each color is implicitly assigned an integer value, starting with zero (0), because enums by default are zero-based. If you want different values, you could assign each one its own value, or if you want to start the enumeration at 1, you could just assign `red = 1`, and it would adjust each enum member value accordingly, so `orange` would equal 2, and so on.

But that's about all you can do with enums in C.

Swift enums are value types just like structs and are first-class types. In addition to storing enumerated values like C enums, they can be extended with properties, methods, and more. Let's cover the structure of a Swift enum.

NOTE

First-Class Types

Being a first-class type means that instances of that type can do all the following: be passed as an argument to a function or subroutine, be returned from a function or subroutine, and be assigned to a variable or constant.

Swift Enum Structure

Enums in Swift do not always have to be integer-based. In fact, by default, each enum member is a full-fledged value with its type explicitly defined by the enum. The syntax for enums in Swift is a little different; not only do you not need the trailing semicolon (`;`), but each member must be prefixed with the `case` keyword, unless members are declared on a single line separated by commas. Figure 12.1 illustrates how to declare enums in Swift with multiple members per line, or on a single line.

```
enum EnumTypeName {
    case MemberOne , MemberTwo , MemberThree
    case MemberFour , MemberFive
    case MemberSix
}
```

FIGURE 12.1
The basic structure of an enum in Swift with various ways to declare members.

Figure 12.1 shows the basic structure of a Swift enum declaration, before we get into more advanced ways to empower enums. Basically, a Swift enum has a name and one or more members, which can be declared all on one line separated by commas, or each member declared on its own line prefixed with the `case` keyword. Let's consider an example of grades Kindergarten through Fifth grade as an enum, shown in Listing 12.1.

LISTING 12.1   Basic Enum in Swift

```
01:   enum GradesKTo5 {
02:       case Kindergarten, First, Second, Third
03:       case Fourth, Fifth
04:   }
05:   let thirdGrade = GradesKTo5.Third  // displays ".Third"
```

In line 1 of Listing 12.1, we declare the `enum` called `GradesKTo5`. Then, in lines 2 and 3, we declare our members to consist of grades `Kindergarten` to `Fifth` grade. Notice there is no comma at the end of line 2, even though we continue with another case statement on line 3. After closing the curly brace to end the `enum` definition, we declare a variable `thirdGrade` on line 5 to equal the value `.Third`.

As it is now, our example enum has no backing values; each member is a value in itself and can be compared against or assigned directly without needing a backing value. But there will be times when it is helpful to have backing values, such as for comparison reasons.

Raw Values

As mentioned already, Swift enums do not have backing values, or **raw values**, by default. However, there will be times when you need a raw value, and it is easy to designate an enum to have raw values for its members.

First, give the enum itself a type in the initial declaration statement. Then, you can assign values to each case. In the event of an `Int`-backed enum, Swift automatically does two things for you: sets the first member's raw value to zero (0), and then auto-increments each following member's raw value. Raw values for other types must be explicitly assigned for each member.

Getting Raw Values from Enums

Let's continue with the Kindergarten to Fifth grade example. Listing 12.2 illustrates how to make the enum an `Int`-backed enum and how to retrieve the raw value by using the `.rawValue` instance property.

LISTING 12.2   Assigning and Retrieving Raw Values

```
01:  enum GradesKTo5: Int {
02:      case Kindergarten, First, Second, Third
03:      case Fourth, Fifth
04:  }
05:  var thirdGrade = GradesKTo5.Third
06:  thirdGrade.rawValue  // displays 3
```

Lines 1 through 5 were identical to Listing 12.1, although this time we declared `GradesKTo5` to be of type `Int`. Then, on line 6, we use the `rawValue` computed property to retrieve the underlying raw value of the current member, which is 3. Remember enums are zero-based, so Kindergarten's raw value is 0, First is 1, and so on.

Setting Enum Values from Raw Values

Not only can you use the `rawValue` instance property to obtain the raw value from an enum member, you can set an enum value from a raw value using an enumeration's parameterized initializer, `init(rawValue:)`. Xcode senses the type of enum with its auto-complete functionality and will supply the type hint for you while you type, helping you complete the syntax with the proper type of raw value to use. Figure 12.2 shows Xcode's suggested hint for creating an enum instance from a raw value for our `GradesKTo5` enum scenario.

NOTE

Computed Properties

So far we have discussed instance computed properties, which are special properties that can exist on an instance of a class or struct. Computed properties do not store a value themselves; rather, they return a computed value based on other criteria within the instance. We cover this topic more in Hour 14, "Digging Deeper with Properties."

It is important to notice here that the `init(rawValue:)` initializer returns an optional type. This is because you could easily enter 9 as the grade, and there is no raw backing value equal to 9 in this implementation. The result would be `nil`, and therefore the initializer must return an optional value to account for that potential failure.

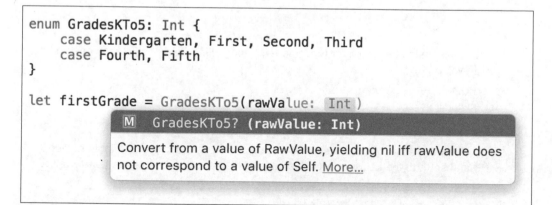

FIGURE 12.2
The raw value initializer in Xcode's auto-complete, suggesting the proper type based on the type of enum chosen.

Enum Shorthand Syntax

As with many things in Swift, enums can utilize shorthand syntax too. Enum shorthand syntax for accessing members is simple; just drop the type name and only enter the member name prefixed with a dot (.). This shorthand syntax can only be used *after* a variable or constant has been defined of an enum type. This example will best be understood by doing it yourself, so follow along in this next Try It Yourself section.

TRY IT YOURSELF ▼

Create an Enum with Raw `String` Values and Shorthand Syntax

Expand upon the `GradesKTo5` example by changing the enum to be backed by `String` raw values, and use shorthand syntax to reassign a variable.

1. Open Xcode and create a new playground. Either a Mac or an iOS playground will work. Clear the contents of the playground.

▼

2. Create the `enum` for `GradesKTo5` of type `String`.

```
enum GradesKTo5: String {


}
```

3. Create cases inside the enum for Kindergarten through Fifth, and assign each one a short `String` value.

```
case Kindergarten = "K", First = "1st"
case Second = "2nd", Third = "3rd"
case Fourth = "4th", Fifth = "5th"
```

4. That's all for the enum. After the enum's closing curly brace, declare a variable named `myKid` and set it to the `Kindergarten` value initially. Call `rawValue` to see its raw value.

```
var myKid = GradesKTo5.Kindergarten
myKid.rawValue    // displays "K"
```

5. One year passes, and your kid grows up. He or she advances to first grade. Change `myKid` to the member value for first grade, using shorthand syntax. Call `rawValue` to see its raw value.

```
myKid = .First
myKid.rawValue    // displays "1st"
```

6. Examine the types when you assign a variable or constant to an enum member or to an enum member's raw value. Create two new constants, `secondGrade` equal to `GradesKTo5.Second` and `thirdGrade` equal to `GradesKTo5.Third.rawValue`. Option-click each constant name and observe the data type of each.

```
let secondGrade = GradesKTo5.Second  // Option-clicking shows type as
    ➥GradesKTo5
let thirdGrade = GradesKTo5.Third.rawValue  // Option-clicking shows type as
    ➥String
```

7. Use the `rawValue` initializer to create a new constant called `fourthGrade`. Then use optional binding to extract the value if it is not `nil`, and display its `rawValue` value.

```
let fourthGrade = GradesKTo5(rawValue: "4th")
if let fourth = fourthGrade {
    print(fourth.rawValue)
}
```

If you finished the Try It Yourself section successfully, your playground should look like what is shown in Figure 12.3.

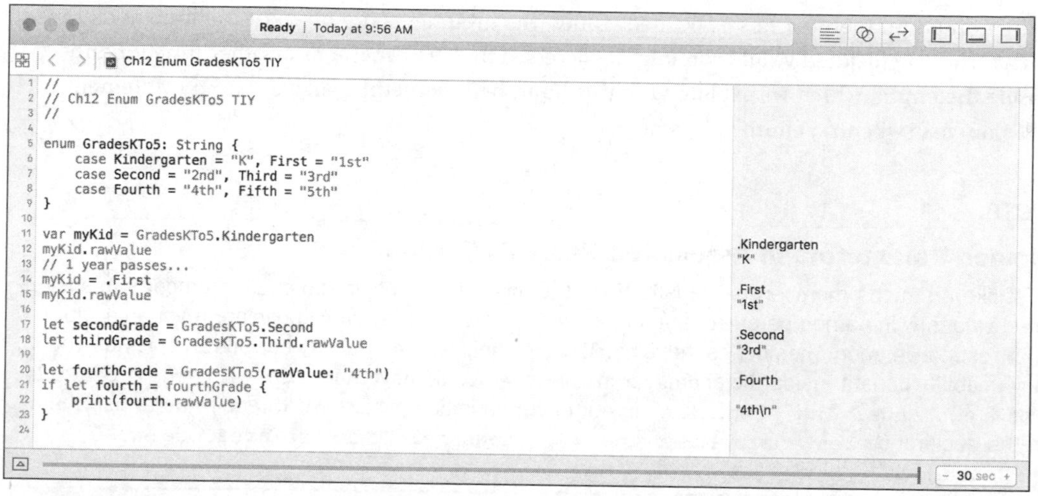

FIGURE 12.3
The completed exercise from the Try It Yourself section for creating a `String`-backed enum, using shorthand syntax and using raw values.

Associated Values

Swift enums have a feature that enables each member to store values called **associated values**. Associated values are a way to store additional information alongside the currently stored enum member value. Associated values can be thought of as if you were storing values, such as in the members of a struct, inside an individual member of an enum.

Associated values are defined with just their types inside parentheses, immediately after the name of a member inside an enum definition. There can be any number of associated values, and any number of types, defined with an enum member. Associated values are useful for when a member of an enum must be chosen, and corresponding information is helpful to be stored, but with a tighter relationship than just another instance property.

Listing 12.3 illustrates how to declare an enum with associated values for its members.

LISTING 12.3 Associated Values in Enums

```
01:   enum PhoneNumber {
02:       case TollFree(Int, Int, Int)
03:       case InternalExtension(Int)
04:   }
05:
06:   let customerService = PhoneNumber.TollFree(800, 555, 1212)
```

When an enum member has associated values, the arguments are given at the time of assignment. These associated values can later be accessed by either methods or other functionality inside the enum, which we explore later this hour, or in something like a switch statement. Let's discuss switching enum values next.

NOTE

Named Parameters in Associated Value Definition

Just like a struct's memberwise initialization, it is possible to declare an enum member's associated values with named parameters, requiring you to use them when you declare a variable with that respective enum member as its value. This can help with readability but doesn't provide you any usability benefit inside the enum. For instance, we could have had case TollFree(areaCode: Int, exchange: Int, ext: Int) in our enum definition, which would require us to use them in the declaration let customerService = PhoneNumber.TollFree(areaCode: 888, exchange: 555, ext: 1212).

Switching Enum Values

In Hour 5, "Controlling Program Flow with Conditionals," the switch statement is a great way to clearly choose a path of execution based on meeting conditional criteria. Enums are particularly nice to switch on, because we can use their member values as the cases, and the Swift compiler is smart enough to sense when all cases have been considered, thus counting the switch statement as exhaustive.

Let's consider the GradesKTo5 example for switching enum member values. Listing 12.4 illustrates how we can do that to print a custom greeting to a student, depending on the student's current grade in school.

LISTING 12.4 Switching Enum Values

```
01:   enum GradesKTo5 {
02:       case Kindergarten, First, Second, Third, Fourth, Fifth
03:   }
04:
05:   let studentGrade = GradesKTo5.First
06:
07:   switch studentGrade {
08:   case .Kindergarten:
09:       print("Welcome to Kindergarten!")
10:   case .First:
11:       print("First grade will be awesome!")
12:   case .Second:
13:       print("You're in second grade? You must be smart!")
```

```
14:   case .Third:
15:       print("You'll master multiplication in third grade!")
16:   case .Fourth:
17:       print("Fourth grade spelling bee tryouts, first day!")
18:   case .Fifth:
19:       print("Fifth graders rule the school!")
20:   }


// displays "First grade will be awesome!"
```

In Listing 12.4, we assign GradesKTo5.First to the constant studentGrade, and then switch on that value in line 7. Line 10 passes the condition, so line 11 is executed. After execution, control is passed to line 20, which ends the switch block. Pretty easy.

We can also use bindings in our switch cases, for when we have associated values. This is when associated values can become valuable. Take a look at Listing 12.5, using the PhoneNumber example with associated values, and using bindings in the case statements to extract individual values from the member's associated values.

LISTING 12.5   Using Bindings with Associated Values

```
01:   enum PhoneNumber {
02:       case TollFree(Int, Int, Int)
03:       case InternalExtension(Int)
04:   }
05:
06:   let customerService = PhoneNumber.TollFree(800, 555, 1212)
07:
08:   switch customerService {
09:   case .TollFree(_, _, let ext):
10:       print("Toll-free number, extension: \(ext)")
11:   case .InternalExtension(let ext):
12:       print("Internal extension: \(ext)")
13:   }
```

Listing 12.5 is largely the same as before, but notice in line 9 how we extract just the ext value from the associated value inside the .TollFree option and bind that value to a local constant called ext so we can use it inside the case statement. This can be useful—as you write more apps, you may have associated values containing RGBa values (Red/Green/Blue/alpha) for making a color, barcode information for 1D or 2D barcodes, phone numbers, or any of a multitude of possibilities for storing values in enums.

You might have figured out on your own that optional values in Swift are a type of enum with associated values. Some languages have a structure slightly similar to this called **Either**, where a value can be either the first value or the second value. A basic implementation of the optional type is represented in Listing 12.6.

LISTING 12.6   Crude Implementation of Optional Enum

```
enum STYOptional<T> {
    case None
    case Some(T)
}
```

As you know, constants and variables in Swift are either optional or non-optional. In previous examples, you've stored optional values inside variables, and it has looked like `Optional(3)`, because the associated value was not `nil`, and it was associated with the `Some` enum member. If a value was `nil`, the `None` member was returned. Swift provides shorthand syntax (the question mark) when indicating an optional, versus using `.Some(value)` or `.None`.

Adding Instance Methods to Enums

By this point, I'm sure you've become comfortable with functions, both by themselves and also as instance methods. It should not come as a surprise to you that enums can also have instance methods inside them. This is a big mental stretch for some who are accustomed to C-style enums where they store a logical progression of enumerated values, and that's it. Swift enums are much more flexible and powerful, and the ability to add instance methods is just one more ounce of proof of that.

Instance methods in Swift enums are basically identical to instance methods in a class or a struct. The structural syntax is the same. They are defined with the `func` keyword; you provide a name for the method, parameters, and a return type, and then the body goes inside curly braces. This enables you to perform actions based on the current instance of the enum, which can make it possible for you to do some pretty powerful things with very little code, since now you can encapsulate a lot of power directly inside an enum.

To access instance methods on an enum instance, you simply use the dot syntax just as with a class's or struct's instance methods. Let's walk through an example in this next Try It Yourself section, so you can get the feel for how enums can add powerful capabilities to your code. In the Try It Yourself section, you'll create a type called `Result`, which is a common enum to create. The basis of it is that the enum instance can represent either a success or failure result of some sort of operation, and it uses associated values with each enum member. For instance, you could use a `Result` type as the return type of a function that parses some data, and if all went smoothly, then your successfully processed data would be the associated value along with the `Success` case. Likewise, an error object would be the associated value along with the `Failure` case, which may contain the information about why the operation failed.

Add Instance Methods to Enums

Create a `Result` enum type that contains two members, one for success and one for failure. The `Success` case should contain an associated value of type `String`, and the `Failure` case should contain an associated value of type `Int`, representing an error code. Extend the enum type by adding an instance method to encapsulate a `switch` statement, utilizing associated values of the enum's members. The function should provide the description for the selected result type.

1. Open Xcode and create a new playground. Either a Mac or an iOS playground will work. Clear the contents of the playground.

2. Create the `Result` enum in your playground to look like the following.

```
enum Result {
    case Success(String)
    case Failure(Int)
}
```

3. After the `case` statements, but before the enum's closing brace, declare a function called `description` that takes no parameters and returns a `String`.

```
func description() -> String {

}
```

4. Inside this method, switch the current value (`self`, because we're dealing with the current instance) and use binding to obtain the relevant data from either case. Use a `String` variable inside the method to keep track of the result to be returned.

```
switch self {
case .Success(let value):
    return "Successful. Value: \(value)"
case .Failure(let value):
    return "Failed. Error code: \(value)"
}
```

5. That's all for the instance method, and the enum as well. Now you can reuse the `switch` statement on any instance, not just once per variable or constant like in Listing 12.5. Create a variable instance of `Result`, assign it the `Success` member, and provide a success message for the associated value. Call the `description()` instance method you just created.

```
var result = Result.Success("Response from web service successful!")
result.description()
```

▼   6. Use shorthand syntax to reassign the `result` variable to `Result.Failure`, and provide a single `Int` as an associated value. Call the `description()` instance method again and observe the value.

```
result = .Failure(404)
result.description()
```

Upon completion of the Try It Yourself section, your code should look like the code in Figure 12.4.

Hopefully by now you're starting to see how all the concepts discussed thus far in the book are used and how they can be integrated with other concepts to create a powerful app with not much code. In this Try It Yourself section, we declare an `enum` with two members, each having associated values. We also have an instance method on that enum, with a `switch` block that uses binding to extract values and use them in the `case` statements. Then we declare a variable with an enum value, call the instance method, reassign the variable, and call the instance method again. This is all done in 20 lines of code.

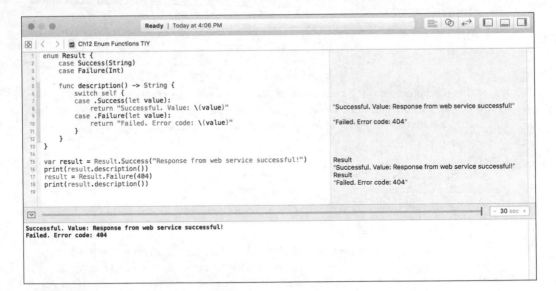

FIGURE 12.4
The completed Try It Yourself section, implementing enum functions.

Summary

This hour introduced a new type not yet used in this book called enums. Enumerations are great type choices when you need a data type to hold a particular value from a set of available options.

You learned that Swift enums can have a backing (or *raw*) value, or they can peacefully exist without one. A raw value can be of type `Int`, `String`, `Character`, `Double`, or `Float`, and Swift auto-increments `Int`-backed raw values, as well as starts them at zero if not explicitly defined. You also learned how to access raw values with the `rawValue` computed property and select an enum member via the `init(rawValue:)` method, which returns an optional.

We also discussed shorthand syntax as a way to quickly and tersely assign an enum member to a variable or constant, while still maintaining meaning and readability. Then we discussed associated values, which are great for storing data alongside an enum member in an instance, rather than storing that data in a property somewhere else. Then we used `switch` statements to execute code based on the current enum value (`self`) and used binding inside switch cases to extract the associated values.

Finally, we discussed adding instance methods to enums, which greatly adds power to enums, a feature not in other languages. Adding instance methods to enums encapsulates enum-specific actions to the enum itself and keeps the responsibility of the code with the enum, rather than as separate entities in code.

In the next hour, we discuss initializers in Swift, and how they can be added and customized within classes, structs, and enums. Because of Swift's type safety, initializers play a big role in ensuring safe type construction and use.

Q&A

Q. What happens if I don't assign raw values to enumerations members of type `Character`?

A. You'll get a compiler error. If you create an enumeration with members of any non-`Int` type, you must assign raw values to each member.

Q. What's the difference between raw values and associated values?

A. You assign raw values to your enumeration's members when you create the enumeration. Once you set them, they cannot change. With associated values, you set the type when you create the enumeration, but no value is assigned until you create a variable based on one of your enumeration's members.

Q. Can an enum have both associated values and raw values?

A. No. Enums can have either associated values or raw values, but not both.

Q. Can I inherit from enumerations like I can from classes?

A. No. Enumerations do not allow inheritance in the way that classes do. You can add functionality with protocols and protocol extensions, however, which are discussed in Hour 17, "Using Protocols to Define Behavior," and Hour 21, "Understanding Protocol-Oriented Programming."

Workshop

The workshop contains quiz questions and exercises to help you solidify your understanding of the material covered. Try to answer all questions before looking at the answers that follow.

Quiz

1. Are Swift enumerations value types or reference types?

2. Which property returns an enum's backing value?

3. What's wrong with the following code?

```
enum Day {
    case Sunday, Monday, Tuesday, Wednesday
    case Thursday, Friday, Saturday

    func isWeekday() -> Bool {
      switch self {
        case .Saturday, .Sunday:
          return false
        default:
          return true
      }
    }
}

let today: DayOfWeek = .Monday
today.isWeekday()
let tomorrow = .Tuesday
tomorrow.isWeekday()
```

4. Which types are legal to use as raw values? Which are legal as associated values?

Answers

1. Swift enumerations are value types. This means that they are copied when they are assigned to a variable or constant or when they are passed as an argument to a function.

2. The `.rawValue` property.

3. We're trying to use enum shorthand notation when we assign a value to `tomorrow` before we establish what type `tomorrow` is. With no type assigned, the compiler doesn't know what `.Tuesday` means.

4. Raw values must be of type `String`, `Character`, `Int`, `Double`, or `Float`. Associated values can be of any type.

Exercise

Create a new OS X playground. We're going to model a standard deck of playing cards. Begin by creating an enum called Suit, with members Hearts, Diamonds, Clubs, and Spades. Write an instance method that determines the color of the card. Remember that hearts and diamonds are red, whereas clubs and spades are black.

Next, write an enum to hold the rank of the card. Valid ranks are One, Two, Three, Four, Five, Six, Seven, Eight, Nine, Ten, Jack, Queen, King, and Ace. Write an instance method that determines whether the card is a face card. Remember that face cards are Jacks, Queens, and Kings.

Last, create a PlayingCard class with properties of type Rank and Suit. Write a method called Description for the PlayingCard class that returns a string of the form: "The <RANK> of <SUIT> is a <COLOR> <FACE> card." Replace <RANK>, <SUIT>, and <COLOR> with the appropriate strings. Replace <FACE> with the word "face" if the card is a face card and with an empty string if the card is not a face card.

For example, if the card is the Ace of Spades, your description method should print "The Ace of Spades is a Black card." For the King of Diamonds, it should print "The King of Diamonds is a Red face card."

Think about how you might assign raw values to your enums to make this task easier.

HOUR 13
Customizing Initializers of Classes, Structs, and Enums

What You'll Learn in This Hour:

▶ What the goal of initialization is
▶ How to create default and parameterized initializers
▶ How to create failable initializers
▶ How to use initializer delegation
▶ How to use designated and convenience initializers
▶ What the rules of initialization are
▶ How to use and override inherited initializers

Throughout the book thus far, we have made do without mentioning much about initialization as a concept in itself, but we have used it, whether you knew it or not. All instances of any type must be initialized before use, not only for safety, but also to be a usable instance in general; it doesn't do you much good to have an uninitialized instance of anything because you wouldn't be able to reliably interact with the instance in either sending data to or getting data from it. In this hour, we discuss many different methods and concepts of initialization. Initialization is a huge topic in itself, and probably more than what would fit in an hour's worth of reading. But in the interest of keeping the discussion of this topic to an hour while still conveying all pertinent and usable information to you, we cover enough of a foundation of initialization, which later hours extend, due to how they interact with initialization. Without further ado, let's dive into initialization in Swift.

Initialization

Each instance in Swift, whether an enum, class, or struct, must be initialized before use. **Initialization** is the method by which values inside the instance are set to either default values or values passed in as arguments. Initialization takes place in code through something called an **initializer**. An initializer is similar to an instance method, much like the instance methods we have written in the previous several hours, only it has specific syntax that differentiates it from normal instance methods. Let's take a look at the structure of initializers now.

The Goal of Initializers

The goal of initializers is simple: Set a value for every property inside the current instance. That is the *raison d'être* of initializers. They should perform no other actions than to ensure the instance is set up properly before use.

Listing 13.1 illustrates the syntax of a basic initializer. Unlike regular instance methods, the func keyword is not used here. Rather, only the init keyword and a pair of parentheses are used. Inside the curly braces is where you put initialization code.

LISTING 13.1 Basic Initializer Syntax

```
01:  class SampleClass {
02:      var sampleInt: Int
03:      init() {
04:          sampleInt = 0
05:      }
06:  }
```

In Listing 13.1, we create a sample class called SampleClass on line 1, with a single variable property called sampleInt, of type Int, on line 2. On line 3, we declare our initializer with the init() method. Inside the init() method, we simply set our instance property sampleInt to 0, which is a likely and common starting value for many numeric types.

Up until now, if you recall, we have always initialized our properties when we define them; otherwise, we get compiler errors (with the exception of structs, but we'll get to that shortly). An example of the error we would receive if we had neither an initializer nor a default value for sampleInt is shown in Figure 13.1. Notice that Xcode offers a solution, in light gray text to the right of the Int keyword, which is to assign an initial value of zero (0) to sampleInt.

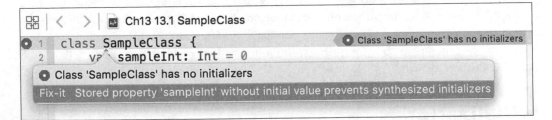

FIGURE 13.1
Xcode error when using uninitialized properties in a class.

Double-clicking the blue Fix-it suggestion auto-completes adding the assignment to zero and silences the compiler error. Setting a value in a variable's or constant's definition statement is called setting its **default property value**. The reason for this is Swift's need for type safety.

Returning an uninitialized instance could potentially cause your app to crash. As you see as we progress through this hour, initializers play a key role in properly setting up instances for use and ensuring your instances begin their lives with the proper initialized values.

We would expect that we would be able to change the value of a variable property, due to it being introduced with `var` rather than `let`. But what about constants, or even optionals? Constant properties can be set in their initializers *only*, if not set directly in their definition, and can only be written to once. The reason for this is that even though it is constant, it still needs an initial value, and inside the initializer or directly in its definition are the only safe places for that to happen. As for optionals, they don't have to be initialized inside an initializer or in their definition statement, because *they are optional*. By being declared optional, its value is `nil` until set otherwise.

There Is Always an Initializer

Swift enums, classes, and structs always have an initializer. Swift provides a **default initializer** for any struct, enum, or base class that provides default values for all its properties and doesn't implement an initializer itself. Because Swift provides a default initializer, we do not see it, but it is there behind the scenes. The best way to understand this is to examine how we create instances of these types. Recall that when we create a constant or variable of a type, we set the constant or variable equal to the name of the type, followed by a pair of parentheses. Using the parentheses after the type name is actually calling the initializer for that type. In the case of our `SampleClass` example in Listing 13.1, writing `let a = SampleClass()` would assign a new instance of type `SampleClass` to a, with `a.sampleInt` being equal to 0. But in this example, it is easy to see that there is an initializer, because we created it on line 3. Consider the following revised version of `SampleClass`:

```
class SampleClass {
    var sampleInt = 0
}
```

In this shortened version of `SampleClass`, since `sampleInt` is set to 0 upon definition, and there are no other properties to assign, there is no need to explicitly add an initializer. However, Swift implicitly adds an initializer to our class because Swift has to have at least one initializer per type to properly instantiate the instance.

Initializing Value Types

There are some differences between initializing value types, such as structs and enums, and reference types, such as classes. Let's cover value types first to grasp some key concepts and then move on to reference types, where we expand upon these concepts with more that only relate to classes.

Setting Default Values

Setting default values for structs is just as simple as either setting the property value directly in the definition statement, or by setting property values inside the initializer, as we have seen so far in this hour. Let's discuss how structs and enums can set default values.

Memberwise Initialization for Structs

If you recall from Hour 10, "Learning About Structs and Classes," when we created a struct called Point, we created an instance of it by using something called **memberwise initialization**. Listing 13.2 shows our Point struct and an example of creating an instance of Point.

LISTING 13.2 Using Memberwise Initialization on a Struct

```
01:  struct Point {
02:      var x: Double
03:      var y: Double
04:  }
05:  let point = Point(x: 2.0, y: 3.0)
```

Memberwise initialization is something Swift does by default when you do not provide any initializers. A memberwise initializer analyzes the defined properties in a struct and creates a default initializer requiring those properties as parameters. The order of the parameters used in the memberwise initializer is the same as the order of the properties defined in the struct. Listing 13.3 illustrates what our Point struct would look like if we provided the exact same initializer as the memberwise initializer (although I changed the parameters to be xx and yy to show that we're using the new initializer and not the memberwise initializer).

LISTING 13.3 What a Memberwise Initializer Looks Like

```
01:  struct Point {
02:      var x: Double
03:      var y: Double
04:      init(xx: Double, yy: Double) {
05:          self.x = xx
06:          self.y = yy
07:      }
08:  }
09:  let point = Point(xx: 4.0, yy: 2.5)
```

The init(xx:, yy:) method on line 4 is just as it would appear if Swift provided its memberwise initializer explicitly, except xx would be x, and yy would be y. Inside the init(xx:, yy:) method, on lines 5 and 6, we set the struct instance's x and y properties to equal the parameters passed in as arguments, and the struct is initialized fully.

NOTE

Using `self`

In Listing 13.3, we refer to `self.x` and `self.y`, rather than just `x` and `y`. Using `self` refers to the instance itself, so you can interact with other parts of the instance directly. In Objective-C, it was required to use `self` before referring to a property or method inside the instance of a class, but in Swift, using `self` is not required unless the statement could be ambiguous. The `init(xx:, yy:)` method in Listing 13.3 could have read `x = xx` and `y = yy` instead, since Swift knows `x` and `y` are its instance properties. If the `init(xx:, yy:)` method's arguments were `x` and `y`, we couldn't have `x = x` and `y = y`. That is unclear as to which `x` and `y` we are working with on the left-hand or right-hand side of the equation, so we would use `self.x = x` and `self.y = y` in that case instead.

Custom Initializers for Structs

As an alternative to having Swift provide a memberwise initializer for structs, you can provide one or more of your own initializers. By providing an initializer, Swift does not provide a memberwise initializer. Take Listing 13.4, for example. We create a simple `Rectangle` struct with just an `init()` method where we provide default values for the properties `width` and `height`.

LISTING 13.4 Initializing Structs with Default Values

```
01: struct Rectangle {
02:     var width: Double
03:     var height: Double
04:     init() {
05:         width = 1.0
06:         height = 2.0
07:     }
08: }
09: var rectangle = Rectangle()    // rectangle is equal to {width: 1.0,
    ➡height: 2.0}
```

When we declare an `init()` method on line 4, we can no longer use the memberwise initializer. Line 9 shows how we now declare a variable of type `Rectangle`, with an initialized instance.

Custom Initializers for Enums

Enums are a little different than structs. Enums provide different cases that a property value could store, and if they have a raw value, they can be instantiated using the `rawValue` initializer, as we saw previously in Hour 12, "Harnessing the Power of Enums." Because enums are value types just like structs, and Swift provides much more functionality to enums, we can also add our own initializers to enums. Listing 13.5 illustrates adding an `init()` method to an enum and setting a default value.

LISTING 13.5 Initializing Enums with Default Values

```
01:   enum GradesKTo5: String {
02:       case Kindergarten = "K", First = "1st", Second = "2nd"
03:       case Third = "3rd", Fourth = "4th", Fifth = "5th"
04:       init() {
05:           self = .Kindergarten
06:       }
07:   }
08:   let k = GradesKTo5()
09:   k.rawValue              // displays "K"
```

Here, we reused the `GradesKTo5` enum from the previous hour and added an initializer on line 4. The initializer takes no arguments, so its purpose is to simply set a default initial value, which we set to `.Kindergarten`. When we declare a constant value of the enum on line 8, rather than writing `let k = GradesKTo5.Kindergarten`, we simply call the enum's initializer with the parentheses after `GradesKTo5`. On line 9, we call the `rawValue` property to show that our initializer did its job.

Let's walk through an example together to get more practice writing code with initializers in a Try It Yourself section.

▼ TRY IT YOURSELF

Use Initializers to Set Default and Custom Values

Create an enum holding different types of melons, and then create a `Melon` struct, with a property of the enum type, seed count, and weight. Use initializers to help properly set up the instances.

1. Open Xcode and create a new playground. Either a Mac or iOS playground is fine. Clear the contents of the playground.

2. Create an enum, and call it `MelonType`, with a raw value type of `String`.

   ```
   enum MelonType: String {

   }
   ```

3. Inside the enum, create three case members: Watermelon, Cantaloupe, and Honeydew.

   ```
   case Watermelon = "Watermelon", Cantaloupe = "Cantaloupe", Honeydew =
     ➥"Honeydew"
   ```

4. Below the `case` statement, create an initializer without parameters that sets the default melon to Watermelon.

   ```
   init() {
       self = .Watermelon
   }
   ```

5. That's all for the enum. Next, create a struct called `Melon`.

```
struct Melon {

}
```

6. Define three variables inside the struct: one for the melon type, one for the seed count, and one for the weight of the melon.

```
var melonType: MelonType
var seedCount: Int
var weightInPounds: Double
```

7. Create a default initializer that sets all values to zero, or their type's initial default state.

```
init() {
    melonType = MelonType()
    seedCount = 0
    weightInPounds = 0.0
}
```

8. Create a custom initializer that can be called when creating an instance of `Melon` that accepts all three parameters for the properties in our struct.

```
init(melonType: MelonType, seedCount: Int, weightInPounds: Double) {
    self.melonType = melonType
    self.seedCount = seedCount
    self.weightInPounds = weightInPounds
}
```

9. For our struct, create a description method that displays in a friendly format the data inside our `Melon` struct instances.

```
func description() -> String {
    return "My \(melonType.rawValue) has \(seedCount) seeds and weighs
    ➥\(weightInPounds) lbs."
}
```

10. That's all for the struct and enum. Next, declare two instances of `Melon` using both initializers and then call their description methods to see their resulting data.

```
let defaultMelon = Melon()
let customMelon = Melon(melonType: .Honeydew, seedCount: 100,
    ➥weightInPounds: 2.0)
defaultMelon.description()
customMelon.description()
```

After completing the Try It Yourself section, your code and results in the results pane should look like those in Figure 13.2.

```
  1   //
  2   // Ch13 Try It Yourself #1
  3   //
  4   enum MelonType: String {
  5       case Watermelon = "Watermelon", Cantaloupe = "Cantaloupe", Honeydew =
              "Honeydew"
  6       init() {
  7           self = .Watermelon                                          .Watermelon
  8       }
  9   }
 10
 11   struct Melon {
 12       var melonType: MelonType
 13       var seedCount: Int
 14       var weightInPounds: Double
 15       init() {
 16           melonType = MelonType()
 17           seedCount = 0
 18           weightInPounds = 0
 19       }
 20       init(melonType: MelonType, seedCount: Int, weightInPounds: Double) {
 21           self.melonType = melonType
 22           self.seedCount = seedCount
 23           self.weightInPounds = weightInPounds
 24       }
 25       func description() -> String {
 26           return "My \(melonType.rawValue) has \(seedCount) seeds and weighs \   (2 times)
              (weightInPounds) lbs."
 27       }
 28   }
 29
 30   let defaultMelon = Melon()                                          Melon
 31   let customMelon = Melon(melonType: .Cantaloupe, seedCount: 100, weightInPounds:   Melon
          2.0)
 32
 33   defaultMelon.description()                                         "My Watermelon has 0 seeds and weighs 0.0 lbs."
 34   customMelon.description()                                          "My Cantaloupe has 100 seeds and weighs 2.0 lbs."
 35
```

FIGURE 13.2
The completed Try It Yourself exercise for creating default and custom initializers.

External Parameter Names in Initializers

By default, all parameters in initializers behave as both the external and internal parameter names. This means that you do not have to explicitly declare external parameter names in your initializers, and Swift requires the parameter names when declaring an instance of that type.

In some cases, it may not make sense to have to explicitly state the initializer parameter name or names, or for succinctness and clarity the parameter name(s) could be removed. To do this, preface an initializer parameter name with the underscore (_) character and a space to indicate to Swift's compiler that the parameter name is not needed when declaring a new instance of a type. Listing 13.6 shows how this is done.

LISTING 13.6 Hiding Parameter Names in Initializers

```
01:   struct MilesPerHour {
02:       var rate: Double
03:       init(_ rate: Double) {
```

```
04:          self.rate = rate
05:      }
06:  }
07:  let mph = MilesPerHour(60)      // intent is clear, 60 MPH
```

Listing 13.6 looks like a pretty standard struct as we've seen already, but on line 3, we use the underscore (_) to denote that we don't need to enter the parameter name in the declaration on line 7. The intent is clear that we are creating an instance to hold a value representing 60 miles per hour.

Initializing Class Types

The initialization concepts and examples so far in this hour, minus memberwise initialization for structs, are available for classes as well. You get a default initializer when your class is a base class and all properties are assigned values in their definition statements. You can also create custom initializers, with or without parameters. Parameterized initializers require their parameters to be listed inside the parentheses when creating an instance. Finally, you can also hide parameter names with the underscore (_) and a space before the parameter name.

Later in this hour, we discuss some of the more powerful and advanced features of class initialization, such as how it works in multiple phases, delegation, and convenience and designated initializers. These concepts become clearer when we cover them if we cover their less-advanced partners for structs.

Setting Default Initialization Parameter Values

Much like using default parameter values in functions like we did in Hour 8, "Using Functions to Perform Actions," you can also insert default values in-line in the initializer parameter list. If you choose, you can then omit specifying arguments for those parameters when you create an instance. Listing 13.7 illustrates the differences in using and calling initializers with default parameters.

LISTING 13.7 Using Default Initializer Parameters

```
struct Incrementor {
    let startValue: Int
    let byTwo: Bool
    init(startValue: Int, byTwo: Bool = false) {
        self.startValue = startValue
        self.byTwo = byTwo
    }
    func increment(times: Int) -> Int {
        var result = startValue
        for _ in 0..<times {
            result = byTwo ? result + 2 : result + 1
        }
```

```
        return result
    }
}

let incrementor = Incrementor(startValue: 1)
incrementor.increment(5)

let incByTwos = Incrementor(startValue: 1, byTwo: true)
incByTwos.increment(5)
```

In Listing 13.7, you can see that by using the default value byTwo set to false, increment-ing defaults to incrementing by one. If byTwo is true, then the result is incremented by two each time.

Failable Initializers

Remember earlier when I said that the sole reason for the existence of initializers is to ensure that all properties on an instance are set to values before use? Well, it turns out there's a small exception to that statement. I hope I didn't shake your faith in me too much.

In Swift 1.1, shortly after the first edition of this book was printed, the concept of **failable initial-izers** was created. A failable initializer can return nil, rather than a fully instantiated instance of some type, which of course must be wrapped in an optional value. The reason for this is simple, and makes a lot of sense: If a parameter passed in to an initializer cannot guarantee a successful initialization, or the initializer depends on something else that may have failed, then nil is returned.

To define a failable initializer, you simply add either the ! or the ? characters after the word init, but before the parentheses of your initializer. This indicates to Swift that you can return nil if you cannot successfully initialize your instance. Unless there is good reason to use the implicitly unwrapped optional failure indicator, my suggestion is to use the ? character to be more explicit about the opportunity for failure. Implicitly unwrapped optionals are still optionals and can cause your app to crash at runtime if they are accessed at runtime while nil.

A perfect example of this is with creating an enum instance using the rawValue initializer that we saw in Hour 12. If the input argument to the initializer is not valid or doesn't match any of the enum cases, the enum will return nil. Listing 13.8 illustrates creating our own failable initializer.

LISTING 13.8 Using Failable Initializers

```
enum AppleWatch : String {
    case Large = "42 mm", Small = "38 mm"

    init?(watchSize: String) {
        if watchSize == "38 mm" {
            self = .Small
```

```
        } else if watchSize == "42 mm" {
            self = .Large
        } else {
            return nil
        }
    }
}

let goodWatch = AppleWatch(watchSize: "42 mm")   // displays ".Large"
let badWatch = AppleWatch(watchSize: "40 mm")    // displays "nil"
```

As you can see in Listing 13.8, only when you need to fail do you use a `return` statement in an initializer. If you have enough information to successfully create an instance, simply set the properties (or `self`, in this enum's example) of the instance without the need for a `return` statement.

When creating an instance of a type that uses failable initializers, wrapping the creation inside an `if let` statement might serve you best. This way you can do the assignment and check it for `nil`, all in one statement, and then execute code you need if the initialization succeeds.

Advanced Initialization

Now that you have a pretty good foundational understanding of the basics of initializers, it's time to discuss some rules and patterns around initialization in Swift.

Initialization Delegation

Initializers of all types can use something called **delegation**, but the rules and methods of delegating initialization are slightly different for structure types and class types. To begin, we discuss delegation in terms of structs and enums.

NOTE

Initializing Enums

As we know, enums in Swift are value types just like structs. This means that, for the most part, the same concepts should apply to enums as to structs. With that being said, examples in this book, when comparing value types and reference types, largely, but not always, use a struct-versus-class example, because enums and structs behave so similarly in Swift.

What Is Initialization Delegation?

Initialization delegation is the process of a particular initializer within a type partially completing initialization and then passing the remaining initialization responsibility to another initializer.

Delegating Initialization with Structures

In value types like structs and enums, you can only delegate across, meaning to another initializer in the same structure. This should make sense, since structs and enums can neither inherit nor be inherited from, so it should stand to reason that initializers can only delegate across within the same structure. Figure 13.3 shows a visualization of this, and then Listing 13.9 shows this written out in Swift code.

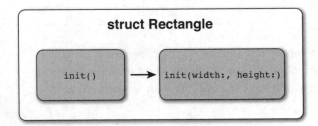

FIGURE 13.3
Diagram of initialization delegation for the Rectangle struct.

In Figure 13.3, the `init()` method points to the `init(width:, height:)` method. That may seem fuzzy to you for now, but examine Listing 13.9 to see how this is written in code.

LISTING 13.9   Initialization Delegation for Structs

```
01:  struct Rectangle {
02:      var width: Double
03:      var height: Double
04:      init(width: Double, height: Double) {
05:          self.width = width
06:          self.height = height
07:      }
08:      init() {
09:          self.init(width: 1.0, height: 2.0)
10:      }
11:  }
12:  print(Rectangle(width: 4.0, height: 6.0))  // displays "Rectangle(width:
   ➥4.0, height: 6.0)"
13:  print(Rectangle())          // displays "Rectangle(width: 1.0, height: 2.0)"
```

Now the arrow pointing from `init()` to `init(width:, height:)` in Figure 13.3 should be clearer. Our `init()` method calls another initializer inside the same struct, `init(width:, height:)`. In other words, the `init()` method delegates the initialization responsibility to the `init(width:, height:)` method. You do not have to structure your initializers this way, but doing so helps keep your code clean and readable, as well as adhering to the Don't Repeat Yourself (DRY) principle for writing code.

CAUTION

Only Call `self.init()` from Inside Initializers

Keep in mind that you can only call `self.init()` (or any other initializer) from within an initializer, and not from anywhere else inside the structure or class. This is for safety and keeps you from re-initializing an instance, as it may be in use and have user data in it already.

Class Initialization Delegation

Classes can delegate the responsibilities of initialization slightly differently than structures can. In addition to delegating across, classes can also delegate up the inheritance chain. This is because classes can inherit from other classes, which means that a subclass inherits the properties and methods of a superclass, and thus all stored properties of the superclass *must* be initialized before use, as well as those in the subclass itself. Because of this, it is important to cover some preliminary vocabulary first.

Initializer Definitions

A **designated initializer** is the primary initializer of the class. The ultimate responsibility of initializing all property values and calling the appropriate superclass designated initializer belongs to the designated initializer. Every class must have at least one, even if it is inferred or inherited, and must be called at most once to properly instantiate the instance. A designated initializer has no special syntax to indicate it is a designated initializer.

A **convenience initializer** is a secondary initializer in a class and is not required like a designated initializer is. A convenience initializer can be used to set some sensible default values, or set properties from arguments passed in to it, by passing them along to the designated initializer or setting them once another initializer has returned execution to the convenience initializer. Convenience initializers are sometimes much nicer to use to create an instance when default values will suffice or if it can reduce code while still providing clear intent. Convenience initializers prefix the `init` method with the `convenience` keyword. Many Objective-C class methods (sometimes called "factory methods") from Cocoa and Cocoa Touch were created as convenience initializers in Swift. One such example is creating an image with `UIImage`. In Objective-C, you could use `[UIImage imageNamed:@"foo"]`, but in Swift, you can use the convenience initializer `UIImage(named: "foo")`.

An **inherited initializer** is an initializer method that gets inherited from the superclass. This can be called directly from the subclass using the `self` keyword rather than `super`. However, it often is treated like a convenience initializer in a subclass due to the subclass having slightly different behavior or needs than its superclass, thus requiring a more custom designated initializer.

Initializer chaining is the process of creating relationships between initializers, whether inherited, convenience, or designated initializers.

The Rules of Initialization Chaining

Apple suggests several rules around initialization chaining, which can be summarized as follows:

▶ Designated initializers must always delegate up to their immediate superclass, if one exists.

▶ Convenience initializers must always delegate across, to either another convenience initializer or designated initializer, in the same class.

NOTE

Full List of Rules, Safety Checks, and Phases for Initialization

The Swift language has safety in mind always, as it is one of the primary cornerstones of the language. Apple maintains a full list of the three rules of initialization chaining, four safety checks initializers must pass, and two phases of initialization that occur before an instance can be used. This information can all be referenced in Apple's iBook *The Swift Programming Language*. For our purposes in this book, we cover key concepts to initialization and delegation that adhere to these guidelines, although we may not take the extensive amount of time to cover each of them in detail.

The Initialization Process

Let's examine what happens when we create an initializer chain with a class hierarchy. We start out with Shape as our base class with one initializer, which is also its designated initializer. Then we subclass that with a class called Rectangle, with a designated initializer and a convenience initializer. After that, we subclass Rectangle with a class called Square, also with a designated initializer and convenience initializer.

Let's look at the diagram of how this would look in Figure 13.4, and then we write the code to show how this looks in practice.

In Figure 13.4, we can see the class hierarchy of Shape => Rectangle => Square. Each blue block (or lighter-colored gray if you are looking at a black and white copy) is a designated initializer for that class, and each red block (or darker gray) is a convenience initializer for that class. If we were to declare an instance of Square using the convenience initializer, our code would call Square's init() method, which delegates to Square's designated initializer, init(length:). Then Square's designated initializer delegates up to Rectangle's designated initializer, which performs steps relevant to the Rectangle class. Then Rectangle's designated initializer delegates up to Shape's designated initializer, which performs steps relevant to the Shape class. All these steps are in *phase one* of initialization.

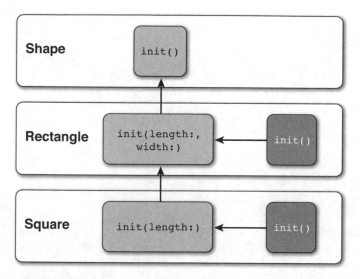

FIGURE 13.4
The diagram illustrating the inheritance chain, as well as initialization chain for initialization delegation.

Phase two of initialization begins on the way back down the initialization chain. After the Shape class's designated initializer finishes, execution returns to the point after which it was called, which is in Rectangle's designated initializer. Any code after the call to Shape's designated initializer is then executed, and control returns to the point after which Rectangle's designated initializer was called. This continues through to the last initializer, at which point the instance is then fully initialized and able to be used.

Now, let's take a look at implementing this in code, in the following Try It Yourself section.

Implement Initialization Chaining

Create the class hierarchy and initialization chain previously discussed.

1. Open Xcode and create a new playground. Either a Mac or iOS playground works. Clear the contents of the playground.

2. Create a Shape base class, provide a property called numberOfSides of type Int, and inside the class's designated initializer, set numberOfSides to 0. Create a description() method, too, which each subclass overrides.

```
class Shape {
    var numberOfSides: Int
```

```
init() {
    numberOfSides = 0
}
func description() -> String { return "I am a shape with no sides." }
}
```

3. Create a `Rectangle` class that inherits from `Shape`. Create a property of type `Int` for the length and another for the width.

```
class Rectangle: Shape {
    var length: Int
    var width: Int
}
```

4. Inside the `Rectangle` class, after the `width` definition, create a designated initializer for `Rectangle` that takes length and width parameters of type `Int`. Set the class's `length` and `width` properties to the length and width parameter values first and then call `super.init()`, since a designated initializer must always call its immediate superclass's designated initializer. After the call to `super.init()`, set `numberOfSides` equal to 4.

```
init(length: Int, width: Int) {
    self.length = length
    self.width = width
    super.init()
    numberOfSides = 4
}
```

5. Create a convenience initializer called `init()`, which calls `self.init(length:, width:)`. Even though this is a convenience initializer on `Rectangle`, it must be overridden because the superclass's designated initializer has the same name, `init()`. Then set `numberOfSides` to 0, because technically a rectangle with no length or width has no sides.

```
override convenience init() {
    self.init(length: 0, width: 0)
    numberOfSides = 0
}
```

6. The `Rectangle` initializers are created now, so override the `description()` method to show the values of the current instance where we can verify our initializers worked properly.

```
override func description() -> String {
    return "I am a rectangle with \(numberOfSides) sides,
 ➥\(length)x\(width), area: \(length * width)"
}
```

7. That's all for the `Rectangle` class. Next, create a `Square` class that inherits from `Rectangle`.

```
class Square: Rectangle {
}
```

8. Inside the `Square` class, create a designated initializer that takes a length parameter of type `Int`. The initializer only needs to call `super.init(length:, width:)`. Calling `super.init(length:, width:)` sets the `length` and also `numberOfSides` properties, so we don't need to repeat setting those properties inside `Square`.

```
init(length: Int) {
    super.init(length: length, width: length)
}
```

9. Create a convenience initializer that calls our designated initializer. Note that this `init()` method does not need to be prefixed with the `override` keyword because the super-class's `init()` method is not a designated initializer. Then set `numberOfSides` to 0, again because a square with zero length and width has no sides.

```
convenience init() {
    self.init(length: 0)
    numberOfSides = 0
}
```

10. That's all for the `Square` initializers, so override the `description()` method to show the values of the current instance to verify our initializers worked properly.

```
override func description() -> String {
    return "I'm a square with \(numberOfSides) sides,
 ➡\(length)x\(length), area: \(length * length)"
}
```

11. Our classes are done. Create two instances of `Square`, one using the designated initializer and one using the convenience initializer. Call the `description()` method on both instances to view their properties after initialization.

```
let square = Square()
square.description()    // "I'm a square with 0 sides, 0x0, area: 0"
let square2 = Square(length: 5)
square2.description()    // "I'm a square with 4 sides, 5x5, area: 25"
```

12. Create two instances of the `Rectangle` class, one using the designated initializer and one using the convenience initializer. Call the `description()` method on both instances to view their properties after initialization.

```
let rectangle = Rectangle()
rectangle.description()    // "I'm a rectangle with 0 sides, 0x0, area: 0"
let rectangle2 = Rectangle(length: 3, width: 4)
rectangle2.description()    // "I'm a rectangle with 4 sides, 3x4, area: 12"
```

Once you've finished the Try It Yourself section, your code and results should look like those in Figure 13.5.

```
     ● ● ●                    Ready | Today at 9:53 PM              ☰ ⊘ ↩  ☐ ▭ ☐

     ⊞ | ‹ › | ▣ Ch13 Initialization Delegation TIY 2
 1   class Shape {
 2       var numberOfSides: Int
 3       init() {
 4           numberOfSides = 0
 5       }
 6       func description() -> String { return "I am a shape with no sides." }
 7   }
 8
 9   class Rectangle: Shape {
10       var width: Int
11       var length: Int
12       init(length: Int, width: Int) {
13           self.width = width
14           self.length = length
15           super.init()
16           numberOfSides = 4
17       }
18       override convenience init() {
19           self.init(length: 0, width: 0)
20           numberOfSides = 0
21       }
22       override func description() -> String {
23           return "I'm a rectangle with \(numberOfSides) sides, \(length)x\(width), area:   (2 times)
             \(length * width)"
24       }
25   }
26
27   class Square : Rectangle {
28       init(length: Int) {
29           super.init(length: length, width: length)
30       }
31       convenience init() {
32           self.init(length: 0)
33           numberOfSides = 0
34       }
35       override func description() -> String {
36           return "I'm a square with \(numberOfSides) sides, \(length)x\(length), area: \   (2 times)
             (length * length)"
37       }
38   }
39
40   let square = Square()                                           Square
41   square.description()                                            "I'm a square with 0 sides, 0x0, area: 0"
42
43   let square2 = Square(length: 5)                                 Square
44   square2.description()                                           "I'm a square with 4 sides, 5x5, area: 25"
45
46   let rectangle = Rectangle()                                     Rectangle
47   rectangle.description()                                         "I'm a rectangle with 0 sides, 0x0, area: 0"
48
49   let rectangle2 = Rectangle(length: 3, width: 4)                 Rectangle
50   rectangle2.description()                                        "I'm a rectangle with 4 sides, 3x4, area: 12"
51
     ⬚                                                            ⎻ 30 sec ⁺
```

FIGURE 13.5
The completed Try It Yourself section implementing class initialization delegation.

There are a few key points of note in this example. First, notice how the initialization delegation takes place. Creating an instance of Square with the convenience initializer sets all the values in the class instance to zero for us; all we need to do is instantiate it by calling Square(). This calls the same class's designated initializer, which then sets property values and calls its superclass's designated initializer. This repeats until initialization hits the top of the class hierarchy, where it then traverses back down to resume execution.

Notice that when the second phase of initialization (the coming back down the hierarchy) is executing, numberOfSides gets assigned the value 4. Then down in Square, numberOfSides gets assigned back to zero because we used the convenience initializer. That may not be the most efficient method for real-world apps, but I did it this way to make a point; execution resumes after the call to super.init() finishes in the Rectangle designated initializer, which means numberOfSides = 4 gets executed before resuming execution in Square's designated initializer.

You see, when your initializers call another initializer, execution of the current initializer halts until the call to the other initializer returns; then execution resumes. Throughout this example, this happens several times, which ultimately produces our properly instantiated instances. Keep this hierarchy and structure in mind when you are developing apps and planning how your instances should get initialized.

The second thing to note is that `Rectangle`'s `init()` is defined with the `override` convenience modifiers, but `Square`'s `init()` is defined with just the `convenience` modifier keyword. This is because if you are creating an initializer in a subclass with the same name as the superclass's designated initializer, you *must* override it, even if the subclass is using it as a convenience initializer. If the initializer exists in the superclass but is not a designated initializer, the subclass can implement its own version but technically is not overriding it, because convenience initializers cannot call initializers in their superclass.

Summary

The topic of initializers is deceivingly large. What seems like a topic to flippantly say "Yeah, okay, hurry up and initialize my data, because I need to use it!" about turns out to be incredibly deep, as you learned if you made it through this hour. Initializers are important, especially with Swift's requirement for safety. Initialization ensures that instances are appropriately assigned values, whether provided or defaults, before being used. This ensures you'll never get returned an instance that has garbage in it or even `nil` for a non-optional type.

You learned about initialization for structs, enums, and classes, and the similarities and differences therein. Structs and enums can call or delegate to initializers within the same structure, whereas classes can not only delegate across but must also delegate up to their superclass's designated initializer, if one exists. Structs also receive memberwise initializers by default, based on the properties defined within it. You also learned that external parameter names are provided by default, the same as with internal parameter names, or you can hide them by adding an underscore and a space before the parameter name.

Next, you learned about using default initializer values, which are great for allowing callers of your initializer to omit certain parameters if they can be set to a sensible default value. After that, you also learned about failable initializers, how to create them, and how to handle creating instances that use failable initializers.

You also learned about designated initializers, convenience initializers, and inherited initializers, and the rules each one must follow. When using these initializers, you learned what happens to control flow of our apps and how to gauge when to initialize properties of the current class or set properties of a superclass.

The best part of this all is that Xcode can really help you with meaningful messages if you are ever stuck or unsure which initializer is the designated initializer, which should be overridden or not, which should be a convenience initializer, and so on. By doing the examples in this hour, you should have a much clearer understanding of how initializers can help make setting up your instances easier and more efficient.

Q&A

Q. Can I have default values assigned where I declare my properties and still use an initializer to set those properties?

A. You certainly can. As long as each stored property has been assigned a value when class initialization is finished, you won't get an error.

Q. Can a class have more than one designated initializer?

A. Yes, as long as the method signatures are different, a class can have as many designated initializers as you want. Because subclasses can only call designated initializers in super-classes, this can be useful when you want subclasses to have more than one way to initialize your class.

Q. If I'm creating a subclass, when should I call `super.init()` in my initializer?

A. You can only call an initializer in a superclass after you have fully initialized your own stored properties. This is to prevent your superclass from accidentally trying to access a property that has not been initialized and thereby causing an error. Consider the case in which you have overridden a method so that it changes the value of a stored property introduced in your subclass. If `super.init()` calls this overridden method, it invokes the subclass's version instead of its own and tries to set a property that hasn't been initialized yet, which would cause an error.

Q. Are initializers inherited from a parent class?

A. If you provide default values for every stored property in your class and provide no initializers, your class will inherit its superclass's initializers. Otherwise, you will not inherit any initializers and you will have to provide your own.

Workshop

The workshop contains quiz questions and exercises to help you solidify your understanding of the material covered. Try to answer all questions before looking at the answers that follow.

Quiz

1. If you write a custom initializer for a struct, is the default memberwise initializer still available to you?

2. Do you have to use external names for all initializer parameters?

3. What's wrong with the following code?

```
class QuizClass {
  var x: Int
```

```
    init(x: Int) {
      self.x = x
    }

    init() {
      self.init(x: 4)
    }
  }
```

4. Can a convenience initializer call another convenience initializer in the same class?

Answers

1. No, the struct's default memberwise initializer is no longer available, but you can write an initializer that behaves like the default if you want.

2. No. By default, Swift requires that external names be used when calling initializers, but you can override this behavior by explicitly setting the external name to underscore (_).

3. A designated initializer cannot call another designated initializer. The initializer that takes no parameters should be marked with the `convenience` keyword.

4. Yes, convenience initializers can call other convenience initializers in the same class as long as a designated initializer is the last initializer called for the class.

Exercise

Create a new OS X playground. See if you can create a class to store some information about triangles. Create a Triangle class with properties to store the length of each side. Triangles are called scalene when all three sides are of different lengths, isosceles when two sides have the same length, or equilateral when all three sides have the same length.

Create an initializer for your class that takes three arguments and properly sets the class properties. Next, create a second initializer to use when your triangle is equilateral. Remember that all three sides will be the same length, so this method should only take one argument, but should still set all three properties. Try writing this initializer as a designated initializer first and then convert it to a convenience initializer.

Finally, we want an initializer for isosceles triangles that takes two arguments. Think about how you should set up the external names for your parameters to make it clear which value will be used for two sides.

Consider other ways you might solve this problem. Could you use subclasses of Triangle to represent isosceles and equilateral triangles instead of using a single class with multiple initializers? Was setting up the isosceles initializer a good idea, or does it just confuse the class? Would the answers to these questions change if you were working on a larger, more complex program? If so, how?

HOUR 14
Digging Deeper with Properties

What You'll Learn in This Hour:

▶ How to use stored properties and computed properties

▶ What lazy properties are and how to use them

▶ How to customize getters and setters

▶ How to observe changes in properties

▶ How to override getters, setters, and observers

Throughout this book, you have been using properties inside classes and structs without yet learning how they are implemented. That is the job of this hour; we cover the basics of properties for storing data in or providing data from instances, observing changes and taking actions based on change, and more. We also cover properties from an instance perspective, as well as a type perspective. Properties provide a great benefit to classes, structs, and enums, so let's get started and learn how to take advantage of properties in Swift.

Properties are a way to associate values with a particular instance of a class, struct, or enum. Each instance has its own properties, relative to the instance in which they are stored. A quick analogy for this is that we are all humans, and we (for the most part) have similar attributes but just different values for those attributes. We all have a height. I am 6'5", but you may be a different height. I have brown hair, but yours may be black, blonde, red, some other color, or none. Humans share a lot of attributes, but the values of those attributes may be different. That is how properties in Swift are handled, too. You can designate properties in a class, struct, or enum that you are creating, and each instance will have its own values for its properties.

There are two categories of properties in Swift: **stored properties** and **computed properties**. Let's take a look at the differences between them now.

Stored Properties

Stored properties in Swift do just as the name suggests: store values as constants or variables in a specified instance. These properties remain as part of the instance until the instance is deallocated from memory. Stored properties can belong to structs and classes but not enums.

As you are familiar with safety in Swift, you know that properties must be initialized to some value before use. You can set values for stored properties during definition or inside an initializer. If your property is a constant (defined with the `let` introducer), your property cannot change after it has been initialized. But if your properties need to change, use the `var` introducer. Stored properties of the same type and same mutability can be declared on the same line, separated by commas, even with default values.

Stored properties can also be optional, defined with the question mark after the type name. This enables data to be represented in an instance that is not yet known upon instantiation or initialization. If not initialized, optionals contain `nil`.

The code in Listing 14.1 shows an example of declaring several types of stored properties in a sample struct.

LISTING 14.1   **Declaring Stored Properties**

```
struct Square {
    var length = 0.0, width = 0.0
    var name: String?
}
```

Instance Variables

If you are coming from Objective-C, it has **instance variables** that are the backing value to stored properties. The idea is that you have an instance variable that is of a certain type, and it is what stores values in your instances. On top of that, Objective-C has properties (like we know them in Swift) that provide a layer of abstraction on top of instance variables. Objective-C properties provide safety for instance variables, plus they give clues to the compiler (that you must declare) as to how it should handle memory for that particular instance variable. They also enable you to create custom accessors to assist with getting or setting a property's instance variable. The widely accepted practice was to label the instance variable with a prefixed underscore to the property name, so that you could identify the instance variable in code apart from the property.

While Objective-C properties are great, they don't prevent you, the developer, from directly accessing the backing instance variable, which could prove to be unsafe in some cases during execution.

Swift does not allow access to a property's backing store for safety reasons. To enable you to customize a property's behavior or observe changes to it, Swift provides several methods for that, which we discuss later in this hour.

Lazy Stored Properties

Another type of stored property in Swift is called a **lazy stored property**. A lazy stored property, or just a lazy property for short, is a property of a struct or class that is known to have a value when it is needed but won't actually initialize itself until it is first called or accessed. This is useful for situations where you may have a property that has an expensive operation such as loading data from a file on disk, creating or retrieving a lot of data after a particular button is tapped or clicked in an app, or making a lengthy network request, and you don't want this processing happening at the time of initialization.

To define a property as lazy, simply add the `lazy` keyword in front of the var introducer. The lazy property must be a `var` since it may be called after initialization, and all constants must not change after initialization. A lazy property can be assigned an instance of another class, struct, or enum. Listing 14.2 illustrates an example of a lazy stored property.

LISTING 14.2 Lazy Stored Properties

```
01:  class SomeClassWithExpensiveOperation {
02:      func doSomeHeavyLifting() -> [String : String] {
03:          var aDictionary: [String : String] = [:]
04:          // lift heavy things and assign to aDictionary
05:          aDictionary["Test key"] = "Test Value"
06:          return aDictionary
07:  }
08:
09:  class SomeClassWithLazyVar {
10:      lazy var dataFromNetwork = SomeClassWithExpensiveOperation()
11:  }
12:
13:  let someClass = SomeClassWithLazyVar()              // nothing yet...
14:  someClass.dataFromNetwork.doSomeHeavyLifting()  // displays
   ➥["Test Key" : "Test Value"]
```

The example in Listing 14.2 uses a lazy property in the `SomeClassWithLazyVar` class, and it is defined on line 10. Line 13 declares and initializes an instance of our class, but the `dataFromNetwork` property is not initialized until we access it on line 14, because it is lazy. Since the method we call, `doSomeHeavyLifting()`, returns an instance of type `[String : String]`, we see the resulting dictionary in the results pane of a playground.

Lazy properties can also be assigned a closure instead of an instance of a class or struct. The closure can have whatever code may take a substantial amount of time or processing power. Then after the closing curly brace, you must add open- and closed-parentheses, which executes the closure. Remember, closures are just unnamed functions, and executing a function requires the parentheses to call it.

Listing 14.2 could be rewritten to move the heavy lifting tasks from the
SomeClassWithExpensiveOperation class to inside the dataFromNetwork
lazy property as a closure. Let's see how that's done in Listing 14.3.

LISTING 14.3 Using Closures with Lazy Stored Properties

```
01:  class SomeClassWithLazyVar {
02:      lazy var dataFromNetwork: [String : String] = {
03:          var aDictionary: [String : String] = [:]
04:          // lift heavy things and assign to aDictionary
05:          aDictionary["Test key"] = "Test Value"
06:          return aDictionary
07:      }()
08:  }
09:
10:  let someClass = SomeClassWithLazyVar()
11:  someClass.dataFromNetwork                  // displays ["Test Key" :
   ➥"Test Value"]
```

In the preceding example, on line 2, we define the dataFromNetwork to be lazy as was done
in Listing 14.2, but then we assign a closure rather than another class instance. The code that
once was executed as part of another class is now inside the closure on lines 3 through 6.
Line 7 ends the closure and appends the parentheses to execute the closure once the lazy
property is accessed.

Now that we have done this, it is interesting to note the results in lines 10 and 11. On line 10,
we declare someClass and assign it to an instance of SomeClassWithLazyVar and initialize it.
But the results pane reads SomeClassWithLazyVar. Why is that? Swift playgrounds show the
type name of a variable created, regardless of its properties, rather than a dictionary-esque key-
value pair representation of the instance created before Swift 2. Once we access the lazy property
dataFromNetwork on line 11, the closure executes, and we now have data.

Using a lazy property with a closure reduces the number of lines of code we need, and also
removes a class, thus removing potential places where we could introduce bugs. Doing more
with fewer lines of code is always a great feeling!

Computed Properties

The concept of stored properties is easily understood: They simply store values related to the
instance to which they belong. Another type of property in Swift is called a **computed property**.
Computed properties do not actually store any value. Rather, they return a calculated value
each time they are called. Also, unlike stored properties, computed properties can belong to not
only structs and classes but also enums. Computed properties cannot be declared with the lazy
modifier—that would result in a compiler error.

There is no difference in the way you access a stored property or a computed property. Both use dot syntax, and Swift's compiler analyzes when you are retrieving data or assigning data and calls the respective getter or setter. Let's look at property accessors now.

Property Accessors

Computed properties enable you to provide a **getter** method to retrieve data, and optionally you can provide a **setter** method to set values of other properties indirectly. These are called **property accessors**. The property accessors of stored properties are inherently created for you, and you cannot alter them; they are provided by Swift so that you have the capability to get and set data inside the property. Computed properties, however, enable you to customize the behavior of a property.

Getters

A getter is a method that returns a value for a computed property. Getters are denoted with the `get` keyword and a pair of curly braces surrounding the code calculating the return value. If you only provide a getter for your computed property, your computed property is treated as read-only, and no assignment can occur. This is useful for when you have a property that you want to provide to external instances, but you do not want them changing the value. Listing 14.4 shows a struct named `Square`, and we use a computed property to calculate and retrieve the area of the `Square` instance.

LISTING 14.4 Using Getters in Computed Properties

```
01:  struct Square {
02:      var length: Double
03:      var area: Double {
04:          get {
05:              return length * length
06:          }
07:      }
08:  }
09:
10:  let square = Square(length: 4)
11:  square.area                          // displays 16
```

The struct in Listing 14.4 is straightforward, and you already learned everything included, outside of lines 3 through 7. Line 3 introduces the computed read-only property, `area`, of type `Double`. A computed property then has curly braces surrounding the code that will be computed and returned. On line 5, we return the product of `length * length`, which gets returned when the `area` property is called on line 11.

NOTE

Omit `get` Keyword in Read-Only Computed Properties

If you are only providing a getter for your computed property, you can safely omit the `get` keyword and curly braces. The resulting effect would turn lines 3 through 7 into one line, `var area: Double { return length * length }`.

Setters

A setter is a method with which you can set the values of other stored properties, based on the value given to the setter. The syntax for creating a setter is the same as a getter, although the `set` keyword is used, and curly braces surround the setting code. You can designate a name for the new value sent to the computed property by including it inside parentheses after the `set` keyword; otherwise, Swift provides the `newValue` constant for you, which includes the value assigned to the computed property. Either `newValue` or the name of the value you designate can only be used within the setter; otherwise, you get a compiler error.

If you provide a setter, you must provide a getter, and you cannot omit the `get` keyword.

Let's expand our Square example by adding a setter in the following Try It Yourself example.

▼ TRY IT YOURSELF

Provide Custom Setter for `Square` Struct

Take the preceding `Square` struct example and expand it to add a custom setter to alter the `length` property in the `Square` struct.

1. Open Xcode and create a new playground; either iOS or Mac works. Clear the contents of the playground.

2. Import the Foundation framework, as we need the square root function later in this example.

   ```
   import Foundation
   ```

3. Create the `Square` struct and provide a `length` variable property of type `Double`.

   ```
   struct Square {
       var length: Double
   }
   ```

4. Create a computed property named `area`, of type `Double`, and provide the same getter as in Listing 14.3 for returning the area of the square.

   ```
   var area: Double {
       get {
           return length * length
           }
   }
   ```

5. After the getter's closing curly brace, add a setter with the `set` keyword, and inside the setter's curly braces, set the `length` property to equal the square root of the new value.

```
set(newArea) {
    length = sqrt(newArea)
}
```

6. That's all for the struct. Create an instance of `Square` and give it an initial length of 4.

```
var square = Square(length: 4)    // Swift converts the Int 4 to a Double 4.0
```

7. Accessing the `area` property should now return the proper area of the square.

```
square.area      // displays 16
```

8. Now set the area of the square to 25.

```
square.area = 25
```

9. Call the `length` property of the square to ensure that the `length` property changed accordingly.

```
square.length        // displays 5
```

The completed Try It Yourself code and results should look like those in Figure 14.1.

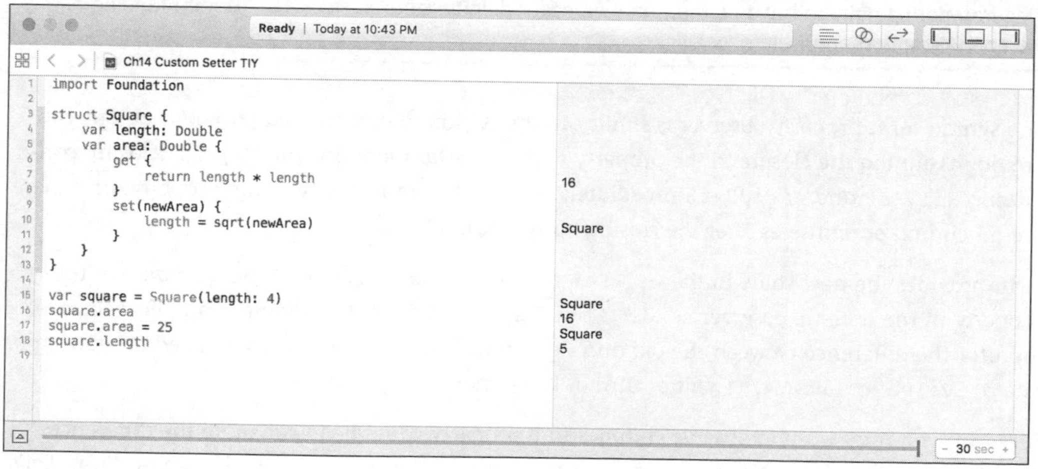

FIGURE 14.1
The completed Try It Yourself example with computed property accessors.

Notice in step 5 of the preceding Try It Yourself example that we explicitly declared the name for the newly assigned value for our setter, with `set(newArea) {...}`. If we had not specified newArea, and just written set {...}, we could use newValue instead. Adding an explicitly named parameter in the setter is more for self-documentation, so your code is clearer about what its intent is, and it is not mandatory to provide a custom name for the value to be set.

Computed properties are great for things that should be properties, yet perform some actions or calculations to derive their data, such as the area property in our example. Other examples would be a description property or a center coordinate of a square on a Cartesian coordinate graph. A function might not make sense for these values, since functions are more geared toward performing a particular action, not returning or setting a simple value.

Property Observers

To observe changes in property values, Swift provides **property observers** that you can customize. There are two ways to observe changes in a property: before the change happens and after the change happens. To respond before the change takes place, use the willSet keyword, followed by a closure encapsulating the code to execute before the property value changes. To respond after the change takes place, use the didSet keyword with a closure, such as willSet.

NOTE

Initialization Does Not Trigger Property Observers

Properties that get their values at definition or via an initializer do not trigger property observers. Observers are only triggered when a property is set after initialization. Observers are not triggered during deinitialization either, and we cover deinitializers in Hour 16, "Understanding Memory Allocation and References."

The syntax for a property observer is similar to the syntax of a computed property, except you are not assigning the closure to the property with an assignment operator (=). The closure containing willSet and/or didSet immediately follows the defined type of the property, and there are no ending parentheses after the closing curly brace.

Swift provides the new value in the willSet observer as newValue, and the old value of the property in the didSet observer as oldValue. This enables you to validate a property change, monitor the difference between the old and new values, or use it however you need for your app. The oldValue and newValue values cannot be changed.

A reason you may want to observe changes in a property could be to calculate the difference between the old and new property values upon a given interval, such as with a speed limit. Let's say we are driving on a highway, and the speed limit is 65 miles per hour (MPH). To be good law-abiding citizens, we are also driving 65 MPH. But suddenly the speed limit decreases to 55 MPH as we enter city limits. We need our app to respond to the change and decrease our speed limit to 55 MPH. Let's look at how this is done in Listing 14.5. If you're following along in a playground, either an iOS or Mac playground will work, as this example does not require any external frameworks.

LISTING 14.5 Observing the Speed Limit

```
01:  class Vehicle {
02:      var speed: Int
03:      var speedLimit: Int {
04:          willSet {
05:              print("Preparing to change speed to \(newValue) MPH")
06:          }
07:          didSet {
08:              let changeSpeed: () -> () = (speed > speedLimit) ? slowdown
➡: speedup
09:              while speed != speedLimit {
10:                  changeSpeed()
11:              }
12:              print("Now I'm driving \(speed) MPH because the speed limit
➡changed to \(speedLimit) MPH from \(oldValue) MPH\n")
13:          }
14:      }
15:      init(speedLimit: Int, speed: Int) {
16.          self.speedLimit = speedLimit
17:          self.speed = speed
18:          print("Speed limit is \(speedLimit) MPH, I'm driving:
➡\(speed) MPH")
19:      }
20:      func speedup() {
21:          print("Speeding up to \(++speed) MPH...")
22:      }
23:      func slowdown() {
24:          print("Slowing down to \(--speed) MPH...")
25:      }
26:  }
27:
28:  let car = Vehicle(speedLimit: 65, speed: 65)
29:  car.speedLimit = 55
30:  car.speedLimit = 70
```

There is a lot happening in the preceding example, so let's break it down. We create a `Vehicle` class, with two properties: `speed` and `speedLimit`. `speed` and `speedLimit` are both stored properties, and `speedLimit` has custom observers in place, as seen by `willSet` and `didSet` on lines 4 and 7, respectively. This is because we want to have some action (either speed up or slow down) occur when the speed limit changes.

The `willSet` observer simply tells the driver to prepare to change speed to the new speed limit and uses `newValue`, which is provided by Swift and holds the new value assigned to speedLimit. The didSet observer creates a variable on line 8 of type () -> (), meaning a function that has no parameters and returns nothing, and then uses a ternary conditional operator to gauge whether the speed should decrease or increase and assign the corresponding function slowDown or speedUp to changeSpeed. Finally, we use a simple while loop to execute while speed is not equal to speedLimit and call the changeSpeed() function inside on line 10, which changes the speed of the car until the driver is driving the speed limit.

Opening the console output viewer in the Assistant Editor by pressing Command+Shift+Y shows that our speed limit started at 65 as well as our speed, since those are the values we provided in our initializer. Changing the speedLimit property on lines 29 and 30 displays the results of our property observer performing the actions needed to change our speed to match the speed limit. The console output should look like Figure 14.2.

```
Speed limit is 65 MPH, I'm driving 65 MPH
Prepare to change speed to 55 MPH
Slowing down to 64 MPH...
Slowing down to 63 MPH...
Slowing down to 62 MPH...
Slowing down to 61 MPH...
Slowing down to 60 MPH...
Slowing down to 59 MPH...
Slowing down to 58 MPH...
Slowing down to 57 MPH...
Slowing down to 56 MPH...
Slowing down to 55 MPH...
Now I'm driving 55 MPH because the speed limit changed to 55 MPH from 65 MPH

Prepare to change speed to 70 MPH
Speeding up to 56 MPH...
Speeding up to 57 MPH...
Speeding up to 58 MPH...
Speeding up to 59 MPH...
Speeding up to 60 MPH...
Speeding up to 61 MPH...
Speeding up to 62 MPH...
Speeding up to 63 MPH...
Speeding up to 64 MPH...
Speeding up to 65 MPH...
Speeding up to 66 MPH...
Speeding up to 67 MPH...
Speeding up to 68 MPH...
Speeding up to 69 MPH...
Speeding up to 70 MPH...
Now I'm driving 70 MPH because the speed limit changed to 70 MPH from 55 MPH
```

FIGURE 14.2
The Assistant Editor console output for the speed limit example in Listing 14.5.

Inheriting and Overriding Accessors

Not only can you create custom accessors in your class, but you can override them in any subclass. If you create a subclass, any source properties can be overridden in the subclass, whether stored or computed. As we saw in Hour 11, "Implementing Class Inheritance," to access anything in the superclass, you use the `super` keyword, followed by the name of the property or method.

Because Swift only needs to know the name of the property and its type, it doesn't care whether the property you are overriding is stored or computed; you can create your own computed version in your subclass. If a property is read-only in the superclass, you can make the property read-write in the subclass, but you cannot make a read-write property in the superclass a read-only property in your subclass.

NOTE

Preventing Override

Remember from Hour 11 that to prevent a property from being overridden in a subclass, you must prefix the definition in the superclass with the `final` keyword.

Overriding accessors only applies to classes and not structs or enums. This is because it requires you to inherit from another class, and structs and enums cannot inherit from other structs and enums.

Let's work through overriding a property in the following Try It Yourself example.

TRY IT YOURSELF ▼

Override a Property and Create Custom Accessors

Inherit a class called `Square` from a base class called `Shape`, and override the `area` property on the superclass with a custom getter and setter relative to the area of a square.

1. Open Xcode and create a new playground; either a Mac or an iOS playground works. Clear the content of the playground.

2. Because we need the square root function, import the Foundation framework at the top of the playground.

```
import Foundation
```

▼

3. Create the base class, called `Shape`, with a property named `area`, assigned to 0.0.

```
class Shape {
    var area = 0.0
}
```

4. Create the subclass, called `Square`, and provide a `length` property of type `Double`. Add an initializer that takes a length parameter of type `Double` and assigns it to our `length` property.

```
class Square: Shape {
    var length: Double
    init(length: Double) {
        self.length = length
    }
}
```

5. Override the `area` property and provide both a getter and setter. Use the default `newValue` keyword in the setter to access the value assigned to the `area` property. Place the overridden property after the `length` property, before the `init` method, to keep the properties all together.

```
override var area: Double {
    get {
        return length * length
    }
    set {
        length = sqrt(newValue)
    }
}
```

6. That's all for the `Square` subclass. After the closing curly brace, create a constant of type `Shape` and check its `area` property's value.

```
let shape = Shape()
shape.area            // displays 0.0
```

7. Create a constant of type `Square` with an initial length of 10. Check the `area` property to get its value; then set the value to 49 and check the length.

```
let square = Square(length: 10)
square.area                       // displays 100.0
square.area = 49
square.length                     // displays 7.0
```

After completing the preceding Try It Yourself example, your code and results should look like those in Figure 14.3.

```
import Foundation

class Shape {
    var area = 0.0
}

class Square: Shape {
    var length: Double
    override var area: Double {
        get {
            return length * length
        }
        set {
            length = sqrt(newValue)
        }
    }
    init(length: Double) {
        self.length = length
    }
}

let shape = Shape()
shape.area

let square = Square(length: 10)
square.area
square.area = 49
square.length
```

FIGURE 14.3
The completed Try It Yourself example code and results for overriding a property with custom accessors.

Inheriting and Overriding Observers

You can also override property observers in Swift, and the process is similar to the process of overriding a property. Supply `willSet` and/or `didSet` closures to your inherited property definition, and the structure is exactly the same as the `speedLimit` property in Listing 14.5; just add the `override` keyword in front of the property definition.

If you are overriding the custom getter and setter already, there is no need to provide `willSet` and `didSet` implementations; you can perform the desired actions inside your setter. You also cannot provide custom observers to inherited constant stored properties or to inherited read-only computed properties.

Listing 14.6 illustrates overriding a property that has property observers in it and adding additional property observers in the subclass. When a subclass and its superclass both provide property observers for a property, both observers are called in a chaining fashion much like how initialization occurs; the subclass's `willSet` observer is called and then the superclass's `willSet` observer is called. The property value gets changed, since technically it exists in the superclass. Then the superclass's `didSet` observer is called and then back down the chain the subclass's `didSet` observer is called. It is important to understand this concept so you understand what is happening to properties and you know where to look if you are noticing unexpected behavior when customizing a subclass's property observers.

Extra `print(...)` have been added to the `Vehicle` class to give you visual feedback in the console when different observers are called. If you are following along in your own playground, you can use either a Mac or an iOS playground.

LISTING 14.6 Overriding Property Observers

```
01:  class Vehicle {
02:      var speed: Int
03:      var speedLimit: Int {
04:          willSet {
05:              print("willSet for Vehicle. Preparing to change speed
   ➥ to \(newValue) MPH")
06:          }
07:          didSet {
08:              print("didSet for Vehicle.")
09:              let changeSpeed: () -> () = (speed > speedLimit) ? slowdown
   ➥: speedup
10:              while speed != speedLimit {
11:                  print("Increasing by 1")
12:                  changeSpeed()
13:              }
14:              print("Now I'm driving \(speed) MPH because the speed limit
   ➥changed to \(speedLimit) MPH from \(oldValue) MPH\n")
15:          }
16:      }
17:      init(speedLimit: Int, speed: Int) {...}  // init unchanged from
   ➥Listing 14.5
18:      func speedup() {...}                     // speedup unchanged from
   ➥Listing 14.5
19:      func slowdown() {...}                    // slowdown unchanged from
   ➥Listing 14.5
20:  }
21:
22:  class Porsche : Vehicle {
23:      override var speedLimit: Int {
24:          willSet {
25:              print("willSet for Porsche.")
26:          }
27:          didSet {
28:              print("didSet for Porsche.")
29:              let changeSpeed: () -> () = (speed > speedLimit) ? slowdown
   ➥: speedup
30:              let porscheSpeedLimit = speedLimit + 10
31:              while speed != porscheSpeedLimit {
32:                  print("Increasing by 2 because Porsches are fast.")
33:                  changeSpeed()
34:                  changeSpeed()
35:              }
36:              print("Porsches should always go faster than the speed limit")
37:          }
38:      }
39:  }
40:
```

```
41:   let porsche = Porsche(speedLimit: 65, speed: 65)
42:   porsche.speedLimit = 70
43:   porsche.speed          // displays 80
```

As you can see in the preceding example, our `Porsche` instance increases its speed by 2 on lines 33 and 34. It doesn't happen only by 2, because the superclass's `didSet` observer increments by 1. You need to be aware of this behavior. The `Porsche` instance also adds 10 to the suggested speed limit, because who wants to drive the speed limit in a Porsche? On line 30, we create the temporary constant of a new speed limit, because if we simply set our own `speedLimit` property to `speedLimit += 10`, it would recursively call its property observer infinitely, because setting the value each time would call its own property observers. Finally, we can see the results in the console output in the Assistant Editor by pressing Command+Shift+Y. Figure 14.4 shows the console output for the preceding example.

```
Speed limit is 65 MPH, I'm driving 65 MPH
willSet for Porsche.
willSet for Vehicle. Prepare to change speed to 70 MPH
didSet for Vehicle.
Increasing by 1
Speeding up to 66 MPH...
Increasing by 1
Speeding up to 67 MPH...
Increasing by 1
Speeding up to 68 MPH...
Increasing by 1
Speeding up to 69 MPH...
Increasing by 1
Speeding up to 70 MPH...
Now I'm driving 70 MPH because the speed limit changed to 70 MPH from 65 MPH

didSet for Porsche.
Increasing by 2 because Porsches are fast
Speeding up to 71 MPH...
Speeding up to 72 MPH...
Increasing by 2 because Porsches are fast
Speeding up to 73 MPH...
Speeding up to 74 MPH...
Increasing by 2 because Porsches are fast
Speeding up to 75 MPH...
Speeding up to 76 MPH...
Increasing by 2 because Porsches are fast
Speeding up to 77 MPH...
Speeding up to 78 MPH...
Increasing by 2 because Porsches are fast
Speeding up to 79 MPH...
Speeding up to 80 MPH...
Porsches should always go faster than the speed limit.
```

FIGURE 14.4
The Assistant Editor console output for the Porsche example in Listing 14.6.

Summary

Properties are powerful and flexible constructs in Swift. In this hour, you learned how to define properties with or without initial values, declare lazy properties, and create computed properties. You also learned how to customize behavior when a property is set by creating custom accessors, called getters and setters, as well as observing value changes by providing custom actions before and after a property changes.

Finally, you learned how to override properties, both stored and computed, as well as override observers and the effective chain of observation when a subclass instance's value changes.

In the next hour, we discuss adding type properties and type methods that can function without an instance of a type. We also cover subscripts and more.

Q&A

Q. When would I want to use a lazy property?

A. Lazy properties are useful when you want to delay the calculation or retrieval of a property. Suppose our class provides access to movie reviews from five different sources, but we aren't sure ahead of time whether the user will request all five reviews. Loading them all ahead of time might result in extra network traffic that we didn't actually need. It would be better in this case to only load the information when the user actually requests it and avoid the extra traffic.

Q. If I write my own accessors, when do I have to provide both set and get?

A. If you only provide a get accessor, your computed property is read-only. The only time you have to provide a set is if you are overriding a mutable property. When the property you override is read-write, your overridden property must also be read-write.

Q. Why would I want to explicitly name parameters in my accessors instead of using the default names provided by Swift?

A. Naming your parameters makes your code more readable. It may save you a few keystrokes to use the default `names`, but if it makes it easier for you to understand the flow of your program, it's worth the extra typing. You'll find that you spend much more time getting the logic of your program correct than you do actually typing code, and the extra keystrokes are a small price to pay for more clarity.

Q. How are `willSet` and `didSet` different?

A. Property observer `willSet` is called before your property changes and has a default parameter named `newValue`, where `didSet` is called after your property has been changed and has a default parameter named `oldValue`.

Workshop

The workshop contains quiz questions and exercises to help you solidify your understanding of the material covered. Try to answer all questions before looking at the answers that follow.

Quiz

1. Can constant stored properties be lazy?

2. Of classes, enums, and structs, which can have computed properties?

3. What's wrong with the following code?

```
class QuizClass {
    var xVal: Int = 1
    var x: Int {
        set { xVal = newValue }
    }
}
```

4. If you don't explicitly assign a name to the argument in a setter, what variable name is used by default?

Answers

1. No. All constant properties must have a value assigned at the end of initialization.

2. Classes, enums, and structs can all have computed properties, but only classes and structs can have stored properties.

3. The x property has a setter, but no getter. If a computed property provides a setter, it must also provide a getter.

4. By default, the parameter is named `newValue`.

Exercise

Create a new OS X playground. Create a `Triangle` class with properties to store the length of each side. If you did last hour's exercise, you can use the class you constructed there. Next, add a read-only computed property named `isEquilateral` that checks to see whether all three sides are the same length and returns true if they are and false if they are not.

Next, add observers so that if the length of a side changes and the triangle becomes equilateral, a message is printed to the console.

Add similar read-only properties to check for scalene (all three sides are different lengths) and isosceles (at least two sides have the same length), and then update your observers to watch for these new triangle types.

Adding Advanced Type Functionality

What You'll Learn in This Hour:

▶ How to use type properties and type methods
▶ How to create type aliases
▶ How to create custom subscripts
▶ What is the significance of `Any` and `AnyObject`
▶ How to cast and downcast types

We have discussed types at length over the past several hours, and there are a few smaller but important concepts to combine in this hour. We cover type properties and methods, type aliases, subscripts, and casting types up or down. After this hour is complete, you should feel comfortable in your understanding of types and how important all the different components of types are.

Type Properties and Methods

Let's start this hour with discussing **type properties** and **type methods**. Type properties and methods belong to the type itself, rather than an instance of that type, and can be applicable to all instances of that type.

Type Properties

Properties can belong to a type, and not necessarily an instance of a type. Type properties can come as stored properties or computed properties, and type computed properties can be read-only or read-write. Computed type properties can be overridden by subclasses, much like you saw in Hour 14, "Digging Deeper with Properties."

The syntax for type properties differs slightly between reference types and value types, as well as between stored and computed class properties. Classes prefix a type property with the `class` keyword for computed type properties that can be overridden in a subclass, and use the `static` keyword for both stored type properties and computed type properties that you don't want over-ridden in a subclass. Structs and enums prefix all type properties with the `static` keyword.

Type properties are useful when you want to declare a property that has a value applicable to all instances of a type. For instance, a `Square` struct may have a static property named `numberOfSides`, which is equal to 4, since there will never be greater than or less than four sides to a square. Type properties are also useful if you have a maximum or minimum bound that all instances should not cross, such as music volume levels, bowling scores, and so on.

Listing 15.1 illustrates how to use a type property in a struct. The syntax would be identical if we defined a type property inside a class or an enum.

LISTING 15.1   Type Properties in All Types

```
struct Square {
    static let numberOfSides = 4
}
print("sides of a square: \(Square.numberOfSides)")


enum CardSuits {
    static let description = "The four suits of a deck of cards"

    case Hearts, Diamonds, Spades, Clubs
}
print("suit description: \(CardSuits.description)")


class Pentagon {
    static let numberOfSides = 5
}
print("sides of a pentagon: \(Pentagon.numberOfSides)")
```

Listing 15.1 shows how to use a static constant in a struct, an enum, and a class. Each then prints the value, even without creating an instance of the type. You can integrate type properties and instance properties to be used in an instance of the type, but you cannot access instance properties from any type properties or methods. Take a look at Listing 15.2 for an example that builds on the struct from Listing 15.1, where an instance property accesses a static property.

LISTING 15.2   Accessing Type Properties from Instance Properties

```
01:  struct Square {
02:      static let numberOfSides = 4
03:      var length: Int
04:      var perimeter: Int {
05:          return Square.numberOfSides * length
06:      }
07:  }
```

```
08:
09:   let square = Square(length: 5)
10:   square.perimeter              // displays 20
```

As you can see on line 5 of the preceding example, to access the type property from within an instance property or method, use the `TypeName.typeProperty` style syntax.

Computed Type Properties

The other kind of type property that you can create is a computed type property. Computed type properties are no different than the computed properties you are used to seeing by now, except that they, like stored type properties, belong to the type itself and not any instance of that type.

Structs and enums that use computed type properties use the `static` keyword, whereas classes can have different syntax for different intentions, as mentioned earlier. If you have a computed type property on a class, and you intend for it to be overridden in a subclass, create it with the `class` prefix. If you do not intend for the computed type property to be overridden, use the `static` keyword. The `static` keyword is just like using `class final`, where the word `final` indicates to Swift that the thing you're marking as `final` cannot be overridden in a subclass.

To see the different types of computed properties in action, examine Listing 15.3 to see computed type properties for a struct, a class, and its subclass.

LISTING 15.3 **Computed Type Properties on All Types**

```
struct Square {
    static var corners: Int {
        return 4
    }
}
Square.corners        // displays 4

class Shape {
    static var color: String = "Red"
    class var cornerAngle: Int {
        return 0
    }
    static var desc: String {
        return "shape description"
    }
}
Shape.cornerAngle      // displays 0

class Octogon: Shape {
    override class var cornerAngle: Int {
        return 360 / 8
```

```
    }
}
Octogon.cornerAngle    // displays 45
Octogon.desc           // displays "shape description"
Octogon.color          // displays "Red"
```

The code in Listing 15.3 should be fairly easily recognizable by now to you. Because structs can have no subclass (or sub-struct, really), `static` is the keyword to use for type properties, both stored and computed. With classes, however, notice that we have properties declared with both `class` and `static`. The computed type property declared with the `class` keyword, `cornerAngle`, can be overridden by the `Octogon` class, but the properties declared with `static` cannot. They are still available for use, though, because they get those properties via inheritance.

Type Methods

The structure, syntax, and concept of type methods are not too dissimilar from those of type properties. Type methods, of course, are methods and not properties, but the style of syntax is the same; prefix the definition of a type method with the `static` keyword for a struct or enum, and either the `class` keyword or the `static` keyword for a class type method, depending on whether you want to allow overriding or not, respectively.

A conventional use for type methods is to return an initialized default instance of a particular type, often referred to as a **factory method**. This is common in Apple's Cocoa and Cocoa Touch frameworks. Using type methods for this is useful in that it not only reduces a few lines of code to one single line, but another benefit is that you get returned a properly structured instance of that type. As Swift gains more traction and matures, these factory methods are slowly converting to becoming convenience initializers, rather than type methods.

In type methods, you can use the `self` keyword to reference the type itself. This is in contrast to using the `self` keyword inside an instance method, computed property, or initializer, where the `self` keyword refers to the instance itself. Another feature of type methods is that you do not need to qualify calling another type method from within a type method with the `TypeName.typeMethodName()` syntax. Rather, you can simply call `typeMethodName()` directly.

Take a look at Listing 15.4. In it, we declare a class named `AClass`, with two class methods and an instance method. If you're following along, either a Mac or an iOS playground will do. Once you finish, press Command+Shift+Y to view the console output in the Debug Area to verify your results.

LISTING 15.4   A Class with Type and Instance Methods

```
01:   class AClass {
02:       class func aClassMethod() {
03:           print("I am a class method")
```

```
04:        }
05:        class func bClassMethod() {
06:            aClassMethod()
07:        }
08:        func anInstanceMethod() {
09:            print("anInstanceMethod. Calling bClassMethod().")
10:            AClass.bClassMethod()
11:        }
12:    }
13:
14:    class BClass: AClass {
15:        override class func aClassMethod() {
16:            print("I am an overridden class method in BClass")
17:        }
18:    }
19:
20:    AClass.aClassMethod()          // displays "I am a class method"
21:
22:    let aClass = AClass()
23:    aClass.anInstanceMethod()      // displays "anInstanceMethod. Calling
    ➡bClassMethod()."
                                     //          "I am a class method"
24:
25:    BClass.aClassName          // displays "I am an overridden..."
```

Listing 15.4 shows several points to discuss. There are two class methods, defined on lines 2 and 5, and one instance method defined on line 8. Type methods can be called from outside the class, struct, or enum by using the `TypeName.typeMethodName()` format, such as on line 20, or from within a type method, too. If called from within a type definition, instance methods must call a type method by prefixing the type name and using dot syntax. A type method, though, may call another type method directly any of three different ways:

► Without qualifying the type name, as seen on line 6

► By using `AClass.aClassMethod()`

► By using the `self` keyword with `self.aClassMethod()`

Type methods can alter type properties. Even though type properties do not belong to an instance directly, they can hold state information of a class, struct, or enum. Listing 15.5 illustrates having a static property on a struct and having a static method modifying the static property.

LISTING 15.5 Modifying Type Properties with Type Methods

```
struct Counter {
    static var count = 0
    static func increaseCountByOne() {
        ++count
    }
}

Counter.count                 // displays 0
Counter.increaseCountByOne()
Counter.count                 // displays 1
```

Let's solidify your knowledge of type properties and type methods in this next Try It Yourself section.

▼ TRY IT YOURSELF

Use Type Properties and Type Methods

Create a struct that controls audio volume. Use static properties to set upper and lower volume limits that every instance must adhere to.

1. Open Xcode and create a new playground; either a Mac or iOS playground works. Clear the contents of the playground.

2. Create a struct named `Volume` and initially give it two static constant properties: one named `minVolume` set to 0 and one named `maxVolume` set to 20.

   ```
   struct Volume {
       static let minVolume = 0
       static let maxVolume = 20
   }
   ```

3. Create a stored variable instance property named `volume`, an `Int` set to 0, with an observer after the value has been set to ensure it is not above the max or below the min volume levels. Place this after the two static constant definitions, inside the struct.

   ```
   var volume: Int = 0 {
       didSet {
           if volume > Volume.maxVolume || volume < Volume.minVolume {
               volume = oldValue
           }
       }
   }
   ```

4. Now that we have property validation happening inside the `didSet` property observer, and our `volume` property will never go above `maxVolume` or below `minVolume`, we can set simple methods for increasing or decreasing the `volume` property. Create one for each.

```
mutating func turnItUp() {
    ++volume
}
mutating func turnItDown() {
    --volume
}
```

5. That's all for the struct. Create a new variable instance of the `Volume` struct. Set the `volume` property to 1. Then turn it down to ensure we can adjust our volume properly.

```
var volume = Volume()
volume.volume = 1
volume.turnItDown()
volume.volume          // displays 0
```

6. Call the `turnItDown()` method again on the `volume` instance and ensure the `volume` property remains at 0 and does not equal -1.

```
volume.turnItDown()
volume.volume          // volume.volume should equal 0
```

7. Do the same to test turning up the volume. Set `volume` to 19 and then turn it up. Check to ensure the volume did go up. Then turn it up once more. Did the value change?

```
volume.volume = 19
volume.turnItUp()
volume.volume          // volume.volume should equal 20
volume.turnItUp()
volume.volume          // volume.volume should still equal 20
```

8. Because our struct enables our `volume` property to be set directly, any other part of an app this struct belongs to could set the `volume` value without using `turnItUp()` or `turnItDown()`. But we safeguarded our value with the `didSet` observer. Set `volume` directly to 30 to ensure that the actual stored value does not go above the maximum allowed.

```
volume.volume = 30
volume.volume          // volume.volume should equal 20
```

The completed Try It Yourself example code and results should look like those in Figure 15.1.

```
 1  struct Volume {
 2      static let minVolume = 0
 3      static let maxVolume = 20
 4
 5      var volume: Int = 0 {
 6          didSet {
 7              if volume > Volume.maxVolume || volume < Volume.minVolume {
 8                  volume = oldValue                                          (3 times)
 9              }
10          }
11      }
12
13      mutating func turnItUp() {
14          ++volume                                                          (2 times)
15      }
16      mutating func turnItDown() {
17          --volume                                                          (2 times)
18      }
19  }
20
21  var volume = Volume()                                                     Volume
22  volume.volume = 1                                                         Volume
23  volume.turnItDown()                                                       Volume
24  volume.volume                                                             0
25
26  volume.turnItDown()                                                       Volume
27  volume.volume                                                             0
28
29  volume.volume = 19                                                        Volume
30  volume.turnItUp()                                                         Volume
31  volume.volume                                                             20
32  volume.turnItUp()                                                         Volume
33  volume.volume                                                             20
34
35  volume.volume = 30                                                        Volume
36  volume.volume                                                             20
37
```

FIGURE 15.1
The completed Try It Yourself example of using type methods and properties.

That's enough for type properties and methods. Let's move on and take a look at something called type aliasing.

Type Aliasing

Swift has a concept called **type aliasing**, which means that you can create an alias to an existing type with whatever name you choose. This enables you to use your custom type in a more meaningful manner in your code to provide a clearer intent than with a more generic type name or to provide a shorter name for perhaps something such as a really long type name.

In its simplest form, you use the typealias keyword, followed by the alias you choose, and use the assignment operator (=), and then the type for which you want to create an alias. In the Volume example from the preceding Try It Yourself section, it might have provided a clearer intent if we had set a type alias called VolumeLevel equal to Int. Even though the term VolumeLevel is longer than using Int, it is clearer to anyone reading your code what type the volume property is. Listing 15.6 shows how we could do that, and provides a few examples of type aliasing different types.

LISTING 15.6   Using Type Aliasing

```
typealias VolumeLevel = Int
var volume: VolumeLevel = 0

typealias JSONObject = [String : String]
typealias JSONArray = [JSONObject]
```

In the last two lines of Listing 15.6, we create a type alias JSONObject equal to a dictionary of type [String : String], then another called JSONArray which is an array of JSONObjects. This is very common to do, and you can even use a fast enumeration for-in loop to iterate over each object in the JSONArray object, with something like the following code snippet:

```
for jsonObject in jsonArray { ... }
```

Type aliasing can also be used to better document the type of a function. Sometimes when you are reading through code, function syntax can get a little difficult to decipher. This is where type aliasing can shine. Let's alias a function type and use it in a function parameter in Listing 15.7. Suppose we have a function that receives a function for a completion handler to be executed once our function has finished performing a long process. Our function has one parameter, which is our completion handler, and it is of the type we alias.

LISTING 15.7   Using `typealias` with Functions

```
typealias ArrayCompletion = ([Int]?) -> ()

func downloadLotsOfData(completion: ArrayCompletion) {
    var someData: [Int]?
    // download lots of data
    completion(someData)  // execute the completion handler
}
```

As you can see, type aliasing can be beneficial for maintaining readable and understandable code. Once you know the type that the alias really is, you can read your code more easily like a sentence.

Type Access Control

Access control provides some security around the visibility of certain properties, methods, initializers, or subscripts in classes, structs, and enums. There are three levels of access you can apply to properties, methods, and subscripts in your code: **public**, **private**, and **internal**.

Public access enables your properties, methods, initializers, or subscripts to be accessed and used from anywhere within the module that defines them, or from any external module that imports the module in which the public entity is defined. Public access is often used for elements you want to be visible in the public-facing interface of a framework, as it is the least restrictive. Public access is defined by prefixing the property, method, or subscript with the `public` keyword. The following code snippet illustrates how to declare a class and its instance property as public:

```
public class MyClass {
    public myVar: String = "Hello"
}
```

Private access, denoted with the `private` keyword, restricts visibility to your properties, methods, initializers, or subscripts to only your class, struct, or enum *file*. This means that you can hide implementation from being accessible by other source files in the module or target. This also means that if you declare a second type inside the same .swift file, anything you declare private may still be accessible to that other type, depending on context. The `private` keyword is often used when you declare a helper method that may help a current method with some sort of calculation but shouldn't be visible to instances of that type to use. The following code snippet illustrates how to declare a method as private. Note that if you try this in a playground, you can use `helperMethod()` from an instance, because it is within the same source file.

```
class MyClass {
    private func helperMethod() -> Int {
    // do some calculation and return an Int
    }
    func needSomeHelp() -> String {
        // Doing something, but I need some help
        let myInt = helperMethod()
        return "\(myInt)"
    }
}
```

Internal access, denoted with the optional `internal` keyword, restricts access to any property, method, initializer, or subscript inside a source file to only other source files within the current module. The `internal` keyword is optional because this level of access is the default if no access modifier is declared. For many projects, you may only have one module, so internal access means that any source file elements can access the element declared as internal. All properties, methods, initializers, and subscripts we have used until now have been internal, because we have not declared them to be either public or private, and Swift inferred them to be internal.

Not only can properties, methods, initializers, and subscripts be made public, private, or internal, but so can classes, structs, and enums themselves. The same rules and syntax apply to types as they do to elements inside a type and use the same three access keywords.

Subscripts

Most programming languages provide a way to access elements in an array or dictionary, including Swift, by using something called **subscripts**. A subscript is shorthand for directly accessing or modifying an element at a particular index in an array, dictionary, or collection.

Throughout this book, we have used subscripts, and the concept should be familiar to you by now. Writing `anArray[3]` would return the fourth element in an array, and writing `aDictionary["username"]` would return the value for the "username" key. Likewise, you can use subscripts to modify elements at an index of an array or add or modify elements at a particular key in a dictionary.

Swift enables you to create your own subscripts for any class, struct, or enum you create. This can be useful when you want to create a custom grid, such as for a board game, a quick way to perform a calculation through a particular mathematic equation, or whatever functionality your app needs. The syntax for creating a subscript in Swift is almost identical to defining an instance method or computed property. The only difference is that you use the `subscript` keyword rather than the `func` keyword, and subscripts do not have names. Subscripts take parameters with names and types, and even return a value or values with provided type or types. As with instance methods, subscripts can also receive variadic parameters.

Listing 15.8 illustrates how we can create a subscript to calculate the power of a given number. If we know that we want to cube any number that comes to us, we can create a subscript that returns any number we provide to the power of three. Creating a subscript for this purpose gives the impression of behaving like a pre-populated array of cubes, just without needing to store the actual values.

LISTING 15.8 Creating a Subscript to Cube a Number

```
01:   struct CubeANum {
02:       subscript(num: Int) -> Int {
03:           return num * num * num
04:       }
05:   }
06:
07:   let cubeANum = CubeANum()
08:   cubeANum[2]         // displays 8
09:   cubeANum[5]         // displays 125
```

In Listing 15.8, we declare the subscript on line 2, taking only one parameter of type `Int` and returning an `Int`. Like a computed property, there is an implicit getter, since we are only writing a read-only subscript.

Let's do an example together in the following Try It Yourself section. Suppose the user of your app is a second grade teacher, and he has assigned his class of six students to write a paragraph about their favorite topic. Because the teacher is busy, he can only grade three papers at a time from the stack of papers. Let's create an example of using subscripting to retrieve a particular number of papers from the stack at a time, rather than one at a time. If you are unfamiliar with stacks in computer programming terms, stacks are **LIFO** (last-in-first-out), meaning you can only remove the top item. You **push** items onto a stack to add, and **pop** them off to remove, one at a time.

▼ TRY IT YOURSELF

Use Subscripts to Help a Teacher Grade Papers Faster

Create a stack of papers and use subscripts to allow the teacher to get any number of papers at a time.

1. Open Xcode and create a new playground; either a Mac or iOS playground works. Clear the contents of the playground, as we will not need it.

2. Create a struct named `Paper` to store each student's paper. To keep the example brief, only create `student` and `topic` properties, constants of type `String`.

```
struct Paper {
    let student: String
    let topic: String
}
```

3. Create a class named `StackOfPapers`. Create a variable array of type `[Paper]` and initialize it to an empty array.

```
class StackOfPapers {
    var papers = [Paper]()
}
```

4. Inside the `StackOfPapers` class, after the `papers` definition, create a method named `push` that takes an item of type `Paper` and adds it to the `papers` array.

```
func push(paper: Paper) {
    papers.append(paper)
}
```

5. After the `push` method, create a method named `pop` that takes no parameters but returns an item of type `Paper` that it removed from the end of the `papers` array.

```
func pop() -> Paper {
    return papers.removeLast()
}
```

6. Create the `subscript` method inside the `StackOfPapers` class after the `pop()` method that takes a parameter of type `Int` and returns an array of type `[Paper]`.

```
subscript(number: Int) -> [Paper] {
    var tempPapers = [Paper]()
    for _ in 0..<number {
        tempPapers.append(pop())
    }
    return tempPapers
}
```

7. Create a computed property below the subscript named `count` so we can easily see how many papers are left to grade.

```
var count: Int {
    return papers.count
}
```

8. That's all for the stack. Declare an instance of `StackOfPapers` and add six students and their topics to the stack.

```
let stack = StackOfPapers()
stack.push(Paper(student: "Susie", topic: "Sea Creatures"))
stack.push(Paper(student: "Bobby", topic: "Music"))
stack.push(Paper(student: "Madeline", topic: "Jungle Cats"))
stack.push(Paper(student: "Blake", topic: "Soccer"))
stack.push(Paper(student: "Cole", topic: "Bicycling"))
stack.push(Paper(student: "Marion", topic: "Boating"))
```

9. Call our `count` computed property to ensure there are six papers in the stack. Then grab the top three papers to be graded.

```
stack.count        // should equal 6
stack[3]           // should display three students and topics,
  ➥in reverse order
```

10. Call our `count` property again, to ensure there are three papers left. Grab the next stack of papers to be graded.

```
stack.count        // should equal 3
stack[3]           // should display three more students and topics
```

11. Call our `count` property once more, to ensure it is now 0.

Upon completion, the code and results from the preceding Try It Yourself example should look like those in Figure 15.2.

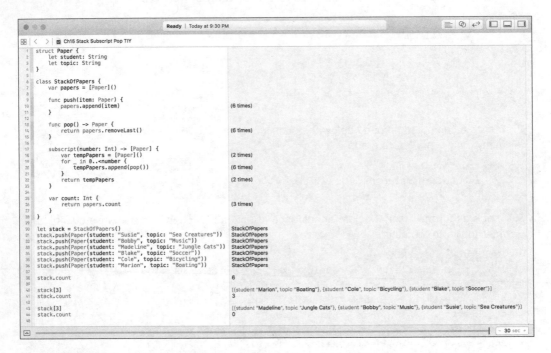

FIGURE 15.2
The completed Try It Yourself section creating a stack with subscripts for grading papers.

Subscript Overloading

Suppose we not only want to return the cubed value of integers but also of floating-point numbers. We can overload subscripts, just like we did with functions in Hour 8, "Using Functions to Perform Actions," with different parameters. Taking the cube example from Listing 15.8, let's re-implement the structure with another subscript that takes a parameter of type `Double` (see Listing 15.9).

LISTING 15.9   Overloading Subscripts

```
01:   struct CubeANum {
02:       subscript(num: Int) -> Int {
03:           return num * num * num
04:       }
05:       subscript(num: Double) -> Double {
06:           return num * num * num
07:       }
```

```
08:    }
09:
10:    let cubeANum = CubeANum()
11:    let dblCube = cubeANum[2.5]                // displays 15.625
12:    let intCube = cubeANum[2]                  // displays 8
```

Listing 15.9 has two subscripts now: one that takes an `Int` and returns an `Int`, and another that takes a `Double` and returns a `Double`. On line 11, we call the subscript that takes a `Double` and returns a `Double` on line 5, because we provided a value of type `Double` inside the subscript, and the results pane displays 15.625. On line 12, we call the subscript that takes an `Int` and returns an `Int`, because we provided a value of type `Int` inside the subscript. Hold down the Option key and click `dblCube` and also `intCube`; notice that `dblCube` is inferred to be `Double` and `intCube` is inferred to be `Int`, so you can easily see that the proper overloaded subscript was called.

NOTE

Don't Repeat Yourself

The Listing 15.9 is functional, but repeating code like that is a sign of poor implementation. These two subscripts do exactly the same thing; they return the parameter provided to the third power. There is a much more succinct and reusable way to express this—by using generics. You learn about generics in Hour 20, "Introducing Generics."

Overriding Subscripts

Subscripts can be overridden as well in a subclass that inherits from a superclass that contains a subscript. The same rules of overriding apply as discussed in previous hours in this book. All you must do is provide the `override` keyword in front of your subscript definition in the subclass. Remember, this can only be done from classes, because structs and enums do not inherit from any other type.

Type Casting and Non-Specific Types

The term **type casting** refers to treating an instance of a particular type as if it were of a different type in its own hierarchy temporarily. Type casting does not actually change the type of the value, since once a value's type is set, Swift does not allow it to be changed for safety reasons.

Determining an Instance's Type

Swift provides an operator called the **type check operator**, denoted with the `is` keyword. Using this operator enables you to determine whether an instance *is* of a particular type or subclass type. If you are an Objective-C programmer, you may be familiar with this concept from using the `isMemberOfClass:` and `isKindOfClass:` methods.

Suppose you have a room full of marching band instruments, and you want to organize and track them. It would be great to know the name of the instrument, the type (brass, woodwind, and so on), and how many keys or valves it has. We could store these items in an array. But arrays in Swift must have an explicit type, and clarinets have traits that trumpets don't, and vice-versa. How can we do this?

Each item has a common trait; it has a name. Take a look at Listing 15.10 for how to build this by creating a common superclass that both `Woodwind` and `Brass` inherit from and adding them to an array. If you are a percussionist or like any other type of instrument better, feel free to substitute to suit your style.

LISTING 15.10   Determining Type of Marching Instruments

```
class Instrument {
    var name: String
    init(name: String) {
        self.name = name
    }
}

class Brass: Instrument {
    let valves: Int
    init(name: String, valves: Int) {
        self.valves = valves
        super.init(name: name)
    }
}

class Woodwind: Instrument {
    let keys: Int
    init(name: String, keys: Int) {
        self.keys = keys
        super.init(name: name)
    }
}

let marchingInstruments = [
    Brass(name: "Trumpet", valves: 3),
    Brass(name: "Trombone", valves: 0),
    Woodwind(name: "Clarinet", keys: 18),
    Woodwind(name: "Alto Sax", keys: 22),
    Brass(name: "Piccolo Trumpet", valves: 4)
]
```

```
var brassCount = 0, woodwindCount = 0

for instrument in marchingInstruments {
    if instrument is Brass {
        ++brassCount
    } else if instrument is Woodwind {
        ++woodwindCount
    }
}

brassCount        // displays 3
woodwindCount     // displays 2
```

Inside the for-in loop in Listing 15.10 is where we use the type checking operator (is). This is sometimes referred to as **introspection**. By checking the type of each instrument, we can come up with how many of each type of instrument is in our room.

Downcasting

Instances in Swift may be of one type, but under the hood they may actually be of a subclass of that type. For instance, if we have a function that takes a parameter of type Instrument, and we pass an argument of type Brass, the parameter inside the function knows the variable is of type Instrument, but under the hood, it is really a Brass instance. We can find this out by using the **type cast operator**, denoted with the as keyword.

The as keyword can be used in one of three ways: first, by just using the as operator; second, by using the optional type cast operator, as?; or third, by using the force type cast operator, as!. The type of conversion you need to perform, **guaranteed conversion** or **forced conversion**, dictates which type of type casting operator to use.

Prior to Swift 1.2, which was released in February of 2015, the as operator performed both guaranteed conversion and forced conversion. The issue with that, however, was that when reading the code, it was not clear whether the conversion would be forced or guaranteed. A guaranteed conversion is one where the success can be verified by the compiler, such as upcasting to a superclass or specifying the type of a literal expression, like let three = 3 as Double. A forced conversion is one where the success cannot be guaranteed by the compiler and may cause a runtime crash. Such a conversion must be handled differently. These changes in Swift 1.2 are unchanged in the current implementation of Swift 2.0.

When using the as! keyword, you are literally forcing the cast, which may fail if the type you are casting to is not in the class hierarchy of the instance's type, or explicitly convertible to the desired type. In situations where you aren't sure whether casting will succeed, use the optional type cast operator, which returns the casted value or nil wrapped in an optional value. This means that you can check for successful casting and unwrapping with if let syntax. The plain as operator should be used in guaranteed success scenarios only, such as upcasting to a known superclass, or in pattern matching in `switch` statements. In `switch` statements, forcing or taking safety precautions with optional binding is not necessary, because if it doesn't match, execution moves on.

Continuing with the preceding marching instrument example, Listing 15.11 illustrates how we could use type casting in a function to extract type-specific information from the parameter passed in. This is a continuation of Listing 15.10, if you are following along. Place the following code at the end of your playground.

LISTING 15.11　Type Casting

```
func displayInstrumentInfo(instrument: Instrument) {
    if let brass = instrument as? Brass {
        print("Brass: \(brass.name). Valves: \(brass.valves)")
    } else if let woodwind = instrument as? Woodwind {
        print("Woodwind: \(woodwind.name). Keys: \(woodwind.keys)")
    }
}

displayInstrumentInfo(marchingInstruments[0])  // displays "Brass:
  ➥Trumpet. Valves: 3"
displayInstrumentInfo(marchingInstruments[2])  // displays "Woodwind: Clarinet.
  ➥Keys: 18"
```

In Listing 15.11, we use the `as?` operator, because we cannot always be sure that we will know whether we received a `Brass` or `Woodwind` instance, or even `Percussion` if we had implemented that.

Using the `as!` operator forcibly downcasts the type in question. As mentioned earlier, this may fail, so only use this operator when you are sure your downcasting will succeed. Many times, the documentation for an API states that a particular type is used, or your code may be structured well enough for the needs of your app, so you can confidently downcast with the `as!` keyword.

Non-Specific Types

Type casting can be useful when working with Cocoa APIs, because much of the framework is built to use a generic type called **id**. id is a pointer to any type of object. This works well in Objective-C, because Objective-C is not a **strongly typed** language, meaning it does not have to explicitly state what type an object should be at compile time.

To work with the Cocoa and Cocoa Touch frameworks when dealing with type id, Swift provides the **Any** and **AnyObject** keywords for non-specific types. The Any keyword refers to an instance of any type, whether reference or value, including function types. The AnyObject keyword refers to an instance of any class type.

When working with JSON (JavaScript Object Notation), you may not always know what each value's type for each key is, so typically JSON either is stored as `AnyObject` or needs to be casted to `AnyObject` first before being downcasted to an array, dictionary, or any other type.

For instance, you could declare an array of type `[Any]` and append values such as 3.14, 7, "car", and so on. You could also declare an array of type `[AnyObject]` and append values such as instances of `Instrument`, `Brass`, `Woodwind`, or even `Square` and `Circle` from examples in previous hours. Be careful when doing this, because this removes Swift's capability to ensure type safety. It is highly suggested that you always downcast when possible to use a safe type.

Summary

This hour contained a lot of information pertaining to types with respect to the additional capabilities enabled in Swift. You learned about type properties and methods, which enable you to access functionality and stored data appropriate for all instances of a type. You also learned about type aliasing, enabling you to create more succinct and readable code, while simplifying the actual writing of code.

Next, you learned about access control and how to determine which source files should have what level of access to your classes, enums, and structs, and even the properties, methods, initializers, and subscripts of those types, too.

Then you learned about subscripts and how you can leverage their shorthand syntax to access property values inside your types easily. Subscripts can be overloaded and even overridden.

Finally, you learned about type casting, type checking, downcasting, and how Swift handles non-specific types with the `Any` and `AnyObject` keywords.

In the next hour, we discuss memory management in Swift. You learn how Swift manages memory and how to manage different reference types.

Q&A

Q. How are type properties and instance properties different?

A. Each instance of a type has its own set of instance properties, but all instances of a type share the same set of type properties. For example, if you create an `Employee` class, each employee has his or her own name. Changing one person's name should not change the name of any other person in the system, so `name` should be an instance variable. But suppose we want our `Employee` class to know how many employees there currently are. Then we might create a static property named `employeeCount` and increase it by one each time someone joins our company and decrease it by one whenever someone leaves our company. Because there is only one `employeeCount` shared by all employees, we only have to update our count in one place.

Q. Do I set a value for stored type properties in `init()` like I do with stored instance properties?

A. Remember that `init()` is called when a new instance of a type is created, but type properties exist before we create the first instance of a given type. This means that unlike stored instance properties, you must always assign a default value to stored type properties. You can still update or change the value of a type property at initialization, but you don't have to.

Q. Can type methods access instance properties?

A. No, they can't. Type methods are not called using an instance of the type, so it would be unclear which instance variables should be used. Additionally, because a type method can be called before any instance is instantiated, there is no guarantee that any instance property will have a value.

Q. If no access level is specified, which level is used by default?

A. Generally, the internal access level is specified. There are a few specific exceptions to this rule, but they are beyond the scope of this book. Refer to Apple's documentation for more information.

Workshop

The workshop contains quiz questions and exercises to help you solidify your understanding of the material covered. Try to answer all questions before looking at the answers that follow.

Quiz

1. Can a type property be computed, or does it have to be stored?
2. Can you define a type with multidimensional subscripts in Swift?

3. What's wrong with the following code?

```
let myArray:[Any] = [1,2,3,4,5]
let myOtherArray = [1,2,3,4,5]
let x = myOtherArray[1] + myArray[2]
```

4. What keywords do you use to define a type parameter for a struct, an enum, and for a class?

Answers

1. Type properties can be either computed or stored.

2. Yes. Subscripts can take any number of parameters.

3. Even though we assigned an array of integers to `myArray`, it is still of type `[Any]`. When we try to add an element of `myArray` to an `Int` in line 3, we get a compiler error. We can fix the code by changing `myArray[2]` to `(myArray[2] as! Int)` at the end of line 3.

4. For structs and enums, use the `static` keyword. For classes, use the `class` keyword if you want to allow a subclass to override, or `static` to prohibit a subclass from overriding.

Exercise

Create a new OS X playground. Many times, a class will contain an array or dictionary that stores the most relevant data in the class, with the rest of class there to support operations on or with the internal array. When this happens, we might want to use subscripts on the class instance to access the array directly. Let's look at an example by modeling a company's employee database for an HR system.

Create an `Employee` class with properties for name (a `String`), job title (a `String`), and employee ID (an `Int`). Next, create a `Company` class that contains an array of `Employee` objects and methods to add and remove employees to the array. Define a computed property for the `Company` class that takes a job title and returns an array of employees who have the matching job title.

Finally, define a subscript on the `Company` class that takes an integer and returns the employee who has the matching employee ID.

Is there anything you might change about this design? For example, could we have made the job title an enum, and how would that change our class?

Understanding Memory Allocation and References

What You'll Learn in This Hour:

▶ How to deinitialize class instances

▶ The basics of Automatic Reference Counting (ARC)

▶ The difference between strong, weak, and unowned references

▶ How to identify and avoid reference cycles

▶ How to create capture lists inside closures

Reference types in Swift, such as classes and closures, have different rules for memory allocation, retention, and disposal than value types. In fact, value types in Swift do not require any extra attention to these concepts at all. Reference types, on the other hand, require us to be mindful of how we are using them in our code. We haven't yet had a need to specifically manage memory settings in Swift, as our examples thus far have been relatively small and self-contained. But when apps get larger, and dependencies on other instances come into play, you must be more mindful of how memory is managed and sometimes tell Swift explicitly how to manage references to instances. In this hour, we cover these concepts, starting with how any instance gets deinitialized and deallocated.

Deinitialization

In Hour 13, "Customizing Initializers of Classes, Structs, and Enums," we discussed initializers, which are called immediately after memory for an instance has been allocated and provide setup instructions for instances of a particular type. **Deinitialization** is the process of cleaning up anything necessary before an instance gets completely deallocated from memory.

Deallocation is not the same as deinitialization. When an instance gets deinitialized, you still have access to the properties inside the instance and can manipulate them as needed before the instance totally goes away. When an instance gets deallocated, however, it is set to `nil` and removed from memory completely. An instance of a reference type gets deallocated from memory when no other instances hold a **strong reference** to it. More about strong references shortly.

To customize a class's deinitializer, use the `deinit` keyword followed by open and closed curly braces, similarly to an `init` method. However, `deinit` takes no parameters. Superclass deinitializers are inherited from an instance's superclass and are executed immediately following the subclass instance's deinitializer method. Swift's **Automatic Reference Counting** (ARC) mechanism calls `deinit` on instances of reference types automatically, when the last strong reference to the instance is removed.

CAUTION

Never Call a Deinitializer Directly

Swift's ARC mechanism calls `deinit` automatically, so you should never call `deinit` directly.

The following code snippet shows the syntax of a `deinit` method:

```
deinit {
    // code goes here, if any, to free up resources or modify properties
  ➥before deallocation
}
```

When a variable or constant reference to a class instance is set to `nil`, and there are no other variables or constants referencing the instance, its **reference count** (sometimes referred to as a **retain count**) is zero and the instance is deallocated from memory. Swift handles this for us, but it is important to understand what is going on. Let's look at an example of this together in the following Try It Yourself section.

When Swift was first launched, Xcode playgrounds did not use ARC in the same way that an actual compiled app or the REPL does, but now you can test memory management in either the REPL or a playground. Let's examine what happens when we initialize and deinitialize a class instance in memory in a playground in the following Try It Yourself section.

▼ TRY IT YOURSELF

Use Initializers and Deinitializers

Use a playground to examine when initializers and deinitializers are called and observe the results.

1. Open Xcode and create a new playground; either a Mac or iOS playground works. Clear the contents of the playground.

2. Create a class named `TestClass` and provide a variable property named `title` of type `String`.

```
class TestClass {
    let title: String
```

3. Provide a basic initializer that sets the `title` property to the title parameter. Print a line to the console here that tells us when we are in the `init` method.

```
init(title: String) {
    self.title = title
    print("\(title) is initialized.")
}
```

4. Provide a deinitializer that just prints a line to the console that tells us when our instance is about to be deallocated. Then end the class with a final curly brace.

```
deinit {
    print("\(title) is being deinitialized.")
}
}
```

5. Create three variables of type `TestClass?` (*optional* `TestClass`). Do not yet assign anything to these instances; they are assigned `nil` by default.

```
var test1: TestClass?
var test2: TestClass?
var test3: TestClass?
```

6. Initialize `test1`, then assign `test2` and `test3` to `test1`. This effectively creates three references to the same instance of `TestClass`.

```
test1 = TestClass(title: "testing")
test2 = test1
test3 = test1
```

7. Assign each reference to `nil`, one at a time. Observe what happens after each assignment and when the actual deinitialization occurs.

```
test1 = nil
test2 = nil
test3 = nil
```

You may be wondering after performing step 7, "Wait, we assigned a new `TestClass` instance to `test1`, so why did nothing happen when we assigned `nil` to `test1`?" Remember that when an instance gets created, it exists in memory somewhere. And because classes are reference types, our variables don't actually hold an instance themselves; they hold a *reference* to the instance in memory. Figure 16.1 shows what essentially happened in step 6.

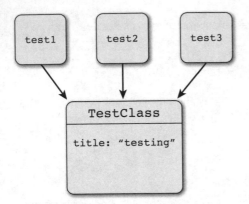

FIGURE 16.1
Three variables referencing the same class instance from the Try It Yourself example.

Even though we declared that `TestClass(title: "my test instance")` is assigned to the `test1` variable, we assigned that same instance's reference to `test2` and `test3`, creating three references to the same instance. Then, once we began assigning `nil` to each variable, each respective reference went away. Assigning each variable to `nil` is like removing each variable's arrow pointing to the `TestClass` instance in Figure 16.1. After the last reference (`test3`) was set to `nil` in step 7, our instance's reference count was zero, and right before ARC removed the instance from memory, it called our `deinit` method, which printed to the console `"my test instance is being deinitialized."` The completed playground code and results should look like the following code and results in Figure 16.2.

```
class TestClass {
    var title: String
    init(title: String) {
        self.title = title
        print("\(self.title) is initialized.")          "my test instance is initialized."
    }
    deinit {
        print("\(title) is being deinitialized.")       "my test instance is being deinitialized."
    }
}

var test1: TestClass?                                    nil
var test2: TestClass?                                    nil
var test3: TestClass?                                    nil

test1 = TestClass(title: "my test instance")            TestClass
test2 = test1                                           TestClass
test3 = test1                                           TestClass

test1 = nil                                             nil
test2 = nil                                             nil
test3 = nil                                             nil
```

```
my test instance is initialized.
my test instance is being deinitialized.
```

FIGURE 16.2
The completed Try It Yourself example of initialization and deinitialization in the playground.

A classic example of the usefulness of deinitialization is when writing content to a file on disk. You don't want the instance doing the writing to get deallocated without closing the file for writing or no one else or no other process can edit the file. Placing code in your class's deinitializer to close or release the file handler would be beneficial, so that any file your instance writes to does not retain a permanent write-lock on the file. Another example could be when a player leaves a game. Their `Player` instance gets deinitialized, and the `deinit` method could return any coins or points the player has to a central bank or repository before the player instance gets deallocated.

Automatic Reference Counting

Several years ago, Apple introduced the aforementioned Automatic Reference Counting (ARC), to manage the allocation and deallocation of objects in memory. Objective-C programmers remember times before ARC, when you had to manually tell the compiler when to retain a reference to an Objective-C object and when to release it with the `retain` and `release` keywords, respectively. This was a point of confusion for a lot of developers, and misunderstanding proper memory management rules led to retain cycles and memory leaks, and even crashing apps. ARC was created to resolve these issues.

How ARC Works

What ARC does is analyze the code for creation of instances, places where they are referenced, and expected lifetimes of the instances via the number of references to them, and automatically keeps track of retaining and releasing references to instances. Then, as mentioned already, once an instance's reference count gets to zero, the instance is deallocated. In other words, when no property, variable, or constant strongly references an instance, ARC deallocates the instance. But what is a strong reference?

Reference Relationships and Behaviors

Rather than explicitly retaining instances ourselves, we tell the compiler the *behavior* a reference should have or what kind of *relationship* to have with another instance. We can do that by telling Swift what type of relationship a property, variable, or constant should have with another class or closure instance. The three types of relationships are **strong**, **weak**, and **unowned**. We will get to weak and unowned shortly; first, let's discuss strong references.

Strong references maintain a strong hold on an instance. As long as at least one strong reference to an instance exists, ARC will not deallocate that instance. When you assign a property, variable, or constant to a class instance, a strong reference is created by default.

Optional type variables behave the same way, but only after a reference to an instance is assigned. Declaring a variable of an optional type sets its initial value to `nil` until it is assigned a reference to an instance. Remember that an optional value is simply an enum with two cases, Some and None, and an associated value for the Some case. An optional class type simply means that a reference to a class type just resides within the Some case, and is a strong reference.

Reference Cycles

Our examples thus far haven't been too advanced, so we haven't had to worry about the implications of strong references. There may be times, though, when you have a class property that strongly references an instance of another class, and that property's class instance needs a reference back to the first instance. Such an occasion could be when a person buys an iPhone; a person would want to strongly hold onto a reference to that iPhone, and likewise the iPhone should only have one owner. Neither instance can get deallocated because each holds a strong reference to the other, creating a **strong reference cycle**.

The code in Listing 16.1 creates two classes, a Person class and a Phone class. After they are created, an instance of each is created.

If you're following along, remember you can use either a playground or the Swift REPL. I will use the playground for the examples in this book but feel free to use the REPL if you like. If you choose to use the REPL, you can either add the code directly in the interactive REPL, or you can add the code to a file with the .swift extension and then run the following command at a command prompt to test your code in the REPL:

```
$ xcrun swift test.swift
```

When using the REPL, I prefer to write my code in a .swift file and then execute it in a separate tab of the Terminal app to avoid constantly closing the .swift file, executing the .swift file, and then reopening the file for editing. Feel free to do whatever is easiest for you.

LISTING 16.1   **Creating Classes with Dependent Properties**

```
enum iPhoneModel: String {
    case iPhone5C = "iPhone 5C", iPhone5S = "iPhone 5S", iPhone6 = "iPhone 6",
  ➥iPhone6Plus = "iPhone 6 Plus"
}

class Phone {
    let model: iPhoneModel
    var owner: Person?
    init(model: iPhoneModel) {
        self.model = model
        print("\(model.rawValue) is being initialized.")
    }
    deinit {
```

```
            print("\(model.rawValue) is deinitializing.")
        }
    }

class Person {
    let name: String
    var phone: Phone?
    init(name: String) {
        self.name = name
        print("\(name) is being initialized.")
    }
    deinit {
        print("\(name) is deinitializing.")
    }
}

var aPerson: Person?
var aPhone: Phone?

aPerson = Person(name: "Steve")    // displays "Steve is being initialized."
aPhone = Phone(model: .iPhone6)    // displays "iPhone 6 is being initialized."

aPerson = nil                      // displays "Steve is deinitializing."
aPhone = nil                       // displays "iPhone 6 is deinitializing."
```

Listing 16.1 shows a standard example of defining two classes, an enum to help with the model of iPhone, and declaring an instance of each class. This example uses optionals so that we can assign to nil for the purposes of illustrating deinitialization and deallocation. Be sure to open the Debug Area by pressing Command+Shift+Y to view the results.

All works as planned in the preceding example, and both instances get deinitialized and deallocated once assigned to nil. But watch what happens if we assign aPerson to aPhone's owner property, and aPhone to aPerson's phone property in Listing 16.2. Place the following code immediately before the lines assigning nil to each variable.

LISTING 16.2 Creating a Strong Reference Cycle

```
// ... the iPhoneModel enum, Phone class, and Person class from Listing 16.1

aPerson?.phone = aPhone
aPhone?.owner = aPerson

aPerson = nil                      // nothing is displayed
aPhone = nil                       // nothing is displayed
```

In Listing 16.2, the only change we made was to assign aPhone to aPerson?.phone and aPerson to aPhone?.owner. Remember, since these are optional values, we had to optionally chain the variables to assign anything to their properties. Look at the results when we assign each variable to nil. Wait, there aren't any results! This is because while we removed the references from our variables (aPerson and aPhone) to their respective instances in memory, each instance also had strong references to each other from their properties.

Figure 16.3 illustrates an abstract of how our instances would look in memory as separate instances and no dependence upon each other, just like Listing 16.1. Figure 16.4 and Figure 16.5 show the same instances with references to each other, creating a strong reference cycle, just like Listing 16.2, and what happens after the variables are assigned nil.

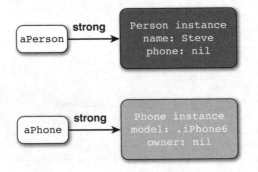

FIGURE 16.3
The Person and Phone instances with only strong references from a respective single variable.

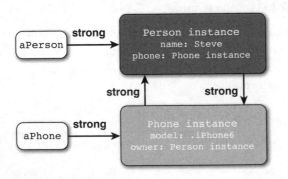

FIGURE 16.4
A strong reference cycle between Person and Phone instances.

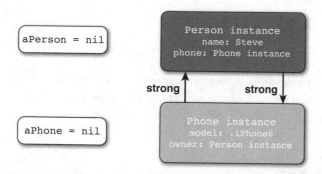

FIGURE 16.5
The strong reference cycle remains even after the variables are assigned to `nil`.

The preceding figures illustrate what happened in our code with respect to the strong references from each variable or property to an instance of a class. Your app's code may need to reference several other instances throughout its lifecycle, so how do we avoid strong reference cycles? There are two other types of memory relationships: weak and unowned.

Resolving Strong Reference Cycles

Strong reference cycles can be resolved by changing the type of relationship that variables and constants have with their instances. Since the preceding example had properties that wouldn't let go of the other instance, neither instance could be deallocated from memory, causing a **memory leak**. A memory leak is when an app never lets go of an instance or instances in memory, so that memory never gets returned to the operating system.

Weak References

To fix this, we can specify one of those references to be a **weak reference**, meaning that property holds a reference to a respective instance as long as some other property holds a strong reference to that instance. If the last strong reference to an instance goes away and only a weak reference remains, the weak reference is set to `nil` and the instance is deallocated.

Using the `Phone` and `Person` example from earlier, modify the `Phone` class so that the `owner` variable property is weak by prefacing the definition with the `weak` keyword. Then execute the .swift file with the REPL, or re-execute your playground. Listing 16.3 illustrates what this change looks like.

LISTING 16.3   Resolving Strong Reference Cycles with Weak References

```
// reusing code from Listing 16.1 and 16.2
class Phone {
    let model: iPhoneModel
    weak var owner: Person?
```

```
    // remainder of Phone class...
}
// remainder of code from example
```

Now that we made the `owner` property a weak reference, the strong reference cycle is bro-ken, and both instances can be deallocated after each variable is set to `nil`. Figure 16.6 shows the new diagram of our instances with a weak reference, enabling both instances to deallocate safely.

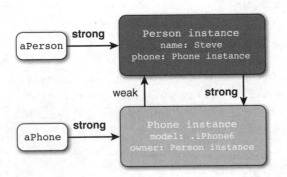

FIGURE 16.6
Using weak references to resolve strong reference cycles.

Weak references must be optional because they may be assigned `nil` at runtime, and because they must be optional, they must be variables, so you cannot have a constant weak reference. Also, because they may be set to `nil` at runtime, you should check whether a reference is `nil` before attempting to access the instance to which it refers.

Consider using weak references when instances do not expect to have the same lifetimes. For example, our `Person` instance could live for years (as we would hope), but iPhones certainly don't live as long as humans. Their life expectancies are different, so it is appropriate to use a weak reference in this case. Also, you should consider using weak references when you would expect a reference to be set to `nil` in the future.

Unowned References

The final type of memory relationship is called an **unowned reference**. Unowned references are a new concept if you are an Objective-C programmer, as you are most likely only familiar with strong and weak references. An unowned reference is a reference that is not strong but yet intends to have the same life expectancy as the instance it references, as the instances depend on each other. An unowned reference behaves as if to say "I depend on you, but I will not strongly hold on to you." To use an unowned reference, insert the `unowned` keyword in front of a prop-erty, variable, or constant definition, exactly the same way you use `weak`.

Since unowned references expect to live as long as the instances they refer to, they cannot be nil. Unowned references must always have a value and be defined as a non-optional type.

For example, let's say at your job, you hire a new employee. That employee will always have an email address as long as they're employed, and that email address will only belong to that employee. They should have the same life expectancy (in terms of employment, not to cast ill will upon your new employee). Listing 16.4 illustrates such a scenario, that when your new employee is created in the HR system, an email instance is also created and attached to the employee.

LISTING 16.4 Creating Reference Cycle with Employee and Email

```
01:  class Employee {
02:      let name: String
03:      var email: Email!
04:      init(name: String, emailAddress: String) {
05:          self.name = name
06:          self.email = Email(address: emailAddress, employee: self)
07:          print("\(name) is being initialized.")
08:      }
09:      deinit {
10:          print("\(name) is being deinitialized.")
11:      }
12:  }
13:
14:  class Email {
15:      var address: String
16:      var server = "imap.company.com"
17:      let employee: Employee
18:      init(address: String, employee: Employee) {
19:          self.address = address
20:          self.employee = employee
21:          print("\(address) is being initialized.")
22:      }
23:      deinit {
24:          print("\(address) is being deinitialized.")
25:      }
26:  }
27:
28:  var employee: Employee? = Employee(name: "BJ", emailAddress:
   ➥"BJ@company.com")
29:  employee = nil

// Displays:
//   BJ@company.com is being initialized.
//   BJ is being initialized.
```

Notice in the initializer for `Employee` that on line 6, we reference `self` by passing it as an argument to the `Email` initializer. We are allowed to do this because the `name` property is given a value on line 5, and the `email` property is an implicitly unwrapped optional (line 3), so its initial value is `nil`, and the `Employee` instance is considered fully initialized after line 5. We cannot use the `self` keyword until the instance is completely initialized, unless it is to differentiate similarly named parameters, such as `self.name = name`.

There is a problem, though. When you execute the .swift file in the REPL or execute the playground, you see that the results show only initialization and no deinitialization when we set our `employee` variable to `nil`.

The proper way to resolve this reference cycle is to use the `unowned` keyword. Because these instances should stay alive as long as the other is alive but not hold each other strongly, we should set one to be an `unowned` reference. Modify the code in Listing 16.4 to add the `unowned` keyword at the beginning of line 17:

```
17:      unowned let employee: Employee
```

Now execute your playground or .swift file again in the Swift REPL. You should see the deinitialization happen as soon as the employee variable is set to `nil` on line 29.

NOTE

Analyze What Behavior and Relationship Is Needed

It is always best to analyze what type of relationship is needed for properties, constants, and variables to instances of reference types. In the preceding example, we could have set the employee as a weak optional `Employee` instance, but that would imply that we could change the employee to another non-`nil` employee at a later time, and we don't want that behavior. This is why you must think about intended behavior of what each property, variable, or constant must have, and also what type of memory management relationship it will have with its respective instance.

Closures and Strong Reference Cycles

Closures in Swift are also reference types. That means that closures are also susceptible to strong reference cycles just like class instances. Since a closure *captures* the properties, variables, and constants from its surrounding context, it has the potential to capture a strong reference to self or another instance that has a strong reference to it, creating a strong reference cycle. We can overcome a strong reference cycle with closures by providing a **closure capture list**.

Closure capture lists are comma-separated lists that go inside a closure at the head, immediately after the opening curly brace and before the parameter list and return type. If there is no parameter list or return type, the closure capture list is placed before the `in` keyword, before the body of the closure. Closure capture lists provide what references should have what type of relationship, all inside a pair of square braces. Since strong is the default, you do not need to specify strong references inside the closure capture list, or anywhere for that matter. Rather, you can specify weak or unowned followed by the reference's name and list as many as needed, separated by commas.

Since closures are reference types just like a class, we can easily think of closures having the capability to create instances of other types inside their braces, as well as reference self, since the closure may need access to properties inside the class in which the closure belongs.

Let's create an example in the following Try It Yourself section that creates a class with a built-in math function, as well as some parameters to accept values upon initialization. In the example, we also create a deinitializer, so we can tell when our instance gets deinitialized before deallocation.

Use Closure Capture Lists to Resolve Reference Cycles in Closures

Using a playground, create a class named MathFunction and provide a mathematical function inside a closure that can be called on an instance of MathFunction. Examine how ARC will or won't deallocate memory when we provide a closure capture list.

1. Open Xcode and create a new playground; either a Mac or iOS playground works. Clear the contents of the playground.

2. Create a class named MathFunction and create two variable properties of type Int.

```
class MathFunction {
    var firstNum: Int
    var secondNum: Int
}
```

3. Create a lazy variable property of type () -> Int and return the product of the two instance properties. This lazy property should be placed after the secondNum definition statement.

```
lazy var multiply: () -> Int = {
    return self.firstNum * self.secondNum
}
```

4. Create an initializer that accepts two integers and assign them to the instance properties.

```
init(firstNum: Int, secondNum: Int) {
    self.firstNum = firstNum
    self.secondNum = secondNum
    print("initializing.")
}
```

5. Create a deinitializer that just prints to the console when the instance is being deinitialized.

```
deinit {
    print("deinitializing. ")
}
```

6. That is all for the class. Create a variable of type *optional* `MathFunction` and assign a newly created instance.

```
var math: MathFunction? = MathFunction(firstNum: 3, secondNum: 5)
```

7. Since the `multiply` property is a lazy property, it has not been initialized yet, even though the instance itself has been initialized. This means the closure is not in memory and there is no reference to it yet. Assign `nil` to the `math` variable and observe ARC initializing and deinitializing our `MathFunction` instance.

```
math = nil
```

8. Now try to print the result of the `multiply` property, right before assigning `nil` to `math` on the last line. The `MathFunction` class instantiates the closure in memory, and since the closure references `self`, a strong reference is created from the closure to the class instance.

```
print(math!.multiply())
math = nil
```

9. At this point, the output in the playground or from executing your .swift (if you are using the REPL) file should be two lines: "initializing." and "15". But we don't see "deinitializing." Try capturing a `weak` reference to `self` in a closure capture list. Execute your playground or .swift file and observe the output. Do you get an error?

```
// Add closure capture list to end of 'lazy var multiply' line
lazy var multiply: () -> Int = { [weak self] in
// remainder of file...
```

10. Executing the file with the weak reference in the closure capture list displays an error, "value of optional type 'MathFunction?' not unwrapped; did you mean to use '!' or '?'?" This is because assigning the reference as `weak` means that we would need to unwrap `self` before using it (as it is of an optional type). While we could do this, `unowned` is a more appropriate choice, because once the lazy variable has been initialized, it should never be `nil` and should exist as long as the class instance exists. Change the `weak` keyword to the `unowned` keyword inside the closure capture list. Then re-execute your playground or .swift file. You should now see "initializing.", "15", and then "deinitializing."

```
lazy var multiply: () -> Int = { [unowned self] in
// remainder of file...
```

Once you've completed the Try It Yourself section, your code and results should look like those in Figure 16.7.

```
                            ☒ Ch16 TIY2 Unowned Closure.playground

  ☷  〈  〉  ☒ Ch16 TIY2 Unowned Closure
  1  class MathFunction {
  2      var firstNum: Int
  3      var secondNum: Int
  4
  5      lazy var multiply: () -> Int = { [unowned self] in
  6          return self.firstNum * self.secondNum
  7      }
  8
  9      init(firstNum: Int, secondNum: Int) {
  10         self.firstNum = firstNum
  11         self.secondNum = secondNum
  12         print("initializing.")                          "initializing."
  13     }
  14
  15     deinit {
  16         print("deinitializing.")                        "deinitializing."
  17     }
  18  }
  19
  20  var math: MathFunction? = MathFunction(firstNum: 3, secondNum: 5)    MathFunction
  21  print(math!.multiply())                                              "15"
  22  math = nil                                                           nil
  23

  ▽ |_____|    – 30 sec +

  initializing.
  15
  deinitializing.
```

FIGURE 16.7
The completed Try It Yourself example code and REPL results for using unowned references inside a closure capture list.

Summary

In this hour, you learned about deinitialization and how to clean up instances before they are deallocated. You also learned about Automatic Reference Counting (ARC), and how it is an automated mechanism for managing the number of references to instances in memory, allocating memory for them, and deallocating them from memory when done.

From ARC, you learned about strong, weak, and unowned references, the behaviors they maintain, and when it makes sense to use each one. You then learned how to identify and resolve strong reference cycles in memory.

Finally, you learned about closure capture lists as a way to mitigate risks of strong reference cycles in closures. Since closures are reference types just like class instances, they are susceptible to strong reference cycles as well. Providing closure capture lists suggests to Swift how you would like to manage the relationships between instances and closures.

While memory management isn't the most glamorous of topics, it is important as you write software for any platform, let alone for mobile platforms, which are more resource-constrained than desktop platforms and for which the implications of poorly managed memory can be noticed more frequently.

Although a lot of memory management is handled for you in Swift's ARC mechanism, you certainly still have a lot of power at your fingertips with this knowledge. Make sure you understand these concepts and their implications, because you want happy users of your apps, and apps crashing from poor memory management make for unhappy users.

In the next hour, we discuss protocols. Protocols enable you to add functionality to types to define what a particular implementation should provide, so that the instance asking for information can guarantee that appropriate information is provided.

Q&A

Q. Do structs have `deinit` methods?

A. Structs do not have deinitializers in the same way that classes do. If you try to declare one, Swift gives you a compiler error.

Q. When does my class need a deinitializer?

A. Unfortunately, it's not possible to provide a comprehensive list of when a `deinit` method is required; most of the time, your class won't need a deinitializer. Generally, you need a deinitializer when you perform some manual cleanup and release extra resources when your class is about to be deallocated. For example, if your class has open network connections, you'll want to close them before your class becomes unavailable.

Deinitializers can also be useful in debugging your application. It is sometimes helpful to have a class display or log information about itself just before it is deallocated so you can check that its state is as it should be.

Q. What causes a memory leak and how can I find them?

A. A memory leak occurs when an application allocates memory for an object but never releases it. Strong reference cycles are the most common cause of memory leaks in reference-counted languages such as Swift. Xcode provides excellent debugging and analysis tools, but they are beyond the scope of this book. If you're interested, look into the Instruments application, which comes bundled with Xcode.

Q. When should I use an unowned reference instead of a weak reference?

A. You should only use an unowned reference when you're sure that the reference will never be `nil`. Weak references should be used when the instance can be set to `nil` at any time.

Workshop

The workshop contains quiz questions and exercises to help you solidify your understanding of the material covered. Try to answer all questions before looking at the answers that follow.

Quiz

1. What are the three reference types available in Swift?

2. If no reference type is specified, which type is used by default?

3. Can weak references have an optional type?

4. Does a deinitializer have access to the class's properties?

Answers

1. Strong, weak, and unowned.

2. By default, references in Swift are strong.

3. Not only *can* weak references have an optional type, they *must* have an optional type.

4. Yes. Deinitialization occurs before deallocation, so all properties in the class are still available to `deinit`.

Exercise

For this exercise, you can either work in a playground or use the REPL like you did for the Try It Yourself sections of this hour.

Let's take a look at how deinitializers are called in a class and its subclasses. Create a class called `Parent` with a `title` property and write an `init` and `deinit` method for your class. These methods should print messages containing the `title` to the console and indicate that the object was initialized or deinitialized.

Next, write a subclass of `Parent` called `Child`. `Child` should have a property called `subtitle` and should have its own set of `init` and `deinit` methods. These should print messages containing the `subtitle` to the console and indicate that the object was initialized or deinitialized. Don't forget to call `super.init(title:)` and pass on the `title` parameter.

Create an optional `var` of type `Child` and assign a child object to it. It shouldn't surprise you that the superclass's `init` message appears before the subclass's. This is the same thing we saw when we covered initializers in Hour 13. Now, set your `var` equal to `nil` and watch the `deinit` messages.

Think about the code you just wrote. Did you have to use the `override` keyword in any of your `init` methods? How about in the `deinit` methods? Why do you think that is? Were you surprised by the order of the `deinit` messages? Why or why not?

Using Protocols to Define Behavior

What You'll Learn in This Hour:

▶ How to define protocols
▶ How to adopt protocols in classes, enums, and structs
▶ How to conform to protocols and check for conformance
▶ How to use protocols as types
▶ How to inherit protocols

In this hour, we discuss protocols as a way to define additional behavior a type should exhibit. Protocols are not a new concept if you are familiar with Objective-C. Even other languages have similar constructs called contracts or interfaces. Protocols are used frequently throughout the Cocoa and Cocoa Touch frameworks, so the knowledge you learn here will help you gain a better understanding of how to interact with different areas of Mac and iOS development.

Defining Protocols

Let's begin the topic with a definition of protocols. A **protocol** is an outline, rule set, or contract, of behavior that a type can implement. A protocol by itself does not have any implementation; it is only a blueprint of methods and properties. Any type can **adopt** a protocol to help give it extra functionality to accomplish a particular task or set of tasks.

Adopting a protocol is similar to a class inheriting from a superclass, although there is nothing to inherit with protocols. Rather, you adopt a protocol as a way of agreeing to abide by the contract it defines. Also, adopting protocols is not limited to classes like it is in Objective-C; Swift structs and enums can also adopt protocols. A type that adopts a protocol and implements its defined behavior is said to **conform** to the protocol. Before we go any further with adopting and conforming to protocols, let's take a look at how a protocol is structured.

The syntax of a protocol is similar to type definitions we have seen already, just with the `protocol` keyword, the name to give the protocol, and a pair of curly braces. Inside the curly braces are the properties, methods, and any other information that should be implemented by whatever type adopts the protocol. The following snippet shows the basic syntax of defining a protocol:

```
protocol MyProtocol {
    // ...property definitions, method definitions, and so on go here
}
```

NOTE

Default Implementations in Protocols

Although protocols themselves do not have any default implementation, you can use something called a *protocol extension* to provide default implementations. This is discussed at length in Hour 21, "Understanding Protocol-Oriented Programming."

Creating and Adopting Protocols

To declare that a type adopts a protocol, you use the same syntax as if you were inheriting a class from a superclass. Append the name of your type with a colon and then the name of the protocol. If you are inheriting a class from a superclass but also need to conform to a protocol, list the superclass first, then any protocols second, and so on, separated by commas. Then, inside your type's implementation, fulfill the defined behavior of the protocol. But what does it mean to fulfill the defined behavior of the protocol? Let's start with a basic protocol with only a few properties defined. Then we create a struct to adopt the protocol and make our struct conform to the protocol by fulfilling the protocol's definition. We do this in Listing 17.1. If you are following along, you may use either a playground (Mac or iOS is fine) or the Swift REPL.

LISTING 17.1   Creating and Adopting a Protocol

```
protocol Rentable {
    var title: String { get }
    var barcode: String { get set }
}

struct Book : Rentable {
    let title: String
    var barcode: String
    let chapterCount: Int
}

let book = Book(title: "Sams Teach Yourself Swift in 24 Hours",
  ➥barcode: "12345678", chapterCount: 24)
```

The syntax for defining a property in a protocol looks a bit strange, but that's because there is no implementation. It is structured exactly as a computed property is, just without any implementation. Let's discuss properties in protocols in greater detail now.

Fully Conform to Adopted Protocols

If your class, struct, or enum declares that it adopts a particular protocol, you must implement all required defined functionality in the protocol. Failing to do so results in a compiler error. Figure 17.1 shows an example of what you might see if your type does not conform to a protocol.

```
16   protocol MyProtocol {
17       var myVar: String { get }
18   }
19
20   struct MyStruct : MyProtocol {          ⓘ Type 'MyStruct' does not conform to protocol 'MyProtocol'
21
22   }
```

FIGURE 17.1
A type not fully conforming to a protocol results in a compiler error.

Properties

To require a gettable property, you simply provide the get keyword inside the curly braces, like the title property in Listing 17.1. To require a gettable and settable property, provide both the get and set keywords inside the curly braces, separated by a space, such as { get set }, like the barcode property. Property requirements are always introduced with the var keyword inside a protocol, even if they may be declared as constants in the conforming type.

Properties in a protocol designed to be read-write must be implemented with the var introducer and also must provide a getter and setter in the conforming type's implementation. By default, you are providing get- and set-ability with a property when you declare it in your implementation with var. Read-write properties cannot be implemented as constants or with just a getter. Conversely, a protocol property defined as read-only, with just a getter, can be implemented in the conforming type as read-write, with a getter and a setter, if it makes sense to do so.

Notice in Listing 17.1 that the title property is defined with just a getter, and the barcode property is defined with a getter and a setter, but neither property has a custom accessor in the implementation. The title property's implementation is as a constant, and a value is assigned during initialization, so it is read-only and satisfies that requirement. The barcode property's implementation is as a variable, and even though it is set during initialization, it can be reassigned at any time during runtime, so that requirement is satisfied as well. You can, however, provide custom accessors, if it makes sense to do so.

Notice also in Listing 17.1 that the Book struct has an extra property, chapterCount. Types that adopt and conform to protocols often have more implementation than just what is defined in the protocol or protocols they adopt.

Protocols can define instance properties and type properties. Type properties are defined in protocols with the static keyword, even if the conforming type is a class. In the actual implementation inside your type, use the appropriate type property attribute (class or static) as discussed in Hour 15, "Adding Advanced Type Functionality." Type properties in protocols could be useful if you are creating a game and you want the maximum number of damage sustainable to be provided to not only your player but also any enemies. That way, each type can define its max, and because each type conforms to the protocol, you know each instance is guaranteed to be able to access that value.

Defining Methods in Protocols

Method definitions inside protocols look exactly like they do in a class, struct, or enum; they just don't have any implementation, just like properties. You still use the func keyword, give the method a name, and then a list of parameters and a return type—no curly braces, no implementation.

When you provide your implementation, you do not need to write the override keyword, because you are not inheriting the method from a superclass; you are merely implementing a method you promised you would implement when you adopted the protocol. Listing 17.2 adds to our example in Listing 17.1 by adding a method signature to the protocol, which requires any conforming type to implement that method.

LISTING 17.2 Adding Methods to Protocols

```
protocol Rentable {
    var title: String { get }
    var barcode: String { get set }
    func rent()
}

struct Book : Rentable {
    let title: String
    var barcode: String
    let chapterCount: Int
    func rent() {
        print("Please return \(title) in 3 weeks.")
    }
```

```
}

let book = Book(title: "To Kill A Mockingbird", barcode: "87654321",
    ➥chapterCount: 31)
book.rent()       // displays "Please return To Kill A Mockingbird in 3 weeks."
```

We could also add parameters to the function and specify a return type in the protocol. The syntax to do this is exactly what you would expect, minus the implementation. Listing 17.3 continues with our `Rentable` scenario to add parameters and a return type to the protocol, and conforming type, `Book`.

LISTING 17.3   Adding Parameters and a Return Type to Protocol Methods

```
protocol Rentable {
    var title: String { get }
    var barcode: String { get set }
    func rent(forWeeks weeks: Int) -> Bool
}

struct Book : Rentable {
    let title: String
    var barcode: String
    let chapterCount: Int

    func rent(forWeeks weeks: Int) -> Bool {
        print("Please return \(title) in \(weeks) weeks.")
        return true
    }
}

let book = Book(title: "Goodnight Moon", barcode: "12344321", chapterCount: 1)
book.rent(forWeeks: 2)     // displays "Please return Goodnight Moon in 2 weeks."
```

To define mutating functions, such as those required in structs to alter the state of a property inside an instance, you provide the `mutating` keyword in front of the definition inside the protocol. This is true for any method that needs to mutate properties, even if the conforming type is a class, where the `mutating` keyword is not necessary. You must add the `mutating` keyword in the protocol, but in the case of a conforming class, you can safely omit the `mutating` keyword in front of method declarations.

As with type properties, you must declare a type method with the `static` keyword in the protocol. Then in the conforming type, use the appropriate type attribute (`class` or `static`) in your type implementation.

You can also define initializers in protocols. When implementing an initializer from a protocol, the initializer must be prefixed with the `required` keyword. Everything else about the initializer is the same as you have learned about initializers.

Using Protocol Names as Types

Although protocols are not a fully implemented type, they can be used as a type in parameter lists, return types, constants, and variables, as an indication that no matter what class, struct, or enum an instance is, it is expected to have a certain set of behaviors based on conformance to a protocol. This can be useful when you have arrays or dictionaries with instances of heterogeneous types but yet which conform to a common protocol, for example.

Let's say we need to encapsulate any rentable types into an array. Listing 17.4 creates two new structs, DVD and AudioCD, both adopting the Rentable protocol, and we create an array of instances with all the different types.

LISTING 17.4 Using Protocol Names as Types

```
protocol Rentable {
    var title: String { get }
    var barcode: String { get set }
    func rent(forWeeks weeks: Int) -> Bool
}

struct Book : Rentable {
    let title: String
    var barcode: String
    let chapterCount: Int

    func rent(forWeeks weeks: Int) -> Bool {
        print("Please return \(title) in \(weeks) weeks.")
        return true
    }
}

struct DVD: Rentable {
    let title: String
    var barcode: String
    let lengthInMinutes: Int

    func rent(forWeeks weeks: Int) -> Bool {
        print("Please return \(title) in \(weeks) weeks.")
        return true
    }
}
```

```
struct AudioCD : Rentable {
    let title: String
    var barcode: String
    let audioTracks: Int

    func rent(forWeeks weeks: Int) -> Bool {
        print("Please return \(title) in \(weeks) weeks.")
        return true
    }
}

let brownBear = Book(title: "Brown Bear, Brown Bear, What Do You See?",
    ➥barcode: "13243546", chapterCount: 1)
let clue = DVD(title: "Clue: The Movie", barcode: "64534231", lengthInMinutes: 94)
let incubus = AudioCD(title: "If Not Now, When?", barcode: "09876543",
    ➥audioTracks: 11)

let items: [Rentable] = [brownBear, clue, incubus]

for item in items {
    print("Item: \(item.title) is rentable. Barcode is \(item.barcode)")
}
```

The example in Listing 17.4 shows how we can have multiple types conforming to a single protocol, and then have an array of type `Rentable`. The array is represented by instances of three different structs. Yet they all commonly adopt and conform to the `Rentable` protocol, so the array is of type `[Rentable]`. Since we can guarantee that each item can provide a `title` and a `barcode`, as they are specified in the protocol's definition, we iterate through the array and ask each item for its `title` and `barcode` without any problem. This is part of what makes protocols so powerful; they can make disparate types behave in a common fashion.

There should be something wrong staring you in the face in the preceding example: We repeated the same code in all three structs. One way we could simplify this implementation could be to extract the repeated code into a common superclass, which adopts the `Rentable` protocol. This calls for not only class inheritance but also protocol inheritance.

Adopting and Inheriting Multiple Protocols

To fix the preceding example, we still need the individual properties particular to each type, such as `audioTracks` on `AudioCD`, but the protocol methods and properties can be offloaded to the superclass to reduce redundancy. Also, we need to change the types from structs to classes to take advantage of inheritance. And to show that we can create types that not only inherit from a superclass but also adopt multiple protocols, we add a protocol named `Optical` to identify what type of disc we have. Let's build this example in the following Try It Yourself section.

▼ TRY IT YOURSELF

Implement Class Inheritance and Multiple Protocol Inheritance

Recreate the Library example from preceding examples to create classes rather than structs to implement a class hierarchy, as well as to adopt multiple protocols.

1. Open Xcode and create a new playground; either an iOS or a Mac playground works. Clear the contents of the playground.

2. Begin by creating the `Rentable` protocol, same as in earlier examples.

```
protocol Rentable {
   var title: String { get }
   var barcode: String { get set }
   func rent(forWeeks weeks: Int) -> Bool
}
```

3. Create the `Optical` protocol. This is used to define what type of optical media a rentable item is.

```
protocol Optical {
   var discType: OpticalDiscType { get }
}
```

4. Create an enum that holds the types of optical media and satisfies the type of the property in the `Optical` protocol.

```
enum OpticalDiscType {
   case CD, DVD, BluRay
}
```

5. Create the superclass, named `Media`. Adopt the `Rentable` protocol and fulfill the protocol's defined requirements.

```
class Media : Rentable {
   let title: String
   var barcode: String
   init(title: String, barcode: String) {
       self.title = title
       self.barcode = barcode
   }
   func rent(forWeeks weeks: Int) -> Bool {
       print("Please return \(title) in \(weeks) weeks.")
       return true
   }
}
```

6. Create the `Book` class as a subclass to `Media`. Add a `chapterCount` property of type `Int`, along with an initializer. Because `Book` inherits from `Media`, which conforms to the `Rentable` protocol, the `Book` class, by definition of inheritance, also conforms to the `Rentable` protocol.

```
class Book : Media {
    let chapterCount: Int
    init(title: String, barcode: String, chapterCount: Int) {
        self.chapterCount = chapterCount
        super.init(title: title, barcode: barcode)
    }
}
```

7. The `Book` class looks much cleaner. Create the `DVD` class, subclassing from `Media` and also adopting the `Optical` protocol. Then add an `OpticalDiscType` property to conform to the `Optical` protocol. Remember, a class can inherit from only one direct superclass, but it can conform to multiple protocols. You must list the class first if you inherit from both a class and protocol(s).

```
class DVD : Media, Optical {
    let lengthInMinutes: Int
    let discType: OpticalDiscType = .DVD
    init(title: String, barcode: String, lengthInMinutes: Int) {
        self.lengthInMinutes = lengthInMinutes
        super.init(title: title, barcode: barcode)
    }
}
```

8. The `DVD` class now inherits from `Media` and conforms to both the `Rentable` and `Optical` protocols. Do the same by creating an `AudioCD` class, with a property named `audioTracks` of type `Int`, set the `discType` property, and create the initializer.

```
class AudioCD : Media, Optical {
    let audioTracks: Int
    let discType: OpticalDiscType = .CD
    init(title: String, barcode: String, audioTracks: Int) {
        self.audioTracks = audioTracks
        super.init(title: title, barcode: barcode)
    }
}
```

9. Now that our classes are created, let's create instances of them and populate an array with the newly created instances. Also, try to rent *The Notebook* for three weeks. You should be able to do so because of inheritance.

```
let theNotebook = Book(title: "The Notebook", barcode: "44445555",
➥chapterCount: 12)
theNotebook.rent(forWeeks: 3)
```

```
let majorLeague = DVD(title: "Major League", barcode: "66667777",
➥lengthInMinutes: 107)
let incubus = AudioCD(title: "Trust Fall (Side A) EP", barcode:
➥"88889999", audioTracks: 4)

let items: [Rentable] = [theNotebook, majorLeague, incubus]
```

10. Iterate through the array of rentable items and print a basic description to prove that you are able to access protocol properties on any type that conforms to that protocol. Create an `if` statement to check whether a title is equal to a favorite of yours and output your favorite song, scene, or chapter.

```
for item in items {
    print("Item: \(item.title) is rentable. Barcode is \(item.barcode).")
    if item.title == "Trust Fall (Side A) EP" {
        print("My favorite song on \(item.title) is Absolution Calling.")
    }
}
```

A key take-away from the preceding Try It Yourself example is that you can always inherit from and conform to multiple protocols whether your type is a class, struct, or enum. If your type is a class, you can only inherit from one class, but you can still conform to multiple protocols. You just need to list the superclass first before listing protocols your type will adopt.

Another key take-away is that no matter what type an instance is, if it conforms to a protocol, you can ask it for properties and methods defined in that protocol. An example of this is with Apple's MapKit framework. You are probably familiar with seeing a map on an iPhone or iPad and interacting with red pins to show locations of places. Those pins are represented by any instance that conforms to the MKAnnotation protocol. The protocol defines a title, subtitle, and a coordinate location, which is all it needs to place a pin on the map. It is convenient to create an extension on your model types to conform to this protocol, reducing the need to create special instances just of the type MKAnnotation. We discuss extensions in Hour 18, "Using Extensions to Add Type Functionality."

The completed code results from the preceding Try It Yourself example should look like those in Figure 17.2.

```
Please return The Notebook in 3 weeks.
Item: The Notebook is rentable. Barcode is 44445555.
Item: Major League is rentable. Barcode is 66667777.
Item: Trust Fall (Side A) EP is rentable. Barcode is 88889999.
My favorite song on Trust Fall (Side A) EP is Absolution Calling.
```

FIGURE 17.2
The results from the completed Try It Yourself example using class inheritance and multiple protocol inheritance.

If we needed to reference an instance that conformed to multiple protocols, such as for a parameter of a function, and the function body accessed properties or methods from multiple protocols, we could use **protocol composition** to ensure our parameter type was defined properly. This is done using the `protocol` keyword, followed by the protocols needed inside open and closed angle brackets, separated by commas. Protocol composition can be used to define any instance property, constant, or variable, and is not limited to just parameters. Listing 17.5 illustrates an example of protocol composition.

LISTING 17.5 Protocol Composition in Function Parameters

```
protocol ProtocolFoo {
    func foo()
}
protocol ProtocolBar {
    func bar()
}

struct Foo: ProtocolFoo, ProtocolBar {
    func foo() {
        print("foo")
    }
    func bar() {
        print("bar")
    }
}

func someMethod(composedProperty: protocol<ProtocolFoo, ProtocolBar>) {
    composedProperty.foo()
    composedProperty.bar()
}

let foo = Foo()
someMethod(foo)
```

Listing 17.5 shows a struct called Foo that conforms to both protocols, ProtocolFoo and ProtocolBar. Then in the function someMethod, the parameter composedProperty expects to be of a type that conforms to both protocols. After we have an instance that satisfies that type requirement, we can safely call .foo() and .bar() on that instance when we call the someMethod method, and both print statements print their respective output to the console.

Optional Protocol Properties and Methods

Much like protocols in Objective-C, Swift provides the optional keyword to be inserted before a property or method definition inside a protocol. An optional property or method is not the same as an optional type (by adding the question mark character after a type name); an optional property or method inside a protocol means that the conforming type does not *have* to implement that property or method, but it *could*.

A protocol with any optional members must itself be marked with the @objc modifier in front of the protocol keyword. Even though you may not be interacting with Objective-C, the keyword is still required. If you mark your protocol with the @objc attribute, it can only be used by class types, and not structs or enums. This is discussed at greater length in Hour 23, "Adding Interoperability with Objective-C."

An example of this is the MKAnnotation protocol. If you open a playground and import MapKit, type MKAnnotation on an empty line. Then Command+click the word MKAnnotation. You should see the code listed in Figure 17.3.

```
2   //
3   // MKAnnotation.h
4   // MapKit
5   //
6   // Copyright (c) 2009-2014, Apple Inc. All rights reserved.
7   //
8
9   public protocol MKAnnotation : NSObjectProtocol {
10
11      // Center latitude and longitude of the annotation view.
12      // The implementation of this property must be KVO compliant.
13      public var coordinate: CLLocationCoordinate2D { get }
14
15      // Title and subtitle for use by selection UI.
16      optional public var title: String? { get }
17      optional public var subtitle: String? { get }
18  }
19
```

FIGURE 17.3
The MKAnnotation protocol definition, with optional properties.

The only required property is the `coordinate` property of type `CLLocationCoordinate2D`. It is not *required* to implement the `title` and `subtitle` properties, although you can. If you do provide those properties and methods in your conforming type, they can be used in the greater implementation. If they aren't provided by you, the properties are ignored and the method is never called by MapKit.

But wait, where is the `@objc` modifier? Notice on line 3 of Figure 17.3 that `MKAnnotation.h` is written, the ".h" meaning that it is from an Objective-C file. `MKAnnotation` is already an Objective-C protocol, but Xcode makes it look like Swift code for us by automatically generating the Swift representation of an Objective-C protocol. A purely Swift protocol with optional members would look like the example in Listing 17.6, which is my version of the `MKAnnotation` protocol, called `BJMAnnotation`.

LISTING 17.6 Adding Optional Members to Protocols

```
import MapKit

@objc protocol BJMAnnotation : NSObjectProtocol {
    var coordinate: CLLocationCoordinate2D { get }
    optional var title: String! { get }
    optional var subtitle: String! { get }
    optional func setCoordinate(newCoordinate: CLLocationCoordinate2D)
}
```

How to Check for Protocol Conformance

Swift provides a mechanism for checking a type's conformance to a protocol, and it is the exact same syntax for type checking and type casting from Hour 15 using the `is` and `as` operators. The `is` keyword returns true if the given instance conforms to the protocol in question and false if not. The `as!` keyword temporarily downcasts the protocol type forcibly. Remember, forcing a downcast with the `as!` operator can cause a runtime error if the downcasting fails.

You can also use the `as?` operator, which attempts to downcast the instance in question to the protocol's type and returns an optional value of the protocol's type if successful. It returns `nil` if the downcasting is unsuccessful.

The only alteration you must make to the type you are checking for conformance is to preface the protocol's definition with the `@objc` attribute.

Since the syntax and the concept are the exact same as type checking and type casting in Hour 15, see the "Type Casting and Non-Specific Types" section of Hour 15 for a full understanding. Simply substitute the protocol type where there is a regular type when using `is`, `as!`, or `as?`, and you experience the same behavior.

Using Protocols for Delegation

Delegation is a common design pattern, and it is used frequently in the Cocoa and Cocoa Touch frameworks. Apple defines a delegate as "an object that acts on behalf of, or in coordination with, another object when that object encounters an event in a program." This means that an application may have certain events that occur, such as the start or end of a game, that can notify a delegate object to customize the response returned to the application.

Take table views on iOS for example. A table view is a list of items viewed onscreen, such as your music list, or a list of emails. The table view is an instance of `UITableView`, and it has two types of delegates: One is an action-based delegate (simply called its **delegate**) and the other is its **data source** delegate. The table view's delegate can respond to calls such as when a row in a table view is selected or deselected, editing or deleting a row, and tapping on the accessory button on the right-hand side of a table cell to show more information. The table view's data source can respond to calls such as returning a configured cell for an index path in the table view, a title for the header of each section, and number of rows in each section of the table view. The aforementioned delegate and data source responsibilities are typical for their definitions; delegates often are responsible for taking action on behalf of another instance, and a data source is responsible for providing for a particular criteria and not necessarily performing actions.

So what do delegates have to do with protocols? The instance that offloads tasks to its delegate doesn't care what type of instance it is. Delegate instances typically conform to a given protocol, versus relying on a class, struct, or enum structure. As long as whatever type of instance the delegate or data source is conforms to the protocol, both instances happily communicate with each other.

NOTE

Dependency Inversion Principle

The Dependency Inversion Principle is one of the SOLID principles of object-oriented programming. A key point of this principle is to depend on abstractions and not on concretions. While every app is different and some implementations call for different design patterns, the Dependency Inversion Principle is a good guideline to follow to ensure loose coupling of objects in your code, making code more flexible and easier to maintain. Using protocols in Objective-C and Swift is one way to implement this principle. For more information on this topic, see the article on Wikipedia at http://en.wikipedia.org/wiki/Dependency_inversion_principle.

Let's look at a quick example of this in Listing 17.7. We create a class that delegates some actions to a delegate instance that conforms to a protocol we specify.

LISTING 17.7   Delegating Responsibilities

```
protocol ButtonDelegateProtocol {
    func didTapButton(button: Button)
}

class ButtonDelegate : ButtonDelegateProtocol {
    func didTapButton(button: Button) {
        print("You tapped the button labeled \(button.title).")
    }
}

class Button {
    let title: String
    let delegate: ButtonDelegateProtocol

    init(title: String, delegate: ButtonDelegateProtocol) {
        self.title = title
        self.delegate = delegate
    }

    func buttonTapped() {
        delegate.didTapButton(self)
    }
}

let button = Button(title: "Tap Me!", delegate: ButtonDelegate())
button.buttonTapped()     // displays "You tapped the button labeled Tap Me!"
```

As you can see in the Debug Area console if you were following along, when you call
`button.buttonTapped()`, the output is displayed saying what the label is of the button that
was tapped. This is because when we tapped the button, the `Button` class didn't care what
happened when the button was tapped; it offloaded that responsibility to the `ButtonDelegate`
class, which conforms to the `ButtonDelegateProtocol` protocol.

NOTE

Protocols Guarantee Behavior

The `ButtonDelegate` class in the preceding example could very well have implemented the
`buttonTapped()` method if `delegate` was an instance of type `ButtonDelegate`, and the example
would still have worked if no protocols were involved. However, because we introduced the protocol,
it is our way of guaranteeing that the delegate **must** implement that method, plus we loosen the
coupling between our classes, and we program to an abstraction versus a concretion. Without the
protocol, we cannot guarantee that the method would be implemented, and the app may not compile, or even worse, if it sneaks past your compiler, the app could crash at runtime.

Now that you have a better understanding of how protocols and delegates work, let's do a larger example together. This is a mini reimplementation of *The Legend of Zelda* (one of my all-time favorites). If you're not familiar with the game, here's the basic premise: You are Link, and you are saving Princess Zelda from the evil enemy Ganon. You battle different enemies along your journey as you search for Zelda and must gauge your health along the way (determined by how many hearts you have). When you take damage from enemies, your number of hearts decrease, but you can increase your number of hearts by drinking healing potions. The game is over if you have zero hearts.

We create a protocol for objects that can heal Link and for the game beginning and ending. We also create an enemy struct and a class that manages Link and his journey. Let's get started.

▼ TRY IT YOURSELF

Use Protocols for Delegation

Create a small rendition of *The Legend of Zelda* using protocols and delegates.

1. Open Xcode and create a new playground; either a Mac or an iOS playground works. Clear the contents of the playground.

2. Create the `Healable` protocol, with a `healableName` variable of type `String` and a `heartsRestores` variable of type `Double`.

```
protocol Healable {
    var healableName: String { get }
    var heartsRestores: Double { get }
}
```

3. Create a `BluePotion` struct and a `Heart` struct, each identifying itself in the `healableName` property, and restoring four hearts in `BluePotion` and one heart in `Heart`.

```
struct BluePotion : Healable {
    var healableName: String { return "blue potion" }
    var heartsRestores: Double { return 4.0 }
}

struct Heart : Healable {
    var healableName: String { return "heart piece" }
    var heartsRestores: Double { return 1.0 }
}
```

4. Create a simple struct for an enemy, with properties for a `name` and `damage` points.

```
struct Enemy {
    let name: String
    let damage: Double
}
```

5. Create the protocol to manage game events. Name it `GameManagerDelegate` and provide the blueprint for two functions: one for game start and one for game end. Each function should take a parameter of the type that we specify for the game, which we haven't created yet, so just enter the type here. The compiler may give you an error until you declare the type later.

```
protocol GameManagerDelegate {
    func gameDidStart(game: TheLegendOfZelda)
    func gameDidEnd(game: TheLegendOfZelda)
}
```

6. Create the `TheLegendOfZelda` class. This will be a long one, so in the interest of being brief, we create the whole class implementation here. Start with declaring the maximum and minimum heart containers Link can have and then set properties for the delegate, player name, sword, heart containers, and hearts. Validate the `hearts` property in `didSet` to make sure it stays within the number of hearts available. Create an initializer, a function to take damage, and finally a function to heal with a `Healable` item.

```
class TheLegendOfZelda {
    static let maxHeartContainers = 20
    static let minHearts = 0.0
    let delegate: GameManagerDelegate
    let name = "Link"
    var sword: String?
    var heartContainers = 3.0
    var hearts: Double = 0.0 {
        didSet {
            if hearts > heartContainers {
                hearts = heartContainers
            }
            if hearts <= TheLegendOfZelda.minHearts {
                hearts = TheLegendOfZelda.minHearts
            }
        }
    }
    init(delegate: GameManagerDelegate) {
        self.delegate = delegate
        self.delegate.gameDidStart(self)
    }
    func takeDamage(fromEnemy enemy: Enemy) {
        hearts -= enemy.damage
        print("\(name) lost \(enemy.damage) hearts from \(enemy.name),
    and has \(hearts) hearts left.")
        if hearts == 0 {
            self.delegate.gameDidEnd(self)
        }
```

```
    }
    func heal(item item: Healable) {
        hearts += item.heartsRestores
        print("\(name) gained \(item.heartsRestores) hearts from a
    ➥\(item.healableName), and has \(hearts) hearts left.")
    }
}
```

7. The last class we need to implement is the `GameManager`, which adopts the `GameManagerDelegate` protocol. Provide the methods necessary to conform to the protocol.

```
class GameManager : GameManagerDelegate {
    func gameDidStart(game: TheLegendOfZelda) {
        print("It's dangerous to go alone. Take this.")
        game.sword = "Wooden"
        game.hearts = 3.0
    }

    func gameDidEnd(game: TheLegendOfZelda) {
        print("GAME OVER. RETURN OF GANON.")
    }
}
```

8. Now it's time to create an instance of `TheLegendOfZelda` and play the game. Watch your console output as you type each line here, to observe which delegate methods get called, which properties get adjusted, and when the game starts and ends.

```
let link = TheLegendOfZelda(delegate: GameManager())
let keese = Enemy(name: "Keese", damage: 0.5)
let dekuBaba = Enemy(name: "Deku Baba", damage: 1.0)
let ganon = Enemy(name: "Ganon", damage: 2.0)
link.takeDamage(fromEnemy: keese)
link.heal(item: BluePotion())
link.takeDamage(fromEnemy: keese)
link.takeDamage(fromEnemy: dekuBaba)
link.heal(item: Heart())
link.takeDamage(fromEnemy: ganon)
link.takeDamage(fromEnemy: ganon)
```

As you can see, the preceding example is crude, and there is much room for improvement. But it gets the point across about how to use delegates that conform to protocols to make your code less complex and more loosely coupled, rather than depending so tightly on a particular type. Pressing Command+Shift+Y displays the Debug Area with the console output results for you to see your work in action. The results of your code should look like those in Figure 17.4.

```
It's dangerous to go alone. Take this.
Link lost 0.5 hearts from a Keese, and has 2.5 hearts left.
Link gained 4.0 hearts from a blue potion, and has 3.0 hearts left.
Link lost 0.5 hearts from a Keese, and has 2.5 hearts left.
Link lost 1.0 hearts from a Deku Baba, and has 1.5 hearts left.
Link gained 1.0 hearts from a heart piece, and has 2.5 hearts left.
Link lost 2.0 hearts from Ganon, and has 0.5 hearts left.
Link lost 2.0 hearts from Ganon, and has 0.0 hearts left.
GAME OVER. RETURN OF GANON.
```

FIGURE 17.4
The console output results from the preceding Try It Yourself section using delegates that conform to protocols.

Summary

In this hour, you learned about protocols, which are used as a contract to guarantee that a particular conforming type will respond to being asked for property information or execute methods. You learned the basics of the syntax and structure of protocols, and how to make a class, enum, or struct adopt one or more protocols.

Next, you learned how to use protocols as types when specifying that a constant, variable, or property that conforms to a protocol should be used. Using protocols as types can also be used in collection types. You also learned how to adopt multiple protocols mixed with class inheritance. Following that, you learned how to check conformance to a protocol with the is, as!, and as? operators in the exact same way, and how to use the @objc attribute on a protocol if you are checking for conformance during runtime or if your protocol contains any optional members.

Finally, you learned about delegation and the role protocols play in delegation. Delegates and data sources are found throughout the Cocoa and Cocoa Touch frameworks and are typically reliant upon any type that conforms to the respective protocol versus a concrete implementation.

In the next hour, we discuss extensions as a way to add, or extend, functionality in types, along with some neat examples of the power this gives you to create concise, meaningful, and powerful code.

Q&A

Q. Why would I want to use protocols? It seems easier to use subclasses or just make new classes instead.

A. When an object adopts a protocol, it is making a promise that it will provide certain functionality. This allows objects that are otherwise unrelated fill a similar role and reduces extra cruft that may be unnecessarily inherited from a superclass. For example, both a car and a classroom might provide information about maximum capacity, but they probably don't belong in the same class structure.

Swift is a single inheritance language, which means that a class can only have a single superclass. But a class, enum, or struct can adopt multiple protocols, which enables more flexibility in your code.

Q. Can a protocol specify a default implementation of a method?

A. Yes, but we have not covered that yet. We discuss this behavior in Hour 21.

Q. If I use the `@objc` keyword, do I have to write Objective-C instead of Swift?

A. No, `@objc` is just a hint to the compiler that the protocol is doing something that it needs to be aware of. You still write your code in Swift.

Q. Can protocols inherit other protocols?

A. Yes, they can! Protocols can inherit one or more other protocols if you need them to. Any type that adopts the child protocol must also satisfy the requirements of the parent protocol.

Workshop

The workshop contains quiz questions and exercises to help you solidify your understanding of the material covered. Try to answer all questions before looking at the answers that follow.

Quiz

1. Do you need to use the `override` keyword when implementing a method required by a protocol your class adopts?

2. True or false? Properties defined in a protocol must always be defined with the `var` keyword, even when they're constants.

3. What's wrong with the following code?

```
protocol CoolProperty {
 var coolFactor: Bool { get set }
}

class Student {
 var name = "Default Name"
}

class Senior : CoolProperty, Student {
 var coolFactor = true
}
```

4. If a protocol defines a read-write property, can my class implement it as read-only?

Answers

1. No, you can just implement the method in your class.

2. True. Always use `var` in property definitions.

3. In the `Senior` class, the superclass must be listed before any adopted protocols. Here, we list the protocol `CoolProperty` before the superclass `Student`.

4. No, If the property is read-write in the protocol definition, it must be read-write in the adopting class.

Exercise

Create a new OS X playground. Define a protocol named `Nameable` that specifies a `describe` method and a property called `name`. The `describe` method should take no arguments and return a string. Next, define a protocol named `Debugable`, which specifies a method named `showDebug`. This method should take no arguments and return a string. When you adopt these protocols, have `name()` and `showDebug()` display useful information about the object.

Create three classes, one that adopts `Nameable`, one that adopts `Debugable`, and one that adopts both protocols. Now create arrays of types `Nameable`, `Debugable`, and the composition of those two protocols.

Practice adding objects of each type to these three arrays and then calling `describe` and `showDebug` on the contents. What happens if you try to add a class that doesn't adopt `Describable` to an array of type `Describable`? What would be different if you were using enums or structs instead of classes? Can you add a class that adopts both protocols to the `Describable` array? Try it out and see.

Using Extensions to Add Type Functionality

What You'll Learn in This Hour:

▶ How to define extensions

▶ How to add initializers with extensions

▶ How to add methods, computed properties, and subscripts with extensions

▶ How to adopt a protocol to an existing type

In this hour, we discuss a feature of Swift called **extensions**. Types provided by Apple in the Swift programming language are closed, unable to be modified by us, and extensions help overcome that roadblock. You learn how to add functionality of multiple different facets to existing types and the implications of doing so. Let's take a look at what extensions are and how to use them.

Defining Extensions

A Swift extension is a way to add functionality, but not override existing functionality, to an existing type. You can add extensions to types that you create, as well as to types provided by Swift, such as `Int`, `Double`, `String`, `Array`, and so on.

Why would you want to add functionality with an extension? There are several reasons why you might want to add extensions to your types. You might not have access to the actual source implementation of types, which is exactly the case with Swift's built-in types of `Int`, `String`, and so on. Your company might have a policy in place as well that disallows you from accessing standard structures of types for modification. Such examples are said to be *closed for modification*, but with extensions, these types are now able to be extended because they are *open for extension*.

NOTE

Open/Closed Principle

The Open/Closed Principle, coined by Bertrand Meyer, states that "software entities should be open for extension, but closed for modification." In keeping with good software development methodologies, extensions provide a tremendous way to extend existing type functionality without altering the actual implementation of a type.

There are also instances in developing apps for Mac and iOS platforms where you may use a framework called Core Data. Core Data is a way to use model objects and an object graph to persist data, rather than dealing with a SQLite database (or whatever backing store) directly. When you create your model objects with Xcode's visual editor, you then create NSManagedObject subclasses that represent your model objects. These NSManagedObject subclasses can get recreated any time your data model is updated. Since these subclasses get overwritten frequently, it doesn't make much sense to put any extra logic inside them, so extensions are a perfect solution for an example such as this.

Basic Structure of Extensions

Extensions in Swift do not get a special name; they only need to reference the type they are extending. The syntax for defining an extension is simply the extension keyword followed by the type name that you want to extend, and, finally, curly braces to include the code you're extending onto the type. Figure 18.1 shows the general structure of an extension.

```
extension TypeNameToExtend {
    // ... functionality to add
}
```

FIGURE 18.1
The general structure of an extension in Swift.

You can also have more than one extension for a particular type. In fact, in the interest of good software design, it may behoove you to create multiple extensions separated by each having a single responsibility. For example, if you Command+click the Int keyword in Xcode, Xcode navigates you to the definition of the Int struct and all its extensions. There are many extensions, each responsible for providing a single solution, such as for providing the hashValue property and also the description property, as shown in Figure 18.2.

```
3994   extension Int : Hashable {
3995       /// The hash value.
3996       ///
3997       /// **Axiom:** `x == y` implies `x.hashValue == y.hashValue`.
3998       ///
3999       /// - Note: The hash value is not guaranteed to be stable across
4000       ///   different invocations of the same program.  Do not persist the
4001       ///   hash value across program runs.
4002       public var hashValue: Int { get }
4003   }
4004
4005   extension Int : CustomStringConvertible {
4006       /// A textual representation of `self`.
4007       public var description: String { get }
4008   }
4009
```

FIGURE 18.2
Two extensions on the `Int` struct showing how functionality can be extracted out to separate components with extensions and protocols.

Adding Functionality with Extensions

There are several pieces of functionality we can add to types with extensions, which include adding new computed instance and type properties, instance and type methods, subscripts, initializers, nested types, and protocol conformance. Adding these pieces of functionality is treated as if you were adding them directly to the type itself, so there really is no difference in syntax; the only difference is that you're adding them to an extension inside an extension definition. Since we are adding functionality to existing types and dealing with instance properties or instance methods, we can refer to the instance itself with the `self` keyword. Let's discuss each one and cover examples to illustrate how each piece of functionality can be added.

Computed Instance and Type Properties

You may add computed instance and type properties to a type with extensions. You cannot, however, add stored properties. An example of adding computed properties could be if you wanted to add instance properties on the `Double` type to convert gallons to quarts, pints, and cups, or on the `String` type to return the string instance broken into an array of `Character` instances.

NOTE
___

Extensions Add Functionality to All Instances of a Type

Remember that adding an extension to a type adds that functionality to all instances of that type, even if they were created before the instance was created, such as an instance retrieved from permanent storage that was created before the extension was in place.

Let's take a look at how we can add a computed instance property to the `String` type. Remember, adding functionality with an extension is just as if we were adding the functionality directly into the type like normal, so the syntax should all look the same to you for concepts learned thus far.

Listing 18.1 illustrates how to add an extension to the `String` type to return an instance's representation as an array of characters.

LISTING 18.1 **Extending the String Type with Computed Properties**

```
extension String {
    var asArray: [Character] {
        return self.characters.reduce([]) { $0 + [$1] }
    }
}

let chars = "Hello".asArray    // chars is equal to ["H", "e", "l", "l", "o"]
let dog = "Fido"
let dogChars = dog.asArray      // dogChars is equal to ["F", "i", "d", "o"]
```

In the preceding example, we simply add a computed instance property to the `String` type, which builds an aggregate array of `Character` instances that we can then use with dot syntax to get the result. Simple, right? Notice that we can also use our extended computed property directly on a string literal in addition to a variable. This is because string literals are still of type `String`, so any property or method can be accessed just as if it were on a variable or constant.

Let's create another example on a numeric type, to see how extensions can be used to add some powerful functionality in just a few lines of code. Say that we have used the `typealias` keyword to create a type alias to `Double`, for working with miles per hour of a car. We can even extend an aliased type. Listing 18.2 illustrates how to do this.

LISTING 18.2 **Extending Aliased Types**

```
typealias MPH = Double
extension MPH {
    var kmPerHour: Double { return self * 1.60934 }
    var milesPerMinute: Double { return self / 60.0 }
}

let speed: MPH = 60
let kmH = speed.kmPerHour       // kmH is equal to 96.5604
let mpM = speed.milesPerMinute  // mpM is equal to 1.0
```

Creating custom computed properties for types inside extensions can greatly increase functionality of a type and its instances, while keeping code separated by responsibility and modularized.

Think about how computed properties could be added to other types and experiment on your own!

Instance and Type Methods

Methods are another piece of functionality that we can add to types via extensions. Again, methods (both instance and type) are added with their normal syntax, without any special modifications. If you are creating a method that would mutate a struct or enum, you must add the `mutating` keyword, as you normally would.

A classic example of adding a method to a type is by adding a method to the `Int` type with a trailing closure that gets executed as many times as the integer value equals. The method takes a single parameter, of type `() -> ()`, and looks like the example in Listing 18.3.

LISTING 18.3 Adding Methods with Extensions

```
extension Int {
    func execute(closure: () -> ()) {
        guard self >= 0 else { return }
        for _ in 1...self {
            closure()
        }
    }
}

3.execute { print("I'm positive I'll be printed.") }
(-4).execute { print("I'm so negative, I won't be printed!") }
```

That is a common example for extensions on the `Int` type, but how could you use this in a practical application? Listing 18.4 shows how to use this extension for quickly adjusting a player's score in a game. Because the `execute(closure:)` method takes a function with no parameters and returns void, we can send any method or function that fits that description.

LISTING 18.4 Adding Methods with Extensions for a Game

```
// use extension from Listing 18.3
struct Player {
    var score = 0
    mutating func increaseScore() {
        ++score
    }
    mutating func decreaseScore() {
        --score
    }
}
```

```
var player = Player()
// while playing game, player wins 5 points
5.execute { player.increaseScore() }
player.score                // displays 5
```

Adding Subscripts in Extensions

Another functionality that can be added to extensions is the capability to add subscripts. You can give subscripts their own meaning inside your apps by creating custom subscripts to be applied to any type, but with extensions, you can add them to existing types. Let's try an example in the following Try It Yourself section to add subscripting capability to the String type so we can obtain the character at a particular index in the string.

▼ TRY IT YOURSELF

Extend the String Type to Add Subscripts

Add a subscript function to the String type to obtain the character at a particular index.

1. Open Xcode and create a new playground; either an iOS or a Mac playground works. Clear the contents of the playground.

2. Recreate the asArray computed property from Listing 18.1, as that provides a convenience for our subscript extension.

```
extension String {
    var asArray: [Character] {
        return self.characters.reduce([]) { $0 + [$1] }
    }
}
```

3. Now that we have self as an array instance, we can easily return the character at a particular index by using a subscript function inside a new extension. Create a subscript with only a getter to return the character at a given index.

```
extension String {
    subscript(index: Int) -> Character {
        return self.asArray[index]
    }
}
```

4. There's a problem with this subscript, though. Can you see it? What happens if the string is empty or if the index provided is out of bounds? Fix the subscript to check the string and index first, and return nil if these criteria are not met. Because we could return nil, change the return type from Character to Character?.

```
extension String {
    subscript(index: Int) -> Character? {
```

```
            if case 0..<self.characters.count = index {
                return self.asArray[index]
            }
            return nil
        }
    }
```

5. Create an instance of String, and access a subscript on that string. Then create an empty string and try to access a subscript on the empty string.

```
let words = "Cuyahoga River"
let fifthChar = words[4]!
let emptyString = ""
let badIndex = emptyString[0]
```

By using extensions and reusing code, we easily created a powerful construct to use any time we need to quickly access the *nth* element of a string, and we don't need to have a lot of repeated code in our app since our extensions apply to all String instances in our module. The completed Try It Yourself section code and results should look like those in Figure 18.3.

```
 1  extension String {
 2      var asArray: [Character] {
 3          return self.characters.reduce([]) { $0 + [$1] }     (15 times)
 4      }
 5  }
 6
 7  extension String {
 8      subscript(index: Int) -> Character? {
 9          if case 0..<self.characters.count = index {
10              return self.asArray[index]                      "h"
11          }
12          return nil                                          nil
13      }
14  }
15
16  let words = "Cuyahoga River"                                "Cuyahoga River"
17  let fifthChar = words[4]!                                   "h"
18  let emptyString = ""                                        ""
19  let badIndex = emptyString[0]                               nil
20
```

FIGURE 18.3
The completed Try It Yourself example illustrating using extensions on the String type to return the character at a particular subscript.

Adding Custom Initializers with Extensions

By now, you should be familiar with the extension concept and syntax, in that you can add mostly any functionality you need by adding an extension on a particular type. Another piece of functionality that you would expect to be written exactly as it is normally and behave the same way is initializers. And you're right, initializers can be added to types via extensions, but there are two caveats: You cannot add a designated initializer with an extension, and you cannot provide a deinitializer.

If you have a struct that provides default values for its properties without a custom initializer, your extended initializer can call either the default initializer or the memberwise initializer. Let's take a look at how that is done in Listing 18.5.

LISTING 18.5   **Creating Initializers in Extensions**

```
import Foundation

struct Circle {
    var radius = 0.0
    var circumference: Double {
        return 2 * radius * M_PI
    }
}

extension Circle {
    init(circumference: Double) {
        let radius = circumference / (2 * M_PI)
        self.init(radius: radius)
    }
}

let circle = Circle(circumference: 31.42)
circle.radius                              // displays 5.0006483....
```

Since a class type must have a designated initializer inside its main implementation, you cannot add one in an extension. Creating initializers inside extensions of class types must use the `convenience` keyword since they should, by default, be convenience initializers, as the designated initializer must reside inside the class implementation directly. That also means that your convenience initializer *must* call the designated initializer or another convenience initializer in the same type to complete full initialization of the instance before use. Failure to do so generates a compiler error. Listing 18.6 shows adding a convenience initializer in a class extension.

LISTING 18.6   Creating a Convenience Initializer in a Class Type Extension

```
class Person {
    var fullName: String
    init(fullName: String) {
        self.fullName = fullName
    }
}

extension Person {
    convenience init(firstName: String, lastName: String) {
        let fullName = firstName + " " + lastName
        self.init(fullName: fullName)
    }
}

let person = Person(firstName: "George", lastName: "Washington")
person.fullName                    // displays "George Washington"
```

Creating an initializer in an extension for a class type is equally as easy and syntactically the same as if it were inside a class implementation directly. Remember that since you cannot add a designated initializer in an extension to a class type, any initializers you add must be convenience initializers.

Adding Nested Types to Extensions

Although we haven't discussed **nested types** yet, the concepts discussed here pertain just as if they were added directly to a type without an extension. Nested types are types that help support a larger type and are only accessible to instances of that larger type. Nested types are not accessible to types outside the type inside which they are encapsulated, in the exact same way that nested functions are not accessible to functions outside of the containing function.

An example of when you would use a nested type could be with a deck of cards, for a quick and simple way to obtain data whether a card is a face card or a numeric card. Another could be if you are keeping track of your Transformers collection. You may want to add a nested type that is an enum that simply tracks whether a figure is an Autobot or a Decepticon. Listing 18.7 shows how you could use a nested type inside a Transformers enum.

LISTING 18.7   Adding Nested Types in Extensions

```
01:   enum Transformers : String {
02:       case OptimusPrime = "Optimus Prime"
03:       case Bumblebee = "Bumblebee"
04:       case Ratchet = "Ratchet"
05:       case Megatron = "Megatron"
06:       case Starscream = "Starscream"
```

```
07:  }
08:
09:  extension Transformers {
10:      enum TransformerType {
11:          case Autobot, Decepticon
12:      }
13:
14:      var type: TransformerType {
15:          switch self {
16:              case .OptimusPrime, .Bumblebee, .Ratchet:
17:                  return .Autobot
18:              default:
19:                  return .Decepticon
20:          }
21:      }
22:  }
23:
24:  let transformer = Transformers.Bumblebee
25:  switch transformer.type {
26:      case .Autobot:
27:          print("\(transformer.rawValue) is an Autobot.")
28:      case .Decepticon:
29:          print("\(transformer.rawValue) is a Decepticon.")
30:  }
```

Since nested types are new to us in this book, as well as a new concept for us to cover with regard to extensions, let's discuss some key lines in Listing 18.7. We created a standard enum on line 1 with a backing value of type String. But suppose after the Transformers type is created, we want to add a description of whether the Transformers instance is an Autobot or Decepticon. On line 9, we extend the Transformers enum, and on line 10, we create a nested type. The nested type is another enum, and the enum is only available to instances of the Transformers type. A nested type can be added to a main type implementation and used just as you see here if not used in an extension—the syntax and usage are exactly the same.

Then on line 14, we create a computed property to return a value of our nested type. If you were following along in the REPL or in a playground, try changing the enum value from .Bumblebee to another Transformers case on line 24, to watch the switch statement find the appropriate description for the Transformer in question.

Protocol Adoption and Conformance in Extensions

The final concept in this hour with regard to what can be added with extensions is about protocols. As you learned in Hour 17, "Using Protocols to Define Behavior," protocols are a blueprint to functionality and behavior that a type must conform to if it adopts the protocol. It is a contract stating that any type that conforms to this protocol can and will provide the necessary information outlined in the protocol.

Adding adoption and conformance to a protocol in an extension is just as simple as everything else we have done in extensions this hour, combined with the simplicity of declaring and conforming to a protocol. In fact, this is how many of the types we use in the Swift standard library are composed; they start with a simple type declaration and through extensions, protocol conformance adds functionality and flexibility to many of the standard types. Whether you're creating a new protocol to make a type conform to or conforming to an existing protocol, you simply add the protocol name after the type name and a colon in the extension declaration, as shown in the following snippet:

```
extension ExistingType : ProtocolName {
    // ...add protocol properties or methods here...
}
```

If a type already has the properties and/or methods that belong to a protocol's definition but does not yet adopt the protocol, you can simply create an extension of the type that adopts the protocol and then provide an empty pair of curly braces, as shown in the following snippet:

```
extension ExistingType : ProtocolName { }
```

The preceding snippet may be beneficial in cases where you have a model object in your app that contains information about the instance that happens to be the same information required by a protocol. Imagine your model object also has a title, subtitle, and coordinate. Despite having the information needed to drop a pin on a map view, the model object's type may not have adopted the protocol, so the map view cannot use it as a pin annotation on the map. By providing an empty extension for your model's type that adopts the MKAnnotation protocol, it can then be shown on the map as a pin annotation, because the map view can only place instances that adopt and conform to the MKAnnotation protocol to the map.

Let's try a small example of adopting and conforming the Int type to a protocol in the following Try It Yourself example.

Extend Int to Adopt and Conform to a Protocol

Create a protocol that has a function to square an integer. Then extend the Int type to adopt the protocol. Finally, add the method to conform to the protocol.

1. Open Xcode and create a new playground; either an iOS or a Mac playground is fine. Clear the contents of the playground.

2. Start by creating the protocol. Call it Squarable and provide a computed property definition that returns an Int:

▼

```
protocol Squarable {
    var squared: Int { get }
}
```

3. Create an extension for the `Int` type and adopt the `Squarable` protocol. Then conform to the protocol by implementing the `squared` computed property and return the squared value of the given integer.

```
extension Int : Squarable {
    var squared: Int {
        return self * self
    }
}
```

4. Finally, try out your new instance method from your extension on a number.

```
5.squared        // displays 25
```

In just a few lines, you added a lot of power to the `Int` type. Now any instance of an `Int` can call the `squared` computed property and immediately get the squared value of itself. The completed code and results from the preceding Try It Yourself section should look like those in Figure 18.4.

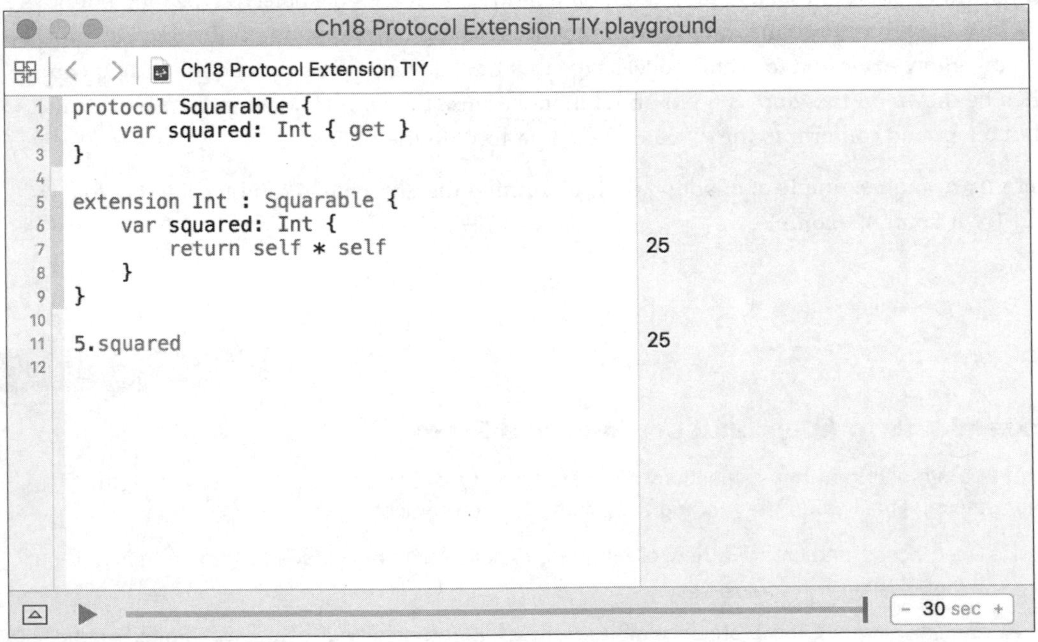

FIGURE 18.4
The completed Try It Yourself example code and results from adding protocol conformance via extensions.

Summary

This hour introduced extensions, a Swift feature enabling you to add functionality to built-in or custom types. You learned about many different capabilities that can be added to types with extensions including computed properties, methods, subscripts, initializers, nested types, and protocols.

As you saw in the many examples in this hour, the code to add these behaviors to types is exactly the same as if they were added directly to the type itself.

In the next hour, we discuss optional chaining, which is a powerful way to traverse paths of optional properties and fail gracefully if `nil` is encountered.

Q&A

Q. When would I want to use extensions instead of just making a subclass and adding the new functionality there?

A. Extensions enable you to modify an existing class without creating a new one. This means that the changes you make are available to every object of the type being extended. If you make a subclass, the new functionality is only available to that new subclass. For example, in this hour, we added new properties to integers, and those changes affected all integers in our program.

Q. Can an extension override a method that already exists in the class, structure, or enumeration type?

A. No. If you try to override a method or property that already exists, you get an invalid redeclaration error.

Q. Can I use access control (public, private, internal) in an extension?

A. Yes. You can specify any level of access control you need to when creating an extension. The same access control rules that we saw in Hour 15, "Adding Advanced Type Functionality," apply to extensions.

Q. If I define an extension on a class, is that extension available to its subclasses too?

A. Yes. Your extension adds new functionality to the base class, and that functionality is passed on to subclasses.

Workshop

The workshop contains quiz questions and exercises to help you solidify your understanding of the material covered. Try to answer all questions before looking at the answers that follow.

Quiz

1. Can there be more than one extension for a single type?

2. True or false? You can add designated initializers using extensions, but not convenience initializers.

3. Can extensions be used to adopt protocols?

4. True or false? Mutating methods are not allowed in extensions for structs or enums.

Answers

1. Yes, as long as the extensions are adding different things.

2. False. You can add a convenience initializer, but just like any other convenience initializer, it must ultimately call a designated initializer.

3. Yes, but if a protocol is adopted, all the normal conformance rules apply. The class, struct, or enum must be extended to implement all required methods and properties.

4. False. Methods defined in extensions can mutate a struct or enum's properties as long as the mutating keyword is used in the method definition.

Exercise

Create a new OS X playground. Create an extension to `String` that produces the string in reverse order. For example, `"My String".reverse` should give us "gnirtS yM" back. If you get stuck, look at the `toArray` method we created earlier.

For more of a challenge, create an extension to `String` that converts a string of digits to an integer. For example, `"1397".toInt` should return the integer 1397. What do you think your extension should do if the string contains something other than integers? This might be a good time for an optional.

HINT: Remember that 1397 = 7 + 90 + 300 + 1000.

Working with Optional Chaining

What You'll Learn in This Hour:

▶ What optional chaining is

▶ When to use optional chaining

▶ How to chain properties, methods, and subscripts

▶ How to verify optional chaining success or failure

In this hour, we cover optional chaining. This concept is new to many programmers, as it only makes sense in the context of working with optional values, which is a new concept itself to some programmers, and sort of new to most Objective-C programmers. You learn the basics of optional chaining, when and how to use it, and how to verify success or handle failure. This hour builds on the concepts of optional values discussed in Hour 6, "Understanding Optional Values," so if you need to brush up on optionals first, I suggest you do so before continuing with this hour. If not, let's discuss optional chaining in Swift.

Defining Optional Chaining

As you recall, Swift provides functionality for dealing with nil, or the absence of a value, called optional values. Think of an optional value as a box. The box may have something inside, or it may be empty. The same goes for optional values in Swift. To continue the box metaphor, if you have an optional String, denoted by String?, the box is of type String?, and inside it may have an actual value (of type String), or it may be empty (nil).

Optional chaining is the process of checking optional values by calling or querying properties, methods, and subscripts of an optional type to perform a specific task or return nil. If an optional value that you call or query is not nil, the call or query succeeds. If the optional value is nil, the call or query fails gracefully and returns nil. Since there is a possibility for the call or query to return nil, the result of an optional chaining is *always* of an optional type. An optional chain can be used instead of several nested optional binding statements.

Optional chaining can be thought of like Matryoshka dolls (also known as Russian nesting dolls). You can see the outer doll, but you don't know whether there is another doll or dolls inside. You open the doll, and if there is another doll, you can attempt to use or open that doll too. If there is no other doll inside, you stop, as if you encountered `nil`.

The reason for stating in the beginning of the hour that this is sort of new to Objective-C programmers is that in Objective-C, you can message or query `nil` and it will fail gracefully, so Objective-C programmers use it to their benefit. There are differences, though, in how Swift handles optional chaining and Objective-C handles messaging `nil`. Mainly, Swift can chain optionals of any type, and return `nil` for any type, not just class instances like Objective-C. You can also have an instance of a class be equal to `nil` in Objective-C without being wrapped, but that is not considered safe in Swift. So all `nil` values must be wrapped, or else the app will crash at runtime.

Optional chaining returns an optional value of the type specified by the instance being called or queried. This means that if you query a property of type `String?`, you receive a `String?` instance back, even if there is a value inside the optional. This is actually helpful, because if you receive `nil` from the call or query, you know that the call or query failed, but you also get the type information that the value would have been if it weren't `nil`. And if the optional contains a value, your call or query succeeded. The same goes for a property, method, or subscript that returns a non-optional type; the result will still be an optional because the call or query could have failed along the chain and returned `nil`.

There are many use cases for optional chaining, and as a Swift developer, chances are you will use this tool many times a day. One such use case is with delegates. Remember using the delegate pattern in Hour 18, "Using Extensions to Add Type Functionality," and how we set the delegate directly in the initializer? That was so that the delegate could not be `nil`. There may be times, however, where the delegate may never be set, because all properties and methods on a particular protocol are optional, and the instance calling the delegate can operate without having a delegate respond to any messages. Using a delegate is a prime example of using optional chaining, by checking whether the delegate is `nil` first before calling or querying any properties or methods on the delegate.

Chaining Optional Properties

Often you have properties in a class, struct, or enum of an optional type. The types that those properties reference or contain could also be optional, and you may find yourself needing to access values two, three, or more levels down the property relationship chain. Optional chaining gives you a safe way to determine whether a value is `nil` at any point along the way to calling or querying your final property, and if so, fail safely by returning `nil`. Not only can you use optional chaining for calling or querying properties, but you can also set properties using optional chaining.

Let's take a look at a simple example of how optional chaining works. Say we have a `Person` class representing a possible owner of a `Dog` instance. The person may or may not have a dog, so we would make this property an optional type. For simplicity's sake, all you dog lovers, we keep the person to one dog for now. Using optional chaining, we try to retrieve the name of the person instance's dog. Listing 19.1 illustrates this example.

LISTING 19.1 Basic Optional Chaining of Properties

```
01:    class Person {
02:        var dog: Dog?
03:    }
04:
05:    class Dog {
06:        let name: String
07:        init(name: String) { self.name = name }
08:    }
09:
10:    let susie = Person()
11:    let dogsName = susie.dog?.name    // returns nil
```

In Listing 19.1, we declare two classes, `Person` and `Dog`, just like normal. On line 10, we declare an instance of `Person` and set it to the constant `susie`. Then on line 11, we try to get the dog's name from `susie`'s dog instance's name property. Since `susie`'s dog property is of an optional type, we need to place the question mark after the dog property before we try to access the dog's name property. `susie` has no dog yet, so `dogsName` is of type `String?` and contains `nil`.

If we were to assign an instance of `Dog` to `susie`'s dog property, we would see the optional chaining call on line 11 with a different result. Let's do that in Listing 19.2 by inserting a creation of a `Dog` instance between lines 10 and 11 from the preceding example.

LISTING 19.2 Assigning a Dog

```
// reuse classes declared in Listing 19.1
let bobby = Person()
bobby.dog = Dog(name: "Cletus")
print(bobby.dog?.name)        // prints "Optional("Cletus")"
```

As you can see, now that `bobby`'s dog property is not `nil`, there is now a name to be accessed via optional chaining. Do you see how the resulting value assigned to `dogsName` is `Optional("Cletus")`? That is because even though there is a value for the `name` property of the `Dog` instance, `bobby`'s dog property is of type `Dog?`, and thus the returned value must be optional, as a `String?`, too.

The preceding examples illustrate how the syntax works for optional chaining, but let's deviate to a larger example, one that may represent an enterprise problem that needs to be solved with your Swift programming expertise. To start, let's discuss accessing and modifying subscripts with optional chaining.

Subscripts

Recall that subscripts are a way to set and get values of types such as arrays and dictionaries, and the syntax for subscript access is implemented by including an integer index or hashable key inside a pair of open- and closed-square brackets.

In my experience, I have worked a lot in the administration realm of Microsoft SharePoint Server. You may have used SharePoint at some point in your career for document management, team collaboration, or any other feature it provides. This book isn't going in the direction of educating you on the inner workings of Microsoft SharePoint Server, but concepts in it can be applied to our topic of optional chaining. Rather than continuing to refer to Microsoft SharePoint Server, I will henceforth refer to it and any similar collaboration tool as simply a *collaboration tool*.

NOTE

The SharePoint Object Model

We discuss objects similar to the hierarchy of SharePoint but not anything specific from the SharePoint Object Model. The concepts here can apply to many other collaborative systems, but I reference SharePoint because of its generally ubiquitous understanding in the tech world.

When accessing subscripts through optional chaining, it is important to take a second to think about what portion or portions of the optional chain should have the optional chaining operator (?), and where in relation to the property, method, or subscript syntax it should be placed. **You should always place the optional chaining operator after the portion or portions that can be optional, not necessarily after the entire expression.** For example, accessing an element at a particular index of an optional array means that you should put the optional chaining operator immediately after the name of the optional array, but before the index, because the array itself is optional, not necessarily the element at the index. In code, it would look like the following code snippet:

```
let someValue = someInstance.someArray?[0] // correct
let anotherValue = anotherInstance.anotherArray[0]? // incorrect
```

Let's say we are writing an app that integrates with a collaboration tool and we need a few classes to store data and perform actions for us, such as a site, document library, and document. Each site can have zero or more document libraries, and each document library can have zero or more documents. There are many other things that these objects could do in real-world collaboration tools, but these few examples are sufficient for this hour. Figure 19.1 illustrates what a collaboration scenario might look like structurally.

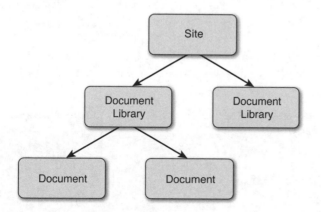

FIGURE 19.1
An example collaboration hierarchy diagram of a site, document libraries, and documents.

Let's create this example in code in the following Try It Yourself section. You walk through creating the classes with optional array properties and then how to access data using optional chaining.

Use Optional Chaining with Subscripts

Create an object model that reflects the collaboration tool hierarchy previously discussed. Then use optional chaining to set and get elements down the chain.

1. Open Xcode and create a new playground; either an iOS or a Mac playground works. Clear the contents of the playground.

2. Start by creating the `Site` class. Provide a variable property named `title` of type `String`. Then create a variable property that is an optional array that contains elements of type `Library`. Don't initialize the array. Provide an initializer to set the `title` property.

```
class Site {
    var title: String
    var libraries: [Library]?
    init(title: String) { self.title = title }
}
```

▼

3. Create the `Library` class. This class has a variable `title` property of type `String` and an optional array that contains elements of type `Document`. Create an initializer for the `title` property.

```
class Library {
    var title: String
    var documents: [Document]?
    init(title: String) { self.title = title }
}
```

4. Create the `Document` class. This class also has a variable `title` property of type `String` and an initializer for the `title` property.

```
class Document {
    var title: String
    init(title: String) { self.title = title }
}
```

5. That's all for the model classes. Create an instance of type `Site` and call it "Accounting".

```
let acctSite = Site(title: "Accounting")
```

6. Create an instance of a document library for documents related to auditing and use optional chaining to append it as the first instance in the `acctSite`'s `Library` array. But before we do that, we have to initialize the `acctSite`'s `Library` array before we can use it.

```
let auditLibrary = Library(title: "Audit Library")
acctSite.libraries = []
acctSite.libraries?.append(auditLibrary)
```

7. That is how we can use optional chaining for assignment. If the `libraries` array was `nil`, `auditLibrary` would not have been appended, and the expression would have returned `nil`, signifying to us that the optional chaining failed. Repeat the concept expressed in step 6 but with creating a document and adding it to the `documents` array in the `auditLibrary` instance, and initialize the `documents` array first.

```
let document = Document(title: "Audit Report November 2015.txt")
auditLibrary.documents = []
auditLibrary.documents?.append(document)
```

8. Now that we have a non-`nil` hierarchy of site > library > document, use optional chaining with subscripts to grab the document name for use in a constant. Use multiple levels of optional chaining to retrieve the document name. Try using `[0]` and also `first` to get the first element. Do this in an optional binding statement, with which the body will be filled in during step 9.

```
if let docName = acctSite.libraries?[0].documents?[0].title { // or...
if let docName = acctSite.libraries?.first?.documents?.first?.title {
```

9. Notice how you had to add ? after `first` also? That is because there may not be an item in the first element, so that computed property returns an optional. Also, even though the `title` property on `Document` is not optional, `docName` *is* optional, because it was retrieved using optional chaining, and any point along the way could have failed and returned `nil`. Use optional binding to extract the value and print an appropriate message.

```
    print("Document name is \(docName).")
} else {
    print("Could not retrieve document name.")
}
```

10. For fun, comment out the line in step 6, `acctSite.libraries = []`. Now what results do you get? You should get `nil`, because optional chaining encountered a `nil` value in its chain before it got to the document's `title` property.

The completed Try It Yourself example code and results should look like those in Figure 19.2.

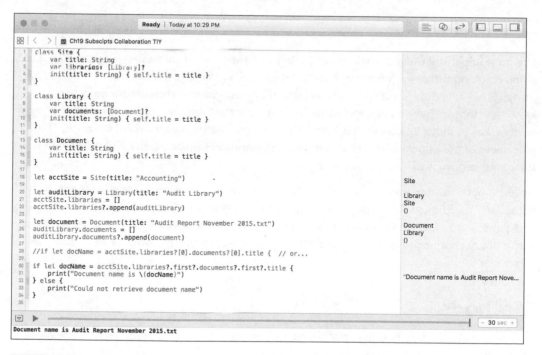

FIGURE 19.2
The completed Try It Yourself example with optional chaining using subscripts and multiple levels of optional chaining.

Another utilization of subscripts with optional chaining is with dictionaries. This is another place where you need to pay close attention to the placement of the optional chaining operator, whether it is before or after the subscript, but luckily Xcode is good about suggesting how to fix your code if you don't put the ? in the right place.

Let's say you are creating an app to track bowling scores, so you have a dictionary with the bowlers' names as the keys and their scores in an array for their key's value. Listing 19.3 utilizes optional chaining using dictionaries to adjust a value of one of the values in a player's array of scores.

LISTING 19.3   Using Optional Chaining with Dictionary Subscripts

```
var bowlingScores = ["Jane" : [190, 180, 172], "John" : [165, 156, 214] ]

bowlingScores    // displays ["John": [165, 156, 214], "Jane": [190, 180, 172]]

// pin counter mis-counted Jane's last game by 1
bowlingScores["Jane"]?[2]++

bowlingScores    // displays ["John": [165, 156, 214], "Jane": [190, 180, 173]]
```

The most important thing to point out in Listing 19.3 is how we incremented Jane's third game score. Breaking this down, we know that bowlingScores["Jane"] itself returns an optional array, [Int]?, because dictionaries always return optional values when obtaining values for keys. Now that we have an optional array, we must use the ? operator before asking the array for its value at index 2. After we have that value, we can use the ++ increment operator. The placement of the ? operator is very important, and you must think carefully about where to put it for your code to work the way you want.

By using optional chaining, we are able to directly set an array's value inside a dictionary's value for a specific key. Remember that a dictionary can return nil when we ask it for a value at a particular key, because that key may not exist yet, so there obviously is no value. We must use optional chaining to access the element at index two of the array stored for key "Jane" to increment it.

Methods

Accessing methods in Swift using optional chaining works in much the same way as accessing properties; you just need to add the parentheses after the method name when you call it. If the method returns a non-optional value, the result will still be an optional value if it was accessed using optional chaining, just as with properties. If the method returns an optional value, the resulting value is not doubly wrapped; a method that returns String? when called using optional chaining does not return String??. A returned value is either optional or non-optional.

Something special happens, however, when you call a function that doesn't have a return type. Swift infers this type of function to return an empty tuple, or (), as we discussed in Hour 8, "Using Functions to Perform Actions." The actual type for this is Void, and since when we use optional chaining we always get a return type as an optional, we are returned Void?. Usually if a function returns nothing, we don't have any need for an empty tuple or anything of type Void, but with optional chaining, we can use this as a way to verify whether our function was actually executed by checking it against nil.

Going back to the collaboration tool example, we can add instance methods to these classes, such as for adding a new document and checking out or checking in a document. By adding a method on Library to add a new document, we can also lazily instantiate the documents array and alleviate the caller of that responsibility, like we had to do in the preceding Try It Yourself example. If you're following along, feel free to open up your playground file from the Try It Yourself example and adjust your code with me, as shown in Listing 19.4. Notice in line 40 of Listing 19.4 that a warning is produced; this is expected and is explained in the paragraph following the listing.

LISTING 19.4   Using Optional Chaining to Call Instance Methods

```
01:  class Site {
02:      var title: String
03:      var libraries: [Library]?
04:      init(title: String) { self.title = title }
05:      func addNewLibrary(title title: String) -> Library {
06:          var library = Library(title: title)
07:          if libraries == nil {
08:              libraries = []
09:          }
10:          libraries?.append(library)
11:          return library
12:      }
13:  }
14:
15:  class Library {
16:      var title: String
17:      var documents: [Document]?
18:      init(title: String) { self.title = title }
19:      func addNewDocument(title title: String) -> Document {
20:          var document = Document(title: title)
21:          if documents == nil {
22:              documents = []
23:          }
24:          documents?.append(document)
25:          return document
26:      }
27:  }
```

```
28:
29:   class Document {
30:       var title: String
31:       var checkedOut = false
32:       init(title: String) { self.title = title }
33:       func checkOut() { checkedOut = true }
34:       func checkIn() { checkedOut = false }
35:   }
36:
37:   let acctSite = Site(title: "Accounting")
38:   acctSite.addNewLibrary(title: "Audit Library")
39:   let addDoc = acctSite.libraries?.first?.addNewDocument(title: "Audit Report")
40:   let checkout = acctSite.libraries?.first?.documents?.first?.checkOut()
```

In the preceding example, we add two new instance methods, one on Site and one on
Library, on lines 5 and 19, respectively. These create a new instance of the type contained
in their array properties and lazily instantiate the arrays if they are equal to nil, on lines 7
through 9 and 21 through 23, respectively. On line 37, we create the site, and then on line 38,
we add a new library to its libraries array. On line 39, we ask the first library in acctSite.
libraries? to add a document using optional chaining, which returns Document? to addDoc.
We could check addDoc for nil to see whether it succeeded. On line 40, we use optional chaining for calling a method again and attempt to check out the first document in the first library in
the site. Xcode provides a warning, stating that the inferred type of our optional chaining call
to checkOut() is ()?, and Xcode warns us that the type ()? may not be expected—but this is
what we expected (see Figure 19.3). You can add a specific type annotation on the checkout
constant (of type ()?) to silence the warning.

```
39   let addDoc = acctSite.libraries?.first?.addNewDocument(title: "Audit Report")
⚠ 40  let checkout = acctSite.libraries?.first?.documents?.first?.checkOut()
41                                   ⚠ Constant 'checkout' inferred to have type '()?', which may be unexpected
```

FIGURE 19.3
Xcode compiler warning suggesting explicit type annotation for ()?.

Summary

In this hour, you learned what optional chaining is and how to understand it by thinking of the
Matryoshka dolls, in that the outer doll wraps around a possible inner doll, and so on.

You also learned how to use optional chaining to perform many different tasks. First, we discussed accessing and setting properties using optional chaining, both at a single level of chaining
and also multiple levels of chaining. A great use case of optional chaining with properties is with

delegates and data sources, by offloading responsibilities to other instances and using optional chaining to determine whether a delegate or data source has been assigned before calling it.

Then you learned how to use optional chaining with subscripts in the collaboration tool example. Remember to think about placement of the optional chaining operator (?) with respect to which expression is optional.

Finally, you learned how to use optional chaining with methods and how to use the `Void?` return type to your advantage, in addition to any return type other than `nil`, to verify that calling a particular method succeeded.

In the next hour, we discuss using generics to create functions that can operate the same set of tasks on many different types. This can be used to significantly reduce the amount of repeated code in your app. When you feel comfortable with the content in this hour, let's move on to generics!

Q&A

Q. Why do I need optional chaining? Aren't `susie.dog?.name` and `susie.dog!.name` doing the same thing?

A. No. Suppose that Susie doesn't have a dog and so `susie.dog - nil`. In that case, `susie.dog!.name` is forcing the unwrapping of an optional and trying to access the `name` property on a `nil` value. This results in a runtime error. When you use `susie.dog?.name`, optional chaining is used, and instead of a runtime error, your code returns an optional value containing `nil`.

Q. When I call `susie.dog?.name`, the name property is a `String`, not an optional `String`. Does that mean that I'll get a non-optional `String` back?

A. No. The result of optional chaining is always an optional, even when the final property or return type is not an optional.

Q. When should I use optional chaining?

A. Any time you need to access properties or methods contained in an optional type, you should use optional chaining.

Workshop

The workshop contains quiz questions and exercises to help you solidify your understanding of the material covered. Try to answer all questions before looking at the answers that follow.

Quiz

1. True or false? If the result of optional chaining is not `nil`, the value is automatically unwrapped for you, so you only get an optional when the result is `nil`.

2. Which of the following is the correct way to perform optional chaining on an element of an optional array:

   ```
   01: var myInt = myObject.intArray[0]?
   02: var myOtherInt = myObject.intArray?[0]
   ```

3. True or false? Optional chaining can only be used to retrieve values, not to set values.

4. If a function has no defined return value, what does it return when you're calling it using optional chaining?

Answers

1. False. The result of optional chaining is always an optional.

2. Line 2 is correct.

3. False. Optional chaining can be used to both set and retrieve values.

4. A function without a defined return value returns an optional empty tuple, which is written as `()?`.

Exercise

Create a new OS X playground. We're going to create a model for a message board. Our model consists of a single class that contains an array of replies.

Create a class called `Post` with string properties for the post's `author`, `title`, and `body`, and an integer property for the post's `score`. Add a property called `replies`, which should be an array of post objects.

Test your new class using the following code:

```
let rootPost = Post(author: "Christine", title: "My First Post", body: "This is
➥the body of my post!")

var replyAuthor = rootPost.replies.first?.author // Should be nil

let firstReply = Post(author: "Sarah", title: "Great Post!, body: "That's one
➥heck of a post!")

rootPost.addReply(firstReply)

replyAuthor = rootPost.replies.first?.author // Should be "Sarah" as a
➥String? instance
```

If you've done everything correctly, you get the indicated output.

HOUR 20
Introducing Generics

What You'll Learn in This Hour:

▶ How to create generic functions
▶ How to create generic types
▶ How to set type constraints
▶ How to extend generic types
▶ How to add associated types for generic protocols

This hour focuses on a concept in Swift called **generics**, which Apple calls one of Swift's most powerful features. Generics exist in other languages such as C# and Java, and also in C++ where they are called templates. You have come a long way in learning the Swift language and its concepts, and by now you are hopefully familiar with many core principles and rules utilized in Swift. And with that knowledge, throughout this book you have hopefully thought to yourself "that example seems to repeat a lot of code," or "couldn't that example be done in a much more concise way?" This is the hour you've been waiting for. There are many places where generics can solve these problems, so let's get going and learn how to understand and use generic code to solve these problems and write better code.

An Introduction to Generics

Generics are a way to create flexible and reusable code to avoid a lot of repetitive code that exists merely to satisfy type requirements. Generics enable you to create code that works with any type or any kind of types you specify. As you see shortly, generics can also increase type safety by setting expected types during declaration and using those expected types throughout the function, class, struct, or enum.

Recall that in Hour 9, "Understanding Higher Order Functions and Closures," we created a function called `mapEachElement(inArray:, withFunc:)`, which iterated over an array of `Int`s and returned a new `Int` array. This function worked well for arrays of type `[Int]`, but what if we need to perform the same function on each element of an array of type `[Double]`? Or even `[String]`?

This is the big problem that generics solve. You may have several types of data that could benefit from using the same functions, classes, structs, or enums, and it is inefficient and error-prone to create a separate function and so on for every single case you can think of. Let's take a look at the structure of a generic function.

Type Parameters and Placeholder Types

A key to generics in Swift is their flexibility. Remember that Swift is a strongly typed language, meaning that outside of using `Any` or `AnyObject`, every instance has a specific type. To create generic functions, we must specify a **placeholder type** inside a **type parameter list** at the beginning of the function, class, struct, or enum definition. A placeholder type can be any unused term you choose (typically a single capital letter, such as T, U, and so on), and the type parameter list is a list of placeholder types inside angle brackets, with multiple placeholder types separated by commas, such as `<T, U>`. The type parameter list is inserted immediately after the name of the function, class, struct, or enum, and before the function's parameters, if any. The best way to understand placeholder types is to imagine the letter `T` talking to you, saying "I don't care what type I am, but whatever type you tell me to be, I will be that type wherever you see me."

Think of type parameters as you would think of parameters to a function—you are just providing types instead of values. A generic function, class, struct, or enum needs to know what types will be represented by its placeholder types. Placeholder types can be used in functions as parameter types, return types, or types used within the body of the function.

Before we get into reconstructing the `mapEachElement(inArray:, withFunc:)` function mentioned earlier, let's take a look at a small example to illustrate the syntax for defining generic functions. Listing 20.1 shows a generic function that prints the value of any given argument of any type.

LISTING 20.1 Generic Function Structure

```
func printWeather<T>(value: T) {
    print("Today should be \(value)")
}

let val1: String = "beautiful"
let val2: Int = 72

printWeather(val1)          // displays "Today should be beautiful"
printWeather(val2)          // displays "Today should be 72"
```

As mentioned, the placeholder type `T` is inside the type parameter list immediately following the name of the function and before the function's parameter list. Then, inside the parameter list, we define a parameter named `value` of type `T`. This means that whatever type we designate as `T`, `value` will be of that type. If our function called for it, we could declare variables or constants of type `T` inside the function, and the `T` placeholder type would represent the given type from the type parameter list.

You may look at that example and think, "What's the big deal? The `print()` function already does that for us!" And you're right; it does—because it is a generic function. Suppose we had a more detailed function. We would have had to implement `printWeather(value: Int)`, `printWeather(value: String)`, and so on. Implementing a generic function potentially saved us a great amount of code.

A different function would be to compare equality of two instances. Let's examine how that would look as a generic function in Listing 20.2. First, create two functions that have identical functionality but take parameters of different types, and then create the generic function that will replace them. If you're following along in your own Swift REPL or playground, watch to see what error you get and on what line you receive the error.

LISTING 20.2 Comparing Equality with a Generic Function

```
01:  func areIntsEqual(first: Int, _ second: Int) -> Bool {
02:      return first == second
03:  }
04:
05:  func areStringsEqual(first: String, _ second: String) -> Bool {
06:      return first == second
07:  }
08:
09:  func areTheseEqual<T>(first: T, _ second: T) -> Bool {
10:      return first == second
11:  }
```

Did you get an error on line 10? The error is a little cryptic, stating "Binary operator '==' cannot be applied to two 'T' operands." This means that Swift cannot infer what *is equal to* means (with the == operator) with certain types, and since `T` can literally mean *any* type, Swift does not have enough information to know when some types are equal or not. To get this to work, we need to add **type constraints**.

Specifying Type Constraints

Type constraints are used to specify what behavior a type should exhibit or what class a type should inherit from. The syntax for type constraints is similar to how you specify a variable or constant of a certain type—you use a colon after the placeholder type name, and then either the protocol or protocol composition that the type should adopt and conform to, or the class the placeholder type should be a subclass of. Writing this inside the type parameter list looks similar to the following snippet:

```
func someFunction<T: ProtocolA, U: ClassB> { ... }
```

To fix Listing 20.2 to be able to create the generic equality function we wanted, we need to ensure that whatever type T represents adopts the Swift standard library protocol called Equatable. The Equatable protocol enables Swift to determine whether two values of the same type are considered to be equal by ensuring each instance of the given type implements the == operator. If a type adopts the Equatable protocol, it must implement a function for the == operator to properly conform to the protocol.

Let's fix the error in Listing 20.2 by adding the type constraint to the generic function of making sure our placeholder adopts the Equatable protocol, and then add some examples in Listing 20.3. The areIntsEqual() and areStringsEqual() functions have been omitted for brevity but are used for reference.

LISTING 20.3 **Adding a Type Constraint**

```
func areTheseEqual<T: Equatable>(first: T, _ second: T) -> Bool {
    return first == second
}

let a = 6, b = 7, c = 6
areIntsEqual(a, b)                          // returns false

let hi = "hi", hello = "hi", bonjour = "bonjour"
areStringsEqual(hi, hello)                  // returns true

areTheseEqual(a, c)                         // returns true
areTheseEqual(hello, bonjour)              // returns false
```

By refining the broad range of types that T could be, we limit it to only those types that conform to the Equatable protocol. If you try to create two dictionaries, whether containing equal key-value pairs or not, and try to compare them in the areTheseEqual() function, you get an error that the dictionaries' types do not conform to the Equatable protocol. So, you can see that this equality function works for many types, but not all, since Dictionary does not conform to the Equatable protocol.

Try out what you learned so far in the next Try It Yourself example. This example combines declaring a generic placeholder type inside the type parameter list, constraining it to conform to a protocol, and using the placeholder type inside the function parameter list, return type, and body. In this example, you return an array of unique elements from an array passed in with potentially duplicate elements. To do this, you need to create a hash table (dictionary) with the elements of the array as the keys in the hash table. Because they will be keys, they need to be hashable, so we have to have our generic type placeholder constrained to only allow types that conform to the Hashable protocol.

Create a Generic Function to Return a Unique Array

Using the concepts discussed so far, create a generic function that produces an array with unique elements.

1. Open Xcode and create a new playground; either a Mac or an iOS playground works. Clear the contents of the playground.

2. Create a function called `unique` and accept a placeholder type `T` that conforms to the `Hashable` protocol inside its type parameter list. The function should take one parameter of type `[T]` and a return type of `[T]`. Leave the function empty for now.

   ```
   func unique<T: Hashable>(array: [T]) -> [T] {

   }
   ```

3. Declare a temporary variable dictionary for us to use inside the function as our hash table. Since the elements in the array parameter will be the keys of the hash table, they should be of type `T`. The value can be anything non-`nil`, since we only care to know whether a value exists or not, so `Int` will do for the value type.

   ```
   var results = [T : Int]()
   ```

4. Use the `forEach` array instance method for performing a function on each element in an array and provide a closure that sets the value at the current key in the results table to 1. Use shorthand closure syntax `$0` to access the current item being used.

   ```
   array.forEach { results[$0] = 1 }
   ```

5. Now that the hash table has keys for every unique element in the array, return the keys of the hash table as an array of type `[T]`. Remember that the `keys` property in a dictionary is of type `LazyMapCollection` and not an array itself, so we need to create a new array by passing keys into an `Array` initializer.

   ```
   return Array(results.keys)
   ```

6. That's all for the function. Create three arrays of differing types with some duplicate elements in each.

   ```
   let numbers = [-8, 0, 1, 3, -8, 5, 3]
   let greetings = ["Aloha", "Hello", "Aloha", "Bonjour", "Ciao", "Ciao"]
   let bools = [true, false, true]
   ```

7. Call the generic `unique` function with each array and examine the results. You should see unique arrays for each type, since each array contains hashable types.

   ```
   let uniqueNumbers = unique(numbers)
   let uniqueGreetings = unique(greetings)
   let uniqueBools = unique(bools)
   ```

As you can see, generics are a powerful concept and implemented with not too much extra code. The syntax can get a little difficult to understand sometimes, but it always helps to read it aloud since most things in Swift are structured to read easily: "a function named `unique` that handles data of some type `T` which conforms to the `Hashable` protocol, accepts an array of type `[T]`, and returns an array of type `[T]`."

The completed Try It Yourself example code and results should look like those in Figure 20.1.

```swift
func unique<T: Hashable>(array: [T]) -> [T] {        (3 times)
    var results = [T : Int]()                       (19 times)
    array.forEach { results[$0] = 1 }               (3 times)
    return Array(results.keys)
}

let numbers = [-8, 0, 1, 3, -8, 5, 3]               [-8, 0, 1, 3, -8, 5, 3]
let greetings = ["Aloha", "Hello", "Aloha", "Bonjour", "Ciao", "Ciao"]   ["Aloha", "Hello", "Aloha", "Bonjour", "Ciao", "Ciao"]
let bools = [true, false, true]                     [true, false, true]

let uniqueItems = unique(numbers)                   [5, -8, 0, 1, 3]
let uniqueGreetings = unique(greetings)             ["Ciao", "Aloha", "Bonjour", "Hello"]
let uniqueBools = unique(bools)                     [false, true]
```

FIGURE 20.1
The completed Try It Yourself example using a generic function to return a unique copy of a provided array.

You may have realized that `Array` and `Dictionary` are generic types, too. They can contain any type of instance for their values. Take a look at the `Dictionary` type definition, by typing `Dictionary` onto an empty line of Xcode, and then press Command and click the word `Dictionary`. You see that the type parameter list for the `Dictionary` type is `<Key: Hashable, Value>`. You are not constrained to just a single letter (such as `T`) when defining placeholder types inside your type parameter list; you can have meaningful names too, as long as they are defined inside the type parameter list, make sense, and are used consistently throughout your generic implementation. Also a suggested best practice is to use `UpperCamelCase` when defining generic placeholder types, rather than `lowerCamelCase`, which is designated for instances of types.

NOTE

Conforming Custom Types to the `Hashable` Protocol

You are not limited to Swift's built-in types when you need a hashable value to serve as a key in a dictionary or anywhere else a hashable value is required. You can adopt the `Hashable` protocol in any type you create and implement the `hashValue` computed property defined in the `Hashable` protocol to ensure your type conforms to the protocol. Your `hashValue` computed property should always return a unique value.

Creating Generic Types

So far this hour, we have created generic functions, and while they are useful, they may be better served inside a struct, class, or enum to provide a greater benefit. So, if we can put generic functions inside types, can we make the types themselves generic? Yes, we can!

Generic types are just that; they are types that can use a placeholder type throughout their implementation for properties, methods, and subscripts they provide. You have used generic types already by using `Array` and `Dictionary`.

Recall in Hour 15, "Adding Advanced Type Functionality," in the second Try It Yourself example, you created a collection called a **stack** that contained instances of type `Paper` so the teacher could grade a stack of papers. A stack is a great example of a type that can be generic so that you can reuse that structure for any type that needs the capability to have a last-in-first-out storage characteristic to it.

Listing 20.4 illustrates a basic stack implementation to show what a generic type implementation might look like. If you are following along in a playground or the REPL, note that the last line is just an example to show that any custom type we have can be used.

LISTING 20.4   Generic Stack Type Implementation

```
struct Stack<T> {
    var items = [T]()
    mutating func push(item: T) {
        items.append(item)
    }
    mutating func pop() -> T? {
        guard !items.isEmpty else { return nil }
        return items.removeLast()
    }
}
var myIntStack = Stack<Int>()
var myStringStack = Stack<String>()
var myCustomStack = Stack<SomeCustomType>()   // just an example

myIntStack.push(5)
myIntStack.push(7)
myIntStack.push(9)
let poppedNum1 = myIntStack.pop()      // 9
let poppedNum2 = myIntStack.pop()      // 7
let poppedNum3 = myIntStack.pop()      // 5
let poppedNum4 = myintStack.pop()      // nil
```

Declaring an instance of a `Stack` is easy, as seen in the three lines following the `Stack` struct definition in Listing 20.4. This stack implementation is fairly common; there is an instance property to contain all the values and functions to push and pop values. Adding the type parameter list after the type name enables us to reuse this collection for any type of data we want to store in it.

Creating generic types is just as simple as creating generic functions. However, the scope of the placeholder types reaches throughout all methods, properties, and subscripts inside the type, rather than just a single function.

A different example of a generic type to create is a **queue**, a data structure in which items in the queue collection are kept in the order they were inserted. Queues are First-In-First-Out, or FIFO. The only operations you can perform on a queue are to insert an item at the **back**, called **enqueueing**, or remove the last item from the **front** of in the queue, called **dequeueing**. You should also be able to query the queue for the number of elements it contains. The Queue struct needs an empty initializer, a variable array of type [T] to store its values, a computed property to return the current count of items, and mutating functions to add items to and remove items from the storage array. To make this example more interesting, let's only add items to our queue if they don't already exist. This means that we should use a type constraint on our queue's generic placeholder type to make sure that each item is able to be compared for equality, so we can perform a calculation on it before adding any item.

▼ TRY IT YOURSELF

Create a Queue **Type to Store Unique Values**

Create a type called Queue that stores a collection of values. It should have the capability to add and remove values, as well as provide a computed variable to return the current count.

1. Open Xcode and create a new playground; either a Mac or an iOS playground works. Clear the contents of the playground.

2. Define the Queue struct with an equatable placeholder type T in the type parameter list.

   ```
   struct Queue<T: Equatable> {

   }
   ```

3. Define the private array variable property and the count computed property. Mark the array as private; even though it doesn't make a difference in a playground, it would in a real application, and it's good to practice good habits.

   ```
   private var items = [T]()
   var count: Int { return items.count }
   ```

4. Create the `enqueue` function. This takes a value of type `T` as its only parameter and has no return value. Ensure that the item does not exist before adding it. (Hint: Use a `guard` statement and the instance method on `Array` called `contains(predicate:)`.)

```
mutating func enqueue(item: T) {
    guard items.contains({ $0 == item }) == false else { return }
    items.insert(item, atIndex: 0)
}
```

5. Create the `dequeue` function. The `dequeue` function first checks that the internal storage sequence has at least one item, and if so, returns it, else returns `nil`.

```
mutating func dequeue() -> T? {
    guard items.count > 0 else { return nil }
    return items.removeLast()

}
```

6. That's all for the `Queue` type. Create an instance of `Queue`. Add items, remove items, and check the count to ensure the proper number is being added. Try adding duplicate items to ensure uniqueness. Then, create an empty queue, and try to dequeue an item, and ensure you get `nil` returned to you.

```
var queue. Queue<String> = Queue()
queue.enqueue("iPhone")
queue.enqueue("iPhone")
queue.enqueue("new")
queue.enqueue("a")
queue.enqueue("need")
queue.enqueue("I")
queue.items      // displays ["I", "need", "a", "new", "iPhone"]
queue.count      // displays 5

var emptyQueue = Queue<Bool>()
let emptyItem = emptyQueue.dequeue()      // returns nil
```

I hope you can see how the `Queue` struct could be beneficial to you in your career as a programmer. But we're not done with it yet. As you continue learning a few more concepts about generics in this hour, we add more functionality to it to make it even more useful.

The completed Try It Yourself example code and results look like what you see in Figure 20.2.

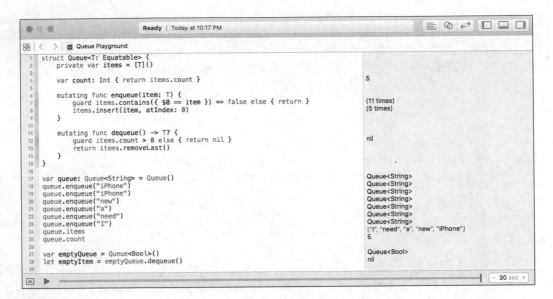

FIGURE 20.2
The completed Try It Yourself example creating the basis of a `Queue` struct.

Extending Generic Types

Extending a generic type is done in the exact same manner as if you were extending a regular type. There is no special syntax in the extension definition, and all the same placeholder types are available to you in addition to what is normally available to you in extensions such as the type's properties, methods, and subscripts.

Let's say we want to add the ability to create a queue from an array. This would be best served in an extension to our `Queue` struct, because this capability is a convenience, and not particularly fundamental to a queue data structure. Listing 20.5 shows how we can do that in Swift using native Swift syntax and utilizing our placeholder type `T`.

LISTING 20.5 Extending the `Queue` Struct

```
// reuse the Queue struct from the Try It Yourself example
extension Queue {
    init(array: [T]) {
        self.init()
        array.reverse().forEach { self.enqueue($0) }
    }
}
let items = [1, 2, 3, 3, 3, 4, 5]
let queue = Queue(array: items)
queue.items       // displays {[1, 2, 3, 4, 5]}
```

In Listing 20.5, we simply create a convenience initializer in the struct's extension that creates a queue from an array of elements. To retain the same ordering of the array's elements into the queue, we reverse the array first before enqueuing each element. Reversing the array is just to keep the illustration easy to understand via seeing the array and the queue in the same order. If you implement a queue, you may have different ordering rules.

You may be thinking at this point, "This is great, but what if I have too many items in the queue, and after a particular number goes through, I want to purge the rest?" That's a good question, and it's one we can solve by extending the Queue struct and doing so by conforming to a protocol. We can create a protocol that defines a function that allows us to flush the queue, and return the remaining items into an array for later use, if so desired. We can also add functionality for returning the current placement of an element in a queue. Creating this functionality in a protocol enables us not only to extend the Queue struct, but also to add the same functionality to other types that could prove useful later.

NOTE

Why Are We Extending Queue **Versus Modifying It Directly?**

The initializer accepting an array not have to be added via an extension, and you could modify the Queue struct to add them directly. However, you may not have access to the Queue source code where you work, or it may not be open for modification; thus, an extension is a perfect solution.

Using Associated Types in Protocols

Before we go straight into the code to add the properties, we need to discuss **associated types** in protocols. Associated types are a way to have generic placeholder types in protocols. This is similar in effect to, but slightly different syntax than, the type parameter list you learned about so far.

To use an associated type in a protocol, you declare the type with the typealias keyword inside the protocol definition. Anywhere in the protocol you need to reference the generic type, you provide the associated type you defined in the typealias expression. Then, in the implementation that conforms to the protocol, you set the associated type equal to whatever type you need, if it is not inferred by Swift. From that point on, anything defined in the protocol uses your type as its associated type, and the protocol is happy, and Swift remains type-safe.

Now that you know how protocols behave with respect to generic types by using associated types, let's create one protocol to enable us to flush a queue after a particular number of elements from the front, and a second protocol to return the current placement of an element from the front of the queue, and then extend the Queue struct to conform to both protocols. Because these two pieces of functionality don't really relate to each other, it makes sense for them to be in two separate protocols and extensions.

As seen in Listing 20.6, adding the two protocols and then extending the Queue struct to conform to those protocols really makes the Queue struct more robust and powerful. Perhaps these examples are a tad simplistic, but consider when you may want to add the same functionality to many different types at once; protocols and extensions will enable you to quickly and easily conform multiple types to a particular set of behaviors and add a great deal of functionality with a few lines of code.

LISTING 20.6 Using Associated Types in Protocols

```
// reuse the combined Queue struct and the extension from Listing 20.5
protocol Flushable {
    typealias ItemType
    mutating func flush(afterNthElementFromFront index: Int) -> [ItemType]
}

protocol CollectionItemInspectable {
    typealias ItemType
    func placementFromFrontForElement(element: ItemType) -> Int?
}

extension Queue: Flushable {
    typealias ItemType = T
    mutating func flush(afterNthElementFromFront index: Int) -> [ItemType] {
        let position = items.count - index
        let result = Array(items[0..<position])
        items[0..<position] = []
        return result
    }
}

extension Queue: CollectionItemInspectable {
    func placementFromFrontForElement(element: ItemType) -> Int? {
        guard let foundIndex = items.indexOf(element) else { return nil }
        return (items.count - 1) - foundIndex
    }
}

var queue = Queue<Int>(array: [1, 2, 3, 4, 5, 6, 7])
queue.flush(afterNthElementFromFront: 2)     // displays [1, 2, 3, 4, 5]
queue.items                                  // displays [6, 7]

queue.placementFromFrontForElement(6)        // displays 1
```

Notice that, in the extension in which we conformed CollectionItemInspectable to the Queue struct, there is not a typealias assignment. This is because it has already been assigned to T once, in the extension conforming to `Flushable`, and Xcode will provide an error stating that you are attempting to redeclare `ItemType` if you typed that line in each extension.

When I was learning about generic programming, it took me a little while to understand the when, how, why, and so on, especially with protocols. Here are a few good tips to keep in mind:

▶ Classes, structs, enums, functions, and protocols can all be generic.

▶ When making a class, struct, enum, or function generic, you can use a placeholder type (such as `T`, `Key`, and so on), and use that placeholder type within the corresponding scope.

▶ When making a protocol generic, define a type alias, and then assign that type alias in the actual implementation.

Because protocols themselves don't have the implementation information that a class, struct, enum, or function does, having a placeholder type as the others do doesn't make sense. This is why you define a `typealias` for whatever generic type you want, and the object responsible for implementing that protocol will assign the aliased type.

Summary

In this hour, you learned about the basics of generic programming in Swift. You learned how to define and use generic functions by using type parameter lists and placeholder types to represent the type that will be used at runtime. You then learned how to use those placeholder types inside functions in the parameter list, as return types, and inside the body if necessary.

Then you learned how to use type constraints to refine what kind of type could be used in a generic function. You can constrain placeholder types by declaring that they must be a subclass of a particular class or conform to a protocol or protocol composition.

You also learned that not only can generics be used in functions, but with class, struct, and enum types as well. The placeholder types defined in the type parameter list can be used within the scope of the type, not just a single function. Once you learned that, you learned how to extend generic types with extensions, as well as extensions that adopted protocols.

Finally, you learned about associated types and how they can be used as generics inside protocols to be defined fully by the conforming type. This allows for many different types to adopt protocols and still implement the required functionality, but also enables generic types to adopt and conform to the protocols as well.

In the next hour, we take a look at something called protocol-oriented programming, which is a slightly different way to think about structuring data models and behaviors in your applications than a purely object-oriented manner.

Q&A

Q. What if I need to use more than one generic type in a single function?

A. You can use as many generic types as you need. Just use multiple type parameters. For example, `func foo<T,U>(first: T, second: U) { ... }` would take two generic type placeholders, `T` and `U`.

Q. If I use more than one generic type, does the order that I list the placeholder types in the type parameter list declaration matter?

A. No. As all of the generic types are listed, the order doesn't matter. For example, if we rewrite `foo` from the previous question this way: `func foo<T,U>(first: U, second: T) { ... }`, it functions exactly the same way.

Q. If my method takes two parameters, and the first is a generic type, does the second one have to be generic too?

A. No. You can mix generic **types** in with non-generic parameters if you want. For example, `func foo<T>(first: T, second: Int) { ... }` defines a function that takes a generic type `T` and an `Int` as parameters.

Q. Are generics in Swift the same as generics in C# and Java?

A. Swift's generics are similar to generics in C# and Java, and to templates in C++. There are some minor differences, which are beyond the scope of this book, but they serve roughly the same purpose in each language.

Workshop

The workshop contains quiz questions and exercises to help you solidify your understanding of the material covered. Try to answer all questions before looking at the answers that follow.

Quiz

1. Do generic placeholder types have to be declared with a single letter?

2. Can we write extensions that use generic types?

3. True or false? Only functions and methods can use generic types.

4. True or false? We can use classes, protocols, or protocol compositions as type constraints.

Answers

1. No, it is customary to use a single capital letter as a placeholder type, but you can use longer names if you want.

2. Absolutely. Extensions for generic types work in the same way as other extensions.

3. False. You can use generic types with classes, structs, and enums as well.

4. True. Classes, protocols, and protocol compositions are all valid type constraints.

Exercise

Create a new OS X playground. In this hour, we created a `Queue` struct that maintained a list of elements sorted in FIFO order. `Queue` defined methods for enqueuing and dequeuing elements, as well as extensions for flushing a queue after a particular position, and querying for the position of a particular element.

For this exercise, extend the `Queue` struct to add two new pieces of functionality. First, add another mutating function to the `Flushable` protocol that flushes the entire queue, and then create that implementation in the extension that conforms `Queue` to `Flushable`.

Next, let's say you are using this `Queue` struct to manage the waiting line at an amusement park, like Cedar Point. You are allowed to take riders two at a time and put them into the roller coaster cars, so you need to create a method that allows you to dequeue two elements at a time, in the form of an array. Create a new protocol called `DoubleDequeuable`, and then extend `Queue` to conform to the protocol.

Understanding Protocol-Oriented Programming

What You'll Learn in This Hour:

▶ How to extend protocols with default behavior

▶ What types of problems protocol extensions solve

▶ How to constrain type requirements in protocol extensions

At the World Wide Developer Conference (WWDC) this year, there was a particular session that gained a lot of popularity. That session was titled "Protocol-Oriented Programming in Swift," by Dave Abrahams. In the talk, he discussed a conversation he had with someone named "Crusty" about the pros and cons of using all reference types in object-oriented programming and how much of the same functionality can be achieved, with less code, and in a much safer manner using protocol-oriented programming than using an inheritance model with classes. This hour aims to explain and expand upon this discussion, and provide practical examples to help you understand this important topic. By the end of this hour, you should feel more comfortable thinking in terms of composed objects with protocols rather than creating an inheritance hierarchy.

A Quick Recap of Protocols

Recall from Hour 17, "Using Protocols to Define Behavior," that protocols are a way to define an interface, or a blueprint, to which a particular type that adopts the protocol should conform. By conforming to a protocol, the type implements all requirements that the protocol defines. This concept is important when decoupling your code from types being tied too tightly to each other. If you need to refactor your code later, separating entities can cause a headache because they know too much about, and rely too heavily on, the implementation of another class, struct, or enum. When using protocols to declare an interface, and dependencies of your type depend on protocol definitions rather than an actual class, struct, or enum type, then refactoring later is much easier. To do so, you just substitute another type that conforms to the protocol in place, and you have saved yourself some ibuprofen.

Implementing Protocols

Methods with similar behaviors among different types have been implemented in the past in two ways:

▶ With a protocol (well, sometimes) and a method with the same name as the method defined in the protocol on many different types, and that must be implemented separately for each type

▶ As a global function that takes an instance of a particular type or sequence as its first parameter

In the Cocoa framework, the first method is used quite frequently. There aren't always protocols to strictly define a standard interface among shared functionality. However, there are many similar ways to interact with elements of similar types in Cocoa.

The second way, as a global function, started out being the way Swift implemented shared functionality. For instance, the map function was defined as a global function in Swift 1. Its first parameter was a sequence to map over, and then the second parameter was the transform function to perform on each element being mapped over. This was fine, but global functions are difficult to find using the code completion tool in Xcode and are not easily searchable. You also could not override an implementation to fit your needs. There has to be a better solution, right? Fortunately, there is.

Introducing Protocol Extensions

Swift 2 introduced a new concept to the language called **protocol extensions**. A protocol extension is just like it sounds—you create an extension, as discussed in Hour 18, "Using Extensions to Add Type Functionality," to an actual protocol. Previously, you could only extend classes, structs, and enums, but now you can extend protocols, and, as you'll see in this hour, this capability is quite powerful.

A protocol extension enables you to add functionality to an existing protocol with something called a default implementation. Similar to a mixin in the Ruby programming language, the protocol extension provides an implementation that will be shared by any type that adopts the protocol.

As a practical example, Swift 2 utilizes a protocol extension on the CollectionType protocol to provide a default implementation of the map function. What this enables you to do in Swift is call the map function from any type that conforms to CollectionType, such as Array, Set, and Dictionary to name a few, and you can expect the same behavior because it shares the same implementation. Additionally, by using protocol extensions, the new map implementation is available as an instance method on your sequence, which makes it easily findable, and makes calling map seem more natural. This is a huge step for Swift. If you didn't get the full impact of how impressive protocol extensions are from reading this section, re-read it. Then inspect Listing 21.1 for a look at a custom implementation of what the map function implementation might look like in the CollectionType protocol extension.

LISTING 21.1 CollectionType Protocol Extension for map Function

```
extension CollectionType {
    func styMap<U>(transform: Self.Generator.Element -> U) -> [U] {
        var result: [U] = []
        self.forEach {
            result.append(transform($0))
        }
        return result
    }
}
```

In Listing 21.1, we created a function called styMap (*sty* is short for Sams Teach Yourself), which is one possible way the map function might be implemented in the CollectionType protocol extension, without seeing the actual implementation. After Swift is open-sourced later this year, we may be able to see how map and other functions are actually implemented.

Notice also that the return type of the styMap function is an array, as [U]. The standard map return type is similar; it just uses the existing generic placeholder type T, as [T]. This is even the case for dictionaries, oddly enough. Figure 21.1 shows the map signature for a Dictionary instance.

```
1   //: Playground — noun: a place where people can play
2
3   let myDict = ["name" : "BJ"]
4   myDict.map( transform: (Self.Generator.Element) throws -> T )
       [T] map(transform: (Self.Generator.Element) throws -> T) rethrows
   Self.Generator.Element? maxElement(isOrderedBefore: (Self.Generator.Element, Self.Generator.Element) throws -> Bool) rethrows
   Return an Array containing the results of mapping transform over self.
```

FIGURE 21.1
The signature for the map function on a Dictionary instance.

Even though the map function is being performed on a Dictionary instance, the return type is still [T], but notice also the throws and rethrows keywords. These indicate that the map function could accept a transform function that could throw an error, which could be rethrown by the greater map function. We discuss throwing errors in Hour 22, "Handling Errors." I wanted to mention the return type here specifically because it is important that you understand the parameter types and return types of the transform closures you send into functions and the functions themselves so that you know how to form your transform closures and know what to expect from the greater function.

Creating Protocol Extensions

It is one thing to see the custom implementation of map in a protocol extension, but I want you to get used to creating your own. First, let's talk about how methods and properties defined in protocol extensions relate to and behave toward those defined (or not defined) in the protocol they extend.

Protocols are useful when you want to define a guaranteed interface to which an instance of some type must conform. The required behavior is listed in the protocol, such that a conforming type can interact with whatever object is calling it, and it will satisfy the requirements defined in the protocol. What this means is that any type conforming to a protocol must implement all required functionality defined in that protocol. You know this already from reading Hour 17.

Let's start with an example of how we might redesign the mammal inheritance hierarchy with protocols, as discussed briefly in the platypus problem from Hour 11, "Implementing Class Inheritance," in the "When to Use Class Inheritance" section. The platypus problem is that a platypus is a mammal, but it doesn't give live birth. Rather, it lays eggs. So inheritance would be less than ideal because we would be inheriting behavior that isn't correct. Listing 21.2 shows an example of how we could define MammalType, LiveBirthable, and EggLayable protocols, rather than a class hierarchy, to allow types to adopt only what they need.

LISTING 21.2 Creating Protocols for Composing Types

```
protocol MammalType {
    var name: String { get }
    var givesLiveBirth: Bool { get }
}

protocol LiveBirthable {
    var pregnancyTermInWeeks: Int { get }
}

protocol EggLayable {
    var clutchSize: Int { get }
}

struct Lion : MammalType, LiveBirthable {
    let name: String
    let givesLiveBirth = true
    var pregnancyTermInWeeks: Int { return 15 }
}

struct Human : MammalType, LiveBirthable {
    let name: String
    let givesLiveBirth = true
    var pregnancyTermInWeeks: Int { return 40 }
}
```

```
struct Platypus: MammalType, EggLayable {
    let name: String
    let givesLiveBirth = false
    var clutchSize: Int { return 3 }
}

Lion(name: "Lucy").givesLiveBirth        // displays true
Human(name: "Hazel").givesLiveBirth      // displays true
Platypus(name: "Patty").givesLiveBirth   // displays false
```

First, we define a MammalType protocol that describes some attributes about mammals, and then we define two protocols that define behavior about an attribute or attributes, with LiveBirthable and EggLayable protocols. The givesLiveBirth property belongs in the MammalType protocol and not the LiveBirthable protocol, because anything that conforms to the LiveBirthable protocol is assumed to give live birth, and some mammals may have that property equal to false.

Protocol Naming Conventions

Protocols are typically named using nouns or adjectives. Naming with nouns gives an impression of what a conforming type *is*, such as MammalType, CollectionType, ErrorType, and so on. Naming with adjectives gives the impression of what a conforming type *does*, such as LiveBirthable, EggLayable, CustomStringConvertible, and so on.

None of the types we created in Listing 21.2 inherited any properties from a superclass via inheritance. In fact, we used structs, so we can't use inheritance at all. But we can use protocols to compose the interfaces of our types that describe how our types should behave and what we can expect from them. This is pretty straightforward; there is nothing new here that we didn't cover in Hour 17.

But if you have a keen eye, you can see that we would need to set givesLiveBirth equal to true for *every single struct* for *every single live-birthable mammal* we define. That's a lot of code duplication, and where there is code duplication, there is room for error and accidents—perhaps not with a simple Boolean value, but you can imagine in larger or more complex applications that this may be a problem. If you are saying to yourself, "I wish there were a way we could set that to be the default for every mammal!," then you're starting to think like a protocol-oriented programmer!

Let's extend the MammalType protocol to define a default behavior for the givesLiveBirth property. Listing 21.3 shows what this code looks like. Place the MammalType extension immediately after the MammalType protocol, and then you can remove the givesLiveBirth property from all three mammal structs.

LISTING 21.3 **Extending the Mammal Protocol**

```
protocol MammalType {
    var name: String { get }
    var givesLiveBirth: Bool { get }
}

extension MammalType {
    var givesLiveBirth: Bool { return true }
}

protocol LiveBirthable {
    var pregnancyTermInWeeks: Int { get }
}

protocol EggLayable {
    var clutchSize: Int { get }
}

struct Lion : MammalType, LiveBirthable {
    let name: String
    var pregnancyTermInWeeks: Int { return 15 }
}

struct Human : MammalType, LiveBirthable {
    let name: String
    var pregnancyTermInWeeks: Int { return 40 }
}

struct Platypus: MammalType, EggLayable {
    let name: String
    var clutchSize: Int { return 3 }
}

Lion(name: "Lucy").givesLiveBirth       // displays true
Human(name: "Hazel").givesLiveBirth     // displays true
Platypus(name: "Patty").givesLiveBirth  // displays true! Uh oh!
```

In Listing 21.3, we add an extension onto a protocol, something we could not do prior to Swift 2. This is immensely powerful, as any conforming type simply needs to adopt the protocol and they get any properties or methods implemented in the protocol extension for free.

But wait a minute—our functionality regressed, didn't it? Patty the platypus now gives live birth, according to our app. We can't have her adopt the MammalType protocol and accept that default implementation because it isn't the truth. In this case, we have two options. The first option is to override the default implementation by providing our own, or the second option is to use type constraints, similar to the way we did in Hour 20, "Introducing Generics," to constrain the extension type to only apply in certain scenarios. Overriding is easy, so do that first to get Patty back to her old self, but then we need to discuss what you can and can't do with protocols and extensions. Simply add the property declaration back to the `Platypus` struct, as in the following line:

```
let givesLiveBirth = false
```

What Is and Isn't Customizable

When defining what you want in a protocol, you place those properties and methods in the protocol definition. If you want to provide default implementations for anything listed in the protocol, simply provide an implementation for it in the protocol extension. There is nothing fancy to see here. If you do not want your conforming type to adopt the default implementation but still conform to the protocol, then you can simply redefine the implementation you want inside your conforming type. If you are familiar with Objective-C, this should be familiar to you as a form of polymorphism in a concept called **dynamic dispatch**.

Dynamic dispatch is a term used to describe how a function gets called at runtime. Any time a function gets overridden, the runtime must perform a lookup to find out which function you actually intended to call, because it has the exact same signature as the function it is overriding. So if you have a class that has a method called `foo()`, and your subclass overrides `foo()`, the runtime has to inspect the type of object in question to decide whether it should execute the method in the superclass or the subclass.

But a second kind of dispatching is available here called **static dispatch**. Static dispatch looks up the memory address of the function at compile time because there is no question of which method should be called, so there is no need to perform a lookup at runtime, saving extra CPU cycles and potentially wasted energy.

At this point, you may be scratching your head and wondering why I'm telling you this. When you define a function or property in your protocol, and also give it a default implementation in your protocol extension, you are then able to override that default implementation in your conforming type because the protocol still says you will provide it, whether by your type or by the protocol extension. The items you override will get dynamically dispatched.

If you create a protocol, and in the protocol extension you provide a default implementation for a function but do not define it in the actual protocol itself, your adopting type gets that default implementation without any extra effort on your part—but the function cannot be overridden. The items you get for free cannot be overridden because they aren't formally defined in the protocol, and they are therefore statically dispatched. The benefit of static dispatch is that you gain some efficiency by saving a potentially great number of runtime lookups. Also, because they don't need to depend on the Objective-C runtime, these protocols and their extensions can apply to all Swift types, not just class types.

To get a good grasp of these concepts, do the following Try It Yourself example of what methods get called when you're defining them in a protocol and an extension, or just the extension, and when a conforming type's implementation gets called or not.

▼ TRY IT YOURSELF

Override Default Protocol Implementations

Practice creating protocols and protocol extensions, and understand which methods get called when providing implementations for methods that are and are not part of the protocol definition.

1. Open Xcode and create a new playground; either a Mac or iOS playground works. Clear the contents of the playground.

2. Create a protocol definition that has one method signature in it. The function does not need to take any parameters or return any values.

```
protocol SomeProtocol {
    func funcOne()
}
```

3. Extend the `SomeProtocol` protocol to define two methods. The first method will be a default implementation for the `funcOne` function defined in the protocol. The second method will be a default implementation for `funcTwo`, but this function is not defined in the protocol. For this purpose, simply have each function print a line stating which function it is and that it is the default method.

```
extension SomeProtocol {
    func funcOne() {
        print("default funcOne")
    }
    func funcTwo() {
        print("default funcTwo")
    }
}
```

4. After creating the protocol and an extension on it, create a struct called `SomeType` that adopts the `SomeProtocol` protocol. Provide implementations for both `funcOne` and `funcTwo` functions, each printing a line stating that it is a custom implementation, to make it easier to see our results in the console.

```
struct SomeType : SomeProtocol {
    func funcOne() {
        print("customized funcOne")
    }
    func funcTwo() {
        print("customized funcTwo")
    }
}
```

5. Create an instance of `SomeType` and call each function on it. Inspect the console by pressing Command+Shift+Y and look at what methods get called.

```
let someInstanceA = SomeType()
someInstanceA.funcOne()
someInstanceA.funcTwo()
```

6. Create another instance of `SomeType`, but this time specifically annotate the type to be of the protocol's type. Call the same two methods, and inspect the output in the console. What is different?

```
let someInstanceB: SomeProtocol = SomeType()
someInstanceB.funcOne()
someInstanceB.funcTwo()
```

The results from the Try It Yourself section should look like those in Figure 21.2.

```
                    Ch21 TIY1 Overriding Defined Defaults.playground
      <   >   |  Ch21 TIY1 Overriding Defined Defaults
 1    // Ch21 Try It Yourself 1 — Overriding Defined Defaults
 2
 3    protocol SomeProtocol {
 4        func funcOne()
 5    }
 6
 7    extension SomeProtocol {
 8        func funcOne() {
 9            print("default funcOne")
10        }
11        func funcTwo() {
12            print("default funcTwo")                    "default funcTwo\n"
13        }
14    }
15
16    struct SomeType : SomeProtocol {
17        func funcOne() {
18            print("customized funcOne")                 (2 times)
19        }
20        func funcTwo() {
21            print("customized funcTwo")                 "customized funcTwo\n"
22        }
23    }
24
25    let someInstanceA = SomeType()                       SomeType
26    someInstanceA.funcOne()                              SomeType
27    someInstanceA.funcTwo()                              SomeType
28
29    let someInstanceB: SomeProtocol = SomeType()         SomeType
30    someInstanceB.funcOne()
31    someInstanceB.funcTwo()
32
```

```
customized funcOne
customized funcTwo
customized funcOne
default funcTwo
```

FIGURE 21.2
The resulting playground from the Try It Yourself section overriding default implementations from protocol extensions.

As you can see in your console output, although having the same name as the function in the protocol extension, the struct's implementation of `funcTwo` was executed for `someInstanceA`. Despite conforming to the protocol, `someInstanceA` is of type `SomeType`, and its implementation of `funcTwo` was executed and not the protocol extension's implementation. However, when we forced `someInstanceB` to be of type `SomeProtocol`, and gave it an instance of `SomeType`, which conforms to `SomeProtocol`, the protocol extension's implementation of `funcTwo` was executed.

The bottom-line rules to remember are these: If you adopt a protocol, you must provide all implementation defined in it, unless default implementations are provided in a protocol extension. Then those are optional for you to provide. You get all default implementations from protocol extensions, but you can only substitute your own implementations if they are defined in the protocol itself.

Type Constraints in Protocol Extensions

Thinking back to the mammal example where we left it, we had quickly just reset a property on the `Platypus` struct to set `givesLiveBirth` to `false`. While we could keep this solution, platypuses aren't the only monotremes—there are four species of echidnas that also lay eggs. We should really add the `givesLiveBirth` property a home in protocol extensions, so let's do that with **type constraints**.

The concept of type constraints applies the same way to protocol extensions as it did in Hour 20. You can simply constrain a protocol extension with the `where` keyword and provide whatever constraint you need. Listing 21.4 builds on the mammal example from Listing 21.3 but adds two extensions using type constraints to appropriately set the `givesLiveBirth` property depending on whether a conforming type is also `LiveBirthable` or `EggLayable`. If you are following along in your own playground, insert the code from Listing 21.4 after the `MammalType` protocol but before the `LiveBirthable` protocol. Also remove the `givesLiveBirth` property from the `Platypus` struct.

LISTING 21.4 Type Constraints in Protocol Extensions

```
// protocol MammalType...
extension MammalType where Self : LiveBirthable {
    var givesLiveBirth: Bool { return true }
}

extension MammalType where Self : EggLayable {
    var givesLiveBirth: Bool { return false }
}
// protocol LiveBirthable...
// remove `let givesLiveBirth = false` from Platypus
```

Let's break down Listing 21.4. In both extensions, we extend the `MammalType` protocol because that is where the `givesLiveBirth` property exists. In each extension, we constrain the `MammalType` extension to be conditionally applied. For the conditional application, use the `where` keyword. The `Self` keyword is the protocol's generic representation for the type conforming to the protocol. If you were to speak these conditional extensions aloud, it would sound like "extend the `MammalType` protocol where the conforming type is also `LiveBirthable`/`EggLayable`." The big win here is the functionality gained by adopting different protocols with their respective extensions, as opposed to creating a class hierarchy with potentially many levels. After you create those levels, many depend on each other and the order, making refactoring or flipping inheritance chains a nightmare. Not only do protocol extensions not use inheritance, you are not limited to classes, and you can compose types using protocols and protocol extensions with classes, structs, and enums.

The playground results should now reflect the appropriate values for each respective instance, and look like the playground in Figure 21.3.

```
38
39  Lion(name: "Lucy").givesLiveBirth              true
40  Human(name: "Hazel").givesLiveBirth            true
41  Platypus(name: "Patty").givesLiveBirth         false
42
```

FIGURE 21.3
The playground results after adding type constraints to protocol extensions.

Homogeneous and Heterogeneous Collections

You learned in Hour 17 that you can have collections whose type is `[ProtocolName]`, such as in the `Rentable` example in Listing 17.4. Such a collection is called a **heterogeneous collection**, meaning that its elements could be of different underlying types. The common bonding type is the protocol type, which only has limited information compared to what the conforming types could contain. An example would be if you needed an array of `Rentable` instances, whether they were `AudioCDs`, `DVDs`, `Books`, or any other `Rentable` object. You could represent them as `[Rentable]`, with which you could only access properties and methods available from the `Rentable` protocol definition on each item.

On the other hand, you could have a **homogeneous collection**, meaning that every type inside the collection is the same underlying type. But with potentially not knowing the underlying type and only knowing the protocol type, how can we represent homogeneous collections when we are passing them to functions? The answer is with generic type constraints in a function's signature. Listing 21.5 illustrates how to accomplish this.

LISTING 21.5   Generic Type Constraints

```
// Rentable protocol and structs from Listing 17.4
let book1 = Book(title: "Sams Teach Yourself Swift in 24 Hours", barcode:
➥"9780672337246", chapterCount: 24)
let book2 = Book(title: "Design Patterns", barcode: "0201633612", chapterCount: 6)
let dvd1 = DVD(title: "The Wizard of Oz", barcode: "883929087334",
➥lengthInMinutes: 102)
let dvd2 = DVD(title: "Gladiator", barcode: "883929304127", lengthInMinutes: 155)
let cd1 = AudioCD(title: "Compton", barcode: "111", audioTracks: 16)
let cd2 = AudioCD(title: "1989", barcode: "222", audioTracks: 13)

func displayAnyTitle(rentables: [Rentable]) {
    rentables.forEach { print($0.title) }
}

func displayTitleForOneType<T: Rentable>(rentables: [T]) {
    rentables.forEach { print($0.title) }
}

let all: [Rentable] = [book1, book2, dvd1, dvd2, cd1, cd2]
let books = [book1, book2]
let rentableBooks: [Rentable] = [book1, book2]
displayAnyTitle(all)                    // OK
print("")  // just a blank line to separate the output
displayTitleForOneType(books)           // OK
displayTitleForOneType(all)             // error: not homogeneous
displayTitleForOneType(rentableBooks)   // error: not homogeneous
```

The biggest concept to point out in Listing 21.5 is the difference in the two ways the protocol name is used. One way is as a *type*, and the other is as a *type constraint*. First, we create several instances, two of each type, that conform to Rentable. Then we create a function that displays the title for any Rentable, no matter the underlying type. This function can accept a heterogeneous array of Rentables. The second method, however, has a generic type constraint. It accepts an array of type [T], meaning that the underlying type must be homogeneous, but with the constraint that T must be Rentable. So we can send in an array of [Book], [DVD], or [AudioCD], but not [Rentable].

A different way to look at this is if you had a more generalized protocol, such as Comparable. You could have an array of Ints, Doubles, Strings, and your own custom type Foo, which is Comparable, but comparing an Int to Foo wouldn't make much sense, because they are two totally different types. Despite all conforming to the same protocol, they are still all different types, and their comparability may not make much sense.

It is important to distinguish the differences between collections such as these and to know when you are writing apps which type you need. Ask yourself whether you need a collection of disparate types that all conform to the protocol, or whether you need a specific type (represented by a generic placeholder type, such as T) that is constrained to also conform to a protocol.

Converting Protocol Sequences

If you find yourself with an array or some sequence of protocol types, and you need a more concrete type sequence, you can convert it using map. For instance, say you have [Rentable], but you know that you have Book as the underlying element type. Converting will create a new array of type [Book] for you.

The reason you need to convert using an iterative transformation function like map is that the array of protocol types doesn't have the proper storage information in memory for whatever underlying type may be in the array. An instance of a protocol type is only about 40 bytes in size, whereas an actual concrete type instance may be much larger.

Let's go through a brief example together in the following Try It Yourself example. In the example, you create a protocol named DeviceType, and then create a new type and conform it to DeviceType protocol. You then create an array of several instances of the new type, but as an array of DeviceType. You then use map to convert the instances from the array of DeviceTypes to the array of your type.

TRY IT YOURSELF ▼

Convert Sequences from Protocol Types to Concrete Types

Create a protocol and a type that conforms to that type, and then practice converting that array from one type to another using map.

1. Open Xcode and create a new playground; either a Mac or iOS playground is fine. Clear the contents of the playground.

2. Define a protocol called DeviceType, and provide a title property of type String that should be read-only.

```
protocol DeviceType {
    var title: String { get }
}
```

3. Define a struct called iPhone that conforms to DeviceType. The iPhone struct should accept a model property as a String, and the title property should return that as part of its description.

```
struct iPhone: DeviceType {
    let model: String
```

▼

```
         var title: String { return "iPhone \(model)" }
}
```

4. Create two instances of the iPhone struct, passing in different device type strings into the initializers.

```
let i6Plus = iPhone(model: "6 Plus")
let i6 = iPhone(model: "6")
```

5. Create an array of the iPhone instances, but annotate the type to be [DeviceType], rather than Swift inferring [iPhone]. Then use the map function and assign the result to a new array. The transform closure for the map function should simply use as! to cast the current instance to the iPhone type.

```
let alliPhonesAsProtocolType: [DeviceType] = [i6Plus, i6]
let alliPhones = alliPhonesAsProtocolType.map { $0 as! iPhone }
alliPhones
```

After you complete the Try It Yourself exercise, your playground should look like the resulting playground in Figure 21.4.

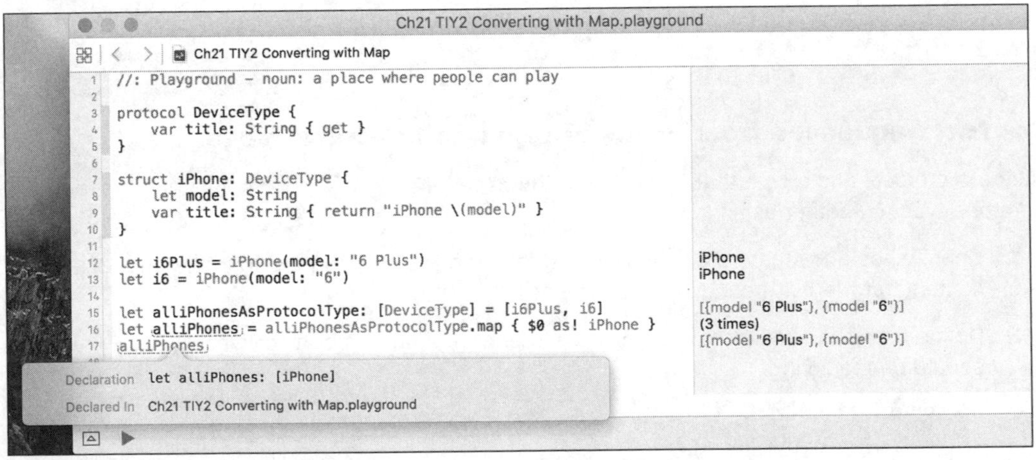

FIGURE 21.4
The completed playground from the Try It Yourself example converting an array of a protocol type to a concrete type.

Summary

This hour covered more in terms of protocols and extensions in Swift. You took what you learned in Hours 17 and 18, as well as some generic concepts from Hour 20, and focused on using protocols not only to define behavior but also extend protocols with default behavior.

You then learned how to use protocol extensions to define default behavior and better identify attributes of mammals that give birth to live young and those that don't. You also used type constraints to extend protocols conditionally, applying an extension only when the type conforming to the protocol also conformed to another protocol or was a particular type.

Additionally, you learned about the differences in the ability to override methods and properties that are and are not defined in the protocol, and how that affects dispatching methods. You learned that dynamic dispatch is where something polymorphic needs to have a runtime lookup to see which implementation to execute, versus a static dispatch, which is identified at compile time.

Finally, you learned about heterogeneous and homogeneous collections with respect to protocols, and how to define methods that accept either type.

Protocol-oriented programming will certainly pick up in popularity, as it is proving to be more flexible and easier to compose than inheritance alone. Indeed, the protocol-oriented programming session was presented twice at WWDC 2015. That's how strongly Apple feels about its importance. Using a protocol-oriented approach in your applications also enables better use of the Liskov Substitution Principle (https://en.wikipedia.org/wiki/Liskov_substitution_principle), part of the SOLID software development principles.

In the next hour, we discuss error handling, and how Swift 2 supports a much nicer and cleaner way to handle errors than some alternatives.

Q&A

Q. Can I override a function from a protocol extension that is not defined in the protocol itself?

A. No. A function can only be overridden if the function implementation in the extension is defined in the protocol.

Q. How can I reference the type conforming to the protocol within the protocol itself, such as in a function signature?

A. Use the `Self` keyword to reference the type conforming to the protocol.

Q. Protocol extensions sound a lot like marking something as optional in a non-extended protocol that had to be marked both as `@objc` and with the `optional` keyword. Are protocol extensions a replacement for this behavior?

A. Perhaps, but not yet officially. It seems that this may be the direction Apple is going. Often the optional methods in a protocol will have a default value because a value is needed but a common default will suffice. However, the opportunity is there to override it. Think of the `UITableViewDataSource` method `numberOfSectionsInTableView:`. You have the opportunity to override that method to provide your own value, but the default is 1.

Workshop

The workshop contains quiz questions and exercises to help you solidify your understanding of the material covered. Try to answer all questions before looking at the answers that follow.

Quiz

1. True or false? Protocol extensions do not need a protocol to be defined first.

2. When creating a protocol extension, is it ok to have an empty protocol definition and have everything in the extension?

3. I don't understand the difference between a function parameter that is `[Ordered]`, versus `[T]`, where `T: Ordered`, for some protocol called `Ordered`. Aren't they the same thing?

4. Is protocol-oriented programming only about creating protocols and protocol extensions?

Answers

1. False. You need a protocol defined first in order to extend one.

2. Yes, the protocol itself can be empty. Any type adopting that protocol will automatically get all default implementations without any extra effort. Just be aware that if nothing is defined in the protocol, nothing can be overridden.

3. No. An array of type `[Ordered]` could contain `Strings`, `Ints`, and `Bools`, for example, if they all conform to `Ordered`. Having the generic type constraint `Ordered` on type `T` ensures that the function parameter can only be `Strings` that are `Ordered`, or `Ints` that are `Ordered`, and so on, but they cannot be mixed types.

4. Not entirely. Protocol-oriented programming is about programming to abstractions versus concretions, composing abilities onto types rather than using an inheritance hierarchy, and referencing protocols for expected behavior rather than a specific type. It enables much more flexibility, and the capability to more easily refactor by substituting one type for another as long as they both conform to a protocol.

Exercise

Create a new playground. Create an extension on `Dictionary` to return an array of the values from each key-value pair, and that are sorted. Remember, to sort an array of something, you want to have each item be comparable to another, so you will need to constrain your type. If you need help knowing which type to constrain, Option-click the `Dictionary` type to find the type names of each key and value. The returned array's elements should be of the same type as the `Dictionary`'s value type.

After you have the extension, you should be able to create a dictionary and ask for its sorted values like the following snippet:

```
let names = ["student1": "Sarah", "student2": "BJ"]
names.sortedValues
```

That computed property should produce an array that looks like `["BJ", "Sarah"]`.

Handling Errors

What You'll Learn in This Hour:

▶ How errors were previously handled
▶ How to create error types
▶ How to throw errors
▶ How to catch thrown errors
▶ How to execute clean up code after throwing

Error handling is never one of the more glamorous topics to cover, or even much fun to implement in an app you're creating, but it is something all programmers should be doing. The concept of handling errors could mean the difference between your app crashing abruptly and leaving your users bewildered, or providing them with a nice message and safely recovering from the error. In this hour, we discuss a brief history of error handling in Cocoa and Objective-C, and how Swift 2's new syntax helps you be clearer and more deliberate about handling errors.

Error Handling

Many different languages have their own ways of handling errors. Some languages use in-out parameters in functions as a way of populating an error if one occurs, such as Objective-C and much of the Cocoa framework. Some languages throw exceptions that you are responsible for catching, but many times, there is no compiler assistance. The main idea is the same: There may be times when a function call fails, input is invalid, a subscript is out of range, or any other type of imperfect scenario occurs. The developer is responsible for ensuring that these issues are handled appropriately. If they are not handled correctly, data could be lost, or worse yet, users could stop using your app and share their negative reactions with others.

Cocoa Error Handling

The generally accepted way of handling errors in the Cocoa frameworks with Objective-C involves a few steps:

1. The method that could fail *should* return a Boolean value indicating whether or not the method succeeded.

2. The method *should* populate an NSError object upon failure, and then the method *should* return false.

3. After you call the method, you *should* check the Boolean return value to see whether it is true or false, and if it is false, then check the associated NSError object for more details.

That's a lot of *shoulds*, but nothing is enforced by the compiler or at runtime. Listing 22.1 shows an example of what this might look like in Objective-C.

LISTING 22.1   Error Handling Example in Objective-C

```
01:   -(BOOL)someMethodThatCouldFail:(NSError **)error {
02:       // oops, something bad happened
03:       error = [NSError errorWithDomain:@"App domain" code:1
     ➥userInfo:someInfoDictionary];
04:       return NO;
05:   }
06:
07:   NSError *error = nil;
08:   BOOL success = [self someMethodThatCouldFail:&error];
09:   if (success) {
10:       // no need to check error, call succeeded
11:   } else {
12:       // call failed, extract info from the error here
13:   }
```

While it seems like it should be a good solution, there are too many disconnected parts for it to work reliably all the time. In fact, there are times when the return value is false, but the error is nil, or when the method succeeds but the error is not nil. Because Objective-C methods can only return a single value, the use of in-out parameters is used in this solution, as you can see by the &error on line 8. In Objective-C, the NSError ** reference on line 1 means a *pointer to a pointer to an NSError object*, so that's why we pass in the address of error with &error. This way, the error object can get populated by the method on line 3 and its contents will persist after the method completes and can be retrieved inside the else block on line 12.

I have often seen this paradigm misused, and instead of declaring an empty NSError * object to pass into the method, many programmers, including myself many times when I was younger, simply pass `nil` and thus discard any potential error information. The attitude of "I don't care about any errors; I trust that this should succeed all the time" is both naïve and wrong.

Swift Error Handling

Although Swift began its life using the same type of paradigm as shown in Listing 22.1, the same problem still existed. How can Swift make it easier for programmers to not have to deal with pointers to pointers of objects, not so easily discard valuable error information, and make it a cohesive experience rather than several disjointed pieces that don't enforce anything? Listing 22.2 shows the Swift translation of the code in Listing 22.1.

LISTING 22.2   Error Handling in Swift 1

```
01:  func someMethodThatCouldFail(error: NSErrorPointer) -> Bool {
02:      // oops, something bad happened
03:      error = NSError(domain: "App domain", code: 1, userInfo:
   someInfoDictionary)
04:      return false
05:  }
06:
07:  var error: NSError? = nil
08:  let success = someMethodThatCouldFail(&error)
09:  if success {
10:      // no need to check error, call succeeded
11:  } else {
12:      // call failed, extract info from the error here
13:  }
```

The Swift code in Listing 22.2 is almost identical, line for line, to the Objective-C code in Listing 22.1, just with Swift style syntax. The only real difference is on line 1, where the `error` parameter is of type `NSErrorPointer`, which is a reference (pointer) to an object that is a pointer to an `NSError` object. But this still didn't solve the problem that existed where you could easily discard error information, and there were too many disjoint moving parts. Swift 2 introduced a modern error-handling syntax, in addition to a new way for the compiler to enforce error handling, as well as a customizable error type.

One way to handle imperfect cases in Swift is with optionals. If a call fails, you could return an optional value, such as trying to call `Int("one")`. The string "one" is not a number, so an optional value of type `Int?` would be returned, and it would contain `nil`. But that doesn't really give us much information. Sure, in this example, you could deduce that it failed because we couldn't convert a `String` to an `Int`, but what about scenarios that are more complex, such as requesting network resources or attempting to access files on the disk that may or may not exist, or may or may not be corrupted?

We need to cover three concepts about handling errors: defining error types, throwing errors, and catching errors. First, let's discuss the error type and how to tailor it to your app's needs.

Customizing Error Types

Swift's standard library comes with a protocol type named `ErrorType`. This protocol is used to provide a uniform interface for throwing and handling errors. But here's the most interesting thing about the `ErrorType` protocol: It's empty. There is nothing defined in it. The reason is brilliant—you can define any type you want, with any information you want, as long as it adopts the `ErrorType` protocol. This means that Swift can handle data to be thrown of any type, as long as it conforms to the `ErrorType` protocol.

When Swift 2 was first released, the `ErrorType` protocol was automatically compatible with the `NSError` type, and this maintained compatibility with Cocoa's existing frameworks that use the `NSError` class for error handling. In addition to that, Swift allows enums to conform to the `ErrorType` protocol for custom error type creation. Enums are ideal candidates for holding error information due to their nature of being case-based, plus they have the capability to have one or more associated values along with each case for more identifying information. As of Swift 2 beta 5, Swift now allows you to adopt the `ErrorType` protocol for any type you create, whether an enum, struct, or class.

To allow a type to be used as an error type, you simply add the `ErrorType` protocol adoption to either the type definition itself or via an extension, as you saw in Hour 17, "Using Protocols to Define Behavior," and Hour 18, "Using Extensions to Add Type Functionality." Listing 22.3 illustrates adding `ErrorType` adoption to an enum and a struct. Class adoption is omitted but would look identical.

LISTING 22.3 Adopting the `ErrorType` Protocol

```
01:    enum NetworkError: ErrorType {
02:        case BadRequest
03:        case Unauthorized(String)
04:        case Forbidden
05:        case NotFound
06:    }
07:
08:    struct FileError: ErrorType {
09:        let code: Int
10:        let description: String
11:    }
```

Because the `ErrorType` protocol has no methods or properties defined in it, we don't need to do anything special inside our types, but we can provide properties to store helpful information about our types. Lines 1 and 8 add `ErrorType` adoption to both types we define. Line 3 uses an associated value for the Unauthorized case, in the event we want to know what username attempted to contact the network resource that failed.

Also, because the ErrorType protocol can be added to any type, you can use extensions to add adoption to any type. Listing 22.4 adopts the ErrorType protocol to the String type, so that you can use any String instance at all as an error type.

LISTING 22.4 Extending `String` to Adopt the `ErrorType` Protocol

```
extension String : ErrorType { }
```

Now that we have taken a look at the ErrorType protocol, let's see how to use it in code to actually send error information back to the element that called a failing function.

Throwing Errors

The approach that Swift takes with sending error information back to the caller of a failable function is to **throw** an error. When an error is thrown, the method exits, just as if you had typed return, but the error information is sent along back to the caller. You accomplish this with the throw keyword, followed by an instance of whatever type you want that adopts ErrorType.

Functions in Swift cannot throw errors by default. To enable a function to throw an error, you must mark the function as a throwing function, by adding the throws keyword after the parameter list and before the return arrow (->). The reason that you must indicate that a function throws is twofold: It lets Swift know that a function can potentially throw an error, and it also lets you be more deliberate about the possibility of error situations in your code, which the compiler then assists you with later when you need to call this function. Listing 22.5 adds to the NetworkError enum type from Listing 22.3 and creates a function that uses that enum for throwing errors.

LISTING 22.5 Throwing Errors

```
01:   enum NetworkError: ErrorType {
02:       case BadRequest
03:       case Unauthorized(String)
04:       case Forbidden
05:       case NotFound
06:   }
07:
08:   func processNetworkResponse(username: String, code: Int) throws -> String {
09:       switch code {
10:       case 400:
11:           throw NetworkError.BadRequest
12:       case 401:
13:           throw NetworkError.Unauthorized(username)
```

```
14:      case 403:
15:          throw NetworkError.Forbidden
16:      case 404:
17:          throw NetworkError.NotFound
18:      default:
19:          return "OK!"
20:      }
21:  }
```

There are a few things to point out in Listing 22.5. First, notice the function signature on line 8. We indicate that the function throws an error by using the `throws` keyword, but then it also returns a `String`. Notice that this is not `String?`, even though the function may return without returning a `String` instance. The return type of a function is essentially ignored if a function ends up throwing an error, relieving you of the need to require an optional just in case an actual `String` instance is not returned. Neat!

It is also worth noting that we do not specify a throw type like we specify a return type. The reason is that if a function is a throwing function, it just needs to throw something that adopts the `ErrorType` protocol. The types of errors do not have to be homogeneous either. Rather, you can throw a `NetworkError`, `NSError`, or `FileError` all from the same function. Although, if you are throwing too many errors of disparate types from a single function, your function may be trying to do too much.

The next item to point out is that because we expect our error type to be an enum, with the `Unauthorized` case expecting an associated value, we can pass along a `String` value if the error code passed into the function is 401. This helps provide valuable information to our calling function in the event of an error.

Lastly, notice that the only place we return an actual `String` instance is in the `default` case on lines 18 and 19. This is because, in this example, we did not have an error case that we cared about (although in reality there probably are many more we should care about), so then we can assume our response was okay and return a string, which satisfies the function's return type requirement.

Now that we have seen how to create error types and how to throw errors of those types when error situations arise, we need to discuss the process of calling a throwing function and handling any potential errors that get thrown.

Catching Errors

After creating our function in Listing 22.5, and knowing it could potentially throw an error, we cannot just simply call the function as we have with any other function in this book. Swift requires us to be specific about our intention to call a throwing function and handle its potential error or errors by using a special keyword when calling, as well as a simple yet powerful mechanism for catching these thrown errors. Let's break this down into two parts: calling a throwing function, and catching thrown errors.

Calling a Throwing Function

Other languages have functions that can throw errors or exceptions at any time, and without any special indication that they could. This is not only difficult to foresee sometimes, but also can lead to unforeseen crashes due to unhandled exceptions simply because you didn't know that the function being called could throw such an exception, or any at all. We've already seen that Swift requires the `throws` keyword when a function can throw an error, but there's another keyword required when calling a throwing function, and that is the `try` keyword.

The `try` keyword must be wrapped in something called a **do-catch** block, similar in structure to an `if-else` block. The `try` statement goes inside the do block, and exception handling goes inside the `catch` block. You must preface calling the throwing function with the `try` keyword inside the do block, and any successive code that should execute upon a successful return of the throwing function is written after the `try` expression, still inside the do block. Multiple `catch` blocks can be used to catch different types of errors. If you do not specify an error to handle and simply use the `catch` keyword with curly braces, an implicit constant named `error` of type `ErrorType` is usable inside the `catch` block.

Part of the beauty of using `do-catch` blocks to handle errors is that it really helps you take care of the error situations right then and there at the point of calling. You would have to make a conscious decision to ignore the errors with this style, because the compiler will assist you in letting you know that you may not have used a `catch` block to handle the errors from a throwing function.

The code following the `try` expression inside the do block is not executed if the `try` expression fails and an error is thrown; instead, the `catch` block or blocks are then executed. After the entire `do-catch` block execution finishes, any code after that will execute normally, no matter if the `try` expression failed or succeeded. A visualization may help, so let's walk through the next Try It Yourself section and examine how the whole error-handling puzzle fits together.

TRY IT YOURSELF ▼

Catch Errors from a Throwing Function

Build upon the code from Listing 22.5 and use `do-catch` blocks and the `try` keyword to call a throwing function and handle success and failure cases appropriately.

1. Open Xcode and create a new playground; either a Mac or iOS playground works. Clear the contents of the playground.

2. Place the code from Listing 22.5 into the playground, including the `NetworkError` enum type and the `processNetworkResponse` function.

3. After the function, create the do block. Inside the do block, call the processNetwork-Response function and assign the result to a constant named response. Pass a name into the username parameter and 401 for the code parameter. Remember to call the function with the try keyword. Print the response value if the call succeeds.

```
do {
    let response = try processNetworkResponse("cletus", code: 401)
    print(response)
}
```

4. Add the first catch block after the do block's closing curly brace. Just as with using else blocks, putting catch blocks on the same line as the closing brace in the preceding block is customary. Catch a BadRequest error, and print an error message inside this catch block.

```
catch NetworkError.BadRequest {
    print("Hold up! Fix your syntax!")
}
```

5. Add another catch block to catch an Unauthorized error, and use binding to extract the associated value. Print a message using the bound username.

```
catch NetworkError.Unauthorized(let username) {
    print("\(username) couldn't log in")
}
```

6. Add a final catch block with no qualifier and print whatever error is caught. Remember, if you do not specify a certain type of error to be caught, an implicit constant named error of type ErrorType is sent.

```
catch {
    print(error)
}
```

7. Take turns changing the code value sent into the processNetworkResponse function to see the different output in the console by pressing Command+Shift+Y to show the Debug Area.

Upon completion, the Try It Yourself playground should look like the playground in Figure 22.1.

```
●  ●  ●                    Ch22 TIY1 Catching Errors.playground
⊞  <  >  ▣ Ch22 TIY1 Catching Errors
 1  enum NetworkError: ErrorType {
 2      case BadRequest
 3      case Unauthorized(String)
 4      case Forbidden
 5      case NotFound
 6  }
 7
 8  func processNetworkResponse(username: String, code: Int) throws -> String {
 9      switch code {
10      case 400:
11          throw NetworkError.BadRequest
12      case 401:
13          throw NetworkError.Unauthorized(username)
14      case 403:
15          throw NetworkError.Forbidden
16      case 404:
17          throw NetworkError.NotFound
18      default:
19          return "OK!"
20      }
21  }
22
23  do {
24      let response = try processNetworkResponse("cletus", code: 401)
25      print(response)
26  } catch NetworkError.BadRequest {
27      print("Hold up! Fix your syntax!")
28  } catch NetworkError.Unauthorized(let username) {
29      print("\(username) couldn't log in")                  "cletus couldn't log in\n"
30  } catch {
31      print(error)
32  }
33
⊡  ▶
cletus couldn't log in
```

FIGURE 22.1
The completed Try It Yourself example playground using try statements and do-catch blocks to catch errors.

After going through the Try It Yourself example, it should be very clear to you how error handling is structured in Swift. Of course, you may not always have the error code known ahead of time like we do in the Try It Yourself example, but you may get the status code as part of an HTTP response. The point is this—error catching and handling can mean the difference between your app crashing abruptly at different times and potentially losing data, or gracefully handling the errors, letting users know something went wrong and maybe that they may want to try some action again.

Trying Without Catching

In addition to a try statement for trying a statement for success or failure, Swift packs a try! statement (pronounced "force try") to forcibly call a throwing function. However, with try! you take the responsibility of knowing that it should succeed, or else your app will crash at runtime. This is very much like using as! to forcibly cast, or using ! to forcibly unwrap an optional value. If you use the try! keyword, you do not need to wrap it inside a do-catch block, because you are not catching any errors.

The try! keyword can be useful when you know that calling the throwing function will not fail, such as if you have already validated the input that would cause the called function to fail. For example, if you already knew the code was 200 in the previous Try It Yourself section, and it is not input that would throw an error, you can call the function with the try! keyword. Listing 22.6 shows the try! keyword in use in the last scenario.

LISTING 22.6   Using the try! Keyword

```
// use the same NetworkError enum and function from Try It Yourself section
let success = try! processNetworkResponse("cletus", code: 200)
print(success)   // displays "OK!"
```

The try! keyword is perfectly acceptable to use when you know that calling a throwing function will not fail. But do keep in mind that you should only use it when you are sure of its success, much like using the as! operator and also the force unwrap operator on optionals. I don't want to discourage you from using these keywords, but think safety first.

Another way to call a throwing function without catching is with the try? keyword (pronounced "optional try"). Similar to the try! keyword, any thrown error is discarded, but this operator can be safely used with optional binding in if let or guard let statements. The reason you would want to use the try? keyword is to see whether calling a throwing function succeeds without caring about the error thrown. But if there is an error thrown and the function failed, you can simply create an else clause to resume a different path of execution. Remember, just like the try! keyword, the thrown error information is thrown away (sorry, bad pun). Listing 22.7 shows how to use the try? keyword.

LISTING 22.7   Using Failable try? Keyword

```
enum NumError : ErrorType {
    case NotEven
}

func isEven(num: Int) throws -> Bool {
    if num % 2 != 0 {
        throw NumError.NotEven
    }
    return true
}

func squareAnEvenNumber(num: Int) -> Int? {
    guard let _ = try? isEven(num) else { return nil }
    return num * num
}
```

```
squareAnEvenNumber(5)
squareAnEvenNumber(6)
```

The example in Listing 22.7 uses `guard let` syntax to call the throwing function with the `try?` keyword. Because the throwing function returns a `Bool`, we don't need the return value if the function succeeds; success will pass the `guard` statement and return our input number squared. In this case, we didn't care about what type of error occurred, we just needed to know if the call to the throwing function succeeded or failed, so we could either return `nil` or the number squared.

I should mention also that calling a throwing function that returns an optional value with the `try?` keyword will return a doubly wrapped optional. For instance, if you call a function that returns `String?`, and use the `try?` keyword, the return type upon successful completion will be `String??` (which is `Optional<Optional<String>>`). If used in `if let` or `guard let` binding syntax, the return type would be `String?`. Keep this in mind when optionally trying functions with an optional return type—you may need to flatten one layer of optional wrapping to use the return value as intended.

Deferring Execution

When calling a function that can throw, the function is most likely exiting before its natural end of execution. Take, for example, the `processNetworkResponse` function from Listing 22.5. You may use a `guard` statement to trap an error toward the beginning of a function, so the rest of the function never gets executed.

When you throw errors from a function, leaving the throwing function early may not be such a clean break. There may be delegate methods, for instance, that indicate a process has started, and that the caller is expecting another delegate method to execute to indicate that the process ended somehow; or, say you open a file for writing but throw an error mid-use. Your file closing code may never get executed, leaving your file open and causing potential issues later. These are all ideal uses for the `defer` statement we discussed back in Hour 8, "Using Functions to Perform Actions."

Recall that the `defer` statement will execute the code inside its closure no matter when or how the function exits. This is great news, because when you throw an error, the function does not run its normal course and exit at the last curly brace or the final `return` statement. You may also have multiple `defer` blocks if you need to signal multiple clean-up operations or delegate calls.

In the following Try It Yourself example, you use the `defer` statement to provide a final callback to a delegate to indicate processing has finished, no matter how the function exits.

▼ TRY IT YOURSELF

Defer Delegate Execution

Create an enum conforming to the `ErrorType` protocol to have something to throw, a delegate that can identify the beginning and end of a process, a handler that conforms to that delegate protocol, and a struct that has a delegate and a method that performs a lengthy process, informing its delegate of start and completion.

1. Open Xcode and create a new playground; either a Mac or iOS playground works. Clear the contents of the playground.

2. Start by creating an enum that conforms to the `ErrorType` protocol and contains a single case. We only need one case to illustrate this example.

```
enum MyError: ErrorType {
    case Foo
}
```

3. Create a protocol to which a delegate will conform. This protocol will have two methods, one to indicate the beginning and one to indicate the ending of the process.

```
protocol ProcessDelegate {
    func didBeginProcess()
    func didEndProcess()
}
```

4. Create a struct that conforms to the `ProcessDelegate` protocol, and fill in those methods with `print` statements just to see the output in the Debug Area.

```
struct Handler: ProcessDelegate {
    func didBeginProcess() { print("starting") }
    func didEndProcess() { print("ending") }
}
```

5. Create a struct that contains a variable property of type `ProcessDelegate?`, and also a method with the signature `(Bool) throws -> String`. Throw an error if the Boolean parameter is false; otherwise, return a string of your choosing. Also, tell the delegate that you began processing at the start of the method and ended processing right before the return statement.

```
struct SomeStruct {
    var delegate: ProcessDelegate?
    func methodThatCanThrow(shouldThrow shouldThrow: Bool) throws -> String {
        delegate?.didBeginProcess()
        if shouldThrow {
            throw MyError.Foo
        }
```

```
                delegate?.didEndProcess()
                return "too much foo!"
        }
    }
```

6. Declare an instance of `SomeStruct` and pass in a new instance of `Handler` for the `delegate` parameter.

```
let someValue = SomeStruct(delegate: Handler())
```

7. Try calling `methodThatCanThrow` from your `someValue` instance inside a `do-catch` block. Use the resulting value upon success in a `print` statement to the debug console.

```
do {
    let result = try someValue.methodThatCanThrow(shouldThrow: true)
    print(result)
} catch {
    print(error)
}
```

8. Upon executing the playground, you should see two lines in your debug console, "starting" and "Foo". The "Foo" you see is the printed representation of the enum error case. But notice that the `delegate`'s `didEndProcess` function was never called. Add a `defer` block right after the `delegate?.didBeginProcess()` line, and move the `delegate?.didEndProcess()` call into the `defer` block. Ensure the method implementation looks like the following code:

```
func methodThatCanThrow(shouldThrow shouldThrow: Bool) throws -> String {
    delegate?.didBeginProcess()
    defer {
        delegate?.didEndProcess()
    }
    if shouldThrow {
        throw MyError.Foo
    }
    return "too much foo!"
}
```

9. Now with the `defer` block in place, our delegate instance gets properly balanced callbacks. Try changing the `shouldThrow` argument from `true` to `false` to see whether you get the appropriately returned string value.

After you complete the Try It Yourself section, your playground should look like the playground in Figure 22.2.

```
enum MyError: ErrorType {
    case Foo
}

protocol ProcessDelegate {
    func didBeginProcess()
    func didEndProcess()
}

struct Handler: ProcessDelegate {
    func didBeginProcess() { print("starting") }      "starting\n"
    func didEndProcess() { print("ending") }          "ending\n"
}

struct SomeStruct {
    var delegate: ProcessDelegate?
    func methodThatCanThrow(shouldThrow shouldThrow: Bool) throws -> String
        {
        delegate?.didBeginProcess()                   ()
        defer {
            delegate?.didEndProcess()
        }
        if shouldThrow {
            throw MyError.Foo
        }
        return "too much foo!"                        "too much foo!"
    }
}

let someValue = SomeStruct(delegate: Handler())       SomeStruct
do {
    let result = try someValue.methodThatCanThrow(shouldThrow: false)   "too much foo!"
    print(result)                                     "too much foo!\n"
} catch {
    print(error)
}
```

```
starting
ending
too much foo!
```

FIGURE 22.2
The completed Try It Yourself example using `defer` blocks to ensure clean-up code executes no matter how a function exits.

Summary

In this hour, we covered the important topic of error handling. You learned the basics of Cocoa error handling and how error handling looks in Objective-C. Then you saw how to do similar error handling in Swift 1.

You then learned how Swift 2 drastically improved error handling such that it is now a uniform experience, easy to customize, and you get assistance from the compiler, too. You learned about the ErrorType protocol and how to customize any type to become an error type by adopting that protocol. Swift enables you to create error types that adopt `ErrorType` to be an enum, class, or struct.

Then you learned how to throw errors from a function. You learned that not just any function can throw an error, but a function that needs to throw an error must be marked with the `throws` keyword. A throwing function can throw any type of error it needs, as long as the error conforms to the `ErrorType` protocol.

After learning how to throw errors, you then learned different techniques for calling functions that can throw errors by using `try`, `try!`, and `try?`. You also learned how to catch errors in `do-catch` blocks. Because throwing functions exit a function earlier than you may sometimes want, you learned how to use `defer` blocks to execute code no matter when or how a function exits. This can be very useful for when you open resources that need to be closed or handled when an instance is finished using them.

The topic of error handling is large, and there is much more to learn about it than what could be covered here in one hour's time, so I encourage you to do more research online about error handling in Swift in various scenarios, such as in asynchronous programming, or even *rethrowing* errors.

In the next hour, we discuss interoperability between Swift and Objective-C, which you will no doubt encounter in your career as a Swift developer. When you feel comfortable with the content of this hour, let's move forward to the next hour.

Q&A

Q. **If I have two different error types, both adopting the `ErrorType` protocol, can I throw either in a single function?**

A. Yes, as long as your error types adopt the `ErrorType` protocol, you can throw an instance of any type.

Q. **If I call a throwing function with the `try!` keyword, can I still catch an error?**

A. No. If you use either `try!` or `try?`, the error information is discarded.

Q. **I have older Objective-C code that used the in-out style error parameter of type `NSError **`. Do I have to update that code or can I still call that function from Swift?**

A. No, you should not need to update the code, and yes, you should be able to still call that function using a `do-catch` block and a `try` statement. Swift is able to translate that for you behind the scenes.

Workshop

The workshop contains quiz questions and exercises to help you solidify your understanding of the material covered. Try to answer all questions before looking at the answers that follow.

Quiz

1. True or false? Using the `try?` keyword to call a function that returns an optional value results in a doubly wrapped optional.

2. What are the three key concepts behind making error handling in Swift work?

3. True or false? Code inside a `defer` block will not get executed if a function exits early by throwing an error.

Answers

1. True. A function that returns `Int?` would result in `Int??` when called using the `try?` keyword.

2. Creating an error type using the `ErrorType` protocol, throwing errors, and catching errors.

3. False. The code inside a `defer` block will execute no matter how a function exits.

Exercise

Create a new playground, and in this exercise, you will create the code necessary to validate user login information. This validation will serve as a pre-check before it would ever go to a web service.

First, create an error type that can handle several different cases, such as username length, empty input, and so on. Then create a function that will validate input sent into it and will either return a value of type `String` with a special message for the user, or throw an error for whatever criteria failed your validation. You should catch errors accordingly and display appropriate error messages to the user depending on what type of error was thrown.

HOUR 23
Adding Interoperability with Objective-C

What You'll Learn in This Hour:

▶ How to create a basic Objective-C class

▶ How to translate types between Swift and Objective-C

▶ How to use bridging headers

▶ How to use `id` and `AnyObject` between languages

▶ How to call Objective-C methods and properties from Swift

In this hour, we discuss several concepts with regard to interoperability between Swift and Objective-C. The encompassing topic is huge in and of itself, and we will not be able to cover everything in just one hour. Throughout this book, I have made the assumption that you do not necessarily have an Objective-C background, so some of the concepts in this hour may be too basic for you if you do; feel free to skip anything you may already know. The position taken this hour is to familiarize you with Objective-C by comparing certain aspects of it to what you have learned in Swift thus far. Also, I want you to have a basic understanding of Objective-C when you see it, so that you know how to access an existing Objective-C code base from Swift. If you plan to be a Swift developer, you will doubtless encounter Objective-C code, and you must know how to integrate Swift and Objective-C. Let's start with some basics.

Objective-C Basics

Before we begin integrating Swift and Objective-C, let's take a few minutes to cover some quick basics about Objective-C. Objective-C notoriously uses a lot of @ signs, square brackets ([]), and semicolons (;), so I hope that doesn't bother you.

Also, since Xcode playgrounds are not compatible with Objective-C, we do not use any playgrounds in this hour. There is a project on GitHub set up for you to clone to your computer that we will walk through, adding Swift functionality to an existing app written in Objective-C. You can find the project at https://github.com/STYSwiftIn24H/ExamplesV2/ in the Ch23 folder.

File Structure

The first thing to note about Objective-C is that, unlike Swift class files, there are two files: a **header file** (filename.h) and an **implementation file** (filename.m). The header file, sometimes called the **public interface file**, is where you define publicly accessible properties and methods of your class. The implementation file is where your implementation code is written. You can also have an optional **private interface** at the top of the implementation file, which is a place to define private properties and methods to be used inside the implementation but not publicly accessible. Elements inside the implementation file are not accessible publicly unless publicly defined in the header file. Listing 23.1 illustrates a simple model object interface. We cover the implementation shortly. Both Song.h and Song.m appear in the Models group in the Xcode project, if you are looking at them in the project.

LISTING 23.1   Sample Objective-C Model Interface

```
01:   //Song.h
02:   #import <Foundation/Foundation.h>
03:
04:   @interface Song : NSObject
05:   @property (nonatomic, copy, nonnull) NSString *title;
06:   @property (nonatomic, copy, nullable) NSString *artist;
07:   @property (nonatomic, strong, null_resettable) NSNumber *rating;
08:   - (instancetype _Nonnull)initWithTitle:(NSString * _Nonnull)title
                                  artist:(NSString * _Nullable)artist
                                  rating:(NSNumber * _Nullable)rating;
09:   @end
```

A lot happened in Listing 23.1, so let's break it down so you understand all the pieces. Lines 1 through 9 define the public interface for the Song class, inside the Song.h file. Breaking each down further, let's start with the header interface.

Objective-C Header Files

Line 2 imports the Foundation framework, similarly to what we have done with the `import Foundation` statements in Swift. That is necessary to create a class in Objective-C since all classes in Objective-C must have a root class, which is most often NSObject (or a subclass thereof), and NSObject is part of the Foundation framework. Did you see that there is no `class` or `@class` keyword to define a class, rather just an `@interface` statement? That is how Objective-C creates classes and ends the interface with the `@end` statement.

Inside the `@interface` section is where we declare any properties and/or methods that we want to publicly expose. On lines 5 through 7, we define three properties of type NSString * (the * is important—see the next note) that have several different property attributes, `nonatomic`, `copy`, `strong`, and several varying nullability attributes. `nonatomic` means that we simply want to return or set the property values directly without any locking mechanism, which would prevent multiple process threads from accessing or changing the value while we may be reading or writing the property's contents. You don't have to specify this in Swift because all Swift properties are nonatomic. The `copy` attribute means a copy of the property will be returned when requested rather than a pointer to the instance directly. This is used in cases of mutability, and even though `NSString` is an immutable class, an `NSMutableString` could be set to the property and then later change when you don't expect it. Having the `copy` attribute helps prevent this accidental mutability.

The `strong` keyword is exactly the same as the `strong` keyword we discussed in Hour 16, "Understanding Memory Allocation and References," in that we tell Objective-C that we want to retain a strong reference to that property. We must specify this in Objective-C, whereas in Swift, `strong` is the default. Sometimes you may see the `copy` attribute as opposed to a `strong` attribute, which still is a `strong` reference but a copy of the object is returned. This helps keep the actual model object safe from accidental mutation. For our example, using `strong` is perfectly fine. Lastly, as for all those words that start with *null*, we'll discuss those shortly in the section "Nullability."

NOTE

Why Is the Asterisk Important?

Remember that Objective-C is a strict superset of the C language, and to reference memory in the heap (which is where all Objective-C instances are stored), you must reference that memory location by using the `*` character. The type is often said to be "an `NSString`," but strictly speaking, the type is `NSString *`, meaning a pointer to an `NSString` object.

NOTE

Custom Getters and Setters

Objective-C provides default getters and setters in a process called **synthesizing**. Prior to auto-synthesizing properties, Objective-C programmers had to write getters and setters for every property, or just use the backing instance variable directly, which is often not safe. Lines 9–11 in Listing 23.3 show what a custom setter might look like. If you want to provide custom getters *and* setters, you can, but you need to add `@synthesize propertyName;` in the implementation file so Objective-C could create a backing instance variable to be used by your properties and handle its memory management. Xcode is fairly good about warning you when you need to specifically synthesize properties.

On line 8, we define a custom initializer that we provide code for inside the implementation. All methods in Objective-C are prefaced with either a plus sign (+) for a class method or a minus sign (-) for an instance method. After the class/instance sign, the return type is listed inside parentheses. This is different from Swift where the return type is at the end of the function or method definition. Inside the parentheses is the keyword instancetype, which is a special return type for init methods and is a reference to the type of the receiver object. Since a class could be subclassed but use the superclass's initializer, instancetype returns the proper type of object.

Notice the syntax of the initializer on line 8. The parameter names and types are intermixed with the arguments just like in Swift, just without commas. Listing 23.2 shows the same initializer definition in Swift and Objective-C.

LISTING 23.2   Initializers in Swift and Objective-C

```
//Objective-C
- (instancetype _Nonnull)initWithTitle:(NSString * _Nonnull)title
                                artist:(NSString * _Nullable)artist
                                rating:(NSNumber * _Nullable)rating;


//Swift
init(title: String, artist: String?, rating: NSNumber?)
```

The functionality of these two init methods is identical. Swift's method syntax is a little more succinct than Objective-C's, but the Objective-C init method should be easily readable now that you've learned Swift's method syntax with relation to the inline parameter names, types, and arguments. Objective-C's convention for method naming with parameters is to provide a meaningful explanation of what the method does, while intermixing the parameters inline, as seen by initWithTitle:(NSString * _Nonnull)title artist:(NSString * _Nullable) artist rating:(NSNumber * _Nullable)rating. Notice also that Objective-C does not separate parameters with commas like Swift. Rather, a single space separates the parameters.

Objective-C Implementation Files

The implementation of the Song class in Objective-C from Listing 23.1 is shown here in Listing 23.3.

LISTING 23.3   Sample Objective-C Model Implementation

```
01:  //Song.m
02:  #import "Song.h"
03:
04:  @interface Song ()
05:  //this is where the private interface code goes, if any
06:  @end
07:
08:  @implementation Song
```

```
09:    - (void)setRating:(NSNumber *)rating {
10:        _rating = (!rating) ? @0.0 : rating;
11:    }
12:
13:
14:    - (instancetype)initWithTitle:(NSString *)title artist:(NSString *)artist
    ➡rating:(NSNumber *)rating {
15:        if (self = [super init]) {
16:            _title = title;
17:            _artist = artist;
18:            _rating = rating;
19:        }
20:        return self;
21:    }
22:
23:    @end
```

The file begins by importing the Song.h header file on line 2, so that the implementation file can use the information from the public header in case any properties or methods are declared publicly and used in the private implementation.

Lines 4 through 6 define a private interface, where private properties and methods can be declared before being used. This section is particularly useful when you need to maintain private data that you don't want to expose to other classes but need to use inside this class. In our example, nothing is listed there, but declaring private properties and methods is identical to declaring them in the public interface. However, the Objective-C compiler knows not to expose them. This is akin to using the private attribute in Swift.

Line 8 begins the implementation with the @implementation keyword, denoting the beginning of our class's implementation. Lines 9 through 11 define a custom setter for the rating property, which is required because we defined it as null_resettable. Then on line 14, we define our initializer's implementation. First, we ask our superclass to perform its initialization process and assign self to the result with self = [super init]. We check the result of that inside an if statement, because in Objective-C, like Swift, the initialization process could fail and return nil. If our superclass initializes properly and is assigned to self properly, we finish our own class's initialization by setting our instance variables directly, with the underscore in front of the property name. Using the instance variables in the initializer is customary, because technically the instance is not fully initialized until you return self from the initializer, so you shouldn't reference self.title until after initialization; rather, you should use _title. After the if statement, we return self, but we return self after the if statement because if our call to [super init] failed, return self would return nil, which is 100% okay in Objective-C.

NOTE

Order of Initialization

Did you see that in Objective-C we call [super init] first before initializing any of our own class's properties? This is because the object needs to get allocated in memory first, which our superclass chain takes care of, before we can set any properties of our own. This is different from Swift, where our instance needs to be initialized before calling super.init(). Swift classes do not need a superclass, so Swift handles the memory allocation automatically, and you are responsible for initializing your instance first before calling super.init().

Nullability

Remember that Objective-C uses nil differently than Swift does, and when working in a project that is all Objective-C, you interact with nil, message it, assign it, and your app (with a few exceptions) continues to run and be happy. When interacting Objective-C with Swift, however, giving the compiler some directives on how to handle **nullability**, or the capability to become null/nil at some point, becomes very helpful. There are different directives to provide for property definitions than method signatures, so let's cover those now.

Nullable Property Definitions

As you saw in Listing 23.1, three nullability attributes were defined: **nullable**, **nonnull**, and **null_resettable**. nullable lets the compiler know that the property can be set to nil in the future, and the property is treated as an optional value when used in Swift. nonnull lets the compiler know that this property will not be nil, and the property is treated as a non-optional value when used in Swift. null_resettable lets the compiler know that the property could be set to nil, but if it is, it should immediately default to a known good value. In other words, null_resettable can be assigned nil, but it will never be nil. When using an Objective-C property that is null_resettable from Swift, it is treated as an implicitly unwrapped optional. The null_resettable property is also required to have a custom setter that ensures the property has a value at all times, even if being set to nil. This could come in handy when you may want to have a color property, and setting it to nil would simply reset it to its default color value.

You do not have to set nullability attributes in your Objective-C code. If you do set a nullability attribute for at least one property or method, you are then required to do so for the remainder of the properties and parameters in the rest of the class. As a shortcut measure, if you want all properties to never be nil, you can enclose all code in your header inside two define statements, NS_ASSUME_NONNULL_BEGIN and NS_ASSUME_NONNULL_END. If you do not set any nullability attributes or state the aforementioned BEGIN and END defines, all properties port over to Swift as implicitly unwrapped optionals.

Nullable Method Parameters

Also notice in Listing 23.1 the initializer method definition and how the nullability attributes are different from those we just mentioned for properties. The nullability attributes you can use for methods are **_Nonnull** and **_Nullable**. There is technically a third, **_Null_unspecified**, but we won't discuss it here. The _Nullable and _Nonnull attributes are exactly what they sound like, based on their similar counterparts from the previous section. The only differences are that they are prefaced with an underscore (_) and have a capital *N*. These nullability attributes behave the same way and just indicate that a property can or shouldn't be nullable. If a function parameter is marked _Nonnull, then any argument passed into it can be assumed not to be nil, and you don't need to check it for nil before interacting with it.

Allocation and Initialization

While Swift takes care of the memory allocation for you, as discussed in Hour 16, Objective-C does not do that for you. Listing 23.4 shows the differences in instantiating objects in Swift and Objective-C.

LISTING 23.4   Instantiating Objects

```
//Objective-C

Song *song = [[Song alloc] initWithTitle:@"Happy" artist:@"Pharrell", rating:@4.5];

//Swift
let song = Song(title: "Happy", artist: "Pharrell", rating: 4.5)
```

In Objective-C, we have to pass the alloc message to the Song class, which allocates a space in memory for a new object of type Song. Then we pass initWithTitle:artist:rating: to the newly allocated object, which initializes the object and sets the values we passed in as arguments.

Notice that to declare a constant or variable of an Objective-C type in Swift, you do not need to enter init or even With. The init keyword is assumed when you use parentheses after a type name. The compiler automatically strips out With as well, because it doesn't make sense grammatically to have a floating With since init was stripped out.

NOTE

Nested Method Calls in Objective-C

The square brackets can get a bit confusing to keep straight sometimes in Objective-C. Each method call is really a *message* sent to the object or class name inside the brackets. Objective-C's runtime executes the nested message first, and the result of that is then used within the outer message. So for instance, [Song alloc] is executed, and the result of that is an uninitialized object of type Song, which is then sent the `initWithTitle:artist:rating:` message. While it looks a little weird at first, it becomes second nature after a while. This type of message sending syntax is structured after SmallTalk.

One more quick note about initializers in Objective-C that are used in Swift is that Objective-C class methods that return an instance of that type (sometimes referred to as **factory methods**) are mapped to be convenience initializers in Swift. Such an example is shown in Listing 23.5. Before ARC, factory methods in Objective-C were helpful with memory management in that they would automatically release an object when it went out of scope, which was one less object for you to manage with `retain` or `release` keywords.

LISTING 23.5   **Objective-C Factory Methods Are Convenience Initializers in Swift**

```
//Objective-C
NSURL *url = [NSURL urlWithString:@"https://github.com"];

//Swift
let url = NSURL(string: "https://github.com")
```

The Objective-C factory method takes care of the alloc/init process for you and returns a reference to a newly instantiated `NSURL` object. As mentioned, this translates to a convenience initializer in Swift. Since you don't have to specifically execute an `alloc` statement, this can all happen in an initializer.

Bridging

In a moment, we get to implementing Swift code in an existing Objective-C app, but first we need to cover a concept called **bridging**. With regard to the interoperability of Swift and Objective-C, bridging takes on a few different meanings under different contexts, the first bridging context being the module or API level and the second being the type level. Let's cover module/API bridging first.

Module Bridging

Any Objective-C framework (or C framework) accessible as a module can be imported into Swift, using the `import SomeModuleName` statement. This makes available to Swift all publicly declared APIs in an Objective-C or C module. You can also make Objective-C classes available to Swift via a **bridging header**, which Xcode automatically creates for you when it senses that you are about to mix languages in the same project. Xcode offers to create a bridging header when you are about to add an Objective-C file to a Swift app or a Swift file to an Objective-C app. We create a bridging header shortly when we get into our example.

When you need to import Swift code into Objective-C, Xcode auto-generates a header file named using a generated filename consisting of the name of the product module plus "-Swift.h". To use this in Objective-C, you would then have a statement at the top of either your .h or .m file, #import "YourProductModule-Swift.h".

Type Bridging

Many of the types used in Objective-C are actually from the Cocoa framework. The Cocoa framework consists of the Foundation Kit, Application Kit (often referred to as AppKit), and Core Data frameworks. The Cocoa Touch framework is similar but contains UIKit instead of AppKit. The types included in these frameworks are mostly recognized by their naming convention of starting with the two letters NS. This naming convention stemmed either from NeXT-Sun's creation of OpenStep or NeXTSTEP's term for the OpenStep framework (Wikipedia, http://en.wikipedia.org/wiki/Cocoa_(API)#History). Unless I need to differentiate between the two, I will henceforth refer to Cocoa and Cocoa Touch as simply "Cocoa."

Most Cocoa types are bridgeable to Swift without much work on your part. For instance, NSString is bridgeable to String and vice versa. Being a bridged data type means that it can be used interchangeably or is convertible to its equivalent counterpart. This is useful if you have an existing Swift type, such as a String or an Array and you are working with an Objective-C API that requests an NSString or NSArray, respectively.

There is one small caveat, however. Cocoa types don't automatically bridge to Swift types any longer; only Swift types automatically bridge to Cocoa types. Listing 23.6 shows a quick illustration of type bridging in action.

LISTING 23.6   Inferred and Explicit Type Bridging

```
import Foundation

let nsString: NSString = "Hello, I'm an NSString"
let string: String = "Hi, I'm a String"

func funcThatTakesAnNSString(text: NSString) { print(text) }

func funcThatTakesAString(text: String) { print(text) }

funcThatTakesAnNSString(string)
funcThatTakesAString(nsString as String)
```

Also, remember in Hour 15, "Adding Advanced Type Functionality," we discussed non-specific type specifiers such as Any and AnyObject. Any and AnyObject aren't really types like we think of them; they are protocols. AnyObject is a protocol that describes any instance of a reference type. Since all objects in Objective-C are reference types, all Objective-C objects are

AnyObject compatible by default when using them in Swift. The Objective-C equivalent to AnyObject is id, which is a pointer to any Objective-C object.

Following are several Swift types and their Objective-C compatible equivalents. There is a lot of information on these topics that could be covered, but here we only cover some main highlights.

String **and** NSString

Swift's String type and Objective-C's NSString class are bridgeable as well as interchangeable. Wherever you see NSString in Objective-C, you can insert a Swift String. Wherever you need to use a String in Swift but you currently have an NSString object, you can use that NSString, as long as you cast it to a Swift String using the as operator (not as!). To enable the bridging in a Swift file, simply import the Foundation framework. You can also cast String instances to NSString without the need to use the optional as? or forced unwrap as! operator since the cast is guaranteed to succeed between the two types. This may seem a little odd at first because technically String is a value type (struct) and not a reference type, yet it is still interchangeable with NSString, which is a reference type. The work to bridge these types has been done for you to provide a seamless coexistence between the two, so just imagine the Jedi-wave with Apple telling you, "You don't need to see Swift's internal implementation."

Numeric Types and NSNumber

Several numeric types in Swift are directly interchangeable with NSNumber objects in Objective-C. These Swift types include Int, UInt, Bool, Double, and Float. Whenever a method or object defines the need for an NSNumber object, you can freely pass in one of the aforementioned Swift numeric types. The difference, however, is that you cannot pass an NSNumber object to a method or object that defines the need for an Int, UInt, Bool, Double, or Float, because the compiler cannot guarantee that the number inside the NSNumber object is compatible with the Swift type. For example, if a function parameter takes an Int, you cannot send an NSNumber object because the compiler cannot guarantee that the NSNumber is not really a Bool, or some other non-Int type.

Array **and** NSArray

When converting an NSArray instance to an Array instance, an array of type [AnyObject] is returned. This is because NSArray objects contain objects of type id, and all Objective-C objects are AnyObject compatible, so Objective-C returns [AnyObject] to Swift to remain type-safe. When converting from Array to NSArray, each element in the array must be AnyObject compatible, meaning it must be of a class type (or reference type).

Once you have an [AnyObject] array, you can downcast it to a more defined type if you need to, such as from [AnyObject] to [Int]. This is done with the as? operator, because the downcast could fail if the types of objects inside are not compatible with the intended casted type. If you are sure of the type cast, you can use the as operator, but just know that if it fails, your app will crash reliably.

Dictionary **and** NSDictionary

Converting an NSDictionary object to a Swift Dictionary results in a dictionary of type [NSObject: AnyObject]. Just as with arrays, you can downcast a dictionary to a more specific type for the keys and values, but the conversion is not always guaranteed to succeed, so use the as? operator for safety. When converting from a Swift Dictionary to an NSDictionary, all keys and values must be instances of classes or bridgeable to instances of classes. In other words, if the keys or values are structs (like String), they should be bridgeable to an Objective-C class type (like NSString).

Integrating Swift into an Objective-C App

In lieu of separate Try It Yourself sections, let's take the remainder of this hour to build an app together that uses both Objective-C and Swift. This way, I can explain things a lot better along the way, and with screenshots, and basically make one long Try It Yourself section. So follow along, and let's get rolling.

Download the Starter Project

To start, clone the repository for this book's example code from GitHub. Open Terminal.app, or whatever app you use to access a Unix shell, and enter the following command:

```
$ git clone git@github.com:STYSwiftIn24H/ExamplesV2.git
```

Once the cloning has completed, change the directory to the Examples/Ch23/ObjCInterop folder and then open the Xcode project by entering the following commands:

```
$ cd Examples/Ch23/ObjCInterop
$ open ObjCInterop.xcodeproj
```

Xcode should now be open to the ObjCInterop project. Don't feel too overwhelmed by everything in Xcode if you're not familiar with it; I will walk you through what you need to do for this app.

TIP

Completed Project Is Available for Reference

If you get stuck or need to see the project in its entirety, the completed project is available in the Examples/Ch23/ObjCInterop-Final folder. Only use it if you need to!

The ObjCInterop project lists a few songs, with the artist and rating information below it (the ratings are made up). So far, it is written solely in Objective-C. Hold down the Command key and press R to run the app. The app opens in the iOS Simulator, and an app appears that looks like the one in Figure 23.1.

FIGURE 23.1
The ObjCInterop app upon first run, as solely an Objective-C app.

Clicking on any of the list items pushes, or **segues**, a new view controller onto the screen, showing detailed information about whatever song you tapped. Right now, what is displayed should look similar to <Song: 0x7fd0b1e5bb40>, because the app hasn't implemented a pretty way to display the tapped song. We implement that in Swift shortly. Hold the Command key and press Q to quit the iOS Simulator.

In the Xcode Navigation Pane on the left-hand side, expand the ObjCInterop grouping and then expand the Models grouping. Inside the Models grouping, you see two files: Song.h and Song.m. Click Song.h, and in the content area, you see the public header interface for the Song class. In it, song title, artist, and rating properties are defined, as well as a custom initializer. Notice that the Song class inherits from NSObject, since all Objective-C classes must have a superclass, most commonly NSObject or a subclass thereof. Next, click on Song.m and notice that we have nothing in the private interface, and we provide a simple implementation for our initializer. Song is our model class and is used to populate the elements in each cell in the table view.

Our MasterViewController class provides the list of songs to the table view interface, and the DetailViewController class currently displays detailed information about whatever element belongs to the cell tapped in the master view controller. Right now, the DetailViewController class is not implemented, so select both DetailViewController.h and DetailViewController.m and delete them. If Xcode prompts you to remove references or move to trash, select Move to Trash. We recreate this class in Swift.

Create a Swift Class and Bridging Header

In Xcode, click to select the ObjCInterop grouping (with the yellow folder icon, not the blue project icon, at the very top of the Navigation Pane). Click File > New > File (or hold down the Command key and press N). In the template picker under iOS, select Source, choose Swift File, and then click Next, as shown in Figure 23.2.

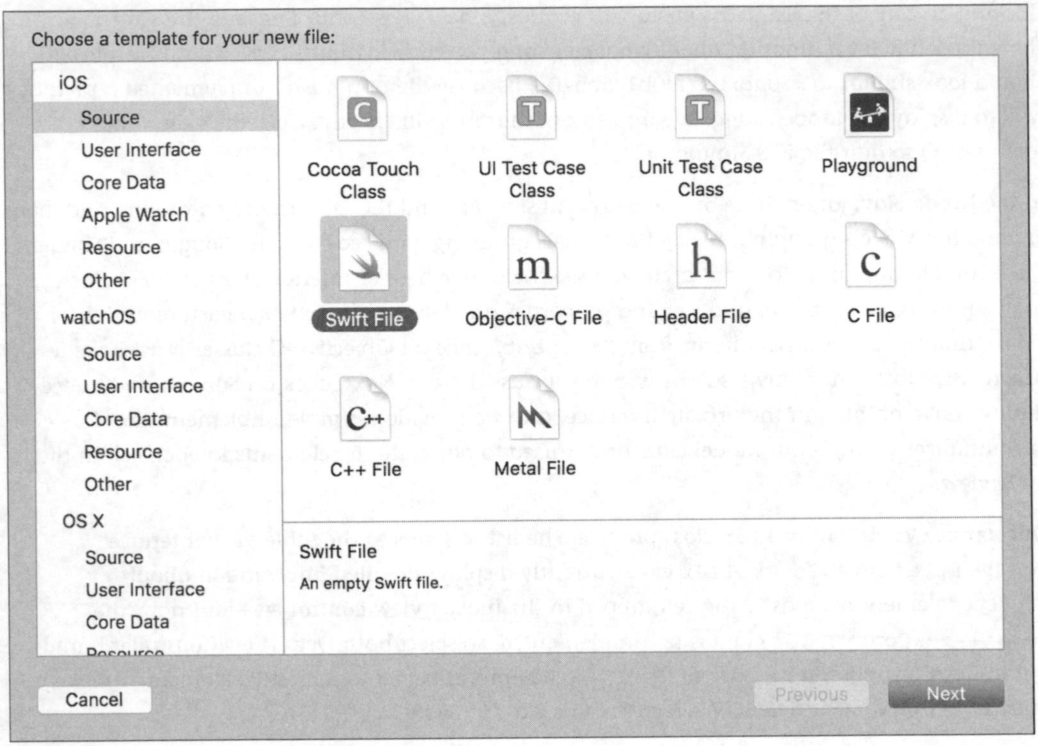

FIGURE 23.2
Choosing to create a Swift file from Xcode's template picker.

On the next dialog, in the Save As text field, name the file DetailVC and then click Create, as shown in Figure 23.3. DetailVC is short for DetailViewController, but I wanted to name it differently to illustrate using the Swift file versus anything left over from the `DetailViewController` Objective-C class we deleted.

FIGURE 23.3
Save the new Swift file with the name DetailVC.

Xcode prompts you with a question about whether you want to configure an Objective-C bridging header. Click Create Bridging Header, as shown in Figure 23.4.

The newly created DetailVC.swift file is shown in the content editor with a simple `import Foundation` statement inside it. Select the ObjCInterop-Bridging-Header.h file and notice there is nothing in it yet but some comments. We add to this file later.

Would you like to configure an Objective-C bridging header?

Adding this file to ObjCInterop will create a mixed Swift and Objective-C target. Would you like Xcode to automatically configure a bridging header to enable classes to be accessed by both languages?

Cancel   Don't Create   Create Bridging Header

FIGURE 23.4
Click Create Bridging Header to create an Objective-C bridging header.

Now we can create the `DetailVC` class inside the DetailVC.swift file. Click to select the DetailVC.swift file in the Navigation Pane. In the content area, create the class by entering the code exactly as listed in Listing 23.7.

LISTING 23.7   Creating the `DetailVC` Class in Swift

```
01:  import UIKit
02:
03:  class DetailVC: UIViewController {
04:      @IBOutlet weak var detailDescriptionLabel: UILabel!
05:
06:      var detailItem: AnyObject? {
07:          didSet {
08:              configureView()
09:          }
10:      }
11:
12:      func configureView() {
13:          detailDescriptionLabel?.text = detailItem?.description
14:      }
15:
16:      override func viewDidLoad() {
17:          super.viewDidLoad()
18:          configureView()
19:      }
20:  }
```

On line 1, we replace the Foundation framework with the UIKit framework so we can have our `DetailVC` class be a subclass of `UIViewController` (necessary for controlling the scene in the storyboard and displaying a view onscreen) and also have access to types such as `UILabel`. Then on line 3, we define the `DetailVC` class as a subclass of `UIViewController`. You should be familiar with everything on line 4 except that weird `@IBOutlet` attribute. `@IBOutlet` declares to Xcode that this property will be used as an **outlet** to an interface element and will be responsible for changing that UI element. The outlet property is set to be weak, because when the UILabel gets placed onscreen, a strong reference will be held on to it already, so we don't need another strong reference ourselves. It is also an implicitly unwrapped optional, which is by default set to nil, because the outlet gets set after the view controller's initializer completes.

On lines 6 through 10, we define a stored property called detailItem of type AnyObject?. Ultimately, detailItem will be an instance of Song. The reason for this is that if you open MasterViewController.m and look at the prepareForSegue:sender: method, it sends the setDetailItem: message to the destinationViewController object, passing a Song instance, and the interface *segues* to the destination view controller, as seen on line 35 in Figure 23.5. The detailItem property was from the DetailViewController class that we deleted, so we just redefined it here in Swift. We also use a property observer to notify our interface to update when the property gets set.

```
34
35   - (void)prepareForSegue:(UIStoryboardSegue *)segue sender:(id)sender {
36       if ([[segue identifier] isEqualToString:@"showDetail"]) {
37           NSIndexPath *indexPath = [self.tableView indexPathForSelectedRow];
38           Song *song = self.songs[indexPath.row];
39           [[segue destinationViewController] setDetailItem:song];
40       }
41   }
42
```

FIGURE 23.5
The prepareForSegue:sender: method that gets executed before segueing a new view controller on screen.

Continuing the explanation of Listing 23.7, lines 12 through 14 define the configureView() method, which simply updates the detailDescriptionLabel's text property (which is what gets updated in the UI) using optional chaining assignment and sets it equal to the optionally chained value on detailItem called description. We haven't implemented any description computed properties yet, but we will do that shortly.

Finally, on lines 16 through 19, we override a method from UIViewController called view-DidLoad(). This important method gets called immediately before the view comes onscreen, after every outlet has been connected to an interface element, if necessary. Inside the method, we simply call its superclass implementation to make sure any other view hierarchy setup gets executed, and then we call configureView() to update the UI.

Running the app right now would not prove fruitful, because we have to tend to a few errors and also update the UI to use our new Swift class. Let's do a few more things to finish our implementation, starting with some housecleaning.

Housecleaning

Now that we have created the Swift `DetailVC` class and file, we need to remove references to the `DetailViewController` files we removed and update `#import` statements with our new Swift file. Select the MasterViewController.m file from the Navigation Pane to edit it. Xcode should be greeting you with an error already, which is good. Remove the `#import` `"DetailViewController.h"` line and replace it with the following:

```
#import "ObjCInterop-Swift.h"
```

ObjCInterop-Swift.h is the **generated header file** that Swift creates for interoperating with Objective-C. You do not need to create this header file; it is automatically regenerated any time there is a change to anything publicly or internally declared in any Swift file.

CAUTION

Xcode Auto Complete May Suggest Incorrect Header

Be careful not to choose the ObjCInterop-Bridging-Header.h file that is auto-suggested by Xcode. This is the wrong header file, and the rest of the project will not work correctly if you import the bridging header instead of the generated header file. Make sure your import statement reads `#import` `"ObjCInterop-Swift.h"`. At the time of this writing, the bridging header is the only file suggested by Xcode, and not the Swift-generated header file, but that may change by the time you are reading this. Just be careful when using autocomplete to ensure the correct file is being imported.

Next, select AppDelegate.m from the Navigation Pane, and you see a similar error in Xcode. This `#import` statement, however, does not need to be replaced for our needs, so just remove it.

Exposing Objective-C Classes to Swift

To add the `description` computed property to the `Song` class as an extension, we need to make the `Song` class available to Swift. In the Navigation Pane, select the ObjCInterop-Bridging-Header.h file to edit the file. Add the following line to the bridging header:

```
#import "Song.h"
```

This statement imports the `Song` class's public interface properties and methods to Swift and enables them to be used by Swift.

Extending an Objective-C Class with Swift

Extending an Objective-C class with Swift is just as easy as adding an extension normally in Swift. To do this, let's create the extension in its own dedicated file.

Hold down the Command key and press N to create a new file. From the template chooser, choose another iOS Swift file and click Next. Name the file `SongDescription` and click Create.

Listing 23.8 shows the code that you need to enter into the extension. Note that you can remove the `import Foundation` statement, as it is not necessary for this extension.

LISTING 23.8   Extending the Song Class

```
01:    protocol STYCustomStringConvertible {
02:        var styDescription: String { get }
03:    }
04:
05:    extension Song: STYCustomStringConvertible {
06:        var styDescription: String {
07:            return "\(artist ?? String()) sings the song \(title),\(rating) stars."
08:        }
09:    }
```

We declare a new protocol, `STYCustomStringConvertible`, which has a sole property called `styDescription` of type `String`. This is our own implementation of the built-in `CustomStringConvertible` protocol, but because `Song` inherits from `NSObject`, it already has that by inheritance, so we just create our own. Next, we create the extension on `Song`, adopting the `STYCustomStringConvertible` protocol. Then on line 7, we simply return the `String` value we want to show in our detail view controller. Notice that we are returning a `String` and not an `NSString`, even though our `Song` class is declared in Objective-C. Notice also that we use nil coalescing when we interpolate the `artist` value. This is because we defined `artist` to be nullable, so it is an optional value in Swift's eyes. Instead of forcibly unwrapping it, we supply an empty string with `String()`.

Because we created our own `styDescription` property and did not override the built-in `description` property provided, we need to update the DetailVC `configureView()` method to use our new `styDescription` property. Open DetailVC.swift and change the following line

```
detailDescriptionLabel?.text = detailItem?.description
```

to

```
detailDescriptionLabel?.text = detailItem?.styDescription
```

Lastly, change the type of `detailItem` to `Song?` from `AnyObject?`. This is necessary because `AnyObject` doesn't understand our new `styDescription` property.

We're almost there—just one more small thing to do and then we can see the fruits of our labor.

Update the Class in the Storyboard

Because we deleted the provided `DetailViewController` class and created our own, we need to change the class type of the scene in the storyboard. Select the Main.storyboard file in the

Navigation Pane to edit it. You may have four panes in this view: the Navigation Pane on the far left, the Scene Pane to its right, the actual storyboard layout in the third pane, and the Inspector Pane on the far right. In the Scene Pane, expand Detail Scene. Click to select Detail (with the yellow icon). Click View > Utilities > Show Identity Inspector, which then shows the Identity Inspector in the right-hand Inspector Pane. In the Class drop-down field, change the value from DetailViewController to DetailVC, as shown in Figure 23.6.

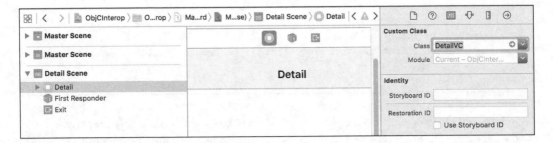

FIGURE 23.6
Change the class in the Identity Inspector to DetailVC.

Run the App

If you have done everything so far as outlined, you should be able to run the app in the Simulator. Hold the Command key and press R to run the app. You may have to choose a device first, which you can do from the device picker in the top bar of Xcode, as shown in Figure 23.7. To the right of the Run and Stop buttons, you see the name of the app (which is the Scheme Picker) and then the device type. Click the device type button, which may say "iOS Device" or any of the devices listed in Figure 23.7. I chose iPhone 6; feel free to choose whichever device you want.

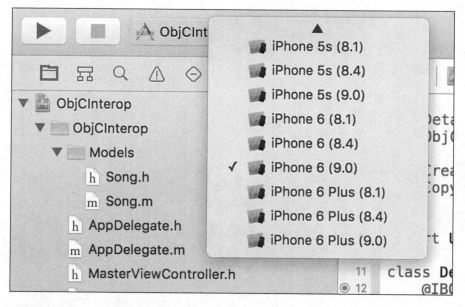

FIGURE 23.7
Choose a Simulator to execute your app on.

Once your app begins running, you should see three songs listed; they are the three songs we hard-coded into MasterViewController.m. Tapping any one of them should perform the segue from the master view controller to the detail view controller, which is our new Swift class, DetailVC. Since we created the extension to Song and provided a styDescription property, we get a nice, easy-to-read output in the detail view controller. The detail view controller should look like Figure 23.8.

FIGURE 23.8
The detail view controller showing the description of the song you tapped.

Summary

The topic of interoperability with Objective-C and Swift is too much to cover within the bounds of this hour. The goal for this hour was to acquaint you with Objective-C, using similarities to what you have learned already with Swift, and to help you learn how to recognize some things about Objective-C to know how to write Swift to integrate with it.

In this hour, you learned some basics of Objective-C including class file structure, the differences between public and private interfaces, and what a class implementation looks like. With this, you learned about Objective-C property definitions and how to create an initializer method. Then you learned the structure of an Objective-C class and how to instantiate an instance of a class using the alloc/init pattern. With that, you learned about defining nullability attributes for Objective-C objects and how that relates to Swift.

Next, you learned about bridging, both in terms of modules and APIs, as well as types. You learned how Swift and Objective-C bridge similar types, such as String and NSString, and how to make APIs available from Objective-C to Swift with bridging headers. There is also an auto-generated header file that the compiler creates to allow Objective-C to access Swift APIs, which is the name of the application or module, plus "-Swift.h". That must get imported using the #import statement wherever you need Swift APIs in an Objective-C class file.

Finally, we walked through adding Swift code to an existing Objective-C app. You learned how to create an extension on an Objective-C class, which you used to display customized output to the detail view controller's user interface (UI). There are many more resources on learning Objective-C if you are interested, such as *Sams Teach Yourself Objective-C in 24 Hours*, 2nd edition, by Jesse Feiler, as well as the highly acclaimed *Objective-C Programming: The Big Nerd Ranch Guide*, 2nd edition, by Aaron Hillegass and Mikey Ward.

In the next hour, you learn more about interacting with user interfaces and Swift. You learn how to create a UI and hook up Swift code to control the UI. Great job making it through this hour! When you're ready to move on to the next hour, let's go!

Q&A

Q. I see that a Swift Bool bridges to Objective-C's NSNumber. Why does that happen?

A. The Bool type in Objective-C is actually a typedef of a signed char, and a signed char is a numeric type. This means that in Objective-C, YES actually has a value of 1 and NO has a value 0.

Q. I see a folder called ObjCInteropTests in the sample project. What is that?

A. When you create a new project, Xcode creates a Tests folder for you automatically. This is where you place your project's unit tests. Unit tests are small bits of code that you can use to make sure that your program is behaving the way you expect it. Unit testing is a deep and interesting topic but is beyond the scope of this book.

Q. **I have an `NSArray` and I know it contains only `NSString` objects, but when I try to use it, Xcode tells me that `AnyObject` is not convertible to `String`. I thought `NSString` bridges to `String` automatically.**

A. Even though `NSString` does not bridge to `String` automatically, `NSArray` itself still bridges to `[AnyObject]`. This means that you have to cast the elements of the array to the correct type before you can use them. You can cast the entire array at once using `myArray as? [String]` or cast the individual elements as you access them. Xcode 7 introduced lightweight type annotations in Objective-C for declaring typed arrays, such as `NSArray<NSString *> *`, but this is outside of the scope of this book.

Workshop

The workshop contains quiz questions and exercises to help you solidify your understanding of the material covered. Try to answer all questions before looking at the answers that follow.

Quiz

1. What are header files (filename.h) used for in an Objective-C project?

2. When converting an `NSDictionary` to a Swift object, what is the type of the resulting dictionary?

3. Which Swift types can you pass to an Objective-C method that expects an `NSNumber`?

4. True or false? If an object is written in Objective-C, you can only create subclasses in Objective-C, never in Swift.

Answers

1. Header files define the publicly accessible methods and properties for a class.

2. `NSDictionary` converts to a dictionary of type `[NSObject: AnyObject]`.

3. `Int`, `UInt`, `Bool`, `Double`, or `Float`.

4. False. You are free to create subclasses of Objective-C objects in Swift.

Exercise

For this exercise, we continue using the project from the hour examples. The `Song` class is written in Objective-C, but we create a subclass in Swift and use it in our project. Add a new Swift file to the project called `PopSong.swift` and in that file define a class called `PopSong`, which is a subclass of `Song`. Don't forget to `import Foundation`.

Add a stored property called chartPosition of type Int to your class. Next, add an initializer that takes title, artist, rating, and chart position as arguments. This initializer is going to be called from Objective-C, so think carefully about what types your init method should take; will you need Int or NSNumber? In the initializer, set the chartPosition variable in the PopSong class and pass the rest of the arguments along to super.init().

Next, override the description method so that it returns a string containing the artist, song title, rating, and chart position. Use the description method in SongDescription.swift as a guide.

Now go to MasterViewController.m and change the song "Happy" to be type PopSong instead of a Song and give it a chartPosition of 1. Don't forget to change the class in the alloc statement too.

After you make the changes, compile and run your application. When you click on Happy, you should see the new description string that you wrote instead of the original one.

HOUR 24
Functional Thinking in Swift

What You'll Learn in This Hour:

▶ What functional programming is
▶ How to identify when functional programming is beneficial
▶ How to chain functions together
▶ How to create custom operators

In this final hour, we explore some functional programming concepts and abilities in Swift. Functional programming is a different way of thinking about approaching problem solving than procedural or even object-oriented programming. Swift was released as a 1.0 with many functional capabilities, but those have become more robust and easily accessible over the past year. I promise not to get too deep in this last hour, but I would be remiss if I didn't cover this topic. Functional programming is a paradigm too large to cover fully in one hour, so if this style of programming interests you, I suggest studying it further. You've already used many of the concepts throughout this book, but in this hour, we take a whole new look at them. Let's get started with some basics of functional programming.

What Is Functional Programming?

Functional programming, as defined in Wikipedia, is a "paradigm that treats computation as the evaluation of mathematical functions and avoids changing-state and mutable data. It is a declarative programming paradigm, which means programming is done with expressions. In functional code, the output value of a function depends *only* on the arguments that are input to the function" (emphasis mine). From that definition, you can see that Swift already values a functional style by virtue of the fact that you are encouraged to use constants whenever possible over variables to avoid mutating state, as well as having functions as first-class objects that can accept arguments as parameters and return data based on those inputs.

Indeed, many languages also value these virtues, even Objective-C, but they are not defined as functional languages. On the contrary, Swift isn't a fully functional language. In fact, Apple calls Swift a protocol-oriented language. However, Swift includes many more functional aspects than other languages do. The goal of this hour is to cover some of the basic functional concepts and see how to use them in Swift.

Thinking in Terms of Functions

Remember that in Swift, functions are first-class values. This means that you can pass them to other functions as parameters, return functions from functions, and even assign a function to a constant or variable. You saw this briefly in Hour 9, "Understanding Higher Order Functions and Closures," so this concept shouldn't be too foreign to you. There is power in knowing this, as it can truly help you write cleaner, leaner code to accomplish powerful results.

One of the reasons you would want to do this type of programming is that you can easily reuse code. When you think of operations as functions, you know that the result will be directly tied to the input, and it helps you understand composing a chain of functions to get a desired result. Or perhaps even when you need to perform the same set of tasks, just with different types of input, then you can leverage generic programming to reduce code even further.

Throughout this hour, I walk you through several common functions used in functional programming and explain the reasons why you would want to use them. Let's start with the `map` function.

Transforming with `map`

You use the `map` function to take a provided transform function and perform that over the item in question. The item in question could be a sequence, such as an array, or even a single value. The `map` function previously was a global function, but it and many other functions have gradually been added onto existing types via extensions to make them not only more findable as instance methods but also more explicit about what types can perform a `map` or other function.

What the `map` function enables you to do is obtain a value of a resulting type that is potentially different from the type of the item being mapped over. You provide a function, called a **transform function**, which the `map` function then applies to each item in its sequence (or just the single value) and returns the transformed object or objects.

The function signature for `map` varies depending on where it is defined, but the behavior is very similar in every invocation. The lines in Listing 24.1 illustrate how `map` is defined for first the `SequenceType` protocol and then on the `enum` type.

LISTING 24.1   Definitions of `map` Functions

```
extension SequenceType {
    public func map<T>(@noescape transform: (Self.Generator.Element) -> T) -> [T]
}

public enum Optional<T> {
    public func map<U>(@noescape f: (Wrapped) throws -> U) rethrows -> U?
}
```

In the `SequenceType` extension, you see the definition for the `map` function. It is public, meaning that you can access it from other modules, and it is also generic. But what's the deal with that weird `@noescape` keyword? The `@noescape` attribute is an attribute that can be used on closures and tells Swift that the closure will only live as long as the call, so there is no possibility for a retain cycle, as covered in Hour 16, "Understanding Memory Allocation and References." Using `@noescape` also alleviates the need to state `self` explicitly before instance property and method names inside the closure, because ARC requires that for memory semantics when you're not using `@noescape`. The following snippet shows that when using a `@noescape` parameter in a function such as `map`, you do not need to use the `self` keyword inside the closure when referencing elements belonging to the instance:

```
func square(num: Int) -> Int { return num * num }
let numbers = [1, 2, 3]
let squares = numbers.map { square($0) }  // not self.square($0)
```

The next weird syntax to look at is the `Self.Generator.Element` syntax. `Self` (with a capital S) refers to the type of the current object conforming to the protocol. `Generator` is a `typealias` inside an inherited protocol that basically returns the type conforming to the protocol; `Element` refers to the type of the individual element. So, for `[String]`, `Self.Generator.Element` would be `String`.

Next, in the `Optional` type, you can see that `Optional` itself is already a generic enum with the type `T` in its placeholder list. The `map` function here takes a non-escaped function `f`, which transforms the current value (if any) inside the optional from `T` to `U`, which then ultimately returns `U?` from the `map` function.

I would imagine these implementations to look somewhat like those in Listing 24.2, without any error handling.

LISTING 24.2   Crude Reenactments of `map`

```
// SequenceType
extension SequenceType {
    func styMap<T>(@noescape transform: (Self.Generator.Element) -> T) -> [T] {
        var generator = self.generate()
        var result = [T]()
```

```
        while let element = generator.next() {
            result.append(transform(element))
        }
        return result
    }
}

let names = ["larry", "my brother darryl", "my other brother darryl"]
let upNames = names.styMap { $0.uppercaseString }
upNames          // displays names in all caps

// Optional
extension Optional {
    func styMap<U>(@noescape f: (Wrapped) -> U) -> U? {
        switch self {
        case .None: return nil
        case .Some(let x): return f(x)
        }
    }
}
let optionalOne: Int? = 1
let optionalNegativeOne: Int? = -1
let maybeOne = optionalOne.map { $0 > 0 }
let maybeNegOne = optionalNegativeOne.map { $0 > 0 }
maybeOne         // displays true
maybeNegOne      // displays false
```

As you can see, map is a very powerful function. My only word of caution with map is to use it when it is appropriate. There may be times when you need to iterate over a sequence and adjust some properties but not necessarily return a new sequence, or returning a sequence is ignored. As of Swift 2, there is a new solution for just these cases.

Iterating with forEach

As discussed in Hour 9, Swift 2 introduced the forEach function. The forEach function is similar to the map function, but the main difference is that forEach does not return a resulting value. You can use forEach to iterate over sequences or ranges and think of it as a substitute for for-in loops. The forEach function, however, does not provide an early exit mechanism like you have with a for-in loop; forEach acts exactly the way map does, just without a return value.

The signature for the forEach function looks like the following code snippet:

```
public func forEach(@noescape body: (Self.Generator.Element) -> ())
```

Notice that there is no return value for the body function or the entire forEach function. This can be very useful when you need to iterate over a range of values to perform a task or set of tasks a certain number of times or do something for each item in a sequence.

Suppose you are writing an app and need to create some buttons programmatically to put in your interface. Creating multiple buttons can be tedious, but if you can isolate the code that is repeated, then you can use the map function. You can also use the forEach function alongside the map function to set multiple properties on those buttons after they are created. Let's take a look at how we might do this in the following Try It Yourself section.

TRY IT YOURSELF ▼

Create and Iterate with map and forEach

Create three buttons and customize their appearance by utilizing the map and forEach functions.

1. Open Xcode and create a new playground; either a Mac or an iOS playground works. Clear the contents of the playground.

2. Because we will be creating UI elements, ensure UIKit is imported. Create the frame that tells the button how big to be, which is stored as a CGRect.

```
import UIKit

let frame = CGRect(x: 0, y: 0, width: 175, height: 44)
```

3. Create a constant array to hold the attributes we will need for each button, which are just a name and a color. Use named tuples so we can easily access their properties inside the map function later.

```
let buttonAttributes = [
    (title: "Save", color: UIColor.blueColor()),
    (title: "Cancel", color: UIColor.redColor()),
    (title: "Dismiss", color: UIColor.grayColor())
]
```

4. Create the array of buttons by using the map function over your array of attributes. Remember that for each iteration of map in your sequence of attributes, that respective sequence element (in this case, a tuple) is the item being worked with, so it is the parameter to the map function's closure. Each iteration will return an instance of UIButton.

```
let buttons = buttonAttributes.map { buttonAttribs -> UIButton in
    let button = UIButton(frame: frame)
    button.setTitle(buttonAttribs.title, forState: .Normal)
    button.backgroundColor = buttonAttribs.color
    return button
}
```

▼

5. Now that you have the three buttons created and stored in an array, use `forEach` to iterate over the array and set the same properties for each button. Remember, the buttons are reference types, so the changes made persist in their respective instances.

```
buttons.forEach { button in
    button.layer.cornerRadius = 15.0
    button.layer.borderColor = UIColor.darkGrayColor().CGColor
    button.layer.borderWidth = 2.0
    button.setTitleColor(UIColor.whiteColor(), forState: .Normal)
}
```

6. After the buttons have been created and customized, it is now time to display them. You can view the buttons in the playground by tapping the icon that looks like an empty circle in the right-hand answer pane of the playground for any line of code. The icon turns into a plus sign when hovered over and also says "Show result" in the tooltip. Create three constants to reference the buttons by name versus by index in the array, and then tap the empty circle-turned-plus icon to the right of the three constants you create.

```
let saveButton = buttons[0]
let cancelButton = buttons[1]
let dismissButton = buttons[2]

saveButton      // tap the Show Result button here,
cancelButton    // here,
dismissButton   // and here
```

The completed Try It Yourself code and results should look like those in Figure 24.1. Certainly, the button customization code in the `forEach` closure could have been included in the `map` closure without the need for the `forEach` statement at all, but I did that to show the difference in syntax and usage of each.

These are simple yet powerful functions. Remember to consider these functions when the need arises, but carefully choose the best option. If you don't need to return a value but need to touch every element in a sequence, `forEach` might be your best option. If you need an early exit, perhaps if some criteria are matched early on in the sequence, then a for-in loop might be the best. If you need to produce a transformed optional or array of a given type, then `map` is a good choice.

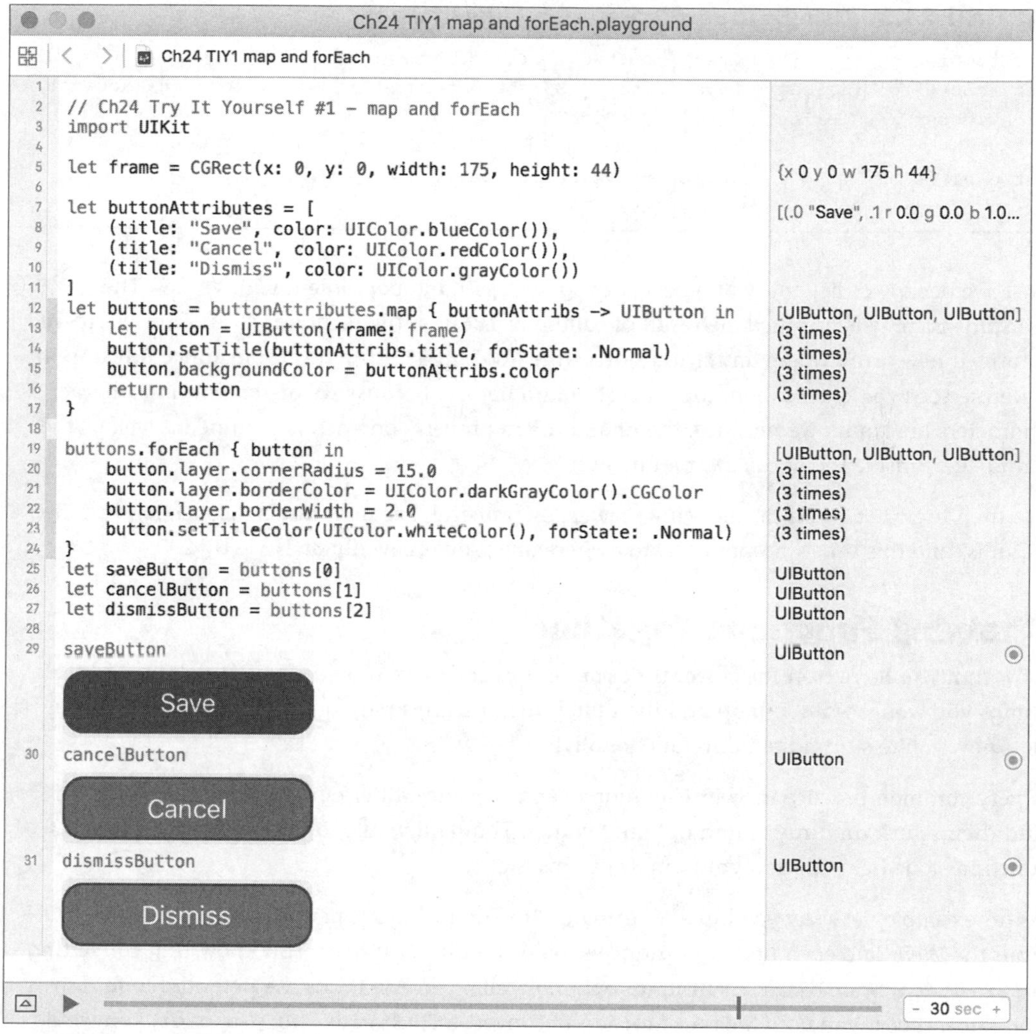

FIGURE 24.1
The completed Try It Yourself exercise using `map` and `forEach`.

Filtering Values

The `filter` function returns a new sequence where each element is filtered either in or out of the new sequence based on the criteria provided in the closure argument. This is akin to using an `NSPredicate` object to filter a collection of items if you've done that with Objective-C at some point. Listing 24.3 illustrates how to use `filter` on dictionary keys and values to return arrays of desired values.

LISTING 24.3 Using `filter` to Return a Filtered Array

```
var fooDictionary = ["fooOne": 1, "two": 2, "fooThree": 3]
let foos = fooDictionary.keys.filter { $0.characters.startsWith("foo".characters) }
Array(foos) // displays ["fooOne", "fooThree"]

let divisibleByTwo = fooDictionary.values.filter { $0 % 2 == 0 }
Array(divisibleByTwo)    // displays [2]
```

First, we declare a dictionary of type [String : Int] and populate it with values. The constant foos gets assigned the result of calling filter on the dictionary's keys property and returns a new array where any string starts with "foo". startsWith is an instance function in a SequenceType extension in the Swift standard library. Because we are comparing whether characters are equal, we must use the characters property on each key name, as well as the string "foo" inside the startsWith function.

We then use filter on the dictionary's values property, because that is a collection just like keys is, and this time we want an array where any value is evenly divisible by 2.

Chaining Functions Together

Now that you have seen the power that map and filter can provide, you may have ideas of things you would want to map and then filter, then perhaps map again. Kudos to you if you do—now you're starting to think functionally!

A very common practice in Swift is to map over a sequence, filter out anything that is not nil, and then return an array of non-optional values. Thankfully, due to the power of chaining functions together with dot-syntax in Swift, this is easy.

As an example, let's say you have an array of String instances, perhaps downloaded as JSON from the Web, and each String instance should contain a number. You know that converting a String to a Double will result in an optional value because it has the potential to fail, so you know that if you used the map function to convert the [String] to [Double], you would really have [Double?]. The next logical step would be to filter out any nil values, resulting in a potentially smaller sequence, but then you want your array to be [Double], not [Double?]. After filtering, you know none of your instances inside the array will be nil, so you can safely map again, this time using a closure much like (T?) -> T. Listing 24.4 illustrates this exact example.

LISTING 24.4 Chaining Functions Together

```
let arrayOfStrings = ["1.1", "2.0", "three point one four", "4.7"]

let doubles = arrayOfStrings
    .map({ Double($0) })
```

```
    .filter({ $0 != nil })
    .map({ $0! })

doubles  // displays [1.1, 2, 4.7]
```

This example should be pretty self-explanatory to you by now. We take our array of strings received from some Web API, map sending each string to the `Double` initializer, filtering out `nil` values, and then map again unwrapping all remaining values. Even though that was really a one-line expression, I separated each operation onto its own line for readability, and not just because it may extend past the margin of this book; many developers separate these operations onto their own respective lines to easily identify just how many, and what, operations are taking place on a sequence.

But this wouldn't be a great Swift example if we couldn't shorten it, right? Recently a very powerful function was introduced, and just like `map` and others, it is in an extension of many commonly used types such as `SequenceType` and `Optional`. This powerful function is called **bind** in other languages, but is called **flatMap** in Swift.

Flattening Objects

As mentioned, `flatMap` is a powerful and very welcomed addition to the Swift standard library. `flatMap` is a bit difficult to define in a sentence or two because it really behaves differently depending in which context it is operating.

flatMap **on Sequences**

The `flatMap` function can take an n-dimensional array and reduce it by one dimension; for instance, `[[1, 2], [3, 4]]` would `flatMap` to `[1, 2, 3, 4]`. It can also flatten an incoming sequence or optional value, perform a transform function, and then re-inflate it or keep it at the same dimensionality. This flexibility is what makes `flatMap` so powerful.

Continuing the example from Listing 24.4, we can use `flatMap` to reduce calling three functions (map, filter, map) into a single `flatMap` call. Listing 24.5 rewrites Listing 24.4 using `flatMap`.

LISTING 24.5 Replacing **map-filter-map** with **flatMap**

```
let arrayOfStrings = ["1.1", "2.0", "three point one four", "4.7"]
let flattenedDoubles = arrayOfStrings.flatMap({ Double($0) })
flattenedDoubles  // displays [1.1, 2, 4.7]
```

By using `flatMap` instead of the `map-filter-map` design, we reduced a lot of code and made our intent even clearer. With this implementation of `flatMap`, we basically told Swift, "iterate over the `arrayOfStrings` array, convert each one to a `Double`, discard what doesn't convert, and give me the ones that did convert in a new array." Option-click on `flattenedDoubles` and you'll see the type is `[Double]`.

flatMap on Optionals

Unsurprisingly, you can also flatMap over optional values. What this function does is take a transform function, flatten the optional (if a value exists), apply the transform, and then return the new value as an optional of that new type. Otherwise, it returns nil, as an optional in the new type. The function signature in the Optional enum looks like the following snippet:

```
public func flatMap<U>(@noescape f: (Wrapped) throws -> U?) rethrows -> U?
```

This looks an awful lot like the map function definition. Indeed, but there is one slight difference: The return value of the transform function is optional here, whereas with the map function, the transform function is of type (Wrapped) -> U. Although this looks trivial, it is actually quite important, and knowing this key difference can assist in chaining together multiple flatMap operations to produce results in powerfully succinct one-line expressions.

Imagine you have a series of URLs your application could communicate with, and they all require you to insert a timestamp and a cryptographically secure hash into the URL as parameters. You know that creating NSURL instances to handle the URL-creation portion of the communication process returns optional values (because a poorly formed URL could return nil). So, you could:

▶ Force-unwrap the optional and hope you don't crash your app.

▶ Do the "nil dance" each time you need a URL by checking whether the object is nil before proceeding.

▶ Leverage the power of flatMap and optional values to perform several operations neatly and in one line—by creating an NSURL object, passing it to a timestamp function that returns an NSURL with the timestamp appended, and then passing that object to the function that appends the hash.

If the object is nil at any point, the expression fails and resumes execution, just like optional chaining does. This is sometimes called **railway-oriented programming** (http://fsharpforfunandprofit.com/rop/).

Let's take a look at this very example in the next Try It Yourself section. You will create a series of URLs, some helper functions for returning time-stamped and hashed URLs, and use flatMap to put them all together.

▼ TRY IT YOURSELF

Chain Together flatMap Functions to Create URLs

Create an array of NSURL objects pieced together by chaining flatMap calls.

1. Open Xcode and create a new playground; either a Mac or an iOS playground works. Clear the contents of the playground.

2. Import the Foundation framework, as that is where the `NSURL` class lives. Then, create the base URL for us to work with because we create URLs later.

```
import Foundation

let baseURLString = "https://www.something.com"
let baseURL = NSURL(string: baseURLString)
```

3. Next, create two helper-computed properties to return both the current timestamp and a random secure string of your choosing. This is just for purposes of this example. Please don't use the following secure hash as your own in a production application!

```
var timestamp: Int {
    return Int(NSDate().timeIntervalSince1970)
}

var secureHash: String {
    return "Sup3rs3cureH4sh"
}
```

4. After creating the computed properties, which will make string interpolation easier in the next step, now create the methods that will append the timestamp and the secure hash to the URL. The function signatures should match those of the `flatMap` parameter, so that we can easily `flatMap` these operations together.

```
func timestampedURL(url: NSURL) -> NSURL? {
    return NSURL(string: "?timestamp=\(timestamp)", relativeToURL: url)
}

func hashedURL(url: NSURL) -> NSURL? {
    let urlString = url.absoluteString + "&secureHash=\(secureHash)"
    return NSURL(string: urlString)
}
```

5. That's all for the functions to create the URLs; now actually create some `NSURL` objects that contain the location of a resource on a remote server.

```
let employeesURL = NSURL(string: "Employees", relativeToURL: baseURL)
    .flatMap(timestampedURL)
    .flatMap(hashedURL)
print(employeesURL?.absoluteString)

let inventoryURL = NSURL(string: "Inventory", relativeToURL: baseURL)
    .flatMap(timestampedURL)
    .flatMap(hashedURL)
print(inventoryURL?.absoluteString)
```

Again, for the sake of readability, I put the `flatMap` expressions on their own line, but feel free to put them on the same line of your app if you like. The completed Try It Yourself example should look like the example in Figure 24.2.

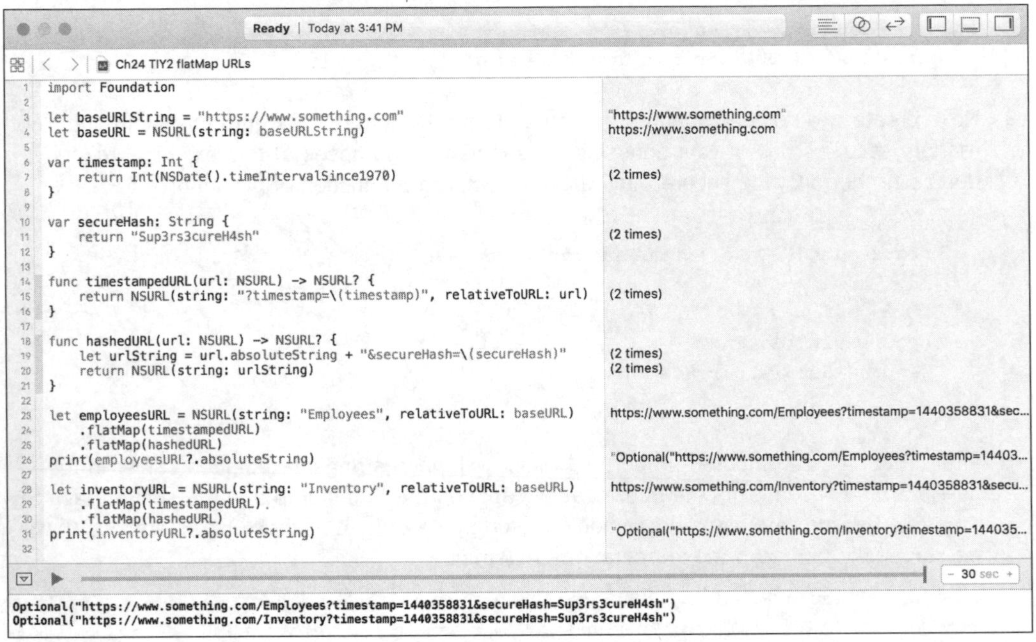

FIGURE 24.2
The completed Try It Yourself example with chained `flatMap` functions.

Because Swift is strongly typed, uses optionals to wrap `nil`, and can chain functions and values easily, the `flatMap` function is by far one of the most powerful and helpful functions in the standard library. It fits in beautifully with the safety, expressiveness, and power that Swift has to offer.

Of course, with Swift being so flexible, you can also take this same example one step further. Let's discuss how to make a custom operator for `flatMap`, which can make readability and flow of operations even nicer. Let's discuss making custom operators next, including what to do, why, and what to be cautious of when creating custom operators.

Creating and Overloading Operators

Swift enables you to create and override operators, something not available in Objective-C. One common use for overloading operators is by adopting protocols in Swift that enable you to define behavior with a uniform interface with which to interact.

Protocols and Overloading Operators

Two protocols, Equatable and Comparable, enable you to do this with basic operators. The Comparable protocol requires that you overload the less-than operator (<) and inherits from the Equatable protocol, which requires that you overload the is-equal operator (==). So if your class, struct, or enum adopts the Comparable protocol, you must also implement both required operators, < and ==.

You can also define your own custom operators in Swift. To do this, you define whether it is an infix, prefix, or postfix operator, and optionally an associativity (left, right, or none) and a precedence value. Custom operators can be very helpful when you have many tasks that repeat or chain to produce an aggregated result and you need a simple operator in between each operation. Be careful, however; this can be a source of contention between some developers, as some people can go overboard with obscure operators that are not intuitive as to the purpose of their implementation. If you need to create a custom operator, I suggest conversing with your team first, if you work on one, and get acceptance first.

CAUTION

Overloading Operators Can Cause Confusion

As mentioned, a great deal of benefit can come from overloaded operators. However, a great deal of confusion also can come along with it, and it deserves mention again. As a general rule, if you overload an operator, make sure that your team knows what it does and why, and that your overloading is documented. Accidental or unknowing use of an overloaded operator can cause unwanted behavior.

First, let's discuss overloading operators for equality and comparability, as this is extremely common. Let's say you have an app in which you need to sort answers to posts by whether the answer is the accepted answer and then by score, highest to lowest. Listing 24.6 illustrates a struct that conforms to the Comparable protocol and overloads both == and <. When you overload ==, you get != by default, and when you overload <, you get > by default. When overloading both == and <, you get <= and >= by default.

LISTING 24.6 Comparable Protocol Operator Overloading

```
struct Answer: Comparable {
    var text: String
    var score: Int
    var accepted: Bool
}

func == (lhs: Answer, rhs: Answer) -> Bool {
    return (lhs.accepted == rhs.accepted) && (lhs.score == rhs.score)
}
```

```
func < (lhs: Answer, rhs: Answer) -> Bool {
    if lhs.accepted {
        return false
    } else if rhs.accepted {
        return true
    } else {
        return lhs.score < rhs.score
    }
}


let answer1 = Answer(text: "I have the answer!", score: 100, accepted: true)
let answer2 = Answer(text: "Mediocre answer", score: 30, accepted: false)
let answer3 = Answer(text: "I have the answer!", score: 100, accepted: true)

answer1 == answer2    // false
answer2 != answer3    // true
answer1 == answer3    // true

answer1 < answer2     // false
answer2 < answer3     // true
answer1 >= answer3    // true
```

Even though our `Answer` struct adopts the `Comparable` protocol, the operator overloads are placed outside the struct's definition. You use the struct's (or class's or enum's) type inside the parameter list for the operator functions, denoted by `lhs` (for left-hand side) and `rhs` (for right-hand side). Because these comparison operators are infix operators, meaning they go in between two operands, labeling the parameters as `lhs` and `rhs` makes sense.

If you do not have access to a type's definition or don't want to clutter up your type definition with all sorts of protocol adoptions, you can achieve the same results by adopting a protocol in a type extension.

Many more protocols are defined in the Swift standard library. To learn more about the protocols defined, Command-click the word `Swift` in an `import Swift` line and search for the word *protocol*.

Creating Custom Operators

Going back to the example in the previous Try It Yourself section with `flatMap` and creating `NSURL` instances, let's take a look at how using a custom operator for `flatMap` can help with code flow and readability.

Our custom `flatMap` operator will be an infix operator, as we will use it to chain operations together with a left- and a right-hand side. We will want it to be left-associative, meaning the left-hand side of the operation will evaluate first before the right. We also provide a precedence to evaluate before or after others in our app (remember order of operations from school?), and we set it to 150 in this example. You may want it higher or lower depending on your needs. For more information on precedence and associativity, read the Apple documentation at https://developer.apple.com/library/ios/documentation/Swift/Conceptual/Swift_Programming_Language/Declarations.html, or this article from the venerable NSHipster, http://nshipster.com/swift-operators/.

After we define the operator attributes, we then provide the operator function implementation. Just like with the == and < operators, custom operators are defined as functions, with a left-hand and right-hand side, as well as a return value. Listing 24.7 builds upon the existing code in the previous Try It Yourself section and illustrates how we can create the setup code for our custom operator.

LISTING 24.7 Creating a Custom `flatMap` Operator

```
01: // insert after the hashedURL computed property
02: infix operator >>- {
03:     associativity left
04:     precedence 150
05: }
06:
07: func >>-<T, U>(value: T?, f: T -> U?) -> U? {
08:     return value.flatMap(f)
09: }
10:
11: // rewrite creating the two NSURL objects with new operator
12: let employeesURL = NSURL(string: "Employees", relativeToURL: baseURL)
    ➡>>- timestampedURL >>- hashedURL
13: print(employeesURL?.absoluteString)
14:
15: let inventoryURL = NSURL(string: "Inventory", relativeToURL: baseURL)
    ➡>>- timestampedURL >>- hashedURL
16: print(inventoryURL?.absoluteString)
```

Before discussing what the lines of code do in the beginning of Listing 24.7, how does that custom operator look to you in your code? Does it read a little better to you, knowing what that operator does and make it a little cleaner by separating operators and operands by spaces instead of dot syntax? I'm definitely a fan of this operator, but I certainly respect that there are those who do not like this; to me, it is a matter of making sure you and your team are on board with custom operators and this style of using them. Ultimately, my goal is to show you different ways of achieving tasks—be judicious in what you choose to use.

In Listing 24.7, we start by defining the custom operator in lines 2 through 5. We define it as an infix operator, state what symbol or symbols you want (in our case, >>-), and then inside curly braces define an associativity and precedence. Then on lines 7 through 9, we create the actual implementation of the operator. Because it is a `flatMap` operator, we only need to call `flatMap` with the given parameters and return the result. Then lines 12 through 16 rewrite the lines where we create two `NSURL` instances. Instead of chaining `flatMap` functions with dot syntax, we put our new custom operator in between the optional value and the `timestampedURL` function, which returns an optional that we can `flatMap` with our operator to the `hashedURL` function.

It may seem a little foreign at first to you because an infix operator is structured and ordered differently from a method call. A simple analogy to how to look differently at this would be with addition: You can easily tell that `add(2, 3)` should add the numbers 2 and 3 and return 5, right? What if we introduce an infix operator instead, such as +? Now 2 + 3 doesn't look so weird, does it? The + operator is really a function that takes a left-hand side and right-hand side, just like our `flatMap` operator.

Summary

This final hour was pretty heavy, and hopefully you were able to follow along without trouble. Functional programming is a terrific programing paradigm, and deserves much more than a chapter in a book, but I hope this was a good start for you. Using functional concepts can certainly help you in your day-to-day work in Swift.

In this hour, you learned about some basic functional concepts and the basics of using some common functions such as `map`, `forEach`, and `filter`. `map` and `forEach` are similar, but the biggest difference is that `forEach` does not return a new value or sequence like `map` does. `filter` is a function commonly used when you need to obtain a smaller subset of items that match particular criteria.

You also learned about the `Equatable` and `Comparable` protocols and how to overload the `==` and `<` operators to perform custom comparison. Be careful, however, when overloading operators. Make sure that they have been clearly defined and documented to help prevent unwanted or accidental misuse of the operators.

Then you learned quite a bit about the `flatMap` function and several different use cases for it. `flatMap` is a powerful function that you will keep in your Swift tool belt frequently. You used `flatMap` over optional values and sequences, and even created a custom operator that performed `flatMap` as an infix operator.

Congratulations are in order for having completed reading this book. I sincerely hope you learned a great deal of information about Swift and good programming practices and feel ready to take on learning more specifics about the Cocoa and Cocoa Touch frameworks to build useful apps for the Mac and/or iOS platforms. Best of luck to you in your endeavors building apps! And remember to check https://github.com/STYSwiftIn24H/ExamplesV2 for up-to-date code examples from this book that will be updated for future revisions of Xcode and Swift. Thank you for reading this book.

Q&A

Q. Is the `map` function okay to use to quickly update settings on a sequence of existing reference instances?

A. You certainly can use `map`, but a better choice might be a `forEach` function or a for-in loop. Use `map` when you want to return that transformed sequence as a new sequence.

Q. What is the difference between `forEach` and for-in loops?

A. There is no difference from a conceptual perspective. However, for-in loops allow you to exit early, whereas `forEach` does not allow that, and will continue looping until the end of the sequence.

Q. The `Comparable` protocol enables me to use `>=` on my objects, but only requires me to implement `==` and `<`. How does it know what to do for `>=`?

A. Apple was clever in creating the protocols in the standard library. Checking for `>=` is the same as checking for `>` or `==`, and checking for `>` is the same as checking for not `<`. This means that all the comparison operators can be constructed using just the two required by the `Comparable` protocol.

Q. Is Swift a functional programming language?

A. Strictly speaking, Swift is not a functional programming language, but it does adopt a number of functional patterns. This enables you to structure Swift code to use functional techniques, imperative techniques, or some combination of the two depending on the requirements of your program.

Workshop

The workshop contains quiz questions and exercises to help you solidify your understanding of the material covered. Try to answer all questions before looking at the answers that follow.

Quiz

1. What is the difference between the `map` and `flatMap` functions?

2. Which function is best if you want to iterate over a sequence and apply the same transformation to each element? `map`, `reduce`, or `filter`?

3. What's wrong with the following code?

```
let cities = ["San Diego", "London", "Dubai"]
let counts = map(cities) { $0.characters.count }
print(counts)
```

4. What value is stored in `result` at the end of this code?

```
let values = [[1,2],[3,4,5]]
let result = values.flatMap { $0 }
```

Answers

1. The `map` function returns a copy of the sequence after performing a transform function over each element but leaves the original sequence unchanged, or transforms over an optional value as well. The `flatMap` function can perform similar functions but also works in another dimension in that it maps, but also flattens, sequences and optionals.

2. The `map` function is best in this case.

3. `map` is not a global function; it is an instance method on any sequence in this case. Changing `map(cities)` to `cities.map` fixes the error.

4. The `flatMap` statement here reduces one dimension of the array, resulting in [1, 2, 3, 4, 5].

Exercise

For this exercise, we use a playground to construct email addresses, and then construct `Employee` instances with those email addresses. Then you'll get to practice filtering employees based on certain criteria.

Start out with a new, empty playground. Create an array of `String` instances that just contain several names, like the following:

```
["professor_prunes", "colonel_ketchup", "miss_crimson", "mister_lime",
 ➡"mrs_ivory", "mrs_pheasant"]
```

Think of a domain name that you could create for these email addresses, and use the `map` function to return a new array of `String` instances with fully formed email addresses. Next, use the `map` function again to create `Employee` instances with these email addresses, and then change any properties individually you want, such as names and/or employee ID numbers. This will serve as your company directory.

Next, try searching your company directory for a particular person to send an email. Use the `filter` function to accomplish this.

For extra practice, add a `salary` property to the `Employee` type, and populate that property in each of your employees. Filter for employees who make less than $40,000 per year so you know who needs a raise. After you accomplish this, try populating the salary properties of the employees from an external source, such as a `Dictionary`, that may have been downloaded as JSON from the Internet. Some data may be missing or malformed, so you would need to account for that and provide default salary values if the data is missing or not convertible to a number. You could use the `flatMap` function to return an array of salaries that are convertible to numbers, perhaps as an array of tuples that contain the employee ID and the respective salary.

Index

Symbols

F

Learning Labs!

Learn online with videos, live code editing, and quizzes

SPECIAL 50% OFF – Introductory Offer
Discount Code: STYLL50

FOR A LIMITED TIME, we are offering readers of Sams Teach Yourself books a 50% OFF discount to ANY online Learning Lab through Dec 15, 2015.

Visit informit.com/learninglabs to see available labs, try out full samples, and order today.

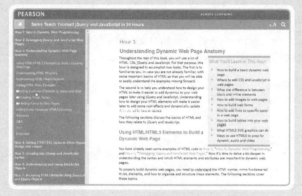

■ **Read** the complete text of the book online in your web browser

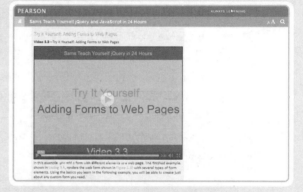

■ **Watch** an expert instructor show you how to perform tasks in easy-to-follow videos

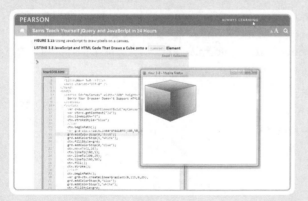

■ **Try** your hand at coding in an interactive code-editing sandbox in select products

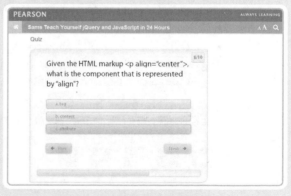

■ **Test** yourself with interactive quizzes